Mystics

Religion and Postmodernism

A series edited by Mark C. Taylor and Thomas A. Carlson

Mystics Presence and Aporia

Edited by MICHAEL KESSLER AND CHRISTIAN SHEPPARD

The University of Chicago Press *Chicago and London*

MICHAEL KESSLER has taught at Purdue University and the University of Chicago.
CHRISTIAN SHEPPARD is a lecturer in the Basic Program at the University of Chicago.

The University of Chicago Press, Chicago 60637
The University of Chicago Press, Ltd., London
© 2003 by The University of Chicago
All rights reserved. Published 2003
Printed in the United States of America

12 11 10 09 08 07 06 05 04 03   1 2 3 4 5

ISBN: 0-226-43209-2 (cloth)
ISBN: 0-226-43210-6 (paper)

Library of Congress Cataloging-in-Publication Data

Mystics : presence and aporia / edited by Michael Kessler and Christian Sheppard.
    p. cm.—(Religion and postmodernism)
Includes bibliographical references and index.
ISBN 0-226-43209-2 (cloth : alk. paper)—ISBN 0-226-43210-6 (pbk. : alk. paper)
    1. Mysticism—History—Congresses. I. Kessler, Michael, 1944– II. Sheppard, Christian.
III. Series.

BV5075. M88 2003
248.2'2—dc21

                                            2003006862

∞ The paper used in this publication meets the minimum requirements of the American
National Standard for Information Sciences—Permanence of Paper for Printed Library
Materials, ANSI Z39.48-1992.

Contents

Preface

MICHAEL KESSLER AND CHRISTIAN SHEPPARD

We were asked if any of the advertised participants would be speaking in tongues, displaying stigmata, or at least levitating. A few days before the conference, David Tracy admitted that although he appreciated the conceptual soundness as well as the rhetorical appeal of our title, he was frankly sick and tired of people asking him to confess he was a mystic. He never claimed to be a mystic. None of our conference speakers claim, as far as we know, to be mystics. The conference, held at the Divinity School of the University of Chicago in the spring of 1999, was titled "Mystics" after the excavation of the term by Michel de Certeau in his *Mystic Fable*. In Europe of the sixteenth and seventeenth centuries, mystics were not only persons, such as Saint Theresa of Avila, who confessed experiences of divine presence. Mystics was also a science, a way of describing and explaining such confessed experiences. "Mystics" names a topic and its interpretation; the interpretation is part of the topography. Just as history refers to both the past and the way we critically reflect on the past, we took "mystics" to name a topic that includes not only mystical personages and their mystical experiences but also what is called mystical theology, negative theology, mystical union, mystery, and mysticism as well as any or all of the many ways of critically reflecting on any or all of the above.

We did not choose "mysticism" as our title, wanting to avoid the totalizing connotations of the suffix "ism," where "mysticism" would be understood as one among many rationally categorizable "isms"—atheism, monotheism, polytheism, pantheism, mysticism. Furthermore, for many now, "mysticism" has come to signify mystical experiences only, extraordinary experiences, and, as such, has been separated both from its interpretation and from ordinary reality. Such a view cannot, for example, seriously consider the idea—an idea sustained in Dionysian mystical theology as well as the new phenomenology—that experience as such, including ordinary everyday experience, is so gracious (or gratuitous) as to be itself somehow mystical. "Mysticism" is especially problematic in today's philosophical milieu, where the mystical is often reduced to a concept of some core experience, transforming it into a problem of etiology rather than theology or philosophy.

Our subtitle "presence and aporia" also raised questions. "Aporia," some suggested, is not exactly a household word. It soon came to be in our households, however, as in the Divinity School and the university at large, when before the conference David Tracy and Jean-Luc Marion held a seminar on philosophy and negative theology. The conference was intended as a coda to this course, which would attract over seventy advanced graduate students of religion, philosophy, history, and literature, all on the same page, all already comfortable using in a sentence terms such as "aporia." Indeed, although mystics often refers to experiences of a "sense of presence" (to use William James's unsurpassed formulation), it also refers to experiences of aporia, what can perhaps helpfully be understood as a sense of a conspicuous lack of presence. Or as Bernard McGinn says, we take mysticism as the element within the Christian religion (as well as within other religious traditions) that concerns the preparation for, the attainment of, and the effect of what is described as an immediately conscious "presence" of God (often presence realized in absence).[1] This "presence realized in absence," this aporia, has its discursive analogue in the aporetic moment thought through by negative theology. Mystics, thus understood in terms of presence and aporia (the aporia of negative theology as well as of the dark night of the soul), surpasses speech and defies conceptual control.

Yet mystics calls for interpretation. Mystics not only has a history—esoteric names associated with errant paths or cloistered places, uncertain dates or dates of certain incarcerations and immolations. Mystics also has a language—a language of many languages—Syrian, Hebrew, Greek, Latin, Italian, French, German, English, and the symbolic languages of mathematics, iconographics, and liturgy (just to reference those mentioned in this collection). Mystics is thus imbued with language's ambiguity.

Certeau describes how "mystics," coined from the adjective "mystical"—a word with a long and important history in theology, going back to Dionysius the Areopagite, and before Dionysius to the Greek "mystery," *musterion*—was used both by theologians seeking to describe the divine presence and by ecclesiastical authorities seeking to identify and control those enthusiasts who claimed to experience such divine presence. Around the same time, the traditional adjective "mystical" came to be identified exclusively with the negative/apophatic aspects of Dionysian thought.[2] Thus the topic was narrowed for the convenience of epistemology and ecclesiastics.

Mystics, defined in terms of presence and aporia, is intended in a very different spirit than that of sixteenth- and seventeenth-century ecclesiastical authority. Finding our title in back-formation, in self-conscious anachronism and semantic oddity, we try to question a separation, that between mystical experience and mystical theology, the event and its interpretation. If we were to identify mystics or mysticism with mystical experience exclusively, then mystics could be mistaken for a matter of mere private experience, and mystical theology would consequently be mistakenly separated from practical experience and spiritual practice and be seen as merely an extraordinary but outer eddy of the theological mainstream. Thus, helpful distinctions between public and private, communal and personal, theory and practice would become misleading separations. Such separations deny the unsettling nuances implied by all such distinct pairings, denying mystics its prophetic power to question and qualify usual categories of thinking. Mystics disrupts totality. Our intentionally ambiguous title, which allowed our speakers (who intended only to reflect critically on the topic) to be mistaken themselves for mystics, was meant to negate terminologically a negation: if not hoping against proverbial admonition that two wrongs could make a right, we meant to stymie a misleading separation and thus render the topic open.

How can this open topic be explored? Certeau offers the model of a four-sided frame with each side a different discipline. This collection frames mystics with philosophy, theology, literary studies, and history. Critical hermeneutics insists that understanding be interdisciplinary. A credible philosophy or theology must take the turns of history and language; history and literary studies in turn must find their foundations and meaningful fruition in philosophy or theology.[3] Yet mystics is a topic where the disciplines encounter their discursive limits. Over mystics, philosophy and theology, taking the turns of history and language, face each other and test themselves: philosophy reserving the test of skepticism, theology formulating the test of faith. (Compare Marion's introduction to this volume and Tracy's afterword.) Mystics troubles the distinction between philosophy and theology. Kevin Hart says that mystics "know what they do not know," echoing Socrates: "I know that I know nothing" (202). So radical skepticisms and hermeneutics of suspicion, such as deconstruction, will also seem to echo negative theology.

Although these essays throw light on mystics from different sides, the more lucidly we describe mystics—analogous to divine presence and aporia—the more elusive it seems. As McGinn quotes Augustine: "God should not be said to be ineffable, because when this is said a statement is made. There results a form of verbal strife in that if the ineffable is what cannot be said, then what is called ineffable cannot be ineffable" (92). Mystics questions what can be said, spreading its "verbal strife" to the disciplines that attempt to question it. Mystics not only occasions a questioning of religion's "extreme cases" (to borrow again from William James) but also questions our modes of questioning. As one might go to the desert for a limit experience, one goes to mystics for limit questions.

One side of our frame is history. How does the historian collect facts—persons, places, and dates—about events that are confessed to transcend space and time, and how can such "facts" be meaningfully narrated? How, for example, do we make sense of the Renaissance cardinal Nicholas of Cusa (1401–64), a major ecclesiastic lawyer and worker for conciliation during a time of great crisis for the Church, who returning by sea to Venice from Greece, received "a celestial gift" and was thus "led to embrace incomprehensibles incomprehensibly in learned ignorance, by transcending those incorruptible truths that can be humanly known"?[4] What can a historian do with such a confession, with such "learned ignorance"? It is this learned ignorance, after all, that Cusa seeks "to set loose in [his] books." Such an experience (if it can be called an experience) was neither the beginning nor the end for Cusa but, rather, an apex in his "mystical pursuit of God" (105). McGinn's essay traces a part of this pursuit. In order to follow Cusa, McGinn admits that one must be both a theologian and a historian. He goes on to show the inseparability of mystical theory from actual mystical practice by focusing on Cusa's arithmetical meditations on the Trinity. Cusa claims that in order to understand the Trinity, we must practice a transcendental mathematics, conceptualizing a coincidence of opposites, *unitrinum seu triunum* (one-in-three). Thus our minds may grasp God's relations to himself as Trinity. By grasping God's being mathematically (using the higher power of *intellectus*), we may come to know ourselves as God's likeness. For each of us is also a trinity, a contraction of unity, equality, and connection (98–99). This knowledge is not an end in itself, however. Theoretical knowing prepares us actually to encounter the divine as absolute infinite love. McGinn explains that Cusa searches for an "incisive formulation" in order to educe "the leap beyond" (104).

Another side of our frame is literary studies. How does the literary critic make sense of, for example, such cryptic utterances and pregnant reticences as those of Joan of Arc? Françoise Meltzer's essay asks, Who speaks at the trial of Joan of Arc? What is the "I," the putative subject of such speech, as we attend to her through texts that have found us half a millennium after her death? Joan's mystic voices and visions instill her with agency to fight for France and authorize her responses to the inquisitorial court. Meltzer's Joan is defined by the experience of a God who commands her to an obedience that is not recognized by the Church. In obeying the authority of her voices, Joan bypasses the Church as sole mediator of the revelation of God to the world. The charges as formulated against Joan implicitly deny her authority to interpret her mystic voices. The ecclesial authorities displace and co-opt whatever Joan says. The Church speaks for Joan and finds her responses unsatisfactory. Her reticence preserves her mystic voices from the inquisitorial probe but cannot protect her body from the flames. The Church court considers, in its own words, "all things which are to be considered" and burns Joan on a blanket charge of disobedience. Never heard or responded to, Joan is herself an aporia, whom we must approach, as Meltzer eloquently said at the conference, "with the double vision of awe and caution."

Philosophy and theology complete our frame. Kevin Hart's essay studies Maurice Blanchot in the context of twentieth-century philosophy, theology, and literature in order to clarify the difference between what theologians call mystical experience and postmodern philosophers call limit experience. Blanchot dwells on the "remarkable power of the negative" revealed to work in literature but discerns beyond literature and language, as beyond experience, the "ground and abyss [of] death" (189). In contrast to both traditional mystical experience and Bataille's limit experience of "inner experience," Blanchot theorizes "the experience of non-experience," the experience toward which literature unconsciously gestures but which remains unrepresentable and ultimately unexperienced: death. "What [death] shows," Hart sums up, "and what neither literary criticism nor theologians have sufficiently realized, is that in terms of textual effects it little matters whether one is responding to the transcendent or the transcendental. Perhaps this begins to account for the uneasy pathos of the postmoderns" (199). Hart draws hope from his turn with the postmoderns, showing us how Blanchot's experience of nonexperience can be experienced as "not so much darkness as openness"(202), openness to new possibilities of philosophy and theology and, most to be hoped for, openness to Otherness.

Beginning to define mystics even as it breaks our interdisciplinary frame, this collection finds a rough timeline for the topic. (Even as we connect the earliest Christian mystics with the latest postmoderns, we have, however, been constrained from drawing other important connections, such as, with Islamic, Jewish, and ancient Greco-Roman mystics.) We begin with Dionysius the Areopagite, who brings the term "mystical" into the lexicon. Alexander Golitzin's essay offers an overview of the Dionysian corpus, locating the place of negative theology in Dionysius's mystical theology. Golitzin not only introduces and interprets the *Mystical Theology* and other specific works, but he also seeks to understand how these works were influenced by Dionysius's Syriac Christian tradition. His essay addresses the relationship between the individual (often ascetic, often solitary) mystic and the ecclesiastical community's liturgical worship. Golitzin shows the extent to which Dionysius is a specifically Christian—and liturgical—thinker, not so easily labeled another Neoplatonist contemplative or, for that matter, not so easily plundered by postmoderns for his fascinating apophaticisms. Golitzin argues that it is only in the sacramental experience of Christ, an event that is ecclesiastically controlled and liturgically circumscribed, that we accomplish the cycle of procession of fallen self from God and the ascetic return of redeemed self to God. Thus, in contrast to Meltzer's Joan of Arc located outside the ecclesia, Golitzin's Dionysius takes his place at the altar.

Great moments of mysticism, Gershom Scholem has pointed out, can be identified with great moments of crisis. A first major crisis in Western Christianity occurs at the time of Dionysius, between the fifth and sixth centuries, the Acacian Schism, the first schism between Rome and Constantinople, which eventually culminates, in the eleventh century, with the East-West schism. A second great crisis for Western Christianity, discussed by Susan Schreiner, is the Reformation. Schreiner studies, in the life and work of Martin Luther and Saint Theresa, how mystical experience relates to the modern "search for certainty." Luther's reformers promised "subjective or experiential certitude of salvation," while Counter Reformation Catholics promised "a certainty based on visible authority," that is, the Church (118). Such a search for certainty implies, of course, some essential uncertainty, philosophical skepticism, and religious doubt, but it also inspires a fear of deception: I John 4:1, "beloved do not believe every spirit, but test the spirits to see whether they are of God"; II Cor. 11:14, "for even Satan disguises himself as an angel of light." The hiddenness of God and the deceptiveness of Satan represent aporias not easily answered. Both Luther and Theresa develop strategies for discerning the divine from the diabolical. To overcome the dangerous possibility of deception and adequately test the spirits we encounter, we must become seasoned spiritual practitioners. Whether guided by the Church or by the Holy Spirit directly, in order to abide mystical experience, we must become experienced with the mystical.

Deception, doubt, authority, certainty, experience: these terms also pre-occupy our present moment, by all accounts another moment of crisis for Western religion. The authors of this volume take Bataille and Blanchot as exemplary of the twentieth century's fascination with mystics, and whether this is a nostalgic fascination (as diagnosed by Meltzer) or a proper fascina-tion offering new possibilities for thinking and living (as hinted at by Hart), the issue of experience remains crucial. Amy Hollywood explains Bataille's Nietzschean understanding of experience in terms of his call for a new mystical theology, a theology without God, a mystical "atheology." Bataille's "Atheological Summa"—comprising *On Nietzsche, Guilty,* and *Inner Experi-ence*—replaces the traditional mystical itinerary culminating in mystical expe-rience with his own quest for limit experiences culminating in inner experi-ence. Bataille revives a medieval understanding of contemplation as a kind of action, a contemplation written and published as a community-establishing communication. He develops his practice from reading the *Book of Visions* by Angela of Foligno (1248–1309), an Italian Franciscan tertiary and mystic, with whom Hollywood offers an extensive comparison. Rather than focus as Angela did upon the Passion of Christ, Bataille bases his practice on realizing the ultimate contingency of his own life, focusing on the absolute random-ness of his survival, specifically through the Second World War. Bataille makes explicit the relationship between crisis and mystics, claiming that his writing on ecstatic anguish was called forth by the war (161). Crisis, for Bataille, be-comes generalized into catastrophe, memorialized by the crucified Christ but emblematized for the postmodern atheologian by the "unnamed specificity" of a photograph of a Chinese torture victim. Hollywood is uneasy with Bataille's seemingly easy appropriation of the feminine and the "oriental" Other but recognizes his work as a genuine provocation to reconsider both premodern and postmodern views of mystics.

Our interdisciplinary frame holds different mystical pictures, from the Neoplatonist diagram of man as cosmos, to the Christ that suddenly appears in the liturgy of Dionysius, to the Triune God of Nicholas of Cusa, to Joan of Arc kneeling in prayer before the crossed hilt of her sword or backlit by the inquisitorial flames, to Theresa of Avila in ecstasy, to Bataille's picture of a Chinese torture victim. To these pictures, Jean-Luc Marion adds a new, apophatically figured God of Thomas Aquinas. Arguing for a reappraisal of Thomas's corpus, Marion rejects the widely accepted reading that Thomas conceptually defines God (the supreme entity of metaphysics) in the same terms as other entities. Marion explains the "onto-theo-logical conception of metaphysics" and submits Aquinas's doctrines to the categories of Hei-degger. He shows that Thomas develops metaphysics as a part of theology, not as a science to which we must submit all inquiry about God. According to his *sacra doctrina,* Thomas studies divine things as they reveal themselves, not simply as they can be conceptualized by the human inquirer. God, for Thomas (as for Marion), is the (given) principle of entities, a principle that cannot be metaphysically deduced (or phenomenologically reduced) but must be assumed, accepted, and gratefully praised. Thomas's project thus escapes Heidegger's criticism of metaphysics. His claims about our knowledge of God answer to a model of incommensurability. We cannot know God in the same terms as we know ourselves. Ours is the human encounter with God primarily accomplished through a knowledge that is never complete for human beings. As Marion shows in his essay and in his introduction to this volume, any attempt to frame God conceptually has the added result of framing the human mind.

Just so, in Regina Schwartz's reading of George Herbert, mystics frames the human mind. Placing Herbert in context with Donne, Sidney, Milton, Luther, and Calvin, Schwartz relates the Eucharist and Christ's Passion in Scripture to Herbert's poems of praise, Word to word. Schwartz traces the mystical to an essential sense of mystery, a sense of mystery inherent in language and expressed in poetry, finding in Herbert a sacramental theory of language derived from Calvin's understanding of signs. "Calvin's etymology of sacrament takes him immediately to mystery" (144). The Word partakes of this mystery, and Herbert's poetry of thanks and praise is a response of the Spirit, making Herbert himself a vessel for the Holy Spirit and his poems an offering. Herbert offers himself as sacrifice and his poems as praise. It is a sacrifice of praise signifying divine grace and human gratitude (146). In "The Altar," "each part of the poet's heart, cut by God, desires only to praise, and so the poem is visibly shaped, not only like an altar, but to form the shape of the pronoun 'I'—the subject is the offering made at the altar" (149). And the offering is praise. Herbert's poem presents poetically (performatively and typographically) the "I" as altar.

The question of the mystical subject, traditionally thought of in terms of the immortal soul, is readdressed by Thomas Carlson to a modern self, thought of as relative, replaceable, and disposable. The modern self (as described by Benjamin, Weber, Heidegger, and Altizer) conceptualizes and controls its world with science and technology. Yet this highly capable agent can only know itself and its world according to a weak understanding of truth. Truth no longer correlates to a transcendent ideal but merely must have the modern agent's acknowledgment. Such "truth" seems insignificant in the face of the immense and incomprehensible totality that the modern rational self has made for itself in its own image. Modern subjectivity shapes itself after disenchantment and the death of a God that cannot be mourned. Carlson (as with Meltzer and Hart) identifies a uniquely modern fascination with mystics. Indeed a "strange shadow of the mystical subject and its God" may appear "in the experience of today's technological subject" (226). Early Christian theologians John Scotus Eriugena and Gregory of Nyssa suggest to Carlson how the mystical experience of a God whose center is everywhere and circumference nowhere may form subjectivity. Most interestingly, Carlson finds among these early mystical thinkers an analogous fascination with the technological. The medieval experience of the *mysterium tremendum* resembles the postmodern experience of alienation before an overwhelming, incomprehensible, relationally conceptualized, yet technologically functioning totality. Carlson's essay culminates in a reading of Don Delillo's novel *Underworld,* where the modern self faces itself in the self-annihilating lights of the Internet and the ignition of a nuclear bomb.

With mystics, subject-object dichotomy fails to help us think about either the divine or our own subjectivity. As Gary Wills sums up the issue in his recent biography of Saint Augustine: "'Since it is God we are speaking of, you do not understand it. If you could understand it, It would not be God' (S 117.5). We seek one mystery, God, with another mystery, ourselves. We are mysterious to ourselves because God's mystery is in us: 'Our mind cannot be understood, even by itself, because it is made in God's image' (S 398.2)."[5] A modern formulation, not necessarily contradicting Augustine's, is that "God" cannot be understood because the mind necessarily frames him in its image. As a result, when we frame mystics, we not only frame fragmented images of the divine, we also find framed our own image fragmented and mysterious.

We would first of all like to thank David Tracy and Jean-Luc Marion without whose inspiration and support this conference and this volume would never have been conceived or realized. We would also like to thank Alan Thomas and Randy Petilos at the University of Chicago Press for their continued and conscientious encouragement; Gareth Gollrad, who translated Marion's introduction; our conference participants and contributors, but especially Regina Schwartz, Françoise Meltzer, and Arnold Davidson; the Martin Marty Center for generous financial support; the staff of the Divinity School of the University of Chicago, especially Marsha Peeler and Sandra Peppers; and, most important, the dean of the Divinity School, W. Clark Gilpin for his guidance and unstinting support. This book is dedicated to Shelly Renee Schable, whose life came to an untimely end during the preparation of this volume, and to Cecilia Rose Sheppard, who was born within days of the conference's beginning.

Notes

1. For this view of mysticism, see Bernard McGinn, *The Foundations of Mysticism: Origins through the Fifth Century* (New York: Crossroad, 1991), xiii–xx.

2. Michel de Certeau, *The Mystic Fable: The Sixteenth and Seventeenth Centuries,* trans. Michael B. Smith (Chicago: University of Chicago Press, 1992), 94–95n. 57.

3. David Tracy, *Plurality and Ambiguity: Religion, Hermeneutics, and Hope* (Chicago: University of Chicago Press, 1987).

4. The letter appended to *On Learned Ignorance* in *Nicholas of Cusa: Selected Spiritual Writings,* trans. H. Laurence Bind (New York: Paulist Press, 1997).

5. Gary Wills, *Augustine* (New York: Viking Penguin, 1999), xii.

Introduction: What Do We Mean by "Mystic"?

JEAN-LUC MARION

Translated by Gareth Gollrad

A certain lack of awareness or even a hint of provocation is needed these days in order to dare to use the term "mystic," especially in the academic domain where rationalism seems to encompass every possible form of rationality. Doesn't using the term "mystic" involve a certain admission of uncontrolled subjectivity? Or perhaps it amounts to a renunciation of scientific rigor by "basing moral concepts on real and yet non-sensible intuitions (from an invisible kingdom of God) and dispersing them within the transcendental," in other words, by recourse to the most unruly sensible impulses?[1] Such accusations are so obvious or at least have such common currency that it almost seems unreasonable to go to such great lengths—and perhaps in vain—to justify the choice of a word that has been devalued.

Nevertheless, the editors of this collection, Michael Kessler and Chris Sheppard, know their world and its academic demands in general. In particular, they know just as well as anyone else that the Divinity School at the University of Chicago, which has supported them in this project, along with the University of Chicago Press, which is publishing this volume, are not recognized for unbridled irrationalism. Furthermore, the excellence of the contributors, the expertise involved in the debates, and the very success of the original conference well enough confirm the strict conceptual rigor of their entire project. We must therefore imagine that the term "mystic" takes on an entirely different value here—in the sense that linguistics defines the meaning of a term according to a value obtained through its delimitation by the near-synonyms that frame it, approximate it, and yet which can never be substituted for it as equals. In fact, it could very well be that these days the term "mystic" carries a differential and nearly polemical semantic value. First of all, the term can be distinguished here from its popular meaning—the individual psychological experience of an ineffable, incommunicable, and irreproducible spiritual state. This is because philosophy no longer supposes that it is able (and thus required) to describe the effects of private language but accepts only what can be elevated to the status of language that is public, shared, and therefore universally thematizable. At the other extreme, "mystic" can be distinguished from its proper usage in theology and the history of religions as "mystery" (*mysterion*), where it covers everything from spiritual (and eventually liturgical) initiation to the passage from life to death (especially in the biblical and more particularly in the Christian tradition, then, more marginally, in the Orphic rites or "mystery religions").[2] Between the restriction drawn from the philosophy of language and the very specific historical usage taken from the history of religious thought, here "mystic" designates, through a dual opposition, a different intention.

This otherwise imprecise intention depends on the properly philosophical rejection of a thesis that is diffuse although it is widespread and can be commonly found within the implicit philosophy of many fields of the humanities and social sciences. We may hazard a description as follows: no fact or phenomenon can produce or receive rational meaning if it is not capable of being constituted as an object. By "object" here, according to the received idea of what a science should be, we shall mean the result of the synthesis (or of the constitution) of a sensible given and of a delimited concept, or the result of the synthesis (or of the constitution) of a sensible given by a determined concept in such a way that this product would be able to be delimited, produced, undone, and reproduced at will (or almost at will) by the mind that takes and maintains the initiative. From this perspective, there is no knowledge other than that which arises through scientific knowledge of an object. The method here is marked by the primacy of the knowing mind over what it knows. This is because the method defines the conditions necessary for both the constitution and the intelligibility of its object. In other words, "the *a priori* conditions for the possibility of experience in general are at the same time the conditions of possibility for objects of experience."[3] Stated succinctly, we only know objects; our experience applies only to objects because it fixes the a priori conditions of their possibility as its own. No phenomenon can be given to knowing, or be admitted into the limited field of knowledge, if it does not accept being made into an object—in other words, if it does not assume as its own the conditions of phenomenality that the limits of our mind assign to it in advance. Therefore, in the situation produced by the end of metaphysics and explored today by phenomenology, pragmatic philosophy, ordinary language philosophy, the history of spirituality, and literary theory among other disciplines, we encounter phenomena (in the broadest sense of the term) that cannot appear according to the a priori conditions that a finite mind imposes on experience—and yet, undeniably, do appear. In effect, certain phenomena are characterized by the uncontrollable excess of intuition within them, above and beyond all of the meanings that we will ever be able to assign them. There is neither a single category nor even any sensible form that can delimit them prior to their appearing (apparition). Thus, one cannot predict them either, because their sensible givenness infinitely surpasses any necessary condition. Within these phenomena, intuition is not limited to filling or to fulfilling the finite measure of the concept and/or the signification but spills over to the point of saturating it. From that point on, the phenomenon appears more than any object will ever appear; to be precise, however, it is withheld from any synthesis and from the least act that could constitute it as an object. It escapes prediction because no quantity can predict its sum from its parts. It bedazzles the gaze because its intensity does not recognize any limit based on an absolute maximum that finite vision could tolerate. It surges forth without equal, and so cannot be inscribed within an equivalent relation with any anterior cause, substrate, or other substance. Its existence ultimately defies all possibility (and all impossibility) since it cannot agree with the conditions of possibility of our finite experience, but it imposes itself on these conditions and contradicts what we would expect from our experience. These phenomena, which we have named saturated phenomena, appear, but as if in opposition to our experience. We shall therefore also call them paradoxes or counterphenomena.

And these kinds of phenomena, or saturated phenomena, are not so rare. In fact we know some of these saturated phenomena very well in daily personal life. At least four types of them are very obvious. (1) The historical event needs continuous interpretation and it is never over; for example, the signification of the American Civil War, even today, is at stake. The intuition was so huge that we need new historians to deal with it, producing new concepts, trying to make sense out of the event. (2) There are paintings that grant such an experience that we have to explain what we see. And the more we see, the more we have to explain. (3) There is our own body, our own flesh, which is a phenomenon giving us an uninterrupted intuition, which is so rich and so overwhelming that we need new words—literature and poetry—to make sense out of it. (4) And there is the face of the other that imposes to me an ever-renewed stream of intuition, challenging any attempt to master it. Thus in *Étant Donné,* my last study, I have suggested that the Revelation (the *mysterion* par excellence) is precisely a saturated phenomenon, and more than that, it is a combination of the four types of saturated phenomenon.[4]

Portrayed in theological words, this issue may be summed up, according to the Greek fathers, in the fact that God is invisible, unspeakable, uncircumscribable, and incomprehensible. Yet the experience of not being able to comprehend, see, or think God can be taken seriously as a positive experience. We can be confronted to something completely outside of our reach and nevertheless present as such, as absent. Such is the meaning of an epistemological rule, which can be found everywhere in the tradition of philosophy and theology, for instance, in Gregory of Nyssa's *Life of Moses* 2.163: "What we have to see is the very fact not to see."[5] We must see, in this experience, the very impossibility of seeing. This is repeated with the same word in the *Mystical Theology* 1.2 by Dionysius.[6] And even Thomas Aquinas argues that "the ultimate point of the human knowledge about God is to know that we don't know God."[7] This was assumed, strangely enough, even by Descartes; when answering Gassendi, who contended that Descartes defines God by the infinite because he could not even give any definition of infinity, Descartes pointed out that God may be incomprehensible, as incomprehensibility is the *ratio formalis,* the very core and a quasi definition of the infinite.[8] So incomprehensibility is a real knowledge fitting exactly what is at stake: the infinite, that is, God. And, let us recall Wittgenstein: "What we cannot speak about we must pass over in silence."[9] But there are different ways to keep silent. We may keep silent in such a way that we refuse to think about a thing, refrain from thinking it, and take it to be kept outside the horizon of our thought. But there is another way to remain silent, which is to worship, to take a thing so seriously that we have only one way to speak about it, which is precisely to keep silent.

What is new now in our situation of philosophy, which amounts to a large extent to the "end of metaphysics," is this: we, after the "death of God," can no more take for granted that our metaphysical concepts may outline the ultimate possible pattern of the intellectual and real world. In our situation of crisis, we should not avoid the hypothesis that, in the case of God, we could question our set of concepts and consider the impossibility of any knowledge of God, not as failure of our inquiry but as a positive opportunity for questioning metaphysical concepts. We no longer have unshaken confidence in our metaphysical concepts, and the impossibility of knowing God according to them looks perhaps less as an evidence of God being out of the picture than as the suggestion that our metaphysical concepts can and should be questioned. So there is another way to be silent than simply giving up speaking about God.

Saturated phenomena should not be constituted at all, and what we experience with them is precisely an intuition overwhelming any possible concept. This is not because the saturated phenomenon is irrational but because we are unable to be rational enough to produce concepts matching the intuition that is nevertheless in fact given. Hermeneutics—I refer here to Paul Ricoeur—is nothing else than the discovery that constitution cannot be achieved before the event of the phenomenon but has to be repeated and slowly, endlessly, repeated after the event of the phenomenon.[10] And as we cannot constitute such a phenomenon, we have to interpret it. But what does it mean, to interpret? Exactly what theology does when interpreting the Scriptures. Why are we charged to interpret the Scriptures? Because the Scriptures show themselves as saturated phenomena. And so we cannot constitute them or explain how they should have been written. For, there is perhaps no one right way that the Bible should have been written. So there should be an infinity of equally possible interpretations of the Bible. To admit this does not mean heresy but precisely mere orthodoxy. Orthodoxy implies a plurality of interpretations, if by orthodoxy we mean to assume that the text of the Bible does, at the end, come from God.

Thus in front of the saturated phenomenon, we must admit our lack of concepts, that is, of rationality. This situation was perfectly explained by Paul (Eph. 3:19) when he argued, "We have to know the charity of Christ which goes beyond any kind of knowledge." So we have to know something that, although beyond knowledge, still remains absolutely real: the charity of God given to us in Christ. Thus our ego is no longer in the situation of the transcendental knower, as in idealist philosophy, equal to itself and perfectly self-sufficient (*Ich* = *Ich,* ego = ego). This equality appears broken and at the same moment garnered by charity. I am no more what I am, but what the grace of God gives me to become (Gal. 2:20): "It is no longer I [ego] who live, but it is Christ who lives in me." The ego still stays in place, but it is no longer its own origin. The ego to some extent received itself as given to itself by grace. What does that mean, to the ego, to be given? There is still a subject in charge to make sense of phenomena, that is, to interpret them. But this subject cannot constitute the phenomena any more because it comes after, not before, them. Being given to itself by the event, that ego appears from now on as constituted as a witness. I take witness here not according to the religious meaning, but in the sense of a witness to a crime or at a marriage, in the legal meaning of the term. As witnesses, we don't any more act as the operators of the saturated phenomenon, but as witnesses who must give their best possible account of them. We are not supposed to make a complete report but, rather, just to make the best report we can.

It is precisely these kinds of paradoxes—saturated phenomena—that the contributions collected here attempt to address and describe. These paradoxes are not always, or even often, strictly religious or spiritual phenomena. In some cases, they involve purely historical, artistic, philosophical, or literary problems. However, they all share a common trait—none of them presents the characteristics of the object: predictability and clear evidence (production), a relation to other similar phenomena and subjection to the conditions of our experience (reproduction). On the contrary, they are given as unpredictable, intolerable, absolute, and unfathomable and are phenomenalized according to these forms of givenness. Certainly, in a number of these essays, one could point to the emphasis placed on what one may be tempted to refer to as "negative theology." However, we should not let ourselves be deceived here. First of all, in Christian theology, strictly speaking, there is no negative theology in and of itself. There is only one "negative way," and it is inseparable from the "affirmative way" that precedes it (one denies only after having affirmed everything that can be legitimately predicated of God), and there is, moreover, a "way of eminence," which, far from returning to the affirmative predication, generally liberates itself from all predication. This involves surpassing the predicative use of language in moving toward another usage—praise, for example, and prayer in general. Furthermore, philosophy today knows how to describe effectively nonpredicative uses of language in such a way that the "mystic" can rightfully reassume its proper place within a broader, more open logic. Second, we should not be taken in because the majority of the essays collected here have no confessional intentions or any ambitions to advance an orthodox position. All of them, however, do obstinately want to bring to light the rationality of facts and doctrines that objectifying rationality will not let us touch. In effect, the stakes here involve the limits of rationality, which we intend to push back, if at all possible. In fact, these efforts concentrate on illustrating a superior kind of rationalism, which metaphysics itself is perhaps unable to conceive, within the limits of the a prioris that it continuously seeks to verify (and through which it no doubt seeks reassurance). We must never despair of reason. Reason never consists in stigmatizing the unthinkable only to be more intent on excluding it. Rather, we must have faith in reason to make thinkable what, without the patient labor of the concept, would have remained unthinkable. There is always more to think, on earth and in heaven, which is something that philosphy is quite willing to admit. These essays undoubtedly have no other ambition than striving to ascertain this.

Notes

1. The quote is from Immanuel Kant, *Kritik der reinen Vernunft*, vol. 5 of *Kants gesam melt Schriften*, ed. Herausgegeben von der Deutschen Akademie der Wissenschaften (Berlin: Walter de Gruyeter, 1902–), p. 71.

2. See, e.g., L. Bouyer, *Musterion: Du mystère à la mystique* (Paris: Éditions du Cerf, 1986).

3. Immanuel Kant, *Kritik der reinen Vernunft*, A.111.

4. Jean-Luc Marion, *Étant Donné: Essais d'une phenomenologie de là donation* (Paris: Presses Universitaires de France, 1998), 452, translated as *Being Given: Toward a Phenomenology of Giveness*, trans. J. L. Kosky (Stanford, Calif.: Stanford University Press, 2002).

5. Gregory of Nyssa, *The Life of Moses*, trans. Abraham J. Malherbe and Everett Ferguson (New York: Paulist Press, 1978), 208.

6. Pseudo-Dionysius Areopagite, *The Divine Names; and, Mystical Theology*, trans John D. Jones, (Milwaukee: Marquette University Press, 1980), 266.

7. Thomas Aquinas, *On the Power of God*, trans. the English Dominican Fathers (Westminster, Md.: Newman Press, 1952).

8. Rene Descartes, *The Philosophical Writings of Descartes*, trans. John Cottingham, Robert Stoothoff, and Dugald Murdoch, 2 vols. (Cambridge: Cambridge University Press, 1984–85). Compare *Œuvres de Descartes*, ed. Charles Adam and Paul Tannery (Paris: J. Vrin, 1964–74), 7:368.

9. Ludwig Wittgenstein, *Tractatus Logico-Philosophicus*, trans. D. F. Pears and B. F. McGuinness (London: Routledge & Kegan Paul, 1963), 151.

10. See Paul Ricoeur, *Time and Narrative*, trans. Kathleen McLughlin and David Pellauer, 3 vols. (Chicago: University of Chicago Press, 1984), *Interpretation Theory: Discourse and the Surplus of Meaning* (Fort Worth: Texas Christian University Press, 1976), 107, and *Essays on Biblical Interpretation*, ed. Lewis S. Mudge (Philadelphia: Fortress Press, 1980).

"Suddenly, Christ": The Place of Negative Theology in the Mystagogy of Dionysius Areopagites

ALEXANDER GOLITZIN

I should begin with a caveat: I represent a minority in Dionysian scholarship. In fact, I stand at the very terminus of a series of progressively shrinking minorities. To shift to an arboreal image, the great trunk of Dionysian studies over the past century has been devoted to my subject's undoubted debt to late Neoplatonism, in which tradition our topic in this volume, apophatic theology, plays a considerable role.[1] A sturdy branch of the scholarly literature does seek to take into account Dionysius's equally undoubted efforts—hence the first-century pseudonym of a disciple of Saint Paul—to supply at least the appearance of a Christian background.[2] Narrower is the offshoot that tries to read him against the setting of specifically Eastern Christian thought, and perilously thin the branch from that branch that has sought to apply to this mysterious, late-fifth- or early-sixth-century writer insights from that Christian Syria that, everyone agrees, represents his at least geographical point of origin.[3] Thinnest of all, really the merest twig at the end of all of these branchings, is my argument, which proposes that the Eastern and especially Syrian ascetico-mystical tradition offers us a kind of royal path to the comprehension of the Areopagitica as a coherent and even emphatically Christian vision.[4] The setting of Syrian monasticism in particular, with its roots extending back into those native traditions of Christian Syria that include the wandering ascetical visionaries known to us, for example, from the gospel and the *Acts of Judas Thomas* and, more distantly still—though this is more speculative—into the vision tradition of apocalyptic literature deriving from Christianity's original matrix in Second Temple Judaism, is, I submit, the *Sitz im Leben* of the *Corpus Dionysiacum*.[5]

I admit that I am quite alone in this view. I am also alone in arguing, elsewhere at greater length than here, that Dionysius's more specific context is the conflict or, at least, tension between the figures of the ascetic holy man and the bishop or, more elaborately, between the personal authority of the monastic visionary, peculiarly beloved by the laity of the Syrian Church, and the ecclesiastical, sacramental thrust of Christian worship and polity. This tension, and sometimes conflict, was several generations old by the time our author set his quill to parchment. It had also elicited an equally venerable and distinctive set of replies from within the ascetic tradition itself, replies from which I believe Dionysius drew, especially in his treatises on, and invention of the word, hierarchy, to which I shall return below.[6]

For now, though, any ecclesial or, indeed, obviously Christian element is not immediately obvious in the *Mystical Theology,* the little treatise that is perhaps the most famous and influential of the Dionysian corpus.[7] True, it begins with a prayer offered to the Christian Trinity and goes on to invoke the biblical account of Moses ascending into the cloud atop Mount Sinai as an image of the mind's ascent into the darkness, *gnophos,* and silence, *sige,* of divinity.[8] The remaining four chapters, however, are devoted to a discussion of negation, *apophusis,* which appears to be largely devoid of any ostensibly Christian elements. As God descends into the world, creating and sustaining it, Dionysius explains in chapter 3, so he acquires many names, from Trinity and Unity at the highest stage to all the attributes of human emotions, bodily form, and even to the names of inanimate creation at the lowest end. This is the realm of positive, or *kataphatic,* theology. "But now," he continues, "as [our discourse] ascends from what is lower to what lies above, it contracts to the extent that it ascends, and, once it has completed its ascent, it will be wholly speechless and wholly united to the Unutterable."[9] In the concluding two chapters, he supplies us with this ascent of negations. In *Mystical Theology* 4, he begins with the denial of the attribution of corporeal and passable aspects to the divinity: "Therefore we say that the Cause of all . . . has neither body [*soma*] nor shape [*schema*] nor form [*eidos*] . . . neither is He a place [*topos*] nor seen . . . nor perceived [by the senses] . . . nor is He troubled by material passions . . . nor is He in need of light . . . nor does He either have nor is He any one of the things which are perceived [by the senses]."[10]

We then proceed to the intelligible names in the fifth and concluding chapter:

Moving yet higher we say that He is . . . neither soul nor mind; neither has He imagination nor opinion nor reason [*logos*] nor intuitive knowing [*noesis*]; neither is He reason nor intuition; neither can He be reasoned or intuited. He is neither life nor does He live; neither is He being [*ousia*] nor eternity [*aion*] nor time. . . . He is neither oneness, nor deity, nor goodness. He is not spirit, as we understand [the term], nor sonship nor fatherhood. . . . He is no one of the things which are not, nor any one of those which are . . . [thus] beyond affirmation . . . and beyond negation is the transcendence of Him Who, simply, is beyond all things and free.[11]

While I shall come back momentarily to a detail or two in my translation of these passages, I should like for now to finish up what we might call the case for the prosecution. In what we have just seen, there seems to be precious little support for declaring Dionysius a Christian thinker and a very great deal for regarding him as a Neoplatonist metaphysician whose Christian trappings this treatise in particular exposes as, to borrow a phrase from Anders Nygren's *Agape and Eros,* "an exceedingly thin veneer."[12] The increase of discourse as it expands through affirmation to cover the divine descent into multiplicity and its corresponding contraction through negation in our ascent to the "cause of all" correspond, furthermore, precisely to the cycle of procession (or emanation) and return, *proodos-epistrophe,* which is the bedrock of Neoplatonist thought and, equally, of the Dionysian corpus.[13] More disturbing still to any who would like to read this author as a Christian writer is the concluding section's apparent denial of the same Trinity with which the *Mystical Theology* began, together with the facts that neither love nor, indeed, Christ himself appear anywhere at all.[14] There would thus seem to be nothing to counter the assertions made forty years ago by Father Jean Vanneste and by John Rist, who were both echoing earlier critics, that the Areopagite's is a purely "natural mysticism"—if, indeed, even the term "mysticism" is at all applicable. Vanneste thought it was not.[15] More recently, Paul Rorem at Princeton and Ysabel de Andia at the Sorbonne have published a number of weighty studies advancing similar views, though with some qualifications in the latter's case.[16] For Rorem particularly, it is the *Mystical Theology* that stands at the center of the Dionysian project, an enterprise that is grounded on the timeless relation obtaining between cause and effect—the Neoplatonist bedrock, in other words—and for which there can in consequence be no real place either for Christian eschatology or, indeed, for Christ himself, whose frequent appearances elsewhere in the *Corpus Dionysiacum* are therefore purely "cosmetic."[17]

In my case for the defense, and with it for the place of the *Mystical Theology* and apophatic theology within the *Corpus Dionysiacum,* let me begin with those details I promised just above. The first concerns the initial negation I cited from *Mystical Theology* 4: God does not have either "body" or "form." I daresay that this must sound to most of us like an unnecessary truism—of course, we think, deity, if it exists at all, is necessarily formless and bodiless. I suggest, however, that this axiom was not so obvious in Dionysius's own time and place. Those ascetic visionaries whom I take to have been at once his targets and, at least in part, his readership may well have held very archaic yet still quite lively views about the divine form and were likely to have understood it as the object of the vision that they sought.[18] The divine form or body features prominently in the throne visions of apocalyptic literature, at the term of the seer's ascent to heaven, and continue to play an important role in the *hekhalot* texts of Rabbinic Judaism that are more or less precisely contemporary with the Areopagitica.[19] While I doubt myself that fifth- and sixth-century Christian monks were reading much rabbinic literature—though, who knows? oral crossover was certainly not impossible, especially in a commonly Aramaic-speaking milieu—I can point to the fact that Christian ascetics were copying and, presumably, reading the apocalypses not only of the biblical canon but also of the Old Testament Pseudepigrapha, for example, *I* and *II Enoch*, the *Apocalypse of Abraham*, and *Apocalypse of Zephanaiah*, together with the second-century Christian apocryphon *The Martyrdom and Ascension of Isaiah*, to name a few. It is not accidental, I think, that we find Dionysius thus concluding his corpus with a letter addressed "To John at Patmos."[20]

This leads me to an initial remark about the first treatise on the hierarchies, *The Celestial Hierarchy*, which is traditionally—and I think correctly—held to begin the corpus. Dionysius himself tells us that he was moved to write it because he "had . . . been troubled by the . . . imagery used by scripture in reference to the angels."[21] He dedicates in consequence both the second and fifteenth chapters to an angelic iconography taken almost entirely from Ezekiel, especially from Ezekiel 1, which is to say, from the vision text par excellence—perhaps even the template for the later apocalyptic throne visions—with its zoomorphic cherubim, its wheeled throne (the divine chariot, or *merkavah*), and the human-like form [*demut*] of God's Glory on the throne.[22] Chapter 13 of the *Celestial Hierarchy* is likewise devoted entirely to a second, nearly as important, throne vision, that of Isaiah 6.[23] Here I think my supposition about monastic fondness for the Pseudepigrapha is somewhat confirmed by the presence of an interesting detail. Dionysius's Isaiah does not see the Glory of God within the earthly temple, as in the biblical text, but is "lifted up" by his angel guide to look upon the heavenly throne and liturgy, which the angel then explains to him. This is the same sequence, much compressed and shorn of the passage through seven heavens, that we find in the *Ascension of Isaiah*.[24] Here something else of interest emerges. Dionysius is not at all interested in denying the theophanies of the Old Testament nor, by extension I think, the visionary experiences of his contemporaries. To the contrary, unlike an Augustine, he affirms them. What he does want to do, though, is define them in such a way as also to affirm divine transcendence as he understands it, that is, as free of all forms and concepts.

It is God's sovereign freedom, a second detail from the *Mystical Theology*, which I sought to underline with a translator's trick at the end of my rendering of chapter 5. The Greek text actually ends with "beyond all things," *epekeina panton*. Trick or no, I think this device justified in that it highlights what I take to be one of Dionysius's two fundamental concerns in stressing the use of negative theology: God is subject to absolutely none of our conceptions. Even the revealed names—Father, Son, Spirit—are finally icons, images, drawn from human experience. They are given us in order to point to a reality in the Godhead, indeed, to a community, but that community in and for itself escapes definition. Note as well a third detail in Dionysius's careful qualification: "not spirit *as we understand* [it]." Here he echoes an earlier Christian writer, Gregory Nazianzus, called "the Theologian" because he was the preferred interpreter of the Trinity for the East after the fourth century, whose remarks concerning the divine names even of the Trinity carry a markedly similar thrust.[25] Elsewhere, in *Divine Names* 2.8, Dionysius deals in a similar way with divine fatherhood and sonship. Here, very interestingly and quite in line with my premise of a monastic *Sitz im Leben*, it is the relationship between spiritual father and son at the heart of Eastern Christian ascetic literature from the time of monasticism's fourth-century emergence that he holds out as his preferred image of the first two persons of the Trinity. Yet, he adds, the latter "supremely transcends" even this most exalted and refined instance of human relations.[26] God cannot be known by our kind of knowing but, instead, only by a special kind of "unknowing," *agnosia*, which leaves us free for the experience of the divine presence. Here, then, is the second thrust of the negations: they open up a way to the *cognitio dei experimentalis*.

They do not do so, however, purely and simply as the result of our efforts. Pace Father Vanneste and Rorem, Dionysius's negations are not a kind of metaphysical-cum-mystical trampoline. Thus my fourth detail, which does not appear in the citations I quoted above but does elsewhere in the *Mystical Theology* and throughout the *Corpus Dionysiacum:* whenever Dionysius speaks of the human experience of God, his verbs are invariably in the passive voice.[27] This points as well to a second aspect of the divine freedom that my hero is concerned to emphasize: not only is God free from circumscription by any of our notions, but he is also thus free to reveal himself, to become present to us when we do open up ourselves to becoming present to him. This reciprocity, which Dionysius occasionally refers to as *synergia*, cooperation, after the example of the Eastern Fathers before him, he elsewhere describes in terms of a symmetry of ecstasies.[28] As God comes out of himself, *exestekos*, in a "departure from His own being," *kat'ekbasin tes ousias*, in his processions [*proodoi*] to create, sustain, and save the world, so we are called to an *ecstasis*, a departure from ourselves, as the act of our return [*epistrophe*] to him.[29] Yet the ecstasies are by no means perfectly reciprocal, since the power enabling our return to him and firing our longing for him is, according to *Divine Names* 4.10–17, the very same divine love that moved him to call us and our world into being. This "single moving power" governing the creation, the divine love of *Divine Names* 4.17, is one and the same, I take it, with "the infinite and selfless sea of the divine light, ever ready to open itself for all to share," quoting from *Celestial Hierarchy* 9.3, and I think is also allied—as we shall see presently—with the divine darkness, *gnophos*, into which Moses ascends in *Mystical Theology* 1.3: "The truly secret darkness of unknowing . . . He [Moses] closes [his eyes] to all perceptions open to knowledge and enters into Him Who is altogether untouchable and invisible . . . he is, in accordance with what is greater and by a cessation of his own activity of knowing, united to Him Who is wholly unknowable."[30] As Dionysius writes in *Divine Names* 2.9 of his alleged mentor, Hierotheus, the final stage of our ascent is in fact to become vessels for God's presence, to "suffer divine things" [*pathon ta theia*].[31]

I have obviously left a few questions hanging. If the Dionysian mystical ascent is not purely the work of the autonomous intellect but, rather, requires and at the end surrenders to the power of divine love acting from within, there is still the matter—or rather, the absence—of Christ in the *Mystical Theology*. Second, there is the nagging question for some scholars of a phrase from *Mystical Theology* 1.3 just cited. What is the "according to what is greater," *kata to kreitton*, by which Moses is finally joined to God? Third and last, if the *Mystical Theology* is not, as in Rorem's view, the "methodological prologue" to the Dionysian hierarchies, and so intended to dissolve the latter's traditional use of scriptures and liturgy, then what is its relation to the other half of Dionysius's works?[32] All three of these questions are related. Let me begin my reply by taking up the last two together, and then move on to the first, in order to finish this chapter with a consideration of the phrase that provides my title, "suddenly, Christ," where I hope to show the various threads of Dionysius's thought coming together in the single remarkable paragraph of his third epistle.

The "greater" according to which Moses is united to God has been identified by Father Vanneste and John Rist, together more recently with Ysabel de Andia, with a certain faculty within the human being and above the capacities of both soul and intellect that Dionysius elsewhere refers to as *henosis,* union, and that is thus also somewhat analogous to Proclus's and other late Neoplatonists' idea of the "bloom" or "blossom of the intellect," *to anthos tou nou.*[33] The latter expression does not occur in the *Corpus Dionysiacum,* but I think it likely that it is in fact akin to Dionysius's *henosis.* This appears to raise yet again, as it did for Vanneste and Rist, the question of a "natural mysticism." The appearance is deceptive. First of all, in both Dionysius and the Neoplatonists the faculty is entirely a passive one, and in the case of the Christian writer I think that we can take it as, second, Dionysius's particular expression of a widespread current in Eastern Christian thought—that is, that the human being is created as somehow "capable of God," *homo capax dei,* intended from Adam to be the receptacle and manifestation of the divine presence. This is, in short, the famous deification, *theosis,* which has long been recognized as a key to Eastern Christian understanding of the salvation offered in Christ and which also appears, stated expressly, at a number of points in the *Corpus Dionysiacum.*[34]

We do, however, touch here, third, on what I take to be an important reason—perhaps even the reason—for Dionysius's undoubted attraction to the late Neoplatonists. The latter did not believe in the autonomous intellect either. Rather, and in contrast to Plotinus, they emphatically denied the soul's capacity to ascend unaided to union with the One and believed that it was only through "ineffable rites" handed down from antiquity that the inherent "weakness of the soul" could be assisted sufficiently to participate in the divine realm.[35] One can even speak of a kind of notion of grace implicit in Iamblichus of Chalcis's and Proclus's insistence that the gods are not coerced but are, instead, free to reply to human prayers by manifesting themselves. Dionysius likewise, perhaps especially in *Divine Names* 3, insists on the necessity of prayer as the path to the experience of God.[36] Now, to be sure, Neoplatonist theurgy was in practice worlds away from Christian liturgy, and Dionysius never uses the term "theurgy" for anything other than the work of Christ—the Incarnation, Death, and Resurrection.[37] Neither does he display any interest whatever in late Neoplatonist devotion to sacred stones, crystals, unpronounceable names, séances, ectoplasm, and moving statues. He does, however, affirm a traditional worship, the Christian liturgy, the antiquity of which came vastly better documented than Iamblichus's and Proclus's sad appeal to the spurious *Chaldean Oracles* and which, in turn, could point to a still more ancient ancestry in the Second Temple and, yet further back, to Solomon's Temple and, finally, to God's own revelation to Moses on Sinai of the tabernacle, the very "pattern" of the heavenly liturgy—surely one of the several reasons for the choice of Moses in the *Mystical Theology* as the exemplar of the mystical encounter.[38]

We arrive thus at the opening chapter of the first treatise in the corpus, the *Celestial Hierarchy,* in which Dionysius begins by stating that we gain access [*prosagoge*] to God through Jesus, "the light of the Father."[39] That which we have been given through Christ to make him present to us is the liturgy, as is spelled out in perhaps the most important passage in the *Corpus Dionysiacum:*

> It would not be possible for the human intellect to be ordered with that immaterial imitation of the heavenly minds [i.e., the angels] unless it were to use the material guide that is proper to it, reckoning the visible beauties as reflections of the invisible splendor, the perceptible fragrances as impressions of the intelligible distributions, the material lights an icon of the immaterial gift of light, the sacred and extensive teaching [of the scriptures] [an image] of the intellect's intelligible fulfillment, the outward ranks of the clergy [an image] of the harmonious condition [*hexis*] [of the intellect] set in order for divine things, and [our partaking of] the most divine Eucharist [an icon] of our participation in Jesus.[40]

The passage speaks of worship in the local church, with its candles, incense, scripture readings, orders of clergy, and sacraments. It claims, first, that this liturgy is an image and reflection of the angels. This is nothing new in either Christian or prior Jewish tradition.[41] Second, however, it also specifies that the outward forms of our liturgy—or, perhaps better, of "our hierarchy," since by the latter phrase Dionysius always means the Church at worship—reflect and, I will add, condition or form the inward shape of the soul or intellect. The visible service is therefore a symbol, bearing in mind that the latter term is always to be understood for Dionysius in a strong sense, uniting and coordinating three levels of being: the heavenly, the earthly, and what Saint Paul refers to as the "inner man." This coordination runs consistently throughout the treatises on the hierarchies. It is, indeed, a key to those passages where Dionysius does in fact speak of the form or likeness of God. For example, there is his definition two chapters later of hierarchy as "a sacred order [*taxis*], knowledge [*episteme*], and activity [*energeia*] assimilated [literally, made like to, *aphomoiomene*] so far as possible to the form of God [*to theoeides*]," whose purpose, he continues, is to make its members "images [*agalmata*] of God . . . clear and spotless mirrors reflecting the primordial light."[42]

The shape or form of God is obviously not corporeal here, but it is just as clearly a meaningful idea for our author as it denotes for him both the shape of the worshipping communities of heaven and earth, together with the nature of the relationships obtaining between their members—ordered, harmonious, and governed by loving care, as Dionysius spells out elsewhere—and the inner shape of the soul "formed" in the same virtues.[43] This emerges with particular force in the long Epistle 8 addressed to the erring monk, Demophilus. The latter's name means "beloved by the mob," and in him I think we find an example of the sort of ascetics, enormously popular and hence powerful in especially (though not uniquely) the Syrian Church of the era, whom it is Dionysius's intent to counter and, perhaps, to convert.[44] Demophilus has upset the God-given order, *taxis,* of the Church by presuming to break in on the confession of a notorious sinner, beat the latter up, chase the confessing priest out of the altar, and then stand guard over the "holy things," presumably the reserved sacrament, in order to prevent a second "profanation." The scenario allows Dionysius to expand on our theme. Demophilus, he says, has broken God's ordinance by going in where none but the clergy are allowed, the sanctuary, and by claiming authority where he has none, that is, over the sacraments. More important, and illustrative of my point above, the monk's pride, anger, and consequent usurpation stand in precise contrast to the meekness [*praotes*], mercy [*eleos*], and love that characterized the great God-seers of the biblical revelation: Moses and David, the angels, and preeminently Christ himself.[45] The sacred order, *taxis,* of the Church has been upset, as Dionysius says in so many words, because Demophilus own inner *taxis* was out of order.[46] He had, in short, failed to allow the shape of the liturgy to shape or form his inner man. The epistle concludes with the story of a certain holy bishop, Carpus, who had permitted anger to overcome his normally meek and loving pastoral care sufficiently to curse two sinners. The good bishop is then favored with a vision. Christ in light appears to him on the heavenly throne carried by the angels but, then, pointedly leaves his throne in order to extend a hand to pull the two penitent malefactors out of the jaws of hell.[47]

The focus on pride and, particularly, on anger is also, I should add, typical of the ascetical literature of the century and more that preceded the Areopagitica. So, too, is the emphasis Dionysius places on meekness and the latter's link with Moses as the God-seer (cf. Num. 12:3–8), together with mercy and love. These are the virtues that the late-fourth-century monk Evagrius of Pontus emphasized as making us coworkers with the angels—a very Dionysian theme—and as the precondition for the *visio dei.*[48] The discussion in Epistle 8 therefore dwells precisely on the formation of that receptacle or capacity within us that allows for God's epiphany. Likewise, God himself is something more for Dionysius than anonymous, impersonal divinity. He has a face and a name, and they are Christ. We shall find this brought out in what I take to be a parallel with Moses' ascent of Sinai in the *Mystical Theology* expressed in a passage at the center of the treatise devoted to the Church, the *Ecclesiastical Hierarchy*, and reinforced by the five epistles immediately following the *Mystical Theology*.

Before I turn to these concluding sections, however, let me pause here to note another fourth-century monastic connection with the *Corpus Dionysiacum*. If I spoke just above of Dionysius's attraction to late Neoplatonism and the latter's emphasis on ritual to make up for the soul's weakness, than I must add that we should also look for his ancestry in this regard to three Syrian Christian ascetic writers in the latter half of the fourth century. Ephrem Syrus (d. 373) and the anonymous author of the *Liber Graduum* wrote in Syriac and the similarly unknown writer of the enormously influential *Macarian Homilies* in Greek. All three were concerned to emphasize the necessary connection between the life of the soul and the public liturgy of the Church as a divinely given image of the transformed "inner man." They were also, I think, anxious to bring those among their ascetical contemporaries who were questioning the necessity of clergy and sacraments—and we know that there were such ascetics, particularly in Syria—into conformity with the *societas ecclesiae*.[49] In other words, they shared the same concerns as we find governing Dionysius more than a hundred years later. The Areopagitica belong within this ascetico-mystical continuum. The effectively immediate reception of the *Corpus Dionysiacum* is otherwise inexplicable, though some scholars have tried to explain it by appealing to the subapostolic pseudonym. This is inadequate and the Eastern monks have always known better: Dionysius was one of their own.

Regarding the specific contributions of my three Syrians, certain elements deserve quoting here. Ephrem, perhaps the earliest of the three, makes his argument through the series of parallels he weaves into his *Hymns on Paradise*. The Paradise Mountain, Sinai, the Jerusalem Temple, the Christian assembly at worship, and the individual Christian are all set in apposition to each other, such that, as we shall see with Dionysius, the entry into the sanctuary of the Church corresponds with Moses' ascent up Sinai and the Christian's discovery, within his or her own heart, of the radiance of the divine presence, the *shekinto* in Ephrem's Syriac (equivalent to the rabbinic *shekinah*) that for him signifies the form of Christ in light.[50] Moses' *ascensus montis dei* is thus a type simultaneously of the *ingressus ad altare dei* both of the worshipping community and of the individual believer, that is, the entry into what we might call the double altar of the Eucharistic presence and of the sanctified heart. I believe that this is precisely the relationship of themes obtaining between

Dionysius's two treatises, the *Mystical Theology* (the *ascensus*) and the *Ecclesiatical Hierarchy* (the *ingressus*).

The *Liber Graduum* speaks of "three churches": the heavenly church of the angels and saints, the earthly church of clergy and sacraments, and the "little church" of the heart. It is the middle term, this writer insists, the earthly church, that enables the believer "to find himself in the church of the heart, and [thence]," even if only momentarily in this life, "in the church on high."[51] Perhaps the most exact anticipation of Dionysius, especially of *Celestial Hierarchy* 1.3 cited above, comes in the *Macarian Homilies,* as in the following: "Because visible things are the type and shadow of hidden ones, and the visible temple [a type] of the temple of the heart, and the priest [a type] of the true priest of the grace of Christ, and all the rest of the sequence [*akolouthia*] of the visible arrangement [*oikonomia*] [a type] of the rational and hidden matters of the inner man, we receive the visible arrangement [*oikonomia*] . . . of the Church as a pattern [*hypodeigma*] [of what is] at work in the soul by grace."[52] By "arrangement," *oikonomia,* the author means exactly the same thing as Dionysius's *taxis,* the ordering of the Church at worship—bishops at the altar, priests around him, deacons ministering, laity in the nave, and penitents and catechumens in the Church porch.[53] Like Dionysius, too, this image is not a mere illustration but, as the homilist puts it, a "pattern" to be internalized. Christ gave us, he says a little earlier, "the icon of the Church" in order "that faithful souls might be made again and, having received transformation [*metabole,* a play on traditional language for the miraculous change of the Eucharistic elements], be enabled to inherit everlasting life."[54] The liturgy is thus, as in the *Corpus Dionysiacum,* not only a sign or projection of the soul but also a transfiguring force molding the soul from within.

Turning thus to the treatise on "our hierarchy," the Church, I would underline, first, the architecture of the piece. It is balanced, a symmetry, with a deliberately central chapter toward which the action of the first three chapters, as it were, ascends and from which the concluding chapters decline or descend. Chapter 2 on baptism, and 7 on Christian burial contrive thus to embrace the whole of the believer's life. Dionysius speaks, in fact, of two deaths and two births, sharing in Christ's death through the figurative death of baptismal immersion and thus receiving "divine birth" through the sacrament, on the one hand, and at our literal, physical death being carried out of the church building in hope of the rebirth, *paliggenesia,* of the Resurrection in fulfillment of the baptismal promise, on the other hand.[55] Chapter 3, on the Eucharist, stands in counterbalance to chapters 5 and 6, devoted respectively to the ordination of the clergy in front of the altar and to monastic tonsure accomplished just outside the sanctuary area.[56] The *ingressus* of chapters 2 and 3 and *egressus* of 5–7 thus pivot on the center of the treatise, chapter 4's meditation on the altar, the focal point of the Church's and the Christian's life on this side of the *eschaton,* and on the sacrament of the chrism, the scented oil used in the Eastern Church both to anoint newly baptized believers and to consecrate, precisely, church altars.[57] It is also in this chapter, I think, that we arrive at a reference to the *cognitio dei experimentalis* that is meant to be taken in parallel with the apophatic ascent of the *Mystical Theology.* It thus deserves a few words.

Dionysius begins his meditation on altar and chrism in *Ecclesiastical Hierarchy* 4.3.1 with, quite significantly, a lengthy consideration of the holy man. It is such people, he tells us, who "*are* the truly divine images of that infinitely divine fragrance" that has chosen to take up its abode "within their intellects." The fragrance, as he makes clear a few paragraphs later, is the presence of Christ.[58] After a lengthy meditation on the seraphim around Christ in heaven as typified by the clergy around the bishop at the altar, and following several references to the Incarnation, he moves to his summary statement;

> The theurgy [i.e., the Incarnation] transcends the heavens and is superessential. It is the origin, essence, and perfecting power of all our divinely-worked sanctification. For if our most divine altar is Jesus, Who is [both] the divine consecration of the heavenly intelligences [i.e., the angels] [and he] in Whom we, being at once consecrated and in mystery wholly consumed [literally, become whole burnt offerings, *holokautomenoi*], have according to the [scripture] saying "our access" [*prosagoge*] [to the Father], let us [then] gaze with supramundane eyes on this most divine altar [Jesus], by Whom all who are in process of perfection are both perfected and made holy, that is, by Him Who is Himself [also] the most divine chrism.[59]

Four things deserve underlining here: first, the reference to the holy man, whom Dionysius understands as typified by the sacrament; second, the coordination between heaven and earth; and, third, the identification of both altars, on high and here below, with Christ. My fourth point lies in what I take to be the relation, and even perhaps the functional identity, between the passage quoted here and Moses' entrance into the divine darkness in the *Mystical Theology.* The altar is the peak, to borrow from Ephrem's imagery, of the "mountain of the Church," the place of the divine presence. That presence is Christ, in whom "wholly consumed" we meet God who, again, is Christ, the divine chrism. I submit that this "holocaust" is deliberately intended as a counterpart to the stripping away of the apophatic ascent in the *Mystical*

Theology. Likewise, I would therefore read the darkness, *gnophos*, into which Moses plunges in *Mystical Theology* 1.3, the "dazzling darkness of divinity," as in fact Christ, "the light of the Father" (*Celestial Hierarchy* 1.2), who appears "suddenly" within the vessels, the "unspotted mirrors" (to recall *Celestial Hierarchy* 3.2), who have been prepared for him.[60]

The stripping in preparation for this encounter has already begun with the cultivation of the virtues we saw stressed in Epistle 8—meekness, mercy, and love—and with the struggle against the passions that Dionysius sketches in his discussion of the catechumenate in *Ecclesiastical Hierarchy* 3.3.7. There is also, and relatedly, the implicit apophaticism of his emphasis in *Ecclesiastical Hierarchy* 6.3.2 on the monks as called to live a life without "fantasy," that is, wholly focused on God.[61] We find the very same emphasis in, again, the earlier monastic literature, particularly in Evagrius Ponticus's remarkable little treatise *On Prayer*, in which the latter insists that the dawning of "the light of the Trinity" within the sanctified intellect requires the putting away of every image and concept, even the most exalted. "Prayer," says Evagrius, "is the negation of concepts"; and elsewhere, "Happy is the spirit that attains to perfect formlessness at the time of prayer." Indeed, for Evagrius prayer is in fact that state or condition of pure receptivity that answers in Dionysius to the notion of the "unspotted mirror," the *capax dei*. It is the condition for God's self-manifestation.[62]

Darkness, light, and manifestation are very much the subjects of the five epistles that, and not accidentally, follow the *Mystical Theology*. Perhaps I should emphasize here that the latter treatise is not the end of the discussion begun in the *Celestial Hierarchy*, especially of *Celestial Hierarchy* 1.3. Were that so, then the series of "nots" concluding the former treatise might indeed be taken as signaling, as in Rorem's account, a "loveless" and "Christless" mysticism. Instead, however, the apophatic ascent is embedded in a larger scheme, the outlines of which I have endeavored to sketch and which carries on to the end of the *Corpus Dionysiacum* in Epistle 10, addressed to "John at Patmos." Dionysius ends with a recollection of the same apocalyptic visionary literature with which we saw him begin in *Celestial Hierarchy* 2, on the throne vision of Ezekiel 1. The whole project of the *Corpus Dionysiacum* may therefore be read as an effort to set this visionary tradition within an ecclesiological and, yes, christological context.[63]

It is that same tradition that I think lies behind what appears at first glance as a harmlessly erudite *scholion* by Dionysius's earliest commentator, the learned sixth-century bishop and polemicist, John of Scythopolis, on the darkness of *Mystical Theology* 1.3. The word *gnophos*, which appears in the LXX of Exod. 20:21, is, John remarks, translating the Hebrew term *araphel*.

He goes on to add, "The Hebrews say that *araphel* is the name of the firmament into which Moses went, for [the Jews] speak of seven firmaments, which they also call heavens."[64] This rather striking evocation of the *hekalot* tradition, the mysticism of the heavenly "palaces" that we find in the rabbinic literature of the era, is not without relevance to Dionysius. The rabbinic-era adepts who hoped to make the *aliyah bammerkavah*, the ascent to the chariot [throne] of God, looked forward at the terminus of their experience to the vision of the divine Glory and its radiance.[65] That it is the tradition of the *visio dei gloriae* that underlies Dionysius's discussion in the *Mystical Theology* and Epistles 1–5 and that he identifies this experience with the *visio christi*, emerges clearly in the epistles.

The first five epistles function as a kind of chiasm that serves to complete the thought of the *Mystical Theology*. Epistle 1 is paralleled by 5 and 2 by 4, with Epistle 3 tying them up and together. Epistle 1 carries on the notes of darkness and unknowing, *agnosia*, which preoccupy the *Mystical Theology*. God's darkness (here *skotos*) is "hidden by the light of knowledge" of existing things, Dionysius says, while "complete unknowing is the knowledge of Him Who transcends all things."[66] This statement is countered or, better, expanded on in the opening line of Epistle 5, "The divine darkness [*gnophos*] is the unapproachable light in which God is said to dwell" (cf. I Tim. 6:16). God's dwelling place, *katoiketerion*, recalls—and again not accidentally— Scythopolis's *scholion* on the *araphel*, the place of the divine throne, which is always characterized by the overwhelming light of the presence, and of the stream of light that proceeds from it. Thus we find Dionysius continuing: "And if it [the *phos aprositon*] is invisible because of its superabundant clarity, and unapproachable because of its superabundant outpouring of light, yet it is here that everyone enters who has been made worthy of seeing and knowing God."[67] He goes on to cite David and, especially, Paul as examples of this experience. Here, too, another *scholion* will help us to identify a key theophany to which Dionysius will shortly be alluding in Epistle 3. On the "unapproachable light," the Scholiast observes that the *visio dei* might be compared to looking at the sun's disk at midday, *mesembria*.[68]

The "transcendent outpouring" of the light stream from the presence in Epistle 5 leads us to the matter of God's self-communication, the subject of Epistles 2 and 4. In the former, Dionysius alludes back to a distinction he had underlined in *Divine Names* 2 and 11 between God *in se* and *ad extra*. Deification is real, the Areopagite argues, because God truly gives himself. Yet, while he is himself the "deifying gift," *theopoion doron*, he still transcends the relations he enters into. His gifts are his powers, *dynameis*, or energies, *energeiai*, but not his essence, *ousia*.[69] Epistle 4 then makes it clear that the source of the gift of deification is Christ. In Jesus, Dionysius tells us, transcendence [*apophasis*] and immanence [*kataphasis*] have been joined. Therefore, he continues, Christ "did not do what is divine as God, nor what is human as man, but instead, as God having become man, he has administered to [or, arranged for, *pepoliteumenos*] us a certain, new, divine-human activity [*theandrike energeia*]."[70] Christ's divine-human activity, I will add, in light of my discussion above of the ecclesial dimension of Dionysius's thought, comes to us in the polity and way of life—the *entheos politeia,* as he puts it elsewhere—of the Church.[71] It is in the latter that we receive the "deifying gift" and are led to the encounter with the mystery of Christ's divinity in a "transcendent outpouring of light."

We have finally arrived at the word and document that inspired the title of this essay, the "suddenly" of Epistle 3, which I quote in full:

> "Suddenly" means that which has come forth from the hitherto invisible and beyond hope into manifestation. And I think that here the Scripture [literally, the theology] is suggesting the philanthropy of Christ. The superessential has proceeded out hiddenness to become manifest to us by becoming a human being. Yet He is also hidden, both after the manifestation and, to speak more divinely, even within it. For this is the hidden of Jesus, and neither by rational discourse nor by intuition can His mystery [*mysterion*] be explained, but instead even when spoken, it remains ineffable [*arreton*], and when conceived, unknowable [*agnoston*].[72]

The first thing we might notice is the reprise of the themes of this volume: *apophasis,* divine unknowability and ineffability, together with the tension between hidden and revealed. Second, there is surely a sacramental echo in the reference to the *mysterion* of the Incarnation. Christ is *the* sacrament, at once the source and terminus of the divine processions to us, and both the vehicle and the goal of our return. Thus, third, we can infer the themes of *proodos-epistrophe,* the transmutation of the Neoplatonist bedrock noted above.

The real force and key to the coalescence of Dionysius's thought here lies in the word "suddenly," *exaiphnes,* which opens the epistle. Modern scholarship has noted his admitted dependence here on the Platonic tradition. In Plato's *Parmenides* the "sudden" indicates the timeless moment of intersection between eternity and time, the Forms and the phenomenal world. In the *Symposium* it appears again at the conclusion of the ascent of *eros,* the vision of Beauty. These are certainly all important Dionysian themes as well, and to them we might add the use to which Plotinus puts the sudden in *Enneads*

5.3.17, 5.5.7, and 6.7.36 to signify the moment of the vision of the One in light.[73] I cheerfully concede the undeniable Platonist impress here.

It is at this point, however, that modern scholars have always stopped. They remain thus entirely insensitive to the use of the sudden in the scriptures and in subsequent Christian literature. There are four appearances of the *exaiphnes* in the New Testament that I believe are of direct relevance: Acts 9:3 and 22:6, Luke 2:13, and Mark 13:36. The first two are functionally identical descriptions of Saint Paul's conversion on the Damascus Road. I quote from the second: "As I was travelling . . . at around midday [*mesembria*] a great light from heaven suddenly [*exaiphnes*] flashed around me." The light, of course, is Christ, Who sends Paul off on his mission to the Gentiles. I note the themes of light, the latter as identified with Christ, the "midday" we saw signaled by the Scholiast, and the mission to the "Greeks." Luke 2:13 links the suddenly to the *gloria in excelsis,* the manifestation of the angelic liturgy to the shepherds at the moment of Christ's birth. The fourth instance, Mark 13:36, occurs at the end of the eschatological discourse where Christ warns his listeners to be watchful lest, returning suddenly, the Master find them asleep. The New Testament thus links the sudden to Christ, light, the angelic liturgy, and the eschaton.[74]

My readings in the Christian literature prior to the *Corpus Dionysiacum* have led me, quite accidentally and not at all systematically, to a number of appearances of the sudden that are also in harmony with what I take to be Dionysius's intentions. The earliest example comes from the Syriac work of the third century, the *Acts of Judas Thomas,* where, in the "Hymn of the Pearl," the Apostle "suddenly" encounters the "robe of glory" woven for him in heaven. The context makes it clear that the "robe" is equivalent to the "luminous image" familiar from Jewish and Jewish-Christian literature and that the speaker's clothing with it represents a mystical experience. The experience is, moreover, one of heavenly ascent: clothed with the robe of light, the Apostle goes up "to the gate of greeting" where he worships "the Splendor [*pheggos*] of the Father," that is, Christ.[75] In Athanasius's *Life of Anthony,* the father of monks is rescued from demonic assault by the sudden beam of light from heaven that then comforts him with the voice of Christ.[76] In Ephrem Syrus, the sudden occurs at least three times. In his *Hymns on Nature* (6.7), Christ is the "star of light Who shone forth suddenly" at the Incarnation, while in the *Hymns on Paradise,* the sudden is linked, first, with the *trisagion* of the Seraphim breaking the silence before the presence in Eden and, second, with the recognition of the Risen Christ at the clearly eucharistic "breaking of the bread" in the Emmaus story of Luke 24: "Bread was the key," says

Ephrem, "whereby their eyes were opened . . . darkened eyes beheld a vision of joy and were suddenly [*men shelya*] filled with happiness."[77] Thus, again, we find the term linked with the mystical vision, Christ, light, and the liturgies of both heaven and earth.

If we were in addition to assume that Dionysius knew Syriac, then still another set of associations comes into play. The *men* of the Syriac translation of *exaiphnes* is merely the equivalent of the Greek *ek*, "from," "out of." *Shelya*, however, denotes "rest," "silence," and "stillness," and in Christian Syriac is usually connected with eremetic ascetics, as is *hesychia* in Christian Greek.[78] It may also be used, as does one contemporary of Dionysius, to signify the divine being or essence.[79] As a bilingual pun playing off of these several resonances, the sudden fits quite well indeed into the several themes of the *Corpus Dionysiacum,* and particularly of the *Mystical Theology,* which I have been at pains to underline. It also reminds me of still another Syrian, Ignatius of Antioch (d.115), who is the only Church Father whom Dionysius felt it safe to quote by name (occasioning one of his commentators some difficulties in defending the pseudonym).[80] Ignatius calls Christ "the Word Who proceeds from the Father's silence [*sige*]" and adds, "It is better to keep silence and to be, than to talk and not to be. . . . He that truly possesses the word of Jesus is able to listen to His silence." His concluding words point us directly to my own concluding remarks: "Let us therefore do all things as knowing that he dwells in us, that we may be his temples and he himself may be in us as our God."[81]

Specifically in Ignatius's call to become Christ's "temples," I think that we arrive naturally at the biblical text that John of Scythopolis tells us Dionysius is quoting in Epistle 3, Mal. 3:1, "And suddenly the Lord Whom you seek will come into His temple, and the Angel of Great Counsel Whom you desire." Another scholiast goes on to connect this passage with John 2:21, the temple of Christ's body.[82] The historical Incarnation certainly is part of the message here, as Werner Beierwaltes rightly observed, but I would also point to the coordination that I have noted throughout this chapter between both the "temple" of the liturgical assembly and the "temple" of the Christian's body and soul, together with those passages in earlier Christian literature, going back to the New Testament itself, which link the sudden with mystical experience and, especially, with a theophany of light.[83] Given these, we can surely say that Dionysius also intends to signify both the presence of Christ on the eucharistic altar and his visitation—"beyond hope," "ineffable," "unknowable"—within the temple of the soul. This sudden flash of the "unapproachable light" within is, I maintain, the purpose and goal of the *Mystical Theology* 4–5, as well as the content both of the darkness into which Moses ascends in *Mystical Theology* 1.3 and of the "consummation" and "access" of *Ecclesiastical Hierarchy* 4.3.12. Epistle 3 is the *Corpus Dionysiacum* in a nutshell: mystical, indeed, but also fundamentally liturgical and christological. In Christ the sudden, the several concerns of the corpus—angels and humans, sacraments and apophatic theology, objective and subjective, hierarchy and personal encounter, clergy and ascetic visionaries, Christian revelation and Platonist philosophy, the present world and the eschaton—all meet and are reconciled.

I do not know, frankly, if I have managed to answer all the questions I raised at the beginning of this chapter in the "case for the prosecution," but I hope that I have at the least begun to show why Dionysius was so rapidly received and cherished by the Christian East and especially by the monks. The apophaticism for which he is so famed was read by the latter as fully in concert with other, earlier writers in the tradition, such as, notably, that Evagrius whom I cited earlier a couple of times. It was certainly not understood as a solvent burning away Christian accretions but, rather, as the last opening up of the soul already formed and prepared, through ascesis and sacramental participation, to become the vessel of God's presence in his Christ. My Dionysius at least, as opposed to the Areopagite of many other scholars, belonged and contributed to a continuum. Just as he is bracketed by the tradition that at once inspired him and recognized him as its own, so, too, are the ascending negations and darkness of the *Mystical Theology* bracketed by a larger thinking and background, the *cognitio dei experimentalis*, to which they are contributing factors, instruments and metaphors of a larger purpose. That purpose is the integration of the personal, ascetical, and mystical current of Christianity with the ecclesial, liturgical, and public nature of the faith. This is undeniably the way in which the *Corpus Dionysiacum* was received and read in the Christian East. I for one cannot but believe that this reading also matches Dionysius's own purposes more closely, certainly, than that of the majority of his scholarly critics over the past century, and I cannot resist the observation, which I have made elsewhere, that those Eastern monks who received him have in fact always known better.[84]

Notes

1. The most complete listing of parallels between Dionysius and late Platonism is still Hugo Koch's *Pseudo-Dionysius Areopagita in seinen Beziehungen zum Neuplatonismus und Mysterienwesen* (Mainz: Franz Kirchheim, 1900). See also H. F. Müller, *Dionysios, Proklos, Plotinos: Ein historischer Beitrag zur neuplatonischen Philosophie*, 2d ed. (Münster and Westfalen: Aschendorff, 1926); E. Corsini, *Il tratto "De Divinibus Nominibus" dello Pseudo Dionigi e i commeti Neoplatonici al Parmenide* (Turin: Giappichelli, 1962); J. Vanneste, *Le mystère de*

Dieu (Brussels: Desclée de Brouwer, 1959); R. Hathaway, *Hierarchy and the Definition of Order in the Letters of Pseudo-Dionysius* (The Hague: M. Nijhoff, 1969); B. Brons, *Untersuchungen zum Verhältnis von neuplatonischer Metaphysik und christliche Tradition bei Dionysius Areopagita* (Göttingen: Vandenhoeck & Ruprecht, 1976); S. Gersh, *From Iamblichus to Erieugena: An Investigation of the Prehistory and Evolution of the Pseudo-Dionysian Tradition* (Leiden: Brill, 1976); P. E. Rorem, *Biblical and Liturgical Symbols in the Pseudo-Dionysian Synthesis* (Toronto: Pontifical Institute of Medieval Studies, 1986), "The Place of the *Mystical Theology* in the Pseudo-Dionysian Corpus," *Dionysius* 4 (1980): 87–98, and *Pseudo-Dionysius: A Commentary on the Texts and an Introduction to Their Influence* (Oxford: Oxford University Press, 1994); and Y. de Andia, *Henôsis: L'union à Dieu chez Denys l'Aréopagite* (Leiden and Cologne: Brill, 1996). On apophatic theology in particular, including Dionysius and the Platonists, see R. Mortley, *From Word to Silence*, vol. 2, *The Way of Negation: Christian and Greek* (Bonn: Hannstein, 1986).

2. See, e.g., R. Roques, *L'univers dionysien* (Paris: Aubier, 1954); the succession of articles by O. von Semmelroth in *Scholastik*, nos. 20–24 (1949), 25 (1950), 27 (1952), 28 (1953), and 29 (1954); E. von Ivanka, *Plato Christianus* (Einsiedeln: Johannes Verlag, 1964), 228–89, and *Dionysius Areopagita: Von den Namen zum Unnennbaren* (Einsiedeln: Johannes Verlag, 1981); and P. Scazzoso, *Ricerche sulla struttura del linguagio dello Pseudo-Dionigi Areopagita: Introduzione alla lettura delle opere pseudo-dionisiane* (Milan: Società Editrice Vìta e Pensiero, 1967).

3. Perhaps the most important defender of Dionysius's place in the Eastern Christian tradition earlier this century is V. N. Lossky. See esp. his "La notion des 'analogies' chez Denys le pseudo-aréopagite," *Archives d'histoire doctrinale et littéraire du moyen age* 5 (1931): 279–309, as well as the opening chapters of his *The Mystical Theology of the Eastern Church*, trans. Members of the Fellowship of St. Alban and St. Sergius (London: J. Clarke, 1957; reprint, London: J. Clarke, 1968). For a massive though not entirely successful attempt to place Dionysius within the current of Alexandrian and Cappadocian Christian thought, see W. Völker, *Kontemplation und Ekstase bei Pseudo-Dionysius Areopagita* (Wiesbaden: Franz Steiner, 1958). H. von Balthasar, *Herrlichkeit: eine theologische Aesthetik* (Einsiedeln: Johannes Verlag, 1962), 2:147–214, supplies a most sensitive analysis of Dionysius's place in Eastern Christian thought, though regrettably without an elaborate apparatus. J. Stiglmayr, "Das Aufkommen der Pseudo-Dionysischen Schriften und ihr Eindringen in die christliche Literatur bis zum Lateranconcil 649: Ein zweiter Beitrag zur Dionysius Frage," in *IV Jahresbericht des offentlichen Privatgymnasiums an der Stelle matutina zu Feldkirche* (Feldkirche: 1895), established the links between the Dionysian corpus and Syria, together with the *a quo* (A.D. 486) and *ad quem* (A.D. 532) of the corpus's composition, which have never since been challenged, while W. Strothmann, *Das Sakrament der Myron-Weihe in der Schrift De Ecclesiastica Hierarchia des Pseudo-Dionysius Areopagita in syrischen Übersetzung und Kommentaren* (Wiesbaden: Harrassowitz, 1978), placed Dionysius's liturgy still more firmly in the Syrian Christian milieu. More recently, A. Louth, *Denys the Areopagite* (Wilton, Conn.: Morehouse-Barlow, 1989), has also taken advantage of scholarship on Syriac-speaking Christianity at different points in the course of his very sympathetic account of the corpus and its place in Eastern Christian thought.

4. My argument is made at greatest length in A. Golitzin, *Et introibo ad altare dei: The Mystagogy of Dionysius Areopagita* (Thessalonica: Patriarchal Institute of Patristic Studies, 1994), esp. 349–92, elsewhere more briefly in "The Mysticism of Dionysius Areopagita: Platonist or Christian?" *Mystics Quarterly* 19, no. 3 (1993): 98–114, and "Hierarchy versus

Anarchy? Dionysius Areopagita, Symeon New Theologian, Nicetas Stethatos, and Their Common Roots in Ascetic Tradition," *St. Vladimir's Theological Quarterly* 38, no.2 (1994): 131–79.

5. I have touched on Dionysius's connection with these traditions briefly in "Revisiting the 'Sudden': Epistle III in the *Corpus Dionysiacum*," *Studia Patristica* 37 (2001): 482–91. The distinctive qualities of Syrian Christian asceticism have been noted for some time in the scholarly literature and, more particularly, its links with prior Jewish traditions. See in this regard, e.g., G. Nedungatt, "The Covenanters of the Early Syriac-Speaking Church," *Orientalia Christiana Periodica* 39 (1973): 191–215, 419–44; R. Murray, "An Exhortation to Candidates for Ascetical Vows at Baptism in the Ancient Syrian Church," *New Testament Studies* 21 (1974): 59–80, and "Disaffected Judaism and Early Christianity: Some Predisposing Factors," in *To See Us as Others See Us* (Chico, Calif.: 1985), 263–81; and S. Griffith, "Monks, 'Singles', and 'Sons of the Covenant': Reflections on Syriac Ascetic Terminology," in *Eulogema: Studies in Honor of Robert Taft SJ*, ed. E. Carr et al. (Rome: Pontificio Ateneo S. Anselmo, 1993), 141–60.

On continuities in the ascetico-mystical vision tradition between Jewish apocalyptic literature and Christian, esp. Syrian Christian, ascetical works, see P. Nagel, *Die Motivierung der Askese in der alten Kirche und der Ursprung des Mönchtums* (Berlin: Akademie Verlag, 1966); G. Quispel, *Makarios, das Thomasevangelium, und das Lied von der Perle* (Leiden: 1967); F.-E. Morard, *"Monachos,* Moine: Histoire du terme jusqu'au IVe siècle," *Zeitschrift für Philosophie und Theologie* 20 (1973): 332–411; A. Guillaumont, *Aux origines du monachisme chrétien* (Maine and Loire: Abbaye de Bellefontaine, 1979); G. G. Stroumsa, "Ascèse et gnose: Aux origines de la spiritualité monastique," *Revue thomiste* 89 (1981): 557–73; S. Brock, "Prayer of the Heart in the Syrian Perspective," *Sobornost* 4, no. 2 (1982): 131–42; R. A. Kraft, "The Pseudepigrapha in Christianity," in *Tracing the Threads: Studies in the Vitality of the Jewish Pseudepigrapha*, ed. J. C. Reeves (Atlanta: Scholars Press, 1995), 55–86; and most recently, A. DeConick, *Seek to See Him: Ascent and Vision Mysticism in the Gospel of Thomas* (Leiden: Brill, 1996).

On themes from Jewish mystical literature in earliest Christian literature, see G. Quispel, "Ezekiel 1:26 in Jewish Mysticism," *Vigiliae christianae* 34 (1980): 1–13, and "The Study of Encratism: A Historical Survey," in *La Tradizione dell'Enkrateia*, ed. U. Bianci (Rome: Edizione dell'Ateneo, 1985), 35–81; C. R. Rowland, *The Open Heaven: A Study of Apocalyptic in Judaism and Early Christianity* (New York: Crossroad, 1982); J. J. Collins, *The Apocalyptic Imagination: An Introduction to the Jewish Matrix of Christianity* (New York: Crossroad, 1984); G. Anderson, "Celibacy or Consummation in the Garden? Reflections on Early Jewish and Christian Interpretations of the Garden of Eden," *Harvard Theological Review* 82, no. 2 (1989): 121–48; J. Fossum, *The Image of the Invisible God: Essays on the Influence of Jewish Mysticism on Early Christology* (Freiburg and Göttingen: Vandenhoeck & Ruprecht, 1995); M. Himmelfarb, *Ascent to Heaven in Jewish and Christian Apocalypses* (Oxford and New York: Oxford University Press, 1993); A. Segal, *Paul the Convert: Apostolate and Apostasy of Saul the Pharisee* (New Haven, Conn.: Yale University Press, 1990); G. G. Stroumsa, "Form(s) of God: Some Notes on Metatron and Christ," *Harvard Theological Review* 76, no. 3 (1983): 269–88, and *Hidden Wisdom: Esoteric Traditions and the Roots of Christian Mysticism* (Leiden: Brill, 1996).

On relations and continuities between the Second Temple, apocalyptic literature, Qumran, and later Rabbinic mystical traditions, see G. Scholem, *Jewish Gnosticism, Merkabah Mys-*

ticism, and Talmudic Tradition (New York: Jewish Theological Seminary of America, 1960); I. Gruenwald, *Apocalyptic and Merkabah Mysticism* (Leiden: Brill, 1980); J. Baumgarten, "The Qumran *Sabbath Shirot* and the Rabbinic Tradition," *Revue de Qumran* 13 (1988): 199–213; S. D. Fraade, "Ascetical Aspects of Ancient Judaism," in *Jewish Spirituality,* vol. 1, *From the Bible through the Middle Ages,* ed. A. Green (New York: Crossroad, 1988), 253–88; J. Levenson, "The Jerusalem Temple in Devotional and Visionary Experience," in *Jewish Spirituality,* ed. Green, 1:32–61; C. R. A. Morray-Jones, "Transformational Mysticism in the Apocalyptic-Merkabah Tradition," *Journal of Jewish Studies* 43 (1992): 1–31, and "Paradise Revisited (2 Corinthians 12:1–12): The Jewish Mystical Background of Paul's Apostolate," *Harvard Theological Review* 86 (1993): 177–217 and 265–92; J. J. Collins and M. Fishbane, eds., *Death, Ecstasy, and Otherworldly Journeys* (Albany: State University of New York Press, 1995); and W. F. Smelik, "On the Mystical Transformation of the Righteous into Light in Judaism," *Journal for the Study of Judaism* 27, no. 2 (1995): 122–44.

6. On Dionysius with regard to the ascetical origins of his invention and use of the word "hierarchy," see A. Golitzin, "Hierarchy versus Anarchy?" 152–70; and *Et introibo* 119–230 and 354–92, and "Liturgy and Mysticism: The Experience of God in Orthodox Christianity," *Pro Ecclesia* 8, no. 2 (1999): 159–86, esp. 168–85.

7. *The Mystical Theology* is found, together with Dionysius's other works, in vol. 3 of J. P. Migne's *Patrologia graeca,* here cols. 997A–1048B. In subsequent references I shall the several treatises—*Mystical Theology, Divine Names, Celestial Hierarchy, Ecclesiastical Hierarchy,* and Epistle—and their chapter numbers, together with the Migne column number and letter. In parentheses, I shall include the page and line numbers of the critical text of the *Corpus Dionysiacum,* published this decade in two volumes: *Corpus Dionysiacum,* vol. 1, *De Divinibus Nominibus,* ed. B. R. Suchla (Berlin and New York: De Gruyter, 1990), and *Corpus Dionysiacum,* vol. 2, *De Coelesti Hierarchia, De Ecclesiastica Hierarchia, De Mystica Theologia, Epistulae,* ed. G. Heil and A. M. Ritter (Berlin and New York: De Gruyter, 1991). The most recent translation of the *Corpus Dionysiacum* into English is that of C. Liubheid and P. E. Rorem, trans., *Pseudo-Dionysius: The Complete Works* (New York: Paulist, 1987). Unless otherwise specified, however, the translations of Dionysius cited below will be my own.

8. *Mystical Theology* 1.1, 997AB (141:1–142:4) for the prayer to the Trinity, and 1.3, 1000C–1001A (143:8–144:15) for Moses' ascent into the darkness and silence of Sinai.

9. Ibid., 3, 1033C (147:12–14). Rorem, *Pseudo-Dionysius: A Commentary,* 194–205, argues for this chapter as "perhaps the most crucial and significant of the entire corpus," here citing 195. For reasons I hope to make clear below, I would instead suggest *Celestial Hierarchy* 1.3 as enjoying that distinction.

10. *Mystical Theology* 4, 1040D (148). See also n. 18 below.

11. Ibid., 5, 1045D–48B (149–50).

12. A. Nygren, *Agape and Eros,* trans. P. S. Watson, rev. ed. (Philadelphia: 1953), 576–93 on Dionysius, here citing 576.

13. On *proodos/epistrophe* in Dionysius, see Rorem, *Biblical and Liturgical Symbols,* 58–65, and in Neoplatonism as embracing at once an objective account of the cosmos and a theory of mind, Gersh, *From Iamblichus to Erieugena,* 27–120.

14. Thus see Rorem, *Pseudo-Dionysius: A Commentary,* 216.

15. Vanneste, *Mystère de Dieu,* 216–24; and J. M. Rist, "Mysticism and Transcendence in Later Neoplatonism," *Hermes* 92 (1964): 213–25; see 214 and 224 for Dionysius (though Rist, in subsequent writings and in conversation with me, has withdrawn his earlier assess-

ment). Vanneste supplied a sketch of his argument against "mysticism" in Dionysius in the article, "Is the Mysticism of Pseudo-Dionysius Genuine?" *International Philosophical Quarterly* 3 (1963): 286–306.

16. De Andia is, in general, much more sensitive than Rorem to Greek patristic literature in her *Henôsis.* See, e.g., her chapter on Moses' ascent into the cloud, *Henôsis,* 303–73, with its impressive assembly and juxtaposition of texts from Philo, Gregory of Nyssa, Evagrius Ponticus, and Isaac of Syria—though the latter two, especially Evagrius, are unfortunately not accorded as much attention as I believe they should have received. Compare thus, in contrast, Golitzin, *Et introibo,* 334–40.

17. Rorem, *Pseudo-Dionysius: A Commentary,* 183–213, on the centrality of the *Mystical Theology,* and cf. his essay, "The Uplifting Spirituality of Pseudo-Dionysius," in *Christian Spirituality,* vol. 1, *Origins to the Twelfth Century,* ed. B. McGinn and J. Meyendorff (New York: Crossroad, 1988), 132–51, esp. 144 on the purely "cosmetic" function of Dionysius's Christ.

18. On Jewish visionary traditions of the divine body of glory, see, e.g., Scholem, *Jewish Gnosticism,* 36–42, and Gruenwald, *Apocalyptic and Merkabah Mysticism,* 213–17; on the continuation of these elements in the New Testament, Segal, *Paul the Convert,* 58–64; Morray-Jones, "Paradise Revisted" and "Transformational Mysticism," esp. 11–31, and M. Fishbane, "The 'Measures' of God's Glory in Ancient Midrash," in *Messiah and Christos,* ed. I. Gruenwald et al. (Tübingen: Mohr/Siebeck, 1992), 53–74, esp. 71–72, on Eph. 4:13 and Phil. 3:21; and in the second and third century, ascetic Christian literature of the *Gospel of Thomas* and *Apocryphal Acts of the Apostles,* A. DeConick, *Seek to See Him,* esp. 99–125, and J. Fossum, "Partes Posteriori Dei: The Transfiguration of Jesus in the *Acts of John,*" in *Image of the Invisible God,* 95–108. I know of no articles that seek to trace these currents into later monastic literature other than my very preliminary efforts in "Temple and Throne of the Divine Glory: Purity of Heart in the Macarian Homilies," in *Purity of Heart in Early Ascetic and Monastic Literature,* ed. H. Luckman and L. Kulzer (Collegeville, Minn.: Liturgical Press, 1999), 107–29, esp. 117 ff., and "'The Demons Suggest an Illusion of God's Glory in a Form': Controversy over the Divine Body and Vision of Glory in Some Late Fourth-, Early Fifth-Century Monastic Literature," *Studia Monastica* 44, no. 1 (2002): 13–43. In any case, the terms "form" [*eidos*], "shape" [*schema*], and "body" [*soma*], which *Mystical Theology* 4 addresses thus echo the materials in the articles and studies cited above. So, too, does a fourth term in *Mystical Theology* 4: "place" [*topos*], which deliberately recalls both the Septuagint version of Exod. 24:10, "the place [*topos*] where stood the God of Israel" (to which Dionysius has already alluded in *Mystical Theology* 1.3, 1000D–1A [144:5, 9]), and of Ezek. 3:12, "blessed is the Glory of God from His place [Greek *topos,* Hebrew *maqom*]." See, thus, E. E. Urbach, *The Sages: Their Concepts and Beliefs,* trans. I. Abrahams (Cambridge, Mass.: Harvard University Press, 1995), 65–79, on *maqom* as a name for God in Rabbinic literature and as overlapping with the term, *shekinah;* and cf. my discussion above of Dionysius's Epistles 1–4 and of the *visio Christi* as light.

19. On the dating of, e.g., the late *merkabah* text, *3 or Hebrew Enoch,* see P. Alexander's introduction to *The Old Testament Pseudepigrapha,* vol. 1, *Apocalyptic Literature and Testaments,* ed. J. H. Charlesworth (New York: Doubleday, 1983), 225–29. He places it in the fifth–sixth century. For an interesting and precisely contemporary (to both Dionysius and *3 Enoch*) exposition of the *markabto* (Syriac, "chariot") of Ezekiel, see Jacob of Serug (d. 521), "On the Chariot That Ezekiel the Prophet Saw," in *Mar Jacobi Sarugensis: Homiliae selectae,* ed. P. Bedjan, 5 vols. (Paris: 1908), 4:543–610; and A. Golitzin, "The Image and Glory of God in

Jacob of Serug's Homily, 'On the Chariot that Ezekiel the Prophet Saw,'" *St. Vladimir's Theological Quarterly* (in press).

20. See Epistle 10, 1117A–20A (208–10), and on monastic use of Old Testament Pseudepigrapha, see, e.g., R. A. Kraft, "The Pseudepigrapha in Christianity"; and M. Himmelfarb, *Ascent to Heaven,* together with Athanasius of Alexandria's explicit mention—in a negative tone—of the apocryphal books of Enoch and Isaiah that were popular in the dissident ascetic circles whom he was, in part, addressing in his "Paschal Epistle" of 367, trans. from the Coptic in D. Brakke, *Athanasius and the Politics of Asceticism* (Oxford: Oxford University Press, 1995), 330–32, and cf. the effectively contemporary letters of Anthony's reputed disciple, Ammonas, esp. Epistle 10 (Syriac version), in *Patrologia orientalis* 10:594, quoting approvingly from the ascent to heaven in one of the same apocryphal works that Athanasius is condemning, the second-century, Christian apocalypse, *The Ascension of Isaiah* 8.21, and then adding himself: "sunt homines super terram qui ad hanc mensuram pervenere!" For the English trans. of the passage in the *Ascension of Isaiah,* see Charlesworth, ed., *Old Testament Pseudepigrapha,* 2:169.

21. *Celestial Hierarchy* 2.5, 145B (16:7–10).

22. Ibid., 2.1–5, 136D–45A (10:2–15:18), and 15.2–9, 328C–40A (51:22–58:22).

23. Ibid., 13.1–4, 300B–308B (43:20–49:20).

24. Ibid., 4, 304C (46:23–47:3): the prophet was "was shown this vision by one of the holy and blessed angels who watch over us and, through his illuminating guidance [*cheragogia*], was lifted up [*anatachthenai*] to that holy vision, according to which he saw the highest beings, so to speak symbolically, established beneath God and with God, and [he saw] that Summit [himself], transcendent altogether ineffably above these [beings] and all things, enthroned amidst His subordinate powers." Compare *Ascension of Isaiah* 7–9, in Charlesworth, ed., *Old Testament Pseudepigrapha* 2:165–72.

25. See Gregory's dismissal of all created analogies as well as of language itself as inadequate to the Trinity in "On the Holy Spirit," 31–33; English trans.: E. R. Hardy, *The Christology of the Later Fathers* (Philadelphia: Westminster Press, 1954), 213–14.

26. *Divine Names* 2.8, 645C (132:6–13). On the idea and practice of "spiritual fatherhood" in Eastern Christianity generally, see K. T. Ware, "The Spiritual Father in Orthodox Christianity," *Cross Currents* 24 (1974): 296–313; and, at greater length citing texts taken from the first millennium A.D., I. Hausherr, *Spiritual Direction in the Early Christian East,* trans. A. Gythiel (Kalamazoo, Mich.: Cistercian Publications, 1990), together with Ware's foreword to the latter, vii–xxxiii. On the phenomenon in three of monasticism's earliest writers, see P. Rousseau, *Pachomius: The Making of a Community in Fourth Century Egypt* (Berkeley: University of California Press, 1985), 77–148; and M. S. Burrows, "On the Visibility of God in the Holy Man: A Reconsideration of the Role of the Apa in the Pachomian *Vitae*," *Vigiliae christianae* 41 (1987): 11–33; H. Dörries, *Die Theologie des Makarios/Symeon* (Göttingen: Vandenhoeck & Ruprecht, 1978), 336–66; and, G. Bunge, *Geistliche Vaterschaft: Christliche Gnosis bei Evagrios Pontikos* (Regensburg: Pustet, 1988), esp. 33–36, 40–44, and 69–72.

27. Rorem makes this point in *Biblical and Liturgical Symbols,* 103; and cf. Golitzin, *Et introibo,* 67nn. 171–72, 89n. 89, and 110–14.

28. I borrow the idea of a reciprocity of ecstasies from R. Roques, "Symbolisme et théologie négative chez le Pseudo-Denys," *Bulletin de l'association Guillaume Budé* 1 (1957): 112. For Dionysius's own use of the phrase, "become co-operator with God," see *Celestial Hierarchy* 3.2, 165B (18:16).

29. On the divine ecstasy, see *Divine Names* 4.12, 712B (159:13–14); 5.8, 824C (188:6);

and Epistle 9.5, 1112C (205:5), together with Golitzin, *Et introibo,* 46–49, and 54–59 on God's *proodoi.*

30. *Mystical Theology* 1.3, 1001A (144:9–15); together with *Divine Names* 4.10–17, 705B–13D (154:7–165:5) on divine love; and *Celestial Hierarchy* 9.3, 261A (38:10–11) on the "infinite sea of divine light." For perhaps the best discussion of Dionysius on love, *eros,* against his Platonist and Christian background, see C. J. de Vogel, "Greek Cosmic Love and the Christian Love of God: Boethius, Dionysius, and the Author of the Fourth Gospel," *Vigiliae christianae* 35 (1981): 57–81.

31. *Divine Names* 2.9, 648B (134:1–2); and cf. Hierotheus again in ecstasy, apparently on the occasion of the funeral of the Mother of God, in *Divine Names* 3.2, 681D–4A (141:10–14).

32. For Rorem on the *Mystical Theology,* see his "Place of the *Mystical Theology*" and, at greater length, *Pseudo-Dionysius: A Commentary,* 187 213.

33. See Vanneste, *Mystère,* 183–89; Rist, "Mysticism and Transcendence," 214 and 224; and, at greatest length, de Andia, *Henôsis,* 212–80 on *henôsis* and the *anthos tou nou.*

34. For Dionysius on *theôsis,* see *Celestial Hierarchy* 1.3, 124A (9:8), 7.2, 208C (29:17); *Ecclesiastical Hierarchy* 1.2, 373A (65:4), 1.3, 376A (66:12–13), 1.4, 376B (66:20–21), 1.5, 376D (67:20), 2.2.1, 393A (70:7), 2.3.6, 404A (77:22), 3.1, 424C (79:10–11), 3.3.7, 433C (86:8–9), 436C (87:23–24), 6.3.5, 536C (119:6–7); and *Divine Names* 2.7, 645AB (131:11–12), 2.8, 645C (132:11), 2.11, 649C (136:13–14), and 8.5, 893A (202:22).

35. See J. M. Rist, "Pseudo-Dionysius, Neoplatonism, and the Weakness of the Soul," in *From Athens to Chartres: Neoplatonism and Medieval Thought,* ed. H. J. Westra (Leiden and New York: Brill, 1992), 135–61; and, on Iamblichus and theurgy in particular, G. Shaw, *Theurgy and the Soul: The Neoplatonism of Iamblichus* (University Park: Pennsylvania State Univeristy Press, 1995), esp. the latter's conclusions 237 ff.

36. *Divine Names* 3.1–2, 680B–D (138:1–139:16), on prayer as making us "present" to the Trinity. Shaw, *Theurgy and the Soul,* 240, underlines essentially the same point on grace in Iamblichus: "Iamblichus made the unconscious presence of the *Nous* and the One radically distinct [in opposition to Plotinus], ontologically other, and therefore inaccessible despite all the efforts of the soul. To reach the superior hypostases the soul needed the aid of the superior entities and these were received from without (*exothen*)," i.e., precisely as gift.

37. On this point, see Rorem, *Biblical and Liturgical Symbols,* 14–15.

38. Here see esp. *Ecclesiastical Hierarchy* 5.1.2, 501A–4A (104:15–106:3), and Dionysius's discussion of the three hierarchies of the Law (i.e., of Old Testament Israel), of the Church, and of the angels. By the first, the Areopagite means precisely the worship of the Tabernacle (and Temple) revealed to Moses on Sinai in Exod. 25:9 ff., "the type shown to him [Moses] on Mt. Sinai" (501C, 105:14–15). The term, "law," in the phrase "*he kata nomon hierarchia,*" can be deceptive to scholars working out of the traditional, Western Christian opposition of "law" and "gospel." What Dionysius is assuming here is not the contrast between "works righteousness" and grace but, rather, the distinction between the external manifestation of God in the Old Covenant liturgy and God's more immediate presence made accessible now in both the Church's liturgy and within the Christian soul. See thus my discussion below on *Celestial Hierarchy* 1.3. For a similar and contemporary comparison of the Old Testament cult and priesthood, revealed on Sinai to Moses, with the Christian Eucharist, see Jacob of Serug, "On the Chariot That Ezekiel Saw," in *Mar Jacobi Sarugensis: Homiliae selectae,* ed. Bedjan, vol. 4, 594:1–600:14, esp. 599:3 ff. That both Jacob and Dionysius were drawing here on much older currents, long established esp. in Christian Syria, see, e.g., N. Séd, "Les

Hymnes sur le paradis de saint Ephrem et les traditions juives," *Le Muséon* (1968), 455–501, esp. 458–65 on Church-Paradise-Sinai, and 476–7 for the interdependence and mutual reflection of Paradise, Sinai, and the angelic liturgy in Jewish midrash.

39. *Celestial Hierarchy* 1.2, 121A (7:9–11); and on Christ and light, see the discussion below on Epistles 1–4.

40. *Celestial Hierarchy* 1.3, 121C–4A (8:19–9:6).

41. For an overview of angels in early Christianity, see J. Daniélou, *Les anges et leur mission d'après les pères de l'Église* (Paris: Éditions de Chevtogne, 1951); together with E. Petersen, *The Angels and the Liturgy,* trans. R. Walls (New York: Herder & Herder, 1964); for Judaism of the Second Temple era, Rowland, *The Open Heaven,* 78–124; and Himmelfarb, *Ascent to Heaven,* 9–46; and specifically on Qumran, C. Newsom, *Songs of the Sabbath Sacrifice: A Critical Edition* (Atlanta: Scholars Press, 1985), 39–72.

42. *Celestial Hierarchy* 3.1, 164D (17:3–4) and 3.2, 165A (18:2–4).

43. See, esp., *Divine Names* 11.1–4, 948D–52D (217:5–220:17) on "peace" for a sketch of this harmony and mutual care, together with Golitzin, *Et introibo,* 97–105, on divine love and providence in Dionysius's thought as properly to be reflected in the reason-endowed creation.

44. Epistle 8, 1084B–1100D (171:3–192:2). On the place of this work in the sequence of Dionysius's epistles, see Hathaway, *Hierarchy and the Definition of Order,* 86–102, who points rightly to it as deliberately out of place in the hierarchically ascending series of addressees: monks (Epistle 1–4), deacon (5), priest (6), fellow bishop (7), the monk Demophilus (8), bishop (9), apostle (10). For Syrian monasticism and its popular, charismatic character, see Golitzin, *Et introibo,* 354–59; and most recently P. Escolan, *Monachisme et Église, le monachisme syrien du IVe au VIIe siècle: un monachisme charismatique* (Paris: 1999), esp. 71–123, on monastic heresies, notably the charismatic claims of the "messalians," and 267–311 on the tensions between monks and clergy.

45. Epistle 8.1, 1084B–88A, and 5, 1096C on Christ (171:3–175:13 and 186:8–187:2).

46. Thus, e.g., Epistle 8.1, 1088C (176:3), Demophilus has overturned the "divinely-given order" [*theoparadoton taxin*], referring to the Church's hierarchy, and is warned in 8.3, 1093A (186:7–8), not to "wrong his own [inner] order" [*ten heautou taxin*]. On *taxis* as a central term for Dionysius's notion of hierarchy, see Roques, *L'univers dionysien,* 36–66, and on the same word as a *terminus technicus* in monastic literature for the inner ordering of the soul, G. Gould, *The Desert Fathers on Monastic Community* (Oxford: Clarendon Press, 1993), 151–52.

47. Epistle 8.6, 1100A–D (190:5–192:2). Note the use of "suddenly," *aphno,* to introduce the vision (190:5), and see my discussion below on the related term, *exaiphnes,* used in Epistle 3. Note, too, that Bishop Carpus is favored with a throne vision of Christ, and again compare with the prior literature related to *exaiphnes* that I discuss below.

48. On the importance of meekness, *praotes,* in Evagrius and his school of monastic literature, see G. Bunge, *Geistliche Vaterschaft,* 42–44, and "Palladiana II: La version copte de l'*Histoire Lausiaque,*" *Studia Monastica* 33 (1991): 117–18. The latter recounts a vision Evagrius is said to have enjoyed, at least according to the Coptic version of the *Lausiac History.* Like Dionysius to Demophilus and the lesson of Bishop Carpus's vision in the same Epistle 8, Evagrius is enjoined by a divine voice especially to cultivate the virtues of mercy [*eleos*] and meekness as precondition for the *visio dei.* Dionysius is clearly writing out a tradition here.

49. For the texts in question, see esp., first, *Des heiligen Ephraem des Syrers: Hymnen de paradiso,* ed. E. Beck, Corpus scriptorum christianorum orientalium, 174 (Louvain: Secrétariat

du Corpus SCO, 1957), esp., 5–12, English trans. Saint Ephraem Syrus, *Hymns on Paradise,* trans. and with an introduction by S. P. Brock (Crestwood, N.Y.: St. Vladimir's Seminary Press, 1990), 84–96 and Brock's introcution, 49–57; second, *mimra XII* of the *Liber Graduum* in *Patrologia syriaca,* vol. 3, ed. M. Kmosko (Paris: Firmin-Didot, 1926), cols. 288–304, English trans. in *The Syriac Fathers on Prayer and the Spiritual Life,* trans. S. P. Brock (Kalamazoo, Mich.: Cistercian Publications, 1987), 45–63; and, third, Homily 52 in *Makarios/Symeon: Die Sammlung I des Vaticanus Graecus 694 (B),* ed. G. Berthold (Berlin: Akademie Verlag, 1973), 2:138–42, English trans. in Golitzin, "Hierarchy versus Anarchy," 176–79. For discussion at greater length than here on these texts as background and predecessors to Dionysius and the latter's hierarchies, see again Golitzin, "Hierarchy versus Anarchy," 152–72, and *Et introibo,* 368–85. On the theme of the inner or "little church" of the soul as mirroring the liturgies of heaven and earth in Syrian monastic literature, see R. Murray, *Symbols of Church and Kingdom: A Study in Early Syriac Tradition* (Cambridge: Cambridge University Press, 1975), 262–76; H. Dörries, *Theologie des Makarios/Symeon,* 367–409; S. P. Brock, "Prayer of the Heart," and "Fire from Heaven: From Abel's Sacrifice to the Eucharist—a Theme in Syriac Christianity," *Studia Patristica* 25 (1993): 229–43; V. Desprez, "Le Baptême chez le Pseudo-Macaire," *Ecclesia Orans* 5 (1988): 121–55, esp. 126–30; and C. Stewart, *"Working the Earth of the Heart": The Messalian Controversy in History, Texts, and Language to* A.D. 431 (Oxford: Oxford University Press, 1991), 218–22.

50. For a chart of the parallels between the Paradise Mountain, Sinai, Temple, and the Christian assembly, see Brock's introduction to Ephrem the Syrian's *Hymns on Paradise,* 53. For the appearance of the *shekinto,* see *Hymns* 2.12 (*Hymnen de paradiso,* 7; English trans., 88); for the Sinai imagery, 10.12 (*Hymnen de paradiso,* 8; English trans., 89); and for the Eden/Temple parallels, 3.5 and 14 (*Hymnen de paradiso,* 9 and 11; English trans., 92 and 95). On Ephrem's relationship to, or at least echo of Jewish *merkabah* traditions, and on Christ for him as Glory/*Shekinah* in the Church and in the believer, see N. Séd, "Les *Hymnes sur paradis,*" 468 and 482, respectively. For instances of the term *shekinto,* used in reference to Christ in Syriac-Christian literature, see also *Aphraatis Sapientis Persae Demonstrationes* in *Patrologia syriaca,* vol. 1, ed. I. Parisot (Paris: Firmin-Didot, 1894), 4.7, col. 152:1–2; 18.4, col. 828:8; and 19.4, col. 857:6–7; Jacob of Serug, *Mar Jacobi Sarugensis: Homiliae selectae,* ed. Bedjan, vol. 4, 569:21; 570:13; and 602:25; together with the passages from Isaac of Nineveh (d. ca. 700) assembled by H. Alfeyev in the latter's study *The Spiritual World of Isaac the Syrian* (Kalamazoo, Mich.: Cistercian Publications, 2000), 45, 165, 167–68, and 170–71. This represents a continuum of discourse, extending in Syrian Christian literature from more than a century before Dionysius (Ephrem and Aphrahat), through the works of a contemporary (Jacob), to around two hundred years after him (Isaac). I therefore read the Areopagite as embedded in the same tradition.

51. Kmosko, ed., *Patrologia syriaca,* vol. 3, 288:23–289:1 and 296:8–10 (English trans., Brock, *Syriac Fathers on Prayer,* 46.2 and 49, respectively).

52. Berthold, *Die Sammlung I,* 140:3–8 (English trans., Golitzin, "Hierarchy versus Anarchy," 177–78).

53. Berthold, *Die Sammlung I,* 141:11–142:17 (English trans., Golitzin, "Hierarchy versus Anarchy," 178–79).

54. Berthold, *Die Sammlung I,* 139:29–140:2 (English trans., Golitzin, "Hierarchy versus Anarchy," 177). For more on Macarius's play on such liturgical terms as *metabole* (change), *synago/synaxis* (to gather, assembly), etc., and parallelism he wishes thus to establish between the visible and inner churches, see Golitzin, *Et introibo,* 379–85.

55. On Baptism as birth and death, see *Ecclesiastical Hierarchy* 2.1, 392B (69:7–12) and 2.3.1, 397A (73:12) on birth, and 2.3.5–6, 401A–4A (76:8–77:23) on dying to sin and sharing in Christ's death. On death as looking forward to "rebirth," *paliggennesia*, see 7.1, 553A (120:22–121:1) and 3, 556B (122:14–15). Note also his later recollection of Baptism in the anointing of the body in the funeral service: 7.3.8, 565A (129:14–22).

56. *Ecclesiastical Hierarchy* 3, 424C–45B (79–94) on the Eucharist, and 5–6, 501A–36B (104:3–120:12) on clerical ordination and monastic tonsure. On the location of ordination within the sanctuary, "in front of the altar," see 5.2, 509A (110:11), and on tonsure and the priest "coming" to the candidate from "before the altar," see 6.1, 533AB (117:2–7). I assume that the candidate is standing in front of the sanctuary gates, since Dionysius indicates that this is the place assigned to the monks (as opposed to the clergy within the sanctuary) in Epistle 8.1, 1088D (176:11–12). Compare, relatedly, the canons of Bishop Rabbula of Edessa (d. 436) forbidding monks entry into the raised sanctuary area in A. Vööbus, *History of Asceticism in the Syrian Orient*, vol. 2, *Early Monasticism in Mesopotamia and Syria* (Louvain: Secrétariat du Corpus SCO, 1960), 334, citing canon 58 of Rabbula.

57. *Ecclesiastical Hierarchy* 4, 473B–84D (95:1–104:2). On the importance of the chrism in the Syrian tradition, see Strothmann, *Die Myronweihe*, xxiii–lx.

58. *Ecclesiastical Hierarchy* 4.3.1, 473B–6A (95:19–97:3) on the holy man and chrism, esp. 476A (96:23–97:1), and 4.3.4, 477C–80A (98:26–99:14), on Jesus as the divine fragrance.

59. Ibid., 4.3.12, 484C–5A (103:2–9). For a more extended discussion of this passage with regard to *Mystical Theology* 1.3, see A. Golitzin, "Liturgy and Mysticism: The Experience of God in Eastern Orthodox Christianity," *Pro Ecclesia* 8, no. 2 (1999): 159–86, esp. 181–85.

60. See above, n. 42, and on the soul as mirror in Ephrem Syrus, see E. Beck, "Das Bild vom Spiegel bei Ephraem," *Orientalia Christiana Periodica* 19 (1953): 5–24.

61. See *Ecclesiastical Hierarchy* 3.3.6–7, 432C–6A (84:22–88:9) on the "incubation" of the catechumens within the church, the Fall, and the struggle with the passions. See *Ecclesiastical Hierarchy* 6.1.3, 532–33A (116:8–19) on the monks as reflecting God through their "singleness" of life and concentration, and 6.3.2, 533D (117:23–5) on their freedom from all "fantasy." R. Roques, "Éléments pour une théologie de l'état monastique selon Denys l'Aréopagite," in *Théologie de la vie monastique* (Paris: 1961), 283–314, rightly stresses these features of Dionysius's portrait of the monk but ascribes them chiefly to Neoplatonist influence. See, in contrast, J. Amstutz, *Haplotes: Eine begriffsgeschichtliche Studie zum jüdisch-christlichen Griechisch* (Bonn: P. Hanstein, 1968), on the importance of "simplicity" and "singleness of heart" in Jewish and early Christian thought from the Second Temple era through the second century A.D., and relatedly, Guillaumont, *Aux origines du monachisme*, 13–58, on the Jewish and Jewish-Christian origins of monasticism; and F.-E. Morard, "*Monachos, moine,*" esp. 335–36 and 405–6, on Dionysius's own debts to the earliest Christian sense—rooted in Jewish thought—of the word "monk" and his more specific debt to the Syriac ascetic tradition and the term *ihidaya* ("single one"), which Morard and others have argued is the likely origin for Christian use of the Greek *monachos*.

62. Evagrius, *On Prayer,* esp. 70 and 117, respectively, Greek in Nicodemus of the Holy Mountain's *Philokalia tôn hierôn neptikôn* (Venice, 1782; reprint, Athens: Astir, 1957), 1:182 and 187; English trans., K. T. Ware et al., *Philokalia: The Complete Text* (London: Faber & Faber, 1979), 1:61 and 68. On Evagrius's use also of an interiorization of the Sinai theophany of Exod. 24:10–11 for the reception of the "light of the holy Trinity" within the soul, which I take to be Dionysius's background as well in *Mystical Theology* 1.3; see his "Epistles" in *Eu-*

agrius Pontikos, ed. W. Frankenberg (Berlin: Weidmannsche Buchhandlung, 1912), 561–633, esp. Epistle 39 (Frankenberg, ed., 593), together with the chapters supplementary to the *Kephalaia Gnostica* (Frankenberg, ed., 429–65), esp. numbers 2 (425), 4 (427), 21 (441), and 25 (449). For discussion, on the one hand, linking Evagrius (and, I would argue, by extension Dionysius) to exegetical traditions in the Aramaic *targumim,* see N. Séd "La *shekinta* et ses amis araméens," *Cahiers d'orientalisme* 20 (1988): 233–42; and, on the other, to Neoplatonism, including the use of the "sudden" in Plotinus's *Enneads* (see my discussion at pp. 31 ff., along with nn. 73–79), see A. Guillaumont, "La vision de l'intellect par lui-même dans la mystique évagrienne," *Mélanges de l'Université St. Joseph* 50, nos. 1–2 (1984): 255–62, together with A. Golitzin, *Et introibo,* 334–40.

63. Thus my argument for accepting the order of the *Corpus Dionysiacum* as the latter has come down to us in all of the Greek manuscripts. On the latter point, see B. M. Suchla, "Eine Redaktion der griechischen Corpus Dionysiacum im Umkreis des Johannes von Scythopolis, des Verfassers von Prolog und Scholien: Ein dritter Beitrag zur Überlieferungsgeschichte des Corpus Dionysiacum," *Nachrichten der Akademie der Wissenschaft in Göttingen* (1985), 1–18.

64. *Patrologia graeca,* vol. 4, 412C, commenting on the *gnophos* of *Mystical Theology* 1.3, 1001A (144:10). I borrow, with slight alterations, the translation of P. Rorem and J. C. Lamoreaux in *John of Scythopolis and the Dionysian Corpus: Annotating the Areopagite* (Oxford: 1998), 244–45. On the antiquity of Moses' ascent to heaven, see W. A. Meeks, *The Prophet King: Moses Traditions and Johannine Christology* (Leiden: Brill, 1967), 122–25 (in Philo), 140–42 (Josephus), 156–59 (Old Testament Pseudepigrapha), 205–11 (Rabbinic midrash), and 241–46 (Samaritan tradition). For *arabot,* related to John's *araphel,* as the name of the highest heaven and locus of the throne of God, see I. Chernus, *Mysticism in Rabbinic Judaism: Studies in the History of Midrash* (Berlin and New York: 1982), 89 and 94–95. My discussion here of this passage in Scythopolis and of the Dionysian Epistles 1–4 can be found in slightly more extended form in Golitzin, "Revisiting the 'Sudden,'" and, without the range of supporting texts, in my *Et introibo,* 222–27.

65. See the references to the scholarly literature in nn. 5 and 18 above. For the original language texts of the Rabbinic *hekalot* tradition, see P. Schäfer, *Synopse zur Hekhalot Literatur* (Tübingen: Mohr/Siebeck, 1988), and for German translation, *Übersetzung der Hekhalot Literatur,* 4 vols. (Tübingen: Mohr/Siebeck, 1987, 1989, 1991, 1994).

66. Epistle 1, 1065A (156–7).

67. Epistle 5, 1073A (162:3–4), and cf. also the identical equation between the "darkness" and "unapproachable light" in *Divine Names* 7.2, 869A (196:11–12), and, in the same text, for entry into the light (162:4–6).

68. *Patrologia graeca,* vol. 4, 536B. The scholiast is evidently not Scythopolis here. On the "midday," *mesembria,* as possibly an expression widely in use for the experience of God, see the same expression in Evagrius, *On Prayer,* 146 (Greek *Philokalia* 1:189, English trans., K. T. Ware et al., *Philokalia,* 1:70), in phrasing reminiscent of the scholiast, and cf. also Evagrius's Epistle 33: "May the Lord grant that the midday of your virtue be radiant and that your tabernacle may become the lodging of the holy angels and of our Savior, Jesus Christ" (Frankenberg, ed., *Euagrius Pontikos,* 589). I am indebted for the first reference to Bunge, *Geistliche Vaterschaft,* 53–54. The second, I think, expresses quite the same idea as we find in the discussion and associations of the sudden that I discuss below: it is the place of the angelic liturgy, of the presence of Christ, and so of the believer as temple or, here, tabernacle.

69. Epistle 2, 1068A–9A (158:4–10). I take this point from John of Scythopolis, *Patrologia graeca,* vol. 4, 529B (English trans., Rorem and Lamoreaux, *John of Scythopolis,* 251), who

directs the reader back to his commentary on *Divine Names* 11.6, 953C–6B (222:3–223:3), and Dionysius's distinction between God's secret being and his "powers," *dynameis,* at work in creation. For discussion of the latter in the *Corpus Dionysiacum,* see Golitzin, *Et introibo,* 54–74 and, on Dionysius's patristic background for this distinction, 289–97 (Cappadocians) and 359–62 (Ephrem Syrus).

70. Epistle 4, 1072BC (161:4–10).

71. For *entheos politeia,* see *Ecclesiastical Hierarchy* 2.2.4, 396B (71:15); 3.3.11, 441C (91:23); and Epistle 11.5, 1113A (206:2).

72. Epistle 3, 1069B (159:3–10).

73. On the Platonist background to Dionysius's use of the sudden, see esp. W. Beierwaltes, "*Exaiphnes* oder die Paradoxie des Augenblicks," *Philosophisches Jahrbuch* 74 (1966–67): 272–82; and R. Mortley, *The Way of Negation,* 236–40. Mortley's discussion includes the references to Plotinus that Beierwaltes does not. All the Platonist echoes (though none of the Christian) can now be found in Heil and Ritter's apparatus to the critical text, *Corpus Dionysiacum,* 2:159.

74. I have looked into a number of New Testament commentaries, including the *Theological Dictionary of the New Testament,* ed. G. Kittel and G. Friedrich, trans. G. W. Boromiles (Grand Rapids, Mich.: Eerdmans, 1969–74) and several devoted to Luke-Acts, and have nowhere found any specific notice taken of *exaiphes,* which I think odd, particularly given the word's presence in the LXX—thus see E. Hatch and H. A. Redpath, *A Concordance to the Septuagint,* 2 vols. (Oxford: Oxford University Press, 1897; reprint, Athens: Ekdoseis "Ophelimov Bibliou," 1983), 1:486—and esp. in the LXX version of Mal. 3:1, discussed above. Luke's use of it in particular seems to me to be a deliberate allusion to theophanic language already extant in the literature of both the Jewish scriptures and of the Hellenistic world (which would certainly include Plato), but no one appears as yet to have thought this worth pointing out in the third Evangelist. With regard to ancient Jewish literature, however, see M. N. A. Bockmuehl, *Revelation and Mystery in Ancient Judaism and Pauline Christianity* (Tübingen: Mohr/Siebeck, 1990), 66: "The theme of heavenly revelation out of silence is common in ancient Jewish thought," citing in particular the Wisd. of Sol. 18:14–15 (and see below, n. 81).

75. *Acta Thomae* 112, in *Acta Apostolorum Apocrypha* ed. M. Bonnet (1903; reprint, Hildesheim: Georg Olms Verlagsbuchhandlung, 1959), 2.1 (223:7–13). Compare also the use of the *exaiphnes* in an identical context (ascent to a throne vision) in a late-third-century Manichaean text, *The Cologne Mani Codex* (*P.Colon.inv.ab 4780): Concerning the Origin of His Body,* ed. R. Cameron and J. Dewey, SBL Texts and Translations 15 (Missoula, Mont.: Scholars, 1979), 55:12–57:16, pp. 42 (English) and 44 (Greek); and, again, on the occasion of an epiphany of Christ as light in the mid- to late-fourth-century *Acta Phillipi,* in *Acta Apostolorum Apocrypha,* ed. Bonnet, 2.2 (10:26–11:5). On the Thomas tradition, including both the *Gospel of Thomas* and the *Acts,* as embodying a light mysticism of the divine form, see G. Quispel, "Sein und Gestalt," in *Studies in Religion and Mysticism Presented to Gershom Scholem,* ed. A. Altmann (Jerusalem: Magness Press, 1967), 190–95, and *Makarios, das Thomasevangelium,* 39–64; and A. DeConick, *Seek to See Him* 99–125, and 163 on the *Acts.* On Manicheanism as an offshoot of the same traditions, see I. Gruenwald, "Manicheism and Judaism in Light of the Cologne Mani Codex," *Zeitschrift für Papyrologie und Epigraphie* 50 (1983): 29–45; J. M. Baumgarten, "The Book of Elchesai and Merkabah Mysticism," *Journal for the Study of Judaism* 17, no. 2 (1986): 212–23; and at length in J. C. Reeves, *Heralds of That Good Realm: Syro-Mesopotamian Gnosis and Jewish Traditions* (Leiden: Brill, 1996),

esp. 5–30. It is thus perhaps of note that Dionysius's scholiasts, both John of Scythopolis and others unnamed, present him as refuting Mani (though usually in the sense of affirming the goodness of creation) on several occasions. See *Patrologia graeca*, vol. 4, 149A, 176A, 181C, 272D, 285B, 288C, 349A, 397C, 545C, and 557B.

76. Athanasius of Alexandria, *Vita Antonii*, in *Patrologia graeca*, vol. 26, 860A.

77. Ephrem Syrus, *Des heiligen Ephraem des Syrers: Hymnen de Nativitate*, ed. E. Beck, Corpus scriptorum christianorum orientalium, 186 (Louvain: Secrétariat du Corpus SCO, 1959), 6.7 (52), English trans., *Ephrem the Syrian: Hymns*, K. McVey (New York: Paulist Press, 1989), 112; *Hymnen de paradiso* 5.11 and 15.4; Syriac in *Hymnen de paradiso* 18:6–11 (*men shelya* on line 7) and 63:3–8 (*men shelya* on line 8) (English trans., *Hymns on Paradise*, ed. Brock, 106 and 183, respectively).

78. On *shelya*, see J. Payne Smith, *A Compendius Syriac Dictionary* (Oxford: Oxford University Press, 1903; reprint, Oxford: Oxford University Press, 1990), 580.

79. See R. Chestnus, *Three Monophysite Christologies* (Oxford: 1976), 63, n.2, and 105 for *shelya* in Philoxenus of Mabbug (d. 519) as denoting, respectively, both the simplicity of the divine nature and that inner condition of the soul necessary for encounter with the divine presence.

80. Dionysius cites Ignatius's *Epistle to the Romans* 7, "My *eros* is crucified," in the discussion on *eros* in *Divine Names* 4.12, 709D (157:10–11). How the Areopagite, supposedly a disciple of Saint Paul, could have cited Ignatius who died ca. 115, taxes one scholiast's ingenuity in *Patrologia graeca*, vol. 4, 264BC. He settles on the improbable dating of Ignatius's death to the reign of Domitian in the 90s A.D.

81. *To the Magnesians* 8 and *Ephesians* 15, respectively. Critical text by P. Camelot, trans., *Ignace d'Antioch/Polycarpe de Smyrne: Lettres, Martyre de Polycarpe*, 4th ed., Sources chrétiennes 10 (Paris: Cerf, 1969), 86 and 70–72, respectively. Thus, to recall Bockmuehl's citation of Wisd. of Sol. 18:14–15 (above, n.74), the text of that late (first-century?) text is perhaps worth citing. In the NRSV translation from the Greek, it reads: "For while gentle silence [*hesychou siges*] enveloped all things . . . your all-powerful word [*logos*] leaped from heaven, from the royal throne, into the midst of the land." Note the movement of the divine word from the heavenly throne, and especially from silence, into the world. In the Syriac Old Testament, the *Peshitta*, the divine word moves thus *men* (from) . . . *shelya* (silence).

82. *Patrologia graeca*, vol. 4, 532AB.

83. Beierwaltes, *"Exaiphnes"* 278–79; and cf. Mortley, *Way of Negation*, 237–38.

84. See Golitzin, *Et introibo*, 401–13, esp. 412–13.

Thomas Aquinas and Onto-theo-logy

JEAN-LUC MARION

Hoc ipsum esse, secundum quod est in creaturis ab ipso removemus; et tunc remanet in quadam tenebra ignorantiae.

—*In Sententiarum Libros* I, distinction 8, question 1, answer 1, ad 4m

The Construction of the Question

Whatever the relevance of the thesis claiming the radical historicity of truth, the greatness of a thought may be measured by its ability to transcend the historical conditions of its appearance and disappearance to go on reappearing in debates and disputes which, at first glance, should not have called it up or welcomed it. In brief, a great thought manages to survive its own epoch so that, as timeless or at least as stubbornly reoccurring, it takes part in epochs that are no more its own and makes itself anachronically contemporary. The thought of Saint Thomas illustrates this paradox in a preeminent way. It has not ceased, from rebirths to rediscoveries, to compel recognition, even during centuries in which it should not have, in principle, seemed able to enter the scene. In a word, Thomism in the strict sense, consists solely in an almost uninterrupted series of "returns to saint Thomas," which are expressed as much in the alleged fidelity as in the unquestionable diversity of the interpretations. And our time is no exception to this reflex, which, like the others, claims (at least in outline) "to return" to Thomas in order to better invest, today, debates as unknown to him as they are unavoidable for us.

What debates are we talking about? We can name several that have followed each other chronologically: realism against criticism, the issue about

the *analogia entis,* then the question of being itself, without even mentioning any debate over "Christian philosophy." To these common threads of discussion in which Thomism never ceases to redefine itself, we add another: the
running debate on onto-theo-logy. With this concept, Heidegger has cast
into play a new definition of the essence of metaphysics; but he has also established a hermeneutic of the history of philosophy so powerful that it could
not be matched, but only by the one used by Hegel. In effect, to the degree
that the concept of onto-theo-logy strictly defines all metaphysics and that
each metaphysics is necessarily characterized by its impotence to think the difference between entity and being, it is necessary to conclude that, by its very
onto-theo-logical constitution, no metaphysics has any access to being as
such but only to being(s) as entity(ies).[1] Metaphysics is thus defined as the
thought that asserts being only so long as it does not think it, which is to say
that it does not reach it. The best indication of this impotence typically comes
from the fact that the formula "being inasmuch as it is being" does not disclose in our real understanding much more than "entity inasmuch as it is entity" precisely because when we claim, too quickly and too superficially, to
think and to speak being, in reality we never reach "to be" but, instead, stick
to nothing but the subsistence and enduring presence of an entity (one out
of the beings). It is not enough to invoke being in order to think it otherwise
than as an entity and its properties (e.g., subsistence, independence, act, eternity, etc.), which obviously never define being ("to be") but always nothing—
no *thing*—else than entity alone, that is, precisely a thing. This much we can
agree on: the facility in qualifying entity with the title of God neither affects
nor improves in the least the result that it is still a question of entity, to which
being remains wholly irreducible and God completely foreign.

Consequently, if it might happen that the thought of Thomas Aquinas
were also to share the common lot of philosophies belonging to onto-theo-
logy (directly or by reliable historical mediaries), it would suffer profound
harm. First, because it would become once again precisely what all Thomistic
philosophers have always intended that it not be: just one more metaphysics
among all the others, so that it would have to give up the claim of dominat-
ing, from its speculative height, all previous metaphysical schemes and their
derivations in subsequent metaphysics (to assume the strongly normative
typology of the history of philosophy asserted by this point of view, e.g., by
E. Gilson). Moreover, since onto-theo-logy by definition never thinks of
being except in relation to entity, that is, confusing being and entity, this
hypothesis, if it were true of Thomas Aquinas, would prevent his thought
from assuming to have achieved the act of being (*actus essendi*) as the correct
definition of God, for, if it were applicable to God, He could remain only

as a supreme entity, but it certainly would not be a question of being. If Thomas's doctrine could be assimilated into an onto-theo-logy, it would lose its privileged position in relation to other metaphysics since it would have to renounce any pretense of having achieved *esse;* whether divine or not matters little, because in the first place even the distinction between *ens* and *esse,* or at least the irreducibility of *esse* to its ontic interpretation, would become problematic. Thus, in addition to the theological suspicion of having given in to idolatry by having reduced God to the rank of *esse,* there would also be this time the philosophical accusation of having confused being with entity and claiming most imprudently to have achieved the former, while having treated only the latter. The truth of this question is, then, a debate that is absolutely decisive for the present and future validity of all thought that would like to call itself Thomistic, as much in theology as in philosophy.[2]

Nevertheless, as essential as it may seem today, this debate has long remained foreign to Thomists, occupied as they have been whether with internal quarrels (types of analogy, the concept of entity, the real composition of *esse* and *essentia*) or ritual polemics against modern philosophy as "subjectivist" and/or "idealist." Even when this debate was taken up, it was most often in the form of a dilemma: either the term "onto-theo-logy" was playing the role of a pure and simple sign of infamy, sufficient for pure ideology to disqualify any Thomistic engagement or, tactically, indeed by bravado, it became a title of glory that one assumed not without courage although often without discernment. Both of these attitudes seem to me equally inadequate and ineffective because they omit two indispensable precautions: first, to define exactly the characteristics of ontology according to Heidegger, then, to measure precisely whether the theses of Thomas Aquinas exemplify certain of those characteristics and how far. Only if these two conditions are fulfilled will it become possible to give a different response to the question or, at least, to measure its dimensions and implications.

The Characteristics of Onto-theo-logy

Since one must understand the question correctly before answering it, it is necessary to define (or redefine) onto-theo-logy. Heidegger, in his lecture titled *The Onto-theological Constitution of Metaphysics,* given and published in 1957, elaborates on such a definition: "The onto-theological constitution of metaphysics stems from the prevalence of that Difference, which keeps Being as the ground [*Sein als Grund*] and entity as grounded [*Seiendes als gegründet*] and what gives grounds as a cause [*begrundendes*] apart from and related to each other; and by this keeping, perdurance [*Austrag*] is achieved."[3] This determination indicates, then, a double intersecting foundation. (1) Being—inasmuch as it differs definitely from every entity—is proclaimed not an entity, thus as having nothing of entity and especially nothing of that particular entity called God.[4] On the contrary, insofar as it is a negation of entity, it is able to ground each and every entity, including that named "God," because it makes them both thinkable (according to entity, indeed to a concept of entity) and possible (conceivable as noncontradictory in a concept). (2) Reciprocally, entity, in particular the first entity proclaimed in each metaphysics, not only grounds the other beings in the name of the first cause that gives an account as well but also grounds the being of an entity by bringing it to perfection and even by bringing into existence the formal characteristics of entitativeness. These two principal foundations (the second one doubling itself) remain, however, intersected by the difference, which distinguishes them as being and entity and, for the same reason, reconciles them.

Such a pattern implies two types of consequences, some explicitly taken up by Heidegger, the others carried on by historians of philosophy. The first implication is that, according to its onto-theological constitution, any metaphysics has to be organized around the multiple meanings of its single foundation because it is decidedly according to the foundation that the two terms are defined—whether it be the conceptual foundation [*Gründung*] of the entities in being or the causal foundation and sufficient reason [*Begründung*] of the entities by a supreme entity. Moreover, it is also this single foundation that makes it possible to link together these two intersecting foundations, conceptual and causal. In fact, if it happens that being itself (and not only entities) could prove to be grounded in a supreme being, it is because the latter fulfills being by exemplarily achieving its characteristics of being in general among entities—that is, by actualizing possible being. But no doubt there is room here not only for redoubling the second foundation, as Heidegger suggests it, but to justify, too, a third foundation: this would deal not only with the other entities but even with being itself (and its conceptual foundation) as grounded by the supreme entity (and its causative foundation). By way of example, let us select the case, neutral because paradoxical, of one of the two Cartesian onto-theo-logies. (1) We shall say that, if being is defined on the basis of thought (as *cogitare*), then being would ground entities conceptually by distributing them into a well-know dilemma: "to be is to think or to be thought" [*esse est cogitari aut cogitare*].[5] Now, obviously, all entities without exception rely on this foundation through being, including in the first place the entity that plays the role of first or supreme entity, "God." (2) Then, we could emphasize here that the preeminent entity, that is, the *ego* that thinks (itself) as *res cogitans* and thus first grounds its own existence (*ego sum, ego existo*), also grounds in reason and produces efficaciously, too, those other entities, which are, only insofar as they are thought by it, considered as an entity that thinks first of all itself before any other. (3) Finally, we may conclude that the conceptual foundation of every entity by thought [*Gründung*] is grounded, in turn, in the causal foundation that the *res cogitans* achieves on all thinkable thoughts, thus fulfilling the being of entities.[6] From this first implication, we shall thus conclude that we could not speak accurately about onto-theo-logy without three foundations being at work: the conceptual foundation of entity as such by being [*Gründung*], the foundation of entities by the supreme entity according to efficient causality [*Begründung*], and finally the foundation of the conceptual foundation by the efficient foundation. Of course, the question remains open (although Heidegger did not determine it explicitly) whether onto-theo-logy requires that these three foundations work simultaneously or just one, or two at a time and, in such a case, which ones. We will have to keep in mind this indecision.

A second implication follows, which was more explicitly drawn out by Heidegger himself. The preeminent entity exercises a foundation on all other beings—indeed upon being and its own foundation—but it cannot do it but by acting immediately as causality and efficacy. It must, therefore, turn back on itself the efficient and causal foundation that it exercises on all other entities; it is defined, no matter what name it bears, by its principal function as *causa sui:* "The Being of entity is represented fundamentally, in the sense of the ground, as *causa sui*. This is the metaphysical concept of God."[7] The fame of this statement has, without any doubt, at times masked some of its features. First, in the strict sense, so long as the very term *causa sui* does not appear before Descartes used it, one could not be allowed to speak properly of *causa sui* unless after him (except carefully to make explicit the implicit, which does not happen of itself). Next, the *causa sui* points essentially to a function of foundation by a supreme entity in a metaphysical system, which does not always or necessarily turn out to be God. Thus the supreme entity that grounds by grounding itself through itself can also take the face of "self-thinking thought" (Aristotle) or of the "Eternal Return of the Same" (Nietzsche), as well of that of the divine *causa sui* or that of the "intelligible Word" (Malebranche) and the "ultimate reason of things" (Leibniz). Heidegger marks this clearly by emphasizing that the *causa sui,* when it brings God into philosophy, first assigns him the name of Zeus and that, even so, "before this God man can neither pray nor offer sacrifice."[8] What used to be called God here thus refers, first of all, to a mere function in the onto-theo-logical constitution, that of the causal foundation grounding itself in the manifestation of a first entity. From this perspective—although historically questionable—the God revealed in Jesus Christ would offer only one case, one candidate, or one claimant among many others (neither the first, nor the last, nor even the best) for the function strictly, indeed exclusively, metaphysical of the *causa sui*. Just one condition rules all of them, however: that they should ground entities and being in the name of the preeminent entity, thus that they could be inscribed precisely without exception or remainder within the onto-theological frame of the ontological difference, which is itself thought in a metaphysical manner, starting with and for the exclusive benefit of the entity.

Thus onto-theo-logy is defined according to some extremely precise characteristics, without which we would remain unable to identify any philosophical thought as metaphysical: (*a*) the "God" must be inscribed explicitly in the metaphysical domain, that is, to allow itself to be determined by the historical determinations of being, inasmuch as it is entity, perhaps beginning with the concept of entity; (*b*) it must establish there a causal foundation [*Begründung*] of all the common entities for which it is the reason; (*c*) to achieve this, it must always assume the function and perhaps even the name of *causa sui*, that is, of supreme founding entity, because it was supremely founded by itself. To ask the question of the relationship of Thomas Aquinas's thought to onto-theo-logy thus amounts, beyond prejudicial and ideological polemics, to examining whether it meets these requirements.

The Object of *Metaphysica*

The definition of metaphysics according to onto-theo-logy implies that God, whatever He is, precisely *is* only under the condition that He ensures the universal establishment in the being of entities (as it were "launched" into being). Thus we need first to measure how far the Thomistic acception of God, assuming the function of a foundation, as he does, would give him the rank of a "God" of metaphysics.

Let us note first that Thomas Aquinas, even if he already uses the concept of *metaphysica*,[9] still uses it with parsimony, without surmising from its usage that the commentary tradition was just attributing to Aristotle. Contrary to the majority of his successors, even the immediate ones, he made of it neither the title of a work nor the focal point of his thought. There is an excellent reason for this prudence: in his eyes, *metaphysica* designates, although not without ambiguity, a strictly philosophical and natural discipline. Defining the title of the books called the *Metaphysics* of Aristotle, he left that word, until this point, undefined or called it simply "haec scientia" and attributes to "this science" no less than three names, none of which, therefore, completely satisfy him: (1) "scientia divina sive theologia," inasmuch as it considers separate substances; (2) "prima philosophia," insofar as it considers the first causes of things; and, (3) finally, "metaphysica" strictly speaking, insofar as it considers entity and what belongs to it ("inquantum considerat ens et ea quae consequuntur ipsum"), that is, inasmuch as it has for its object "ipsum solum ens commune."[10] Nevertheless, could not one raise the objection that we are thus meeting, once again, the reciprocal play between a science of entity in general (*metaphysica*) and a science of the divine inasmuch as it exercises the function of a first cause (*theologia*)? And is that not precisely onto-theo-logy?

This hasty conclusion, however, would lead to a complete misinterpretation because the *theologia* included here in *metaphysica* does not at all amount to the entire notion of theology. Indeed, it is necessary to recognize that "the theology which deals with sacred doctrine" differs generically from the theology that is part of philosophy ("theologia quae ad sacram doctrinam pertinet differt secundum genus ab illa theologia quae pars philosophiae ponitur") or, again, that "theologia sive scientia divina est duplex."[11] In what is this duality rooted? Only theology in the sense of "sacra doctrina" can claim to know divine things in themselves, since it alone receives them "according as they reveal themselves" [*secundum quod ipsae seipsas manifestant*] and "according to what the manifestation of divine things requires" [*secundum quod requirit rerum divinarum manifestatio*]. More precisely, it can take them "as the subject of its science, because it receives them from the outset as such" [*ipsas res divinas, considerat propter seipsas ut subjectunt scientiae*], for "it is that theology which is transmitted in Sacred Scripture" [*haec est theologia, quae in sacra Scriptura traditur*]. With regard, in contrast, to "the theology that philosophers deal with and that, by another name, is called metaphysics" [*quam philosophi prosequuntur, quae alio nomine metaphysica dicitur*], it is not able to attain divine things except through their effects ("secundum quod per effectus manifestantur"), which are the only legitimate subject of *metaphysica*, that is to say, the *ens inquantum ens:* "Divine realities are treated by philosophers only insofar as they are the principles of all things. This is because they are expounded in that part of the doctrine where are assigned the things common to all beings that have for their subject *ens* inasmuch as it is *ens*."[12] The science of entity as such is able to deal with divine things, strictly speaking, but only through their effects as entities and according to their entitativeness. Since their effects (and not the divine things themselves) are said only according to entitativeness and as entities, it is necessary to conclude that divine things are not directly inscribed in the theology of metaphysics as its subject as it would be if they were revealed completely by common entity. Rather those divine things intervene only indirectly as the principles of things (or *substrat*) and not as the things themselves, "non tanquam subjectum scientiae, sed tanquam principia subjecti." In other words, separate substances and divine things are recognized as subjects only to the *theologia sacrae Scripturae,* which can alone reveal them and make them directly accessible. At the same time, the *theologia philosophica* must limit itself to taking note of the effects of divine things in *ens in quantum ens* and to approach them only as the principle of these effects, whereas revealed theology deals with them as its subject.[13] Divine things exceed the theology of metaphysics exactly inasmuch as the principle of the subject exceeds the subject of a science. And as metaphysical theology deals with divine things according to entity inasmuch as it is entity, it is necessary to conclude that the theology of revelation exceeds entity as entity. To sum up, God does not belong to metaphysical theology precisely insofar as He remains the principle of the subject of metaphysics, that is, of entity inasmuch as it is entity.

In this way, according to Thomas Aquinas, God as such does not belong to metaphysics, or to theology, or to *ens commune,* or to *ens in quantum ens.* By making such a radical theoretical decision, Aquinas sets himself, in advance, against his successors, who quickly invert this choice in order to reintegrate God in metaphysics and its object—that is, entity, and shortly thereafter the concept of entity, too. This will be the case as early as Aegidius of Rome, who states it without ambiguity: "Its subject [metaphysics] can be called God because the principle of entitativeness is reserved to God more than to other beings. On account of this, it is said that metaphysical science is divine and of God."[14] Here, metaphysics deals (or claims to deal) with God as such because it does not have the least doubt that entitativeness has the right and the power to rule God. Despite its alleged privileged entity, God plays exactly the same game as all other entities: he goes into the subject of metaphysics and becomes, therefore, able to undertake there an onto-theological function. "When you say that God escapes entitativeness, I reply that this is false and, even more, that it is entirely true that God is an entity."[15] God can neither flee nor escape from the entitativeness—which deprives Him of his transcendence and which clasps Him in the common net where all beings, so to speak, swarm. The privilege of an exceptional entitativeness that is granted Him makes, in fact, no difference since He is rewarded by inscribing Him into the uniform regime of entity.[16]

Duns Scotus will give a more solid foundation to this thesis by stating that "God is thought only under the reason of entity" [*Deus non intelligitur nisi sub ratione entis*] and, moreover, that *ens* can only be understood univocally because "God is naturally knowable to us only if entity is univocal for the created and the uncreated" [*Deus non est cognoscible a nobis naturaliter nisis ens sit univocum creato et increato*].[17] It is indeed, therefore, the object of metaphysics—the entity radically conceived as univocal both for the created and uncreated—that includes God at the same time into the *ens commune* (with only the correction of infinity) and into metaphysics, so that this concept makes metaphysics for the first time fully acknowledgeable.

Far from remaining marginal, this inclusion will be consecrated definitively at the end of medieval scholasticism by Suárez. Replacing the customary commentary on the *Sentences* or the *Summa* with the literary form characteristic of *Disputationes metaphysicae,* he started immediately by defining the *objectum metaphysicae:* "Entity insofar as it is real entity must amount to the adequate object of this science" [*ens in quantum ens reale (debet) esse objectum addequatum hujus scientiae*]. This formula, in appearance harmless enough, is nevertheless supported by a radical ontic and noetic reduction: entity is defined as an objective and, above all, formal concept that grips it in a completely abstract representation. A drastic consequence follows from this: because this concept is understood as universally as its abstraction allows, it may come before God himself ("aliquam rationem entis, quae sit prior natura Deo") and must therefore embrace God. However, the distinction between finite and infinite will come along to mark a distance (and a very real one, as the Cartesian revival will show) and soften the claim made on God, but the infinite remains nonetheless always inscribed within the realm of entity and within the grasp of metaphysics so that the distinction reinforces the submission of God rather than makes an exception of it. From that moment on, God is included within metaphysics and definitively becomes a part of it: "The adequate object of this science [metaphysics] must include God" [*objectum adequatum hujus scientiae* (mainly *metaphysicae*) *debere comprehendere Deum*].[18] The univocal concept of being implies, requires, and achieves, both in fact and in right, the inclusion of God in metaphysics. To oppose that inclusion was precisely the unique achievement of Thomas.

In contrast to the apparently irresistible development of the greatest number of his commentators and followers—who all are inclined to understand God within the concept of entity in order to inscribe Him into the object of metaphysics, thus producing the conditions of a genuine onto-theology in theology through ontology—the unmatched position of Thomas Aquinas appears forcefully. For him, God as such does not belong to the subject of metaphysical theology: He remains only the principle (or creator) of common entity, but alone does not fall under it. "First, inasmuch as other existents depend on common *esse,* but God does not, even more does common *esse* depend on God. . . . Next, inasmuch as all existents are contained in common *esse,* but God is not, even more is common *esse* contained under His power, since this divine power goes beyond created *esse* itself."[19] God embraces metaphysics but cannot be caught within it. This thesis will seem paradoxical only so long as one fails to recognize Thomas Aquinas in his true historical situation, which was essentially opposed to the main trend of Thomistic commentary. Paradoxical or not, it denies an essential requirement of all onto-theology—that "God" (or whatever may exercise the function of grounding) should imply being as much as all the entities that He founds and in the same way.

Esse Commune and the Analogy

Let us consider this thesis further, then: is it simply a matter of uniqueness in conceptual nomenclature, or is it a decisive choice that determines the entire thought of Thomas Aquinas? Is it supported elsewhere in his thought, or is it an isolated doctrine that does not seriously call into question the onto-theology ruling the whole issue?

The onto-theo-logical interpretation of the thought of Thomas Aquinas implies, beyond the inscription of God within metaphysics, that the same concept could govern "God," the supreme entity, just as much as the entity insofar as it is entity: only this intermediary link could secure the foundations that join the one to the other. Can one recognize any similar concept in Thomas Aquinas in such a way that one could anticipate those of Duns Scotus and Suárez? This seems to be the case from the moment that *ens* is so very often defined by its primacy from the point of view of knowledge: "That which is first offered to the conception of the understanding is being, because it is only insofar as it is in act that a thing is knowable . . . ; and entity is the proper object of the understanding and it is thus the first intelligible."[20] Thus *ens* is known, or is better defined, by the fact that it is known before every other determination because nothing is known that in some manner is not. What, therefore, distinguishes this position from those of Duns Scotus and Suárez? Two fundamental points.

First, the conception of *ens* thus disengaged does not define here the subject of metaphysics, or that of theological metaphysics, or a fortiori that of revealed theology but only the known object: the priority remains strictly noetic, without claiming to impose itself as a universal or ontical one.

Next and above all, this conception of *ens* does not affect God, and for at least two reasons. (1) Primarily, this conception does not affect God because the divine *esse* cannot be assimilated to *esse commune;* the *Summa Theologiae* demonstrates this by distinguishing two ways in which *esse* is said "without addition": either because its definition implies it without any addition (the *esse commune* of finite entity negatively understood) or because its definition implies positively that it entails without any possible addition [*divine esse*].[21] The *Contra Gentiles* goes further by emphasizing that the abstract universality of knowledge does not affect God: in effect, since what is common is obtained only by "the understanding that apprehends form . . . stripped of all its individualizing and specifying characteristics" [*intellectu qui apprehendit formam . . . exspoliatam ab omnibus individuantibus et specificantibus*], if God were identified with this abstract *esse commune*, it would be necessary that "there were no existing thing except that alone which is present in the understanding" [*non (esset) aliqua res existens, nisi quae sit in intellectu tantum*]; now God is by definition outside understanding alone; therefore he cannot be confused with *esse commune* such that only representation by understanding suffices to distinguish Him. On the contrary, Aquinas will say that "the divine *esse* is without addition not only in thought, but even in reality; and not only is it without addition, but it cannot even receive addition."[22] Such a rejection of represented *ens* and/or of *esse commune* as the point of departure in the knowledge of God is enough to disqualify in advance all attempts by Duns Scotus and Suárez. Above all, it removes God from the domain of entity that metaphysics claims to open and to delimit. It is precisely because the *esse* proper to God alone is stripped away from metaphysics that it gets free, too, from metaphysical intelligibility, even to the point of appearing from that perspective as altogether completely unknown: "Since the argument [the identity in God of *esse* and essence] understands *esse* as that by which God subsists in Himself, His *esse* remains as unknown to us as His essence."[23] Nothing could be more rigorous and consistent than this conclusion: if, on the one hand, the *esse* of metaphysics, which pertains to created entities, borrows its primacy from any (human) intelligibility, and if, on the other hand, the divine *esse* escapes from metaphysics, then the divine *esse* should and could also be disengaged from its intelligibility. By this essential dichotomy, Thomas Aquinas not only rejects in advance any kind of univocal concept of entity but, more important, he denies the core of every onto-theo-logy that the theological and ontological functions may ground one another thus within a common determination, which the duality of foundations (conceptual and efficient) cannot threaten but, rather, reinforces. The *esse/ens commune* cannot, according to Thomas Aquinas, introduce anything common and, above all, nothing intelligible between entity inasmuch as it is entity and God.

The analogy of being—about which it makes sense to emphasize once again that Thomas Aquinas scarcely uses the term *analogia entis*—has no other function than to dig the chasm that separates the two understandings of *esse* (and not to bridge it).[24] It is even more necessary to underline that, coming from Duns Scotus unto Suárez by means of Cajetan, the inflation of this doctrine has had no other aim than to submit it to the growing empire of the univocal and intelligible concept of *ens*. For Thomas Aquinas, analogy by contrast intended to emphasize that no name, no concept, no determination should be applied in the same sense to the creature and to God, especially *esse*. Analogy does not mean the tangential univocity of *esse commune*, but, on the contrary, it opens a space where the univocity of being must be exploded. To do so, Thomas Aquinas proposes a radical distinction in *esse*: "*Esse* is said in two ways: in the first, to signify the act of being, in the other to signify the composition of a proposition, an act of the soul joining a predicate to a subject."[25] Like the composition of subject and predicate, that of *esse* and essence determines without exception all the field of created entities, but it disappears in God, and in this case alone, essence is no longer distinguished from the act of being: "God is not only his essence but his *esse* as well."[26] This mode of being belongs properly to God and separates Him from every other entity or, rather, from entitativeness in general. God alone, Thomas Aquinas does not cease to emphasize, has nothing in common with entity: "In God alone, His essence is his *esse*" [*soli Deo cujus solius essentia est suum esse*]; or: "It is proper to God alone that the mode of being is his subsistent *esse*" [*Solius autem Dei proprius modus essendi est, ut sit suum esse subsistens*]; and "God alone is His *esse*" [*Solus Deus est suum esse*].[27] The difference between being and essence, what one could call the ousio-ontical difference, that goes "horizontally" through all created entities is not simply nullified in God but becomes the instrument for enforcing a complete difference, which one could call "vertical," between the ousio-ontical difference taken globally, on the one hand, and, on the other, the ousio-ontic indifference of God. This new difference becomes obvious by creation: "It is necessary, therefore, that in which *esse* is other than its essence have *esse* caused by another" [*Oportet ergo, quod illud, cui esse est aliud ab essentia sua, habeat esse causatum ab alio*]—if the essence differs from the *esse*, then the entity shows itself to be caused. Reciprocally, "to create belongs to God according to His *esse*, which is His essence" [*creare convenit Deo secundum suum esse, quod est ejus essentia*].[28] The identity of essence with *esse* becomes here the basis for the power and the character of the creator. This difference (cause/creation) is not identical to the real distinction and composition (*esse*/essence), but its distinct mark is to oppose the real distinction—as well as every *conceptus entis*. The analogy between these two differences does not cease to deepen their dissimilarity in order to guarantee that never will the being of creatures be taken for the *esse* of God.

Thomas Aquinas ensures this, further, through two characteristics given to analogy. (*a*) First, it is a matter of *proportio* and not of *proportionalitas*: "analogiam idest proprotionem."[29] Whereas *proportionalitas* translates and thus recalls a proportion of four terms, which entails a defined, commensurable, and intelligible relation between them, *proportio,* by contrast, has no further ambition than to refer several terms to a focal point without the necessity of any common measure between them. The choice for *proportio* thus implies that one admits the epistemological legitimacy of an incommensurable, undefined, and in this sense unintelligible relation between the connected terms. By having preferred an analogy of *proportio,* Thomas Aquinas would have thus marked that he has *not* confused mathematical analogy with the analogy of reference; rather he has repudiated the commensurability of mathematical analogy in order to establish a reference between incommensurable terms (immeasurable because one term remains immense). The analogy of reference leaves "the reality signified outside every limit and overflows the signification of the name" [*rem significatam, ut incomprehendam et excedentem nominis significationem*].[30] (*b*)Furthermore, *proportio* does not refer to a term standing by its own (*ad aliquod unum*): this pole of reference must not be understood as neutral and abstract, taken outside the series of analogues (as health for sickness, medicine, remedy, etc.), so that it could refer each of them at the same title; rather it refers to another term (*ad alterum*), itself within the series, or even to one of the real terms in the reference (*ad unum ipsorum*), as an effect to its cause or principle, as accidents to their substance.[31] This primary analogical term, a real term, remains at the same time different from its analogues and yet intrinsically constitutive of them. The created thus does not support or claim any commensurable proportion (according to the common concept of entity) with God; but Thomas refers to that *proportio* even to the point of bringing in it this *esse commune* on the same level as any created essence, both being thus trespassed according to the exteriority intrinsic to God.

Analogy thus strongly confirms what the exception of God toward the *esse commune* was already suggesting: if God should happen to be, it would never be as taking the part of any object (or subject) of *metaphysica,* above all as yielding to any kind of univocal concept of entity. The univocity that makes, as a principle and a method, the onto-theo-logy possible (and by the way the metaphysics too, that sometimes embodies it historically) is in advance dismissed by Thomas, who refuses in general the first criterion of onto-theology—that is, the inclusion of "God" in the metaphysical realm unified by and for the sake of entity and, possibly, by one and the same concept of entity. One can guess, nevertheless, the price that God must pay in order to remove Himself from this constitution of metaphysics: since onto-theology holds its authority by a concept of entity that makes it intelligible (by definition, since *ens* is the first intelligible), God, in order to distance Himself from this, will have to make Himself known as incomprehensible. But, then God is not first of all incomprehensible in Himself but precisely in order to escape onto-theo-logy—or to free *us* from it.

Cause and Foundation

Such foreignness of God with regard to a metaphysical concept of entity, even supposing that we grant it, would not yet allow, however, to establish that He eludes onto-theo-logy completely. For the second criterion of onto-theo-logy obviously seems to affirm the contrary, since it defines the metaphysical God by his efficient foundation of all other entities, indeed by the efficient foundation of being in general. Now this seems indisputably the case for what Thomas Aquinas views under the name of cause: "It is then necessary to pose a first efficient cause which all call God."[32]

It hardly seems worthy of discussion that the relations of creation and hence of intelligibility between creature and creator are treated here perfectly in terms of foundation—and of foundation by an efficient cause. For not only does efficient causality make created entities get into the entitativeness (from God into the world), but it also opens in return (from the world to God) a knowledge of the creator as a cause and in relation to causality: "We cannot know God naturally except by arriving at Him through effects."[33] Thus God is only named by the name of the cause and because of the cause ("Deus nominari dicitur a suis causatis"); the names attributed to God only make sense as effects from whence they come; they can be applied to God with this minimum of nonimpropriety, which separates them from pure and simple equivocity only to the degree that the causal relation guarantees that they bear the mark of their cause, at least by virtue of its efficient causality. "Good," "beautiful," "true" and so on doubtless tell us nothing of divine goodness, truth, and beauty except that they proceed from it by an indisputable efficient causation but abstractly and without real content. It is only with regard to this relation of what is caused up to its cause that the community of the names of God is generally founded: "These names have nothing in common, but that they follow the order assigned by the cause to what it causes" [*in hujusmodi nominum communitate ordo causae et causati*].[34] In short, causality rules the two meanings of the relation: first the entitativeness of the created through God and then the knowledge of God through the created entities. In addition, the empire of causality even extends to the relation of analogy, which, as understood as *proportio,* seems only to offer a particular case of it: "The proportion of the creature to God is the same as that of the caused to the cause and of knowing to the knowable."[35] This hypothesis being granted, there may be a great possibility of contradiction between the analogy, the function of which consists of opening and maintaining the difference of a radical ignorance of God according to *esse commune,* and the causality, whose relation of abstract intelligibility extends as far as its efficacy produces effects, that is, universally. Does not the foundation that assures that "God" bears the name of "cause" endow Him with an intelligibility whose withdrawal was precisely what analogy aimed at? Is not the metaphysical intelligibility of God, undermined by the limitation of the *esse commune* to the created and by the difference of analogy, entirely restored by the assignment of the function of foundation through efficient causality to God?

To the very degree that this question imposes itself, to that same degree so does its denial. In fact, Thomas Aquinas does not so much submit God to efficient causality in the way in which subsequent metaphysics has understood its concept as he reinterprets the causal relation between the created and uncreated according to the demands of analogy, that is, by imposing consideration for the gap of ignorance on it so that causality does not amount to a mere foundation, the terms of which could reciprocally ground one another. Several arguments permit us to establish that the issue consists in redefining causality. (*a*) First of all is the fact that *causa* cannot be understood in Thomas Aquinas as the "totalis et efficiens causa," which Descartes crudely assigns to the creative act of God.[36] For Thomas, on the contrary, divine causality, even if it privileges efficient causality, does not become total since it is achieved also according to finality and form. Far from reducing causality to efficient causality, a restriction that *metaphysica,* with the exception of Leibniz, will massively ratify, Thomas Aquinas confirms the Aristotelian multivocity of causes. (*b*) Above all, he adds a more theological precaution to this properly philosophical reluctance by understanding the *causa* also along the lines of the meaning of Dionysius: "God is the universal cause of all things that occur naturally" [*Est autem Deus universalis causa omnium quae naturaliter fiunt*].[37] In this context, the cause appears to be less what produces than what happens to be required by the thing in order for it to be (as already for Aristotle) and, more radically, what happens to be asked on the mode of prayer (αἰτία from αἰτεῶ) by the creature to the creator, as the request that the petitioner makes to the petitioned. This petitioner has less the status of an effect than that of a *causatum,* of something caused that keeps within itself the full mark of the *causa,* according to a relation less transitive than immanent.

From these two corrections to the concept of causality, an important consequence follows: abstract intelligibility, transparent and eventually univocal efficient causality gives way, for Thomas Aquinas (and the contrary is true for his successors), to a causality codetermined by the relation of creation. Thus, if the caused effects remain really grounded in the cause, they are at the same time infinitely exceeded by it ("prima omnium causa excedens omnia sua causata"). Although completely determined by it, or by that very fact, they remain "definitely inadequate" [*effectus Dei virtutem causae non adaequentes*].[38] Such inadequacy of caused effects to the excessive cause—which results directly from the pattern of creation—obviously implies a unilateral not reciprocal foundation: it goes up to the caused from the cause but never back to the cause from the caused. Creation imposes an essential asymmetry on causality (a mixed relation), which, in return, forbids any attempt to establish a reciprocal foundation of being by entity or of entity by entity. Here, God, whether understood still as entity (*ens*) or already as *esse*, grounds entities but does not in any event receive any counterfoundation, neither from entities (since He creates them) nor from entity as such, from entity in general or *esse commune* (since He creates these as well). The cause can thus certainly remain unknown as such, because, even if it can be known as grounding its effects, it nevertheless gets back no foundation that would make it reciprocally intelligible. This Thomistic reform of causality allows the cause to produce the *esse commune* while transcending it completely. Not being contained within it, this kind of cause defeats, before the fact, the metaphysical system in which causality is only exercised within the limits of the field (and of the concept) of the entity: that is, at first effectively grounding the privileged entity on the derived entities, then exposing itself to the (logical) counterfoundation of the privileged entity by entity in general. Here, according to Thomas Aquinas, causality does not return to God, who achieves it using inasmuch as he keeps off of it.

We can now sketch the relation of causality to the *esse commune*. Contrary to the disposition that *metaphysica* is supposed to have imposed, causality does not unfold the very meaning of being (or of entity) according to Thomas Aquinas but, instead, presides over it—it determines it as another than itself, as its debtor, not as its rule. Causality is not set to work by setting being (or entity) in motion, but it determines that being (or entity) as relying on itself and by distinguishing itself from it. While Heidegger supposes that causality, by exercising onto-theo-logical foundation, completes (itself) at one blow (as) the being of entity, we must suppose that, for Thomas Aquinas, causality is exercised *upon* the being of entity, therefore from outside of it, without being exercised *by* or at least according to it. May one suggest that this exceptional causality arises from its nonmetaphysical meaning? Between the two theses, then, a radical difference is drawn: a distance that distinguishes by itself causality and the being of entity rather than identifying them, as *metaphysica* never stopped to do. We may explain this difference with some new arguments.

a) God explains himself as *esse* only by exercising a causality toward entities, which affects their *esse* as much as their essences: "He is in all by essence insofar as He is present to all as *causa essendi*" [*Est in omnibus per essentiam, inquantum adest omnibus ut causa essendi*]. This *causa essendi*[39] strictly speaking causes common entitativeness: "The *ens commune* is the proper effect of the highest cause, namely God" [*ens commune est proprius effectus cause altissimae, scilicet Dei*].[40] What being can mean for entities is now to be seen apart from God (and from what "to be" may mean for him) by the distance of a cause. The cause works only according to that distance, and not playing any more for the *esse commune* but, rather, against and before it—distance upon being, therefore without it.

b) Thomas thus takes up once again a major argument of the Dionysian tradition. In fact, the *Divine Names* had not only defined God as the principle of entities—ἀρχὴ ἐστι τῶν ὄντων ἀφ' ἧς καὶ αὐτὸ τὸ εἶναι καὶ πάντα τὰ ὁπωσοῦν ὄντα—but above all as that on which being depends and which, conversely, does not depend on it—αὐτοῦ ἐστι τὸ εἶναι, καὶ οὐκ αὐτὸς τοῦ εἶναι. Consequently, it is necessary to go so far as to say that God precedes entitativeness and the entity (as already for Plato) because, more radically, He achieves the role of a principle on being as such, verbal and different from entity: καὶ αὐτὸς ἐστι τοῦ εἶναι . . . ἀρχὴ . . . πρὸ οὐσίας ὤν καὶ ὄντος.[41] As the principle of the *esse* of created entities, and in this sense the only *universalis provisor totius entis,* God does not go back to being and, for this very reason being goes back to Him.[42] An essential discontinuity occurs between the possible being of God and the entitativeness of the entities that He causes as its principle: not merely between God and entities but also between God and the being of entities. Thomas Aquinas thus looks as the direct heir of a line of thought that the *Liber de causis* illustrates: if "the first cause is beyond every name with which one names it," its transcendence can neither be asserted nor categorized within being: therefore it exercises itself upon being: "First among created things is being and before it there is no other creature."[43] Or also for Albert: "The first is not created by anyone it is itself the source and cause of every being"; or also: "As for the *esse* that this science considers . . . it is rather the first effusion of God and the first creature."[44] Here again it goes without saying that if the being of entities emanates from the Primary or First, this latter, God, does not depend on it, is not inscribed within it, and is not comprehended in it.

c) If God, as nonreciprocal cause, exceeds *esse* in the guise of a first creature, it is necessary to realize that being, as original as it remains to us, despite or rather just because of this, is still *a parte Dei* second, regional, hypothetical, conditioned, in short that it befalls us as the known effect of an unknown cause. Created *esse* remains definitively still an effect—"the proper effect of the first agent, God" [*proprius effectus primi agentis, scilicet Dei*]—held at a distance by the cause.[45] The intimacy of the *esse* to each entity does not so much open this latter to the transcendence of the cause as it emphasizes, on the contrary, that the most intimate for us does not exceed the rank of a created effect: "*Esse* itself is the first and most common effect, effect more intimate than all the others."[46] What is most intimate in us nevertheless remains in itself an effect, first to be sure, but for this very reason that much more common. The most essential, most internal, most profound in created entity certainly remains *esse*, which it receives from the *actus essendi* of God, but this *esse* befalls it already as a created *esse*. The created entity doubtless receives its *esse* from the divine *esse*, but, precisely because it receives it by virtue of being created, it receives it as created. *Esse* "clears" from the created to the uncreated not as one transfers a sum from one account to another (without really modifying it), but as a face or a sky clears from one tonality to another—by being essentially modified. The *actus essendi* sets the created *essentiae* in act, and it is precisely for that this *esse* befalls them in the relation, aspect, and condition of an effect. Causality has to be seen throughout from creation.

Such causality does not contradict distance but fulfills it. Causality, according to Thomas Aquinas, does not assign God to the system of metaphysics still to come; rather, it separates Him from it. (*a*) Causality distances at first because it does not tolerate any epistemic univocity: if effect can only be understood in reference to the cause, the cause, in return, even if its existence can be inferred from the effects as *viae*, nonetheless preserves an absolutely unknown essence. (*b*) Causality distances, furthermore, because, if it permits and imposes a foundation of entities by a cause (*Begründung*), nonetheless this foundation does not come from an entity, supreme or par excellence, since God is properly called *esse* and not *ens;* consequently, this foundation is not limited to created entities but ascends to their being, at least in the meaning of their *ens commune*, a hypothesis that the Heideggerian topics do not consider. (*c*) Above all, this foundation does not allow any reciprocal foundation in return, using the conception of the foundation (*Gründung*) of the supreme entity (although lacking) by and according to its being because the *esse commune* has nothing to share with such a divine *esse*, and the latter neither admits nor requires any foundation.

Just as we had already established that Thomas Aquinas does not include God within the metaphysical field of a common concept of being and hence that he refuses in advance the first of the fundamental determinations of all onto-theo-logical interpretation of God, should we not also admit that he nullifies the reciprocal causal foundation of entities and being, because he goes back to the analogy between them and does not submit *esse* to the necessity of a foundation by thinking causality from creation and ignoring any "principle of sufficient reason"? According to this double hypothesis, neither of the two first characteristics of onto-theo-logy finds the least confirmation in the thought of Thomas Aquinas. But before finally drawing this conclusion, which still needs essential qualification, it is necessary to consider the pertinence of the last characteristic of onto-theo-logy.

The *Causa Sui*

We could now discuss the third characteristic of every possible onto-theology—that is, that God is featured in it according to the function of *causa sui*. There is certainly no reason to doubt that Thomas Aquinas refused the legitimacy of assigning what he understood by God to this function of *causa sui*, but the difficulty is rather a matter of understanding his arguments.

The first one looks obvious, as is the logical contradiction that it denounces. God cannot be defined as *causa sui* because nothing can cause itself, since it would then not only have to differ from itself but, above all, to come (and to be) before itself.[47] But this logical argument does not tell enough to disqualify the *causa sui*: Descartes was perfectly aware of it nonetheless admitting its validity, without withdrawing from the obligation of introducing a concept that looked, from the very inception, contradictory.[48]

No doubt it is for this reason that a second argument, implicit but more powerful, takes over for the first. It is expressed as follows: for God fully to exercise the cause that distance demands, He must withdraw Himself from causality.[49] The divine *esse* admits of no cause precisely because it exercises causality toward *entia* alone: "The *ipsum esse* cannot, in fact, be caused by the form itself or the *quiddity* of the thing—I mean as an efficient cause—because then a thing would be cause of itself and a thing would produce itself into being, which is impossible. It is thus necessary that everything whose esse is other than its nature receive its esse from an other."[50] Causality may play here a role too, but only for entities whose *esse* differs from essence, therefore, by definition, not for God. Furthermore, the second of the *viae* can only reach up to God as cause insofar as causality is suspended as soon as it comes to God, who simply stops it—not only because "it is necessary for it to stop" there as it may be elsewhere but, above all, because this stop alone allows the second *via* to hold fast there and to hold fast within God. Without this limitation, no *via* would end in God because none would end at all but would go on from effect to cause, in its turn interpreted as an effect, indefinitely. Only the limitation of the causal chain makes the argument of causality conclusive. An indefinite causality would produce no conclusion, since it would never obtain but a provisional cause, always susceptible of being converted once again into a simple effect. In short, for Thomas Aquinas, the infinite and final cause can (i.e., God) only conclude a finite causality. Which implies a rejection not only of all causality without an end but also of all reciprocal causality. Hence also a rejection not only of reciprocal foundation between being and either entity as such or supreme entity (determination of onto-theo-logy) but, above all, of the foundation of oneself as effect by itself as cause, without any further ontic separation (*causa sui* in the strict sense). The logical argument thus certainly goes beyond any formal evidence. In fact, it sustains the whole speculative edifice.

However, the central point is not to be found here. Had Thomas Aquinas admitted, in anticipation of Descartes, the legitimacy of a determination of God as *causa sui*, he would have also and at first assumed the thesis that makes this determination possible and necessary—that is, that nothing makes an exception to the principle of causality, not even God. This thesis could be formulated with an almost tiny appearance, as with Suárez. Since, one might agree that "there is no entity that is not either effect or cause" [*nullium autem est ens, quod non sit vel effectus, vel causa*], God being well known as an entity and a cause, it is necessary to admit this law without exception: "Causality is as it were a property of entity as such: there is no entity that does not participate in causality in some manner" [*ipsa causalitas est veluti proprietas quaedam entis ut sic: nullum est ens, quod aliquam rationem causae non participet*].[51] As a consequence, causality being assumed as an intrinsic exigency of entity should rule God as every other entity. The fact that they oppose each other as the first cause and the final effects does not make any difference according to this universal and univocal law—since the first cause here draws its possibility from the essence of causality itself. From now on, the more radical formulation of Descartes becomes inevitable: "Nothing exists of which one cannot ask by which cause it exists. And that can be asked of God Himself."[52] Here the metaphysical claim raised by the *causa sui* becomes obvious: God gets to existence as the supreme entity only insofar as he no longer makes an exception to the metaphysical rule, the rule that asserts that all existence requires a cause. The stake of the *causa sui* amounts at first to the fact that God, by submitting to a universal rule of entity, renounces his exception to the common regime of entities whose essence differs from *esse*. For Descartes, it will henceforth be the divine essence that will play the role of cause for the divine existence, at the risk, at least implicit, of only existing at the price of the transcendence of its irreducible *esse*. But the stake also amounts to the dispute with (or confirmation of) the prior decision made by Thomas Aquinas to except God from the *esse commune* and hence from *metaphysica*, since it is a matter of submitting or not to causality understood as the common feature of *esse commune*. If one agrees here to this implicit claim (God according to causality [Descartes]), it will be necessary afterward to assign such a God to all the other principles that *metaphysica* will dictate: God according to the principle of order (Malebranche), according to the principle of sufficient reason (Leibniz), according to a priori principles of experience (Kant), and so forth. One also sees the importance of Thomas Aquinas's rejecting (as do, in fact, the majority of the medievals) any a priori proof of the existence of God: such proofs, as Spinoza will deliberately note, imply considering God as a simple part and a simple particular case of the doctrine of the entity.[53] By rejecting the *causa sui,* Thomas Aquinas does not merely reject *a* metaphysical name of God, but, as Heidegger has seen so well, *the* metaphysical name of God, which, by submitting him to a first a priori (causality), constrains him in advance to yield to the "great metaphysical principle" of sufficient reason and hence to all those implied in it.

So, the third and last characteristic of the onto-theo-logical constitution of metaphysics—to assume the name of *causa sui,* that is, of the entity supremely grounding and grounded—gets from Thomas Aquinas the same censure as the two prior ones: God cannot ever be lowered to the function of a *causa sui*. It thus seems consistent to conclude that the thought of Thomas Aquinas does not at all match the requirements of the onto-theo-logical constitution of metaphysics, at least as understood in the strict sense of Heidegger's postulate.

The Horizon and the Name of Being

As well argued as it stands, this conclusion could still appear to be imprudent and hasty as soon as one considers a last objection. The onto-theo-logical constitution in fact requires, beyond the precise features that we have discussed and just put into effect, that the question of God be able to be asked and answered within the horizon of being. In any case, Heidegger has described this constitution only with the opened intention of explaining how God (and especially the Christian God) has come into metaphysics, that is has agreed to take up the role of the grounded grounding God: He yielded to it to the exact measure where—to start with—He lets Himself be set within the horizon of being. In other words, in order to gain supremacy over entity, God must pay a price—no less than to become subjected to the a priori of being. From this moment on, the possibility of inscribing God, such as Thomas Aquinas understands Him, within one of the manifestations of the onto-theo-logical constitution cannot be imposed (and be discussed in detail), but on the presupposition that God, in general and in principle, has to do with being—and that the horizon of being could fit Him as the adequate space for his manifestation.

But this point precisely should not be taken for granted and the majority of Christian theologians prior to Thomas Aquinas had given preference either to the horizon of the Good, in line with Neoplatonism, or to that of love, while subordinating to them in both cases that of being. Thomas Aquinas established, if not the first, at least in the most emblematic way, that the knowledge of God, even theological, can and must be achieved within the privileged horizon of being.[54] The exemplary and radical hermeneutics of Exod. 3:14 definitely does not lead to any "metaphysics of Exodus," since Thomas Aquinas was not, properly speaking, dealing with metaphysics, any more than he would suggest that Exodus could have been aware of metaphysics. Nevertheless, Thomas thus undeniably ends up by closing the theological exodus of God out of metaphysics, or inversely, by making God come out of its reluctance with regard to what would soon take the title of *metaphysica*. In assuming as its first name that of *esse* or *actus essendi*, the Thomistic God does not manifest himself only *in* being (which, even when starting from other horizons, theology has always ended by conceding), but in fact *as* being. The counterargument that this manifestation amounts precisely to being (to be), and not as entity (assuming at least that this ontological difference is still found without loss in the distinction between *esse/actus essendi* and *ens/essentia*, which one could reasonably doubt), takes nothing out of the difficulty but makes it worse: not only is God inscribed in being, but He identifies, singularizes, in a word achieves Himself in the role of making being possible—in such a way that being in act would be enough to accomplish God as such. This decision, absolutely without precedent (and a recent commentator willingly prides himself on it) does not only imply a U-turn in the history of the determination of the divine essence but makes possible for the first time, at bottom, an onto-theo-logy.[55] Consequently, in spite of the concise disagreements, Thomas Aquinas would turn out to be the first and most radical advocate of onto-theo-logy, in the two principal meanings of this word. (*a*) Following Heidegger's meaning, God enters metaphysics to the extent that He speaks of Himself and allows Himself to be spoken of according to being, insomuch as being opens a site where the divine and God could assume their own but designated function. (*b*) Following Kant's meaning as well, for, if one defines as onto-theo-logical the proof that "believes to know His existence [mainly God] on the basis of simple concepts, without any regard to experience," should we not conclude that Thomas Aquinas has given a foretaste for this, since he deduces the being (existence) of God from His definition (concept of essence) as *actus essendi?*[56]

As a consequence, our essay should completely reverse his conclusion. However, if one focused attention only to the internal features of onto-theology as Heidegger has defined it, Thomas Aquinas does not have a connection to it, any more than, in the strict historical sense, does he find a place in metaphysics. But, if we consider the preliminary condition for the possibility of an onto-theo-logy—that is, that God would inscribe Himself without restraint in the horizon of being, in essence and in existence, as an act and by definition—then Thomas Aquinas would become not only the first of the onto-theo-logians but one of the most radical, if not the most radical ever, to the very extent to which he holds neither to a supreme entity (Spinoza, Leibniz, Kant) nor to an indeterminate being (Avicenna, Duns Scotus, Malebranche) but to pure *esse* as such (which Aristotle had only approached). One can see better the blindness of some commentators: not doubting for a moment that being would count enough to express and keep the transcendence of God, not even guessing that one could prefer to affirm it according to another of the transcendentals, they do not furthermore suspect that inscribing the divinity of God within being henceforth imposes on this God to take part in the destiny of being; now being has quickly passed from *esse,* where Thomas Aquinas claimed to lift it up, to a *conceptus univocus entis,* which leaves unthought the infinite divinity of God (Scotus, Ockham, Descartes), then reintegrates it in its common rule on the basis of *ens supremum* or *perfectissimun* (Spinoza, Malebranche, Leibniz, Kant); and it could, keeping the same definition, end up with the "death of God," according to the very movement where the *ontologia* finally exhausts itself into nihilism (Nietzsche). If, since Thomas Aquinas, the destiny of being identifies itself with that of God, this identification remains for the better (Thomism) and for the worse (*metaphysica*). It is not enough to claim in response that one has only to go back to the "authentic" Thomistic conception of *esse* to escape this contract—it would also be necessary to be able to do so. And we may imagine that such an access to the "authentic" *esse* would be for us today neither that easy nor powerful enough to have us resist the inexorable attraction of nihilism, the danger of which consists precisely in the extent to which it devalues the "authentic" *esse.* (In fact, if it were to dissolve only an "inauthentic" *esse,* what would this matter to us?) Not to listen to a question, this is not enough to prove to have already answered it, still less to have gone beyond it. In a large part of "Christian philosophy," being remains the last resort, the supposedly unshakable rock on which apology would always lean. But does not one see that being can also become—and historically has already become—a stumbling block, a millstone attached around the neck of one's enemy before throwing him into the water? Should we blind ourselves to the point of asking being—in a full era of nihilism—to save God? Should we absolutely set aside the opposite hypothesis —only a god, and possibly God could save what, in being, could rise again and without doubt under a totally other aspect than the one metaphysics has inflicted on it? In a word, to free ourselves from onto theo-logy, should we again and always break away from Thomas Aquinas to start with?

Nevertheless, I suggest following a totally different way: Thomas Aquinas might, on the contrary, have left God *out* of being, taken not only in the meaning of *metaphysica* but also in the meaning of onto-theo-logy (and indeed of *Ereignis*), inasmuch as he has displayed an *esse* as radically foreign to *ens* and to *conceptus univocus entis* as to the being foreseen by Heidegger.[57] To put it clearly, the Thomistic *esse* cannot be understood starting from ontological determinations, whatever they might be, but only starting from its distance with regard to all possible ontology, following instead the claims imposed by the transcendence of God on entity as well as on his own being. The being of entity maintains its distance from *esse*, because this *esse* assumes in fact and before anything else the features of the *mysterium tremendum fascinandum* of a God making Himself conceptually manifest. If *esse* truly offers the first name of God according to Thomas Aquinas, this thus signifies for him in the first place that God is called *esse* but as to name only and not as such. For in good theology, the primacy of *esse* implies especially that it is to be understood, more than any other name, starting from God, and not that God can be conceived starting from *esse*. To think *esse* starting from God, but not in inverse order (in the way of *metaphysica* and of Heidegger as well), allows Thomas Aquinas to free the divine *esse* from its—tangentially univocal— comprehension starting from what philosophy understands by being, entity, being of the entity, in a word to mark the distance—an "infinitely infinite distance"—from the creature to God (Pascal).

This distance gets evidences through many precise arguments, which bring out as many differences:

a) The first deals with the difference between God and entity and, therefore, with entitativeness in general: "The divine *esse* that is His substance is not the common *esse*, but it is an *esse* distinct from all other entity. This is why, by His *esse* in itself, God differs from all other entities."[58] One could certainly be inclined to merge, at least formally, this difference with the ontological difference, if a second argument did not intervene.

b) The difference between *ens* and *esse* must be thought through and from creation; in fact, according to this radicality, it plays with three and not two terms: the divine *esse* really only causes the entities because he causes also their entitativeness (their *esse commune*), their *esse* as created. But if the divine *esse* creates the *esse commune*, as well as being, according to onto-theo-logy (and to *metaphysica*) takes the place of *esse commune*, we should conclude that the *esse* that stays at a creational distance from the *esse commune* refers neither to this one, nor to the one of *metaphysica*, nor to the one of onto-theo-logy. Or again, one could say that such *esse* keeps within itself the transcendence that opposes the act of being to the *esse commune* of entities. It is necessary to suggest, against the first evidences—but, we think, according to the intention of Thomas Aquinas—that the *esse* assigned to God excludes itself from the common and created being and consequently from all what we understand and know under the title of being. Therefore, God without being (at least without *this* being) could become again a Thomistic thesis. And to go beyond, unto the *esse* of which God fulfills the act, it would be necessary to think without ontological categories but according to truly theological determinations—as, for example, that of "intensive being."[59] Being taken according to this excellence would thus find itself already outside of being.

c) But another argument definitely emphasizes how the excess of the proper *esse* of God disqualifies all metaphysical (conceptual) meaning of being. Thomas Aquinas brings this out either directly or indirectly. He does it directly by identifying the divine essence with *esse:* "God does not have an essence that would not be His *esse*."[60] Or, "The essence of God is His own proper *esse*."[61] Following this path, God does not have any other essence than *esse*, which stands for it, thus excluding any composition of *esse* and essence, which is required everywhere else. But, indirectly, the same result is expressed even more radically, especially in two texts. (i) "One thing exists, God, whose essence is his proper *esse*, that is why one finds certain philosophers who say that God has neither quiddity nor essence, since his essence is nothing else than his *esse*."[62] There is no question that Thomas Aquinas does not here literally ratify the thesis of the absence of essence in God; but the simple fact that he suggests this absence by alluding to the noncomposition in God of *esse* and essence suggests his accord with those "some philosophers." (ii) "Some say, as Avicenna and Rabbi Moses [Maimonides] do, that the thing that God is is some *esse subsistens,* and that there is in God but only *esse:* as a result they say that He is without essence."[63] What does it mean not to have an essence? Obviously this can only amount be the identity between *esse* and essence. But in its own way what does this identity display? For sure, no essence (or quiddity) can be fitting here for the *esse* of God, who, as a result, remains absolutely and formally without essence. But if we were to admit that it belongs by definition (Aristotle) to metaphysics to bring the questioning about what entity is back around to the question about essence (τί τὸ ὄν, τοῦτό ἐστι τίς ἡ οὐσία),[64] how can we not understand the obliteration of essence with respect to God as a new argument forbidding that God could be taken and thought about according to being, in the meaning which metaphysics uses to give to it? In fact, an *esse* irreducible to any essence signifies an *esse* irreducible, too, to the metaphysical essence of being—as elaborated in onto-theo-logy.

A last argument confirms without the slightest ambiguity the metaphysical exclusion of this *esse:* God's unknowability. In fact, the irreducibility of *esse* to any essence argues for the impossibility of articulating anything about God in a predicative way and, therefore, of speaking of it discursively or, in a word, of understanding it. Thus this pure *esse* reveals itself in principle as unknowable as the God it names. God known as unknown—this implies that his *esse* remains knowable only as unknowable, in sharp contrast to the *esse* that metaphysics has essentially set in a concept to make it as knowable as possible. We are not short of textual evidences. For example, "Just as the substance of God is unknown, so it is for His *esse*." And, "God is known through our ignorance, inasmuch as this is to know God, that we know that we do not know what He is." Or, "The highest and most perfect degree of our knowledge in this life is, as Denys said in his book On *Mystical Theology* (I.3), to be united to God as unknown. This is what happens when we know about God what He is not, since what He is remains profoundly unknown." Or then, "With the exception of a revelation of grace we do not, in this life, know about God what He is and therefore that we are united to Him as unknown."[65] As a pure act of being, without any reference to the ordinary composition proper to the metaphysical entity, the divine *esse* remains as unknown as God, precisely because "being is meant in two ways: in a first, to signify the act of being; in another, to stress the composition of a proposition, which soul works out by joining a predicate to a subject. According to the first meaning, we can no more know the being of God than His essence, but only according to the second."[66] The meaning of the *esse* proper to God is strictly characterized by His unknowability, in contrast to the categorical meaning, perfectly integrated to the metaphysical plurality of meanings of entity according to Aristotle. To be excluded from being in the metaphysical sense and to remain by definition unknown turns out to be perfectly equivalent in God and in God alone.

To be sure, it seems that a powerful objection could still contain these arguments. God certainly receives, according to Thomas Aquinas, a name that is proper and directly conformed to being: "Qui est." But, as it should be noticed, it happens that the text itself that affirms more clearly this privilege confirms equally clearly that God excludes himself from being (according to metaphysics) by his unknowability. (*a*) First, given that we should consider "Qui est" as "the name that is most proper to God" [*maxime proprium nomen Dei*], it is appropriate to immediately specify that *maxime* emphasizes without equivocation that it remains still comparable to other names and, therefore, does not count absolutely. (*b*) Second, even knowing this name, we still do not know the divine essence: "Our understanding, in this life, cannot know the essence itself of God as it is in itself, but whatever it determines that it understands about God, it remains short of what God is in Himself." (*c*) Third, the name "Qui est," finally and especially, manifests its most precise property only in the strict measure in which it recognizes also the incommunicability of God: "The name most proper is the Tetragrammaton, used to signify the incommunicable and, if we can speak thus, singular divine substance itself."[67] Thus follows an obvious paradox: the uniqueness and superiority of the name borrowed from Exod. 3:14 come precisely from the insular incommunicability it manifests in God, therefore from the definitive exclusion with regard to all knowable and common being—in short, with regard to the metaphysical concept of *esse commune*. It must be admitted that it is specifically the naming of God according to the being of the so-called metaphysics of Exodus that offers the best argument for the metaphysical exclusion of God according to Thomas Aquinas.

One can then conclude that he does not think of God in a univocal way within the horizon of being. Or simply: the *esse* that Thomas Aquinas recognizes for God does not open any metaphysical horizon, does not belong to any onto-theo-logy, and remains such a distant analogy with what we once conceived through the concept of being, that God proves not to take any part in it, or to belong to it, or even—as paradoxical as it may seem—to be. *Esse* refers to God only insofar as God may appear as without being—not only without being as onto-theology constitutes it in metaphysics but also well out of the horizon of being, even as it is as such (Heidegger). The statement "God without being" not only could be understood as fundamentally Thomistic, but it could be that no contemporary interpretation of Thomas Aquinas could retrieve its validity without assuming the unconditional exclusion of *esse*—therefore without the wise imprudence of such paradoxes.[68]

Answer to the Question: *Esse* without Being

To the questions originally asked (as to the features of onto-theo-logy), we can now attempt to give an answer. Thomistic thought without any doubt rejects the three features of the onto-theo-logic constitution of metaphysics. (1) God does not go into the field (subject or object) of metaphysics or, a fortiori, into the concept of entity. (2) The foundation for entities and for their being (*esse commune*) in God depends without doubt on causality, but it has nothing that is reciprocal, so that being certainly does not ground (conceptually) God, whose *actus essendi* escapes all concepts, to the strict extent that an act determines being in Him. (3) This is confirmed in the fact that, free from any causality or ground (not even His proper essence, directly identified with his act of being), God denies for Himself the metaphysical figure of self-foundation, for which the *causa sui* designates the paradigm. Yet Thomas Aquinas does not take away all the ambiguities implied by two features of the onto-theo-logic constitution of metaphysics. First, is the nonreciprocity between God and created entities enough to get away with a metaphysical interpretation of creation? Second, and in particular, would not the causal grounds of entities as well as that of the being of entities (as created *esse commune*) by God identify themselves with the metaphysical causation of entities by the supreme entity in metaphysics? One immediately recognizes that the answer to these two questions depends on knowing, first, to what extent God remains tangentially *ens supremum* and, then, to what extent the act of being relies on being itself. (4) Hence the last question: if God, as act of being, transcends all real composition of *esse* and *essentia,* thus the whole of created entitativeness, and if in Him *esse* also transcends all concepts, thus if He remains essentially unknown, must we conclude that His *esse* still belongs to what we can understand as "being" (in its metaphysical meaning as well as in its non-metaphysical meaning), or can we admit that it goes beyond any understanding of "being"? In the first hypothesis, the *esse* assigned to God would still impose on Him the onto-theo-logical burden of causal grounding (of the entities and their *esse commune*); while in the second, the meta-ontological transcendence of *esse* without essence or concept would free Him—even under that name of *esse*—from all connection to onto-theo-logy.

Thus all the answers to the question focus the attention to a precise dilemma: Can *esse* be exclusively understood according to a (historically) metaphysical sense, that is, according to a reopened "question of being," or must it be clarified by a meta-ontological meaning—in a word, be understood as *esse* without being? In fact, since one usually admits that the divine *esse* remains, for Thomas Aquinas, if not for his school, deprived of any concept of being, without an essence, without a definition, without knowability—in a word, amounts to a negative name—why pretend to treat it as an affirmative name, giving the equivalent of an essence, the equivalent of a concept, the equivalent of a knowledge? Why not admit that Thomas Aquinas only held onto this *esse* with the intention of tactically leaning on the term preferred by his philosophical interlocutors, without ever assuming it affirmatively, or raising it to eminence, but by certifying it through apophasis? Obviously, we cannot doubt that Thomas Aquinas did designate God as *esse*. But one must doubt that, once appropriately assigned to God, *esse* could mean only what metaphysics, and even the "question of being," succeeds in conceiving it— and not, on the contrary, aim beyond being itself, whatever it might be. This transgression would not in fact imply ontic, or ontological loss, or any irrationality. It only takes into account that nothing is rationally appropriate to God except what matches infinity.

My hypothesis, I know, might surprise the defenders of Heidegger as much as some among the disciples of Thomas Aquinas. For the former, my hypothesis assumes some points that are hardly acceptable: first that *metaphysica,* taken historically, amounts to metaphysics as a determinant of the history of being; then that *metaphysica,* to speak honestly, starts after Thomas Aquinas (and not much before); and also that the Thomistic attribution of *esse* to a Christian God indicates more an assumption of being in a radically nonontological field than the assignation to God of a place in the metaphysical destiny of being; and finally that an impoverishment of metaphysics by excess can occur at any moment in its history. For the latter, the unacceptable remains that, under the guise of liberating Thomas Aquinas from the burden of *metaphysica,* we could pretend to underline the reshuffling in him of the Dionysian (and "Neoplatonic") subordination of *esse* to a cause, going so far as to interpret in a nonontological way the transcendence of *esse*. These two hesitations may in no way surprise, nor do they lack good arguments: besides the shortcomings in our own knowing, one must admit the weight of traditions and personal commitments as well as the indispensable pluralism of interpretations. It would be enough, therefore, as a first step, if our hypothesis could only be taken in consideration in spite of its obvious limits and its apparent paradox.

But does it go without saying that we could improve our knowledge of God today if we persist in understanding Him starting from what we know—

or believe we know—about being? Does taking Thomas Aquinas seriously require that we should think of God starting with being or think of being starting with God? For a long time, it seemed to be out of the question that God, for Thomas Aquinas, had to be thought from being—in debates dealing only with specifying what this being stands for: existence or concept, intrinsic or extrinsic analogy, metaphysics or transcendentalism, and so on. It also seemed, at the same time, to go without saying that the questioning of the primacy of being, as transcendental or as horizon, implied the questioning of the fundamental position of Thomas Aquinas concerning God. We foresee that from now on these two arguments could be articulated quite differently. The debate on the determination of the *esse*, and first of all of its irreducibility to the concept of entity and its exit out of the object of *metaphysica*, gets its importance only from its result: to allow—or more often to forbid—thinking of this *esse* by starting with the distance of God. It is no longer so much the issue to decide whether it is necessary or not to name God by the title of *esse*, but if we can get such an understanding of *esse* that it could reasonably claim not to reach to but at least to aim toward whatever it might be that we name God. It is not a matter of deciding whether we should speak of God in the name of being, but if being (taken as *esse* or otherwise) still has sufficient quality or dignity to enunciate whatever it might be about God, which would be more of value than straw. Reciprocally, if Thomas Aquinas does not belong to the onto-theo-logy problematic, it is also necessary to give up our claim of him to bridge its characteristic insufficiency—that of never thinking of being, except by starting with and in the light of entity: it seems no longer to the point to try to read the *actus essendi* as an anticipation either of *Seyn* or of *Ereignis*, which prior to this would have conceived of being as such.

The *esse* that Thomas meditates on may deal not with metaphysics, or ontology, or even the "question of being" but, instead, with the divine names and on the "luminous darkness."

Notes

This chapter is a translation of "Saint Thomas d'Aquin et l'onto-théo-logie," first published in the *Revue Thomiste* 95 (1995) by B. Gendreau, R. Rethy and M. Sweeney, revised and completed by the author.

1. I have used the standard translations of Being/entity, but I want to make clear that by "Being" I exclusively mean "to be," *esse, Sein, être,* as opposed to *ens, Seiende, étant.*

2. On those two issues, I would like to take a more balanced position than that of my earlier study, *Dieu sans l'être* (Paris: Fayard, 1982; reprint, Paris: Presses Universitaires de France, 1991). See, too, my acknowledgments in the preface to *God without Being: Hors-Texte,* trans.

Thomas A. Carlson (Chicago: University of Chicago Press, 1991), xvii–xxv, and "Metaphysics and Phenomenology: A Relief for Theology," *Critical Inquiry,* vol. 20, no. 4 (1994).

3. Martin Heidegger, "Die onto-theologische Verfassung der Metaphysik," in *Identität und Differenz* (Pfüllingen: G. Neske, 1957), 63, translated as *Identity and Difference,* trans. J. Stambaugh (New York: Harper & Row, 1969), 71 (modified).

4. Given that, indeed, God should and could be said and thought as a being, even a supreme one. And this raises the question of whether we should doubt the accuracy of naming him according to being in general.

5. I refer, indeed, to George Berkeley, *Principles of Human Knowledge,* ed. Howard Robinson (Oxford: Oxford University Press, 1996), I, secs. 2–3.

6. See a more detailed analysis in my study *On Descartes' Metaphysical Prism: The Constitution and the Limits of Onto-theo-logy in Cartesian Thought,* trans. Jeffrey L. Kosky (Paris: Presses Universitaires de France, 1986; reprint, Chicago: University of Chicago Press, 1999).

7. Heidegger, *Identität und Differenz,* 51 (*Identity and Difference,* 60).

8. Heidegger, *Identität und Differenz,* 61 and 64 (*Identity and Difference,* 69 and 72).

9. See the accurate definitions of "metaphysics" given in the forewords to the commentaries to Aristotle's *Physics, Metaphysics, On Generation and Corruption* (Pro. 2), and to *De Coelo* (Pro.1.1). But first of all, "Suprema vero inter eas [scientia philosophica], scilicet metaphysica, disputat contra negantem sua principia, si adversarius aliquid concedit; si autem nihil concedit, non potest cum eo disputare, potest tamen solvere rationes ipsius" (St. Thomas, *Summa Theologiae* Ia, q.1, a.8). Or, "Aliqua scientia acquisita est circa res divinas, sicut scientia metaphysicae" (*Summa Theologiae* IIa–IIae, q.9, a.2, obj.2). And, "Metaphysica, quae circa divina versatur" (Saint Thomas, *Summa contra Gentiles* I,4). I want to emphasize that this connection between *metaphysica* and the *divina* does not fit the definition produced by the commentary on *Metaphysics* in *In duodecim libros Metaphysicorum Aristotelis expositio,* Proemium, ed. M. R. Cathala (Turin: Marietti, 1964), 1 ff.

10. *In duodecim libros Metaphysicorum,* ed. Cathala, 1 ff.

11.The first quote is from *Summa Theologiae* Ia, q.1, a.1, ad 2. The second quote is from St. Thomas, *Expositio super librum Boethii de Trinitate,* question 5, answer 4, ed. B. Decker (Leiden: Brill, 1959), 195, or *Opuscula omnia,* ed. P. Mandonnet (Paris: P. Lethielleux, 1929), 3:119–20. See "hoc modo [mainly *procedere ex principiis notis lumine superioris scientiae*] sacra doctrina est scientia, quia procedit ex principiis notis lumine superioris scientiae, quae scilicet est scientia Dei et beatorum" (*Summa Theologiae* Ia, q.1, a.2, c.). About this double status of theology, see also M. Corbin, *Le chemin de la théologie chez Thomas d'Aquin* (Paris: Beauchesne, 1974), chap. 2 (and in particular sec. 2), as well as G Kalinowski, "Esquisse de l'évolution d'une conception de la métaphysique," *Saint Thomas d'Aquin aujourd'hui: Recherches de philosophie,* vol. 6 (1963).

12. "Res divinae non tractantur a philosophis, nisi prout sunt rerum omnium principia. Et ideo pertractantur in illa doctrina, in qua ponuntur illa quae sunt communia omnibus entibus, quae habet subjectum ens in quantum ens" (*Expositio super librum Boethhi de Trinitate,* ed. Decker, 194; in *Opuscula omnia,* ed. Mandonnet, 3:119).

13. "Theologia ergo philosophica determinat de separatis secundo modo sicut de subjectis, de separatis autem primo modo sicut de principiis subjectis. Theologia vero sacrae Scripturae tractat de separatis primo modo sicut de subjectis" (*Expositio super librum Boethi de Trinitate,* ed. Decker, 195; in *Opuscula omnia,* ed. Mandonnet, 3:120).

14. "Subjectum in illa [mainly *scientia*] potest dici Deus, quia ratio entitate magis reservatur in Deo quam caeteris entibus. Et inde dicitur quod scientia metaphysicae esse divina et

de Deo" (Giles de Rome, *Commentarium in primum librum Sententiarum, Prologus,* question 1, [Venice: heredum O. Scotus, 1521], fol. 2rb). See A. Zimmermann, *Ontologie oder Metaphysik? Die Discussion über den Gegenstand der Metaphysik im 13. und 14. Jahrhundert* (Leiden: Brill, 1965), 144–47.

15. "Cum dicis 'Deus effugiat rationem entis,' dico quod falsum et immo verisimile [Deus] ens est" (*Commentarium,* question 9, ad 1, fol. 4vb). See Zimmermann, *Ontologie oder Metaphysik?* and J.-F. Courtine, *Suarez et le système de la métaphysique* (Paris: Presses Universitaires de France, 1990), 114 ff. and 128 ff.

16. "Similter dico quod in metaphysicis ens in quantum ens est subjectum principaliter per oo et primo. Ex quia ratio entis melius et verius salvatur in Deo quam in alio ente, propter hoc dico, quod Deus est subjectum principale illius scientiae, non per se et primo, sed ex consequenti" (Giles de Rome, *Quaestiones metaphysicales . . .* q.5 [Venice, n.d.; reprint, Frankfurt am Main: Minerva, 1966], fol. 3rb). What is assumed here is precisely what should have been demonstrated against the authority of Thomas Aquinas, i.e., that the *ratio entis* [*in quantum entis*] is better achieved by God than by any finite entity.

17. John Duns Scotus, *Ordinatio,* I, distinction 3, question 3, numbers 126 and 139, vol. 3 of *Opera omnia,* ed. Carolus Balic (Civitas Vaticana : Typis Polyglottis Vaticanis, 1954), 79 and 87, and, in French, *Sur la connaissance de Dieu et l'univocité de l'étant,* ed. and trans. Olivier Boulnois (Paris: Presses Universitaires de France, 1988), 137 and 148. See also O. Boulnois, "Quand commence l'onto-théo-logie? Aristote, Thomas d'Aquin et Duns Scot," *Revue Thomiste* 95, no. 1 (1995): 85–108.

18. Francisco Suárez, *Disputationes metaphysicae* I, s.1, n.13 and n.26, in *Opera omnia,* ed. Charles Berton et al. (Paris: apud Ludovicum Vivès, 1866), 25:6 and 11. See n.19 ("absolute Deus cadit sub objectum hujus scientia") and n.20 ("Nec D. Thomas unquam oppositer docuit [?], sed solum hanc scientiam [metaphysicam] pervenire ad cognitionem Dei sub ratione principii, non tamen negat eamdem scientiam tractare de Deo ut de praecipuo objecto") (p. 9), which seems obviously (and intentionally?) wrong. And II, s.2, n.11: "Ens, de quo nunc loquimur, est commune enti creato et increato" (p. 73); such a community amounts, in a very consistent way, to destroy the analogy: "Si alterum negandum esset, potius analogia, quae incerta est, quam unitas conceptus, quae veris rationibus videatur demonstrari, esset neganda" (II, s.2, n.36; p. 81). On this issue, see J.-L. Marion, *Sur la théologie blanche de Descartes* (Paris: Presses Universitaires de France, 1981; reprint, Paris: Presses Universitaires de France, 1992), 135 ff.

19. *Expositio in librum Dionysii de Divinis nominibus,* V, II (ed. Ceslas Pera [Turin: Marietti, 1950], par. 660; in *Opuscula omnia,* ed. Mandonnet, 2:499): "Primo quidem quantum ad hoc quod alia existentia dependent ab esse communi, non autem Deus, sed magis esse commune a Deo . . . Secundo, quantum ad hoc quod omnia existentia continentur sub ipso esse communi, non autem Deus, sed magis esse commune continetur sub ejus virtute, quia virtus divina plus extenditur quam ipsum esse creatum."

20. *Summa Theologiae* Ia, q.5, a.2, *resp.:* "Primum autem in conceptione intellectus cadit ens, quia secundum hoc unmquodque cognoscibile est, inquantum est actu . . .; und ens est prprium objectum intellectus et sic est primum intelligibile." See *In Sententiarum Libros* I, distinction 38, question 1, answer 4, ad 4 (and distinction 8, question 1, answer 3), *De Veritate,* question 1, answer 1, c., and *De ente et essentia,* Proemium: "Ens autem et essentia sunt quae primo intellectu concipiuntur, ut dicit Avicenna in V Metaphysica" (in *Opuscula omnia,* ed. Mandonnet, 1:145); *In duodecim libros Metaphysicorum* I, question 2, n.46: "Nam primo in intellectu cadit ens, ut Avicenna dicit" (ed. Cathala, 13). On this issue (and some others), see

E. Gilson's "Eléments d'une métaphysique thomiste de l'être," n. 1, in *Autour de saint Thomas* (Paris: J. Vrin, 1983), 97. Concerning Thomas Aquinas's relations to Avicenna, see G. C. Anawati, "Saint Thomas d'Aquin et al Metaphysique d'Avicenne," avec l'appendice sur "Les notions, définitions ou distinctions d'Avicenne approuvées par saint Thomas," in *Colloque commémoratif saint Thomas d'Aquin: Saint Thomas Aquinas commemorative colloquium (1274–1974)* (Ottawa: Université Saint-Paul, 1974).

21. *Summa Theologiae* Ia, q.3, a.4, ad 2.

22. *Summa Contra Gentiles* I, sec. 26, n.4 and ad 2m.: "Divinum autem esse est absque additione non solum in cogitatione, sed etiam in rerum natura, nec solum in additione, sed etiam absque receptibilitate additionis." See, too, *De Potentia* VII, answer 2, ad 4: "Esse divinum, quod est ejus substantia, non est esse commune, sed est esse distinctum a quolibet alio esse"; or *De Potentia* VII, answer 2, ad 6: "Divinum esse non est ens commune." Or *De ente et essentia* VI: "Nec oportet, si dicamus quod Deus est esse tantum, ut in errorem incidamus qui Deum dixerunt esse illud esse universale quo quaelibet res formaliter est. Hoc enim esse quod Deus est, hujus conditionis est ut nulla sibi additio fieri possit: unde per ipsam suam puritatem est esse distinctum ab omni esse" (in *Opuscula omnia*, ed. Mandonnet, 2:159).

23. *Contra Gentiles* I, sec. 12: "Nam hoc intelligitur de esse, quo Deus in se ipso subsistit, quod nobis quale sit, ignotum est, sicut ejus essentia."

24. See, on the history of the concept of *analogia entis,* J.-L. Marion, ed., "L'analogie," special issue of *Les Etudes philosophiques,* nos. 3–4 (1989).

25. *Summa Theologiae* Ia, q.3, a.4, ad 2: "Esse dupliciter dicitur: uno modo significat actum essendi; alio modo significat compositionem propositionis quod anima adinvenit conjugens praedicatum subjecto."

26. Ibid., Ia, q.3, a.4: "Deus non solum est sua essentia . . . sed etiam suum esse."

27. Ibid., Ia, q.6, a.3; and q.12, a.4; and then q.45, a.5, ad 1m. Too many and too well known texts could be quoted here, which have no need of it.

28. Ibid., Ia, q.3, a.4 and, then q.45, a.6.

29. Ibid., Ia, q.13, a.5 and Ia–IIae, q.20, a.3, ad 3: "Analogiam et proportionem."

30. Ibid., Ia, q.13, a.5. I rely, indeed, on the illuminating study by Bernard Montagnes, *La doctrine de l'analogie de l'être selon saint Thomas d'Aquin* (Paris: Librairie Lecottre, J. Gabalda, 1963), and I disagree with P. Aubenque, "Sur la naissance de la doctrine pseudo-aristotélicienne de l'analogie de l'être" (*Les Etudes philosophiques,* nos. 3–4 [1989], 291 ff.), whose analysis fits better Cajetanus or Suárez than Thomas Aquinas.

31. *Summa Theologiae* Ia, q.13, a.5, and *Contra Gentiles* I, sec. 34.

32. Ibid., Ia,, q.2,a.3: "Ergo est necesse ponere aliquam causam efficientem primam, quam omnes Deum nominant."

33. *Contra Gentiles* I, sec. 31: "Deum non possumus cognoscere naturaliter nisi ex effectibus deveniendo in ipsum."

34. Ibid., I, sec. 34 and sec. 33.

35. In *Expositio super librum Boethii de Trinitate,* question 1, answer 2, ad 3m. (in *Opuscula omnia,* ed. Mandonnet, 3:33). See *Contra Gentiles* III, sec. 54: "Proportio ad Deum . . . secundum quod proportio significat quamcumque habitudinem unius ad alterum, vel materiae ad formam, vel causae ad effectum"; as well as *Summa Theologiae* Ia, q.12, a.1, ad 4m ("proportio creaturae ad Deum being understood ut effectus ad causam"), etc.

36. René Descartes, letter to Mersenne, April 27, 1630 (in *Œuvres de Descartes,* ed. Charles Adam and Paul Tannery [Paris: J. Vrin, 1964–74], 1:151).

37. *In Dionysii De Divinis Nominibus,* IV, 2 (in *Opuscula omnia,* ed. Mandonnet, 2:452).

Concerning the doctrine of Dionysius on αἰτία, see my analysis in *L'idole et la distance* (Paris: Bernard Grasset, 1977; reprint, Paris: Bernard Grasset, 1991), sec. 14, 196 ff. From time to time Thomas Aquinas (more often than does Albert the Great) writes *causatum* in the place of *effectum*, which obviously refers more to Dionysius than to Aristotle.

38. *Summa Theologiae* Ia, q.12, a.12.

39. Ibid., Ia, q.8, a.3. For *causa essendi*, see ibid., Ia, q.45, a.1; *De Potentia*, question 3, answer 6; and *Contra Gentiles* II,sec. 6: "Aliis causa essendi existit."

40. *Summa Theologiae* I, q.65, a.5, ad 4. See Ia, q.45, a.6: "Creare est proprie causare, sive producere esse rerum"; or q.105, a.5: "Ipse Deus est proprie causa ipsius esse universalis in rebus"; and *De Potentia*, question 3, answer 5, ad 1: "Licet causa prima, quae Deus est, non intret essentiam rerum creatarum; tamen esse, quod rebus creatis inest, non potest intelligi nisi ut deductum ab esse divino."

41. Dionysius, *On Divine Names*, V, 7 and V, 8 (Migne, *Patrologia graeca* 3, cols. 821B and 824A). Which is literally commented on by Thomas: "[Deus] non solum est causa quantum ad fieri rerum, sed quantum ad totum esse" (*Expositio in librum Dionysii de Divinis nominibus*, ed. Pera, 235, par. 631; in *Opuscula omnia*, ed. Mandonnet, 2:487).

42. The phrase *universalis provisor totius entis* is from *Summa Theologiae* Ia, q.22, a.2, ad 2.

43. *Liber de causis*, XXI, sec. 166 et IV, sec. 37.

44. First *De causis et processu universitatis a prima causa*, ed. W. Fauser, vol. 17A of *Opera omnia*, (Aschendorff: Monasterii Westfalorum, 1993), 18; then *Metaphysica*, ed. Bernard Geyer, vol. 16, pt. 2, of *Opera omnia*, (Aschendorff: Monasterii Westfalorum, 1964), XI, 1, c.3, p.463 (see I, 1, c.1 [16, pt. 1:3]; I, 4, c.8 [16, pt. 1:57]; IV, 1, c.3 [16, pt. 1:163]). Classical commentary by A. de Libera, *Albert le Grand et la philosophie* (Paris: J. Vrin, 1990), 78 ff.

45. *Contra Gentiles* III, sec. 66. See: "Primus autem effectus est ipsum esse, quod omnibus aliis effectibus praesupponitur et ipsum non praesupponit aliquem aliud effectum; et ideo oportet quod dare esse inquantum hujusmodi sit effectus primi causae solius secundum propriam virtutem" (*De Potentia*, question 3, answer 4, resp.); and also: "Ostensum est autem supra, quod Deus est primum et perfectissimum ens, unde oportet quod sit causa essendi omnibus quae esse habent" (*Compendium Theologiae* I, sec. 68, in *Opuscula omnia*, ed. Mandonnet, 2:37); so, it is only insofar as it is the effect in first place of creation that the *esse* can be said to be "first."

46. *De Potentia*, question 3, answer 7: "Ipsum enim esse est communissimum effectus primus et intimior omnibus aliis effctus."

47. Respectively, *Summa Theologiae* Ia, q.2, a.3, *resp.*: "Nec est possibile quod aliquid sit causa efficiens sui ipsius, quia sic esset prius seipso, quod est impossibile"; and also *Contra Gentiles* I, sec. 18, n.4; or *Summa Theologiae* Ia, q.19, a.5, respectively. The denial of any possible *causa sui* was not restricted to Thomas Aquinas, but a unanimous statement from Anselm (*Monologion* VI) unto Suárez (*Disputationes metaphysicae* I, sec. 1, n.27; XXIX, sec. 1, n.20, 25:11 and 26:27). See my studies on that issue in *Sur la théologie blanche de Descartes*, sec. 18, 427 ff., and "Entre analogie et principe de raison: la causa sui," in *Descartes: Objecter et répondre*, ed. J.-M. Beyssade and J.-L. Marion (Paris: Presses Universitaires de France, 1994), 308–14. One remains free indeed to build up a completely different concept of *causa sui* (as, for instance, S. Breton did in his "Réflexions sur la causa sui," *Revue des sciences philosophiques et théologiques*, vol. 70 [1986]), or even to claim that it would fit better the transcendence of the Christian God. Nevertheless, as Thomas Aquinas carefully shifted away from it, as did Christian theology, why take the risk of an unnecessary ambiguity? In that case, why should the so-called *bullitio* (the overwhelming essence of God according to Eckhart) be named *causa sui*?

48. See *Iae Responsiones,* in *Œuvres de Descartes,* ed. Adam and Tannery, 8:108, 7–18: Descartes did not take seriously the logical inconsistency of the *causa sui,* calling it "nugatoria quaestio," widely known ("quis nescit . . . ?"); but, if the difficulty was so superficial, why did he never answer it?

49. *Summa Theologiae* Ia, q.3, a.7: "Deus non habet causam, . . . cum sit prima causa efficiens"; or *Contra Gentiles* I, sec. 22: "Deus autem est prima causa, non habens causam."

50. *De ente et essentia* V: "Non autem potest esse quod ipsum esse sit causatum ab ipsa forma vel quidditate rei, dico sicut a causa efficiente; qui a sic aliqua res esset causa sui ipsius et aliqua res seipsam in esse produceret, quod est impossibile. Ergo oportet quod omnis talis res, cujus esse est aliud quam natura sua, habet esse ab alio" (in *Opuscula omnia,* ed. Mandonnet, 1:157; ed. Raimondo Spiazzi (Turin: Marietti, 1949), chap. 4, p.13, line 27).

51. Suárez, *Disputationes metaphysicae,* XII, Prologue, 25:372 ff. In the opposite vein, Thomas Aquinas admitted a possible difference between the essence and the cause: "Essentia rei vel est res ipsa, vel se habet ad ipsam, aliquo modo, ut causa" (*Contra Gentiles* I, 21).

52. René Descartes, *Meditationes de prima philosophia, Secundae Responsiones,* in *Œuvres de Descartes,* ed. Adam and Tannery, 7:164 ff.: "Nulla res existit de qua non possit quaeri quaenam sit causa cur existit. Hoc enim de ipso Deo quaeri potest"

53. Benedict de Spinoza, *Korte Verhandeling,* I, sec. 10.

54. Along those lines, see Saint Bonaventura, *Itinerarium mentis in Deum,* VI, 1–2. On the history of that turn, see U. von Strasbourg, *De summo bono,* II, 1, 1–3 (ed. K. Flasch and L. Sturlese [Hambourg: F. Meiner, 1987], 27 ff.) following the commentary by A. de Libera, *Albert le Grand et la philosophie,* 80 ff. Along with my arguments in *God without Being,* chap. 3, sec. 3, see the classical study by A. Feder, "Das Aquinate Kommentar zu Pseudo-Dionysius' *De Divinis Nominibus:* Ein Beitrag zur Arbeitsmethode des hlg. Thomas," *Scholastik,* vol. 1 (1926), reprinted in *Thomas von Aquin,* Wege der Forschung, vol. 188, pt. 1 (Darmstadt: Wissenschaft liche Buchgesellschaft, 1978), 50 ff.; and more recently, U. M. Lindblad, *L'intelligibilité de l'être selon saint Thomas d'Aquin et selon Martin Heidegger* (Berne and New York: Publications de l'Université Européenne, 1987), sec. 3, p. 180. To be fair to Thomas Aquinas, it should be said that even his main argument to submit the name of "good" to the name of "being" remains very careful and balanced: *bonum* is still the first name, if we consider God as a cause (and the cause of the *esse*); but the fact is that Thomas himself is the first to emphasize that God plays the role of a cause, even regarding the *esse creatum;* so, to some extent, he sticks, too, to the traditional primacy of *bonum* over *esse.* One cannot refrain from mentioning the very original definition of "being" formulated by B. Lonergan: "Being . . . is the objective of the pure desire to know" (*Insight* [London: Longmans, 1957], II, 12, p. 348). In that case, too, *esse* implicitly depends on *bonum* as the object of desire.

55. E. Gilson: "La métaphysique thomiste s'accorde mal du nom d'onto-logie, car elle est une considération de l'être plus encore qu'un discours sur l'étant; elle n'est même pas une onto-théologie, pour la simple raison qu'elle pose Dieu au-delà de l'étant, comme l'Etre même" (*L'être et l'essence,* 2d ed. [Paris: J. Vrin, 1962], 372). But it is not enough to go beyond entity for God to avoid going into onto-theo-logy because any familiarity with being ascribes him to this metaphysical constitution. Onto-theo-logy deals with being as well as entities, insofar as metaphysical being remains always oriented toward and questioned for the sake of entity. However, how could God amount to "to be" without assuming the figure of an entity whatsoever? Even if so, this paradox should be explained as such.

56. The quoted material is from Immanuel Kant, *Kritik der reinen Vernunft,* A632/B660. See my "Is the Ontological Argument Ontological?" *Journal of the History of Philosophy,*

vol. 30, no. 2 (April 1992), reprinted in *Questions cartésiennes,* vol. 1, *Méthode et métaphysique* (Paris: Presses Universitaires de France, 1991) and in *Cartesian Questions: Method and Metaphysics* (Chicago: University of Chicago Press, 1998), chap. 7, secs. 1–2.

57. By the way, I directly oppose the tactics of Gilson: "L'être de Heidegger est le vrai, non parce qu'il se définit contre Dieu, mais parce qu'il se définit comme Dieu, n'étant qu'un autre nom du Dieu judéo-chrétien de l'Exode"; and, as a result, Heidegger should be granted among Christians with " des compagnons inconnus sur la voie où l'on dirait parfois qu'il se croit seul" (Gilson, "Dieu et l'être," *Revue Thomiste* [1962], reprinted in *Constantes philosophiques de la question de l'être* [Paris: J. Vrin, 1983], 211, 377). As if Christians were interested, in their quest for God, first and only by being! May not Revelation give us more than being, which, after all, remains still the issue of philosophy? Same diplomatic and at least inappropriate plot in J. B. Lotz (*Martin Heidegger und Thomas von Aquin: Mensch, Zeit, Sein* [Pfullingen: Neske, 1975], and *Martin Heidegger et Thomas d'Aquin: Homme, temps, être,* trans. Philibert Secretan [Paris: Presses Universitaire de France, 1988]); or, with less accuracy, in K. Rahner (*Geist in der Welt: Zur Metaphysik der endlichen Erkenntnis bei Thomas von Aquin,* 2d ed. [München: Kösel, 1957]), II, 3, sec. 6. In any case, the point always amounts to imagining, as a good feature about him, that Thomas Aquinas would have foreseen what Heidegger was first able to express correctly. One may wonder whether this statement is more unfair to Thomas (portrayed as a mere forerunner rather than with achievements of his own) or to Heidegger (depicted as an unconscious Christian when he was consciously non-Christian).

58. *De Potentia,* question 7, answer 2, ad 4: "Esse divinum quod est ejus substantia non est esse commune, sed est esse distinctum a quolibet alio ente. Unde per ipsum suum esse Deus differt a quolibet alio ente."

59. C. Fabro, *Participation et causalité* (Louvain: Presses Universitaires de Louvain, 1961), 253.

60. *Contra Gentiles* I, sec. 22: "Deus igitur non habet essentiam, quae non sit suum esse" (and I, sec. 25).

61. *Summa Theologiae* Ia, q.12, a.2: "Essentia Dei est ipsum esse ejus"; and 13,11: "Cum esse Dei sit ipsa essentia."

62. *De ente et essentia* VI: "Aliquid enim est, sicut Deus, cujus essentia est ipsum suum esse; et ideo inveniuntur philosophi dicentes quod Deus non habet quidditatem vel essentia.m, quia essentia sua non est aliud quam esse suum" (ed. Spiazzi, p.14, line 30; in *Opuscula omnia,* ed. Mandonnet, 2:159). Gilson often quotes that text in *Constantes philosophiques,* 199 (without giving any reference), in "Eléments d'une métaphysique," 109 (with an inaccurate reference: *De ente et essentia* V, 30), in *Le Thomisme: Introduction à la philosophie de St. Thomas d'Aquin* (Paris: J. Vring, 1965), 135, n. 3 (wrong reference), and finally in *L'être et l'essence* (115, correct reference).

63. *In Sententiarum Libros* I, distinction 2, question 1, answer 3, solutio.: "Quidam dicunt, ut Avicenna (*Liber de Intelligentiis* I) et Rabbi Moyses (I, c.57–58) quod res illa quae Deus est, est quoddam esse subsistens, nec aliquid nisi esse in Deo est: unde dicunt quod est sine essentia." This is quoted by Gilson in *L'être et l'essence* (199, without giving any reference) and in "Eléments d'une métaphysique," where he seems to admit that Thomas has agreed with Avicenna and Maimonides (109). What we might wonder about, rather, is that (i) this thesis, so profoundly Christian according to Gilson, could owe so much to "à la perspicacité de certains théologiens musulmans, puis à celle du philosophe Avicenne," more perhaps than to that of the " théologien Thomas d'Aquin"; and (ii) that this thesis was rebuked by "la majorité des théologiens chrétiens, dont d'illustres thomistes" (*L'être et l'essence,* 200). Everything happens

as if the Christian philosophy was ironically first worked out by Jews and Muslims. See Avicenna: "Primus igitur non habet quidditatem" (*Metaphysica* VIII, 4, in *Avicenna latinus,* ed. S. van Riet [Louvain: E.Peeters and Éditions Orientalistes; Leiden: E. J. Brill, 1980], 4:400, 398 and 401). And "Le Premier n'a pas de quiddité autre que l'être (al-anniya)" (*Kitâb al-shifa* VIII, ed. Georges Anawati [Paris: P. Guenther, 1927], 2:86). Commentary by A. Forest, *La structure métaphysique du concret selon saint Thomas d'Aquin* (Paris: J. Vrin, 1931), app. C, 331–60; and by A. Wohlman, *Thomas d'Aquin et Maimonide: Un dialogue exemplaire* (Paris, 1988), chap. 4, 105 ff., establishes close comparisons between Thomas Aquinas, Maimonides, and Avicenna; see also D. Burell, *Knowing the Unknowable God: Ibn-Sina, Maimonides, Aquinas* (Notre Dame, Ind.: Notre Dame University Press, 1986), and "Aquinas and Islamic and Jewish thinkers," in *The Cambridge Companion to Aquinas,* ed. N. Kretzmann and E. Stump (Cambridge: Cambridge University Press, 1993). Other sources, directly coming from Neoplatonism may have also played an actual role (S. Pinès, "Les textes arabes dits plotiniones et le courant 'porphyrien' dans le néo-platonisme grec," in *Studies in Arabic Versions of Greek Texts and Mediaeval Science,* The Collected Works of Shlomo Pinès [Jerusalem: Magnes Press, Hebrew University, 1986]).

64. *Metaphysica* Z,1.1028b2–3. The same question would be without doubt also for *Metaphysica* 7.1072b26 ss. and above all τῇ οὐσίᾳ ὢν ἐνέργεια (*On the Soul* III, 5, 430 a 18).

65. *De Potentia,* question 7, answer 2, ad 1: "Sicut ejus [Dei] substantia ignota, ita et esse"; *In librum De divinis Nominibus* VII, 4: "Cognoscitur [Deus] per ignorantiam nostram, inquantum scilicet hoc ipsum Deum cognoscere, quod nos scimus nos ignorare de Deo quid sit" (in *Opuscula omnia,* ed. Mandonnet, 2:534; in *Expositio in librum Dionysii de Divinis nominibus,* ed. Pera, line 731); *Contra Gentiles* III, sec. 49: "Quid vero sit penitus manet incognitum" (see also I, secs. 11 and 12); *Summa Theologiae* Ia, q.12, a.13, ad 1: "Licet per revelationem gratiae in hac vita non cognoscimus de Deo quid est, et sic ei quasi ignoto conjungamur."

66. *Summa Theologiae* Ia, q.3, a.4, ad 2.

67. Ibid., Ia, q.13, a.11: "Intellectus autem noster non potest ipsam Dei essentiam cognoscere in statu vitae secundum quod in se est, sed quemcumque modum determinat circa id quod de Deo intelligit, deficit a modo quo Deus in se sit" (resp.); "Adhuc magis proprium nomen est Tetragrammaton, quod est impositum ad significandam ipsam substantiam incommunicabilem et, ut sic liceat loqui, singularem" (ad 2).

68. A perfect example of this new effort is P. W. Roseman, *Omne ens est aliquid: Introduction à la lecture du "système" philosophique de saint Thomas d'Aquin* (Louvain: Èditions Peeters, 1996), in particular chap. 2, "*Ipsum esse subsistens:* Dieu a-t-il à être?" [Should God have to be?].

Between Mysticisms: The Trial of Joan of Arc

FRANÇOISE MELTZER

They do not kill you for your actions; they kill you for your secrets.
—The critic Newton Arvin on Hawthorne's *Scarlet Letter*

If, as Michel de Certeau notes, the adjective *mystique* qualifies a literary genre, a "style," what is "mystical," in contrast, is a *modus loquendi,* a "language."[1] The word does not become a substantive, as Maitre points out, until the seventeenth century, so that in principle at least, one cannot refer to "a mystic" until then. As Certeau notes, where we say "mystics" today, a sixteenth-century author would say "contemplatives" or "spirituals." The substantive "mysticism," then, refers globally and somewhat vaguely to that which contains mystical elements.[2]

Two aspects will be shown to emerge importantly in this configuration for our purposes here. First, the notion of mysticism is tied from the Middle Ages on to the contemplation of biblical texts and their images, which was to bring Luther to attack it precisely as an ecclesiastical hermeneutics of the Bible. As Bouyer notes, the early Christian texts in which the word μυστικόξ is used fall into three great groups: biblical, liturgical, and spiritual. But a clear boundary cannot be maintained between these, and the third group is dependent on the first two. Christian mysticism, Bouyer insists, is always text derived, and the text is the Bible and the liturgy. Indeed, by the seventeenth century, as Certeau remarks, all the dictionaries use "mystical" to refer to a kind of exposition of the Scriptures. As Amy Hollywood puts it, in reference to the later Middle Ages, "The evidence we have is texts, and mysticism must—and was meant to be—approached through them."[3]

But on Certeau's account, there is a shift beginning somewhere in the six-teenth century that will be clear by the seventeenth. This shift is a move to-ward experience (as against exegesis, textual hermeneutics, etc.) as a source for making mystical claims, for having a secret, or for making theological claims. The sixteenth century, Certeau notes, already uses "mystic" instead of "spiritual" to designate "a way of reading and a transformation of things into the vocabulary of a doctrinal or moral teaching."[4] By the seventeenth century, only traces of such spiritual textual practice remained, and such a hermeneu-tics was extended to a variety of things. The result was a proliferation of "mys-tic" discourses. If the economy of "mystical" and its adjectival offshoots, then, is initially text centered, by the seventeenth century, experience has been added as a source for the mystical. This aspect is what Certeau sees as "new" in seventeenth-century notions of the mystical. The possessed women of Loudun, for example, have the experience of the satanic and, ultimately, the godly. In this sense, then, Joan of Arc is too early in her claim that her ex-perience should stand as a means to secret knowledge of the divine. The In-quisition wants not only to be the sole interpreter but wants text as well. It is in this way, I believe, that one is to understand the text of any heresy trial. Just as the possessed women of Loudun are forced into producing proper names so as to generate a taxonomy (thus reinforcing the language of the Church and its texts), so Joan's trial produces reams of documentation, the purpose of which is to have a text that the Inquisition can interpret. "All things considered which are to be considered," will be the assertion of the Church's juridical hermeneutics in Joan's trial, as we will see shortly. Such a sentence can also be seen as a mark of resistance to experience as a valid source for theologizing and as an insistence on text—both biblical and juridical—as the only acceptable means of interpreting the divine.

The second aspect of importance in this context is that in the Christian tra-dition, the mystical is tied to what cannot be known directly. This aspect in turn assumes two others: the inadequacy of language to convey the experi-ence (frequently as a sense of union with the divine) and the resulting move to what is understood as "secret." Thus, like the German *Frühromantiker* who filled their texts with words meant to convey the impossibility of lan-guage in expressing the inexpressible (*etwas, unsprechlich, unhörige,* e.g.), so the "mystical" text is frequently a language straining to express what cannot be put into words. Such a strategy suggests what Certeau calls "a play be-tween actors": the one who knows and the one who does not. I would add to this another dual play between actors: the relation between the one who knows and the aspect of the divine that has revealed a metonymy of knowl-edge. In this reading there is a triangle, then: the one who knows (*something, etwas*) in relation to the imparting one, as against the one who seeks to know (which can range on a spectrum anywhere, e.g., from the judges in a heresy trial to a sympathetic reader of a given mystical text). I would suggest that such a triangulation allows for, or at least encourages, a certain textual apophasis.[5]

The case of Joan of Arc complicates and perhaps aids in focusing the variant aspects of mysticism, and for several reasons that I will try to examine here. To begin with, Joan was illiterate and so neither wrote nor read any texts at all. To "hear" her, we need to turn to her heresy trial, wherein she is both explicit and secretive. The trial itself, in other words, inscribed and produced by the forces bent on Joan's destruction, provides us with a text that, in turn, can be approached through *hermeneutica generalis*. This is not a text describing the journey of the soul by the "mystic" herself, where language strains to represent the unrepresentable and one can witness, as it were, the attempts by the recipient of the mystical to convey them. This is rather a text documenting resistance on the part of the defendant to the truth the Church seeks to uphold. Since Joan cannot partake of the textual, she is marginalized from the hermeneutics that the Church wants to force on her. Therefore, they can accept no part of her revelatory experience as mystical, even were it not a priori glossed as heretical.

Foucault comments that history has shifted: from seeing documents as the language of a voice reduced to silence, as a trace possibly decipherable, history now works "within" a given document and no longer attempts to discover where the truth might lie within it. History now is "one way in which a society recognizes and develops a mass of documentation with which it is inextricably linked." For Foucault, the document is no longer memory but rather a means of finding "unities, totalities, series, relations."[6] And yet in an important way, Joan's heresy trial is precisely the trace of a "voice reduced to silence"—fragile but possibly decipherable. Georges Bataille sees just such a possibility in his study of another heresy trial, that of Joan's friend and contemporary Gilles de Rais. "Few human beings," writes Bataille, "have left behind traces permitting them, after five centuries, to speak thus! To cry thus!" It is part of Bataille's genius, in my view, and the strength of his odd moral courage, that he resists fancy theoretical constructs by insisting on the scandal of the heresy trial—this is, he says baldly, the record of things that actually occurred: "Such scenes are not the work of an author. *They happened:* somehow we have the stenography of them."[7] It is the "they happened" of these events that should be borne in mind here, for the many ways in which the trial is not documentation at all but, rather, mufflings and distortions of a lost age, risk accumulating to the point where we forget the trace that even

Freud was willing to accord to memory. The "they happened" can be understood as a historical version of Levinas's—or Blanchot's—*il y a;* that which is, frighteningly and inescapably.

The heresy trial of Joan of Arc unfolded from February through the end of May in 1431, culminating with the burning of Joan at the stake on May 30.[8] We have voluminous documents recounting that trial, and yet the problems are endless. The trial manuscripts contain numerous inaccuracies: the original French was jotted down by the scribes and translated into Latin later the same day. The scribes did not always agree with each other concerning what had occurred, and there is good reason to believe that the chief magistrate falsified and censured some of the testimony and questioning. The manuscripts we have are in fragments, so that until the discovery of the complete French manuscript in the 1950s, scholars had to work with a combination of French and Latin texts of the trial. But the trial is also inaccessible to us as a document in many other ways: by the five centuries that separate us from the events; by the numerous layers of language through which it is filtered down to us (the spoken Middle French is transcribed hurriedly into French, translated the same day into [late medieval] Latin, and since the 1840s, retranslated into modern French and English, etc.); by the fact that the voices we "hear" in the documents have long since died; by the syntax and protocol of fifteenth-century juridical proceedings ("item" precedes every point, and the questions and responses are written down in indirect discourse); by the defamiliarizing late medieval French and vulgate Latin in which the trial is recorded; by the gaps and ellipses in the minutes, including lost documents, fragmented ones, and previous trials that are referred to but that have been lost; by a succession of editors who have altered, interpreted, translated, amended, misrepresented, and otherwise corrupted the "purity" of the original, whatever it may have been; by the Church's own censorship, additions and suppressions of certain parts of the trial; by the ravages of wars and time that have corrupted the text; by the ensuing Trial of Rehabilitation, with its hindsight and rationalizations and justifications; by the beatification and ultimate canonization, five hundred years later, of the figure who is the defendant, and whose condemnation we can no longer read without a constant perspective of backformation, so that every small and great event is doubly reinterpreted in the light of subsequent events. One could go on and on. The caveats do not stop, and while this is the case with any documentation from another era (we return here to Foucault's cautious approach), it is particularly the case for a trial that was such a cause célèbre at the time and had so many paratexts in the form of preceding and subsequent trials that it becomes difficult to access anything about it even with the assumption of Foucault's warnings. And yet *they happened* in some way, these events; and like a photograph that seems to capture a moment in time but can be shown to be as subjective as any painting (a fairly accepted view at present), there are moments of what Barthes, reading photographs, calls *punctum,* in Joan's trial. Let us remain cautious and say that there are moments when the "they happened" seems easier to remember. These are largely moments when we feel that Joan's voice pierces through the fabric of the text.

Joan of Arc's heresy trial is spoken in the words of the Church; her own voice is embedded paradoxically to the point of concealment inside its tortuous theological architecture. Thus in the trial there is a real struggle between the inquisitors who want to know and the accused who conceals. Freud recognized this kind of struggle. Addressing himself to "future judges and defending counsel" at a law seminar in 1906, Freud says that he must draw "an analogy between the criminal and the hysteric. In both we are concerned with a secret, with something hidden . . . the task of the therapist, however, is the same as that of the examining magistrate. We have to uncover the hidden psychical material, and in order to do this we have invented a number of detective devices, some of which it seems that you gentlemen of the law are now about to copy from us."[9] Given the procedures of the Inquisition, it might rather be said that psychoanalysis (unconsciously) mimes the same logic as that earlier court: it will know better once the subject opens herself to allow the ecclesial "therapist" to see "the truth." But to the extent that a secret is the precondition of the hermeneutical, the trial provides us with a discourse that pushes the limits of how we are to understand "mystical," which in the case of Joan we have already delimited as an apophasis.

Joan's trial of condemnation produces a doubled concealment: first, in the more understandable aspect that the "mystical" subject is faced, in the context of ecclesial judiciary, with the demand to translate what is hidden into the light of day. This demand however (which, as we have seen, Freud compared to the psychoanalytic situation), creates a hermeneutics of suspicion precisely because in the text the "mystic" is being forced to reveal herself within the lexicon of the court. It is not her own text, in which one might say that the "I" who writes is also the one who wants to know as well as to convey. Again, one thinks of Freud who likens the search for the unconscious as being both the seeker and the uncharted terrain being explored, a metaphor he shares almost verbatim with Proust. Just before he experiences the epiphany provided by the tea and madeleine experience, Proust will note, "I put down the cup and examine my own mind. It alone can discover the truth. But how? What an abyss of uncertainty, whenever the mind feels overtaken by itself; when it, the seeker, is at the same time the dark region through which it must go seeking and where all its equipment will avail it nothing."[10] Freud will discover the interpretation of dreams as the *via regia* that leads to the knowledge of the unconscious in psychic life, thus performing exegesis on the text of his dreams to reach the unknown part of the "seeker."

One might say that a "mystic" writing her or his own text (Porete, Navarre, Eckhart, e.g.) is both the "seeker" and the "uncharted terrain." The move, one imagines however, is to help or enlighten the reader as well as for the mystic to discover her own understanding, or experience, of the divine. The autobiographical "mystical" text then is one possible *via regia* to explore, reexperience, narrate the inexpressible. But a heresy trial establishes itself precisely as a question of exegesis: whether a mystic can interpret a sacred text or event properly. In this, the trial participates in an old theological question (can a mystic read a prophet, etc.). Here, too, the trial strains to stretch "text" to mean visions, voices that, like Freud's analysis of dreams, need to be understood as events to be "read"—or moments to be exegetically interpreted. Who, however, is doing the interpreting in a heresy trial? Who finally holds, or believes he or she holds, the secret? Why does the trial of Joan insist on text at the expense of what she understands as a (mystic) experience?

Before we turn to this question, however, I want to reiterate the points made thus far: the heresy trial of Joan of Arc is the only text we have by which to do our own hermeneutical work with respect to Joan's story. The text conceals doubly: not only with respect to the secrecy of the mystical event but also in the fact that the mystic's voice is in the text but is itself as hidden as possible by what I have called the "architecture" of the Inquisition.

Moreover, in 1415, fifteen years before Joan's trial, the Council of Constance had issued the decree of *Haec Sancta,* which stated that the Church holds its power directly from Christ. Obedience is thus to be obtained from every person since, in this logic, the Church is both infallible and universal. The Church Militant becomes the sole mediator between God and man, and is therefore the sole interpreter of how that connection is to be understood. Thus any visions, mystical experiences, revelations, and so on had to be confessed to a member of the clergy for interpretation. The clergy become the sole guardians of interpretation, the only ones permitted any hermeneutical move, the single vault for secrets.

Thus, what cannot be known directly (a definition for the "mystical") is rendered as if known by the parameters of the Inquisition's epistemological and hermeneutical blueprint. And given that any experience of other worldliness, or the divine, must be first glossed by the Church, any such experience becomes as text, whether it be ocular (visions), audial (voices), or any other sense. Any experience of the divine becomes as text for the Church to scrutinize, classify, and interpret. Joan may be illiterate, but the Church will "read" her visions and voices as text. The question will be twofold: Do these visions come from God or the devil (their existence is never seriously questioned)? And why did Joan think she could gloss them herself, whereas her duty was to confess them to a member of the clergy so that the status of those experiences could be properly ascertained?

With the Council of Constance, laypeople become inferior to the clergy, and their major virtue must be obedience. Joan's heresy trial betrays here another double economy: the visions/voices as text and the court document as text. The first will be interpreted after the fact, retroactively "reading" Joan's experience through the backformation of ideology. The second, the text of the trial, will be glossed before the fact, setting up an architecture as I have been putting it, the nature of which determines any exit or entrance with respect to that text.

For example: Article 1 of the final twelve drawn up against Joan says that the University of Paris (completely under English rule in 1430) has considered her "apparitions." In other words, they have glossed the text of her experience. The university writes as follows:

> You, Jeanne, have said that from the age of thirteen, you had revelations and apparitions of angels, of Saint Catherine and Saint Margaret, and that you saw them quite often with your corporeal eyes, and that they spoke to you. As to this first point, the clergy of the University of Paris have considered the manner of the aforesaid revelations and apparitions, the ends and substance of the things revealed, and the quality of the person. All things considered which are to be considered [*et, omnibus consideratis quae consideranda erant*], they have said and declared: that all things said about them are lies, deceptions, things of seduction and pernicious; and that such revelations are superstitious, arising from evil and diabolical spirits.[11]

The court is explicit about itself as sole hermeneutical authority. It has considered "all things which are to be considered," an ideological tautology that controls the "texts" to be glossed and the interpretation to be obtained. The court has done an exegesis on "the manner of the aforesaid revelations and apparitions" and on the "ends and substance" of the things revealed. The court has also "read" and glossed Joan ("the quality of the person").

In this way, then, the court has appropriated the mystical for itself; and it has made the acknowledgment of any mystical experience its own purview. The Church positions itself as knowing, in other words, that which is by definition unknowable and unsayable—knowing the secret. The result is clear: either mystical experience will be declared satanic, and thus be rejected and expunged, or an experience declared "mystical" will, by so being declared, be domesticated by the church functionaries and neutralized into the condoned. The scandal that can be said to form the mystical will thus more often than not fall outside the Church, into the diabolical, into "heretical" marginalized groups (which of course for the Church will be the same thing, except that it controls the first group from inside and does not the second), or finally, into individuals whom the Church must accept as pious, but the very excesses of whom it will likewise domesticate through the sanction of sainthood. In this sense, sainthood can be seen as the Church's control over that which is in excess or in danger of escaping its power. The late medieval Church's ideology becomes like a panopticon: what cannot fit in its gaze is eradicated or unacknowledged. Or, as Certeau has shown in his work on the possessed women of seventeenth-century Loudun, the Church can reintegrate those who have been taken over by Satan. In so doing, the Church actually reasserts its power and (again, as Certeau has shown) the necessity of its own taxonomies and texts. We might say that in demanding the names of the devils possessing the Loudun women, the exorcist begins to perform his privilege of hermeneutics: his "read" of the women will demand names so that the language of the Church can be reaffirmed and its interpretation of the ensuing names read back into their proper place, producing (once again) text.

The problem with Joan of Arc, however, is that she does not fit into the Church's various hermeneutics and, thus, can be neither embraced nor, more important, easily rejected on clear grounds. She blurs, as I have shown elsewhere, registers. Not only, as we have seen, does she maintain her experience to be sufficient as mystical (thus, to repeat, foreshadowing what Certeau will call a new element in the seventeenth century); in a corollary to such a stance, she also insists on a private relationship to God. The word *occultus* appears frequently in her trial to describe that relationship.

To begin with, the private relationship she claims with God informs her refusal of a blanket oath in a court of law. In her trial, she is asked repeatedly to swear the oath of truth. Customary as this oath may have been, taking it more than once was not and, indeed, was quite illegal.[12] Already reluctant to swear once, Joan does so with a caveat: "But as to the revelations already mentioned, she would tell them to no one."[13] Thus early on, we have her insistence on a "secret" that the Church cannot, she maintains, force her to reveal. The following day Joan takes the oath, she is asked to take it again but refuses, directly challenging the chief magistrate, Cauchon. John de Montigny, doctor of canon law at the University of Paris at the time of the trial, notes that this move on Cauchon's part was in violation of juridical procedure. Kelly summarizes why the procedure was illegal for two reasons, in

Montigny's view: "First, because she was compelled by oath to respond to all subjects of inquiry, even the most occult [*ad omnia inquisitia, etiam que-cunque et quantumcunque occulta*], and she was compelled to respond generally and absolutely to all things that were to be asked of her, whereas she should have been forced to reply by oath only concerning those points on which she had been defamed or found suspect in the faith; and second, she was forced to swear repeatedly, whereas, according to the law, the oath to tell the truth should be given only once."[14]

It should be noted that the Latin uses the term *occultus*. Indeed, Joan refuses to swear again, and withholds information when she feels it would be disobedient to her voices. "I have sworn enough," she often says, or "Pass on" [*Passez outre*], or again: "Ask me on Saturday." The private relation she claims with God is for her, as we have seen, more important than the Church (Militant) and informs her refusal of a blanket oath in a court of law, even an ecclesiastical one. In fact, two Church scholars at the time of the trial complained that Cauchon had no more right than the Church itself to question Joan on "occult matters" (i.e., on matters that were private or secret in nature—"mystical"). Clearly, the status of the secret (*occultus;* later periods would say "mystical") is a point of contention in the interpretation of late medieval Church law.

The *Oxford Latin Dictionary* gives seven definitions for the adjective *occultus-a-um.* All of these have to do with what is hidden, concealed, secret, inaccessible. The first definition links the word to the secrets of nature: "(of the workings of forces of nature), invisible, secret." If we hear echoes of Freud's uncanny in the Latin notion of *occultus,* it is perhaps because in the trial of Joan too, that which is familiar remains secret. In this case, however, the secret is withheld from the ecclesial court, not from the conscious mind. The "occult" here, then, should be read as the fifteenth-century notion of what we would call privacy: that which has the right to remain secret for the individual. In the fifteenth-century context, this is a right because it is based on the individual's relation to God—just as Joan argues (without, of course, knowing any Latin). It is not a notion, however, that is meant to be applied in cases of divine revelation, wherein, as we have noted, only the Church has the right to interpret. For Joan, here lies the problem.

The distinction between transgressions of a private nature (between the individual and God) and those of a public domain accountable under the jurisprudence of the ecclesial court stem from the codification of the *iniquisitio* by Innocent III. It is a distinction that Joan refuses to recognize, and it is perhaps in this sense that she can be seen as an early modern. In order to explain what I mean by this, we have to keep in mind the medieval Christian notion of the individual, quite a different concept from what we today say constitutes a subject.

Both Louis Dupré and Louis Dumont have noted that the Christian doctrine of individual salvation detached the person from the cosmic because each individual was seen as responsible to God.[15] But this did not mean that the person (a term that I am using in this, its earlier sense) was autonomous, for there was the community of the Church. Whereas the modern notion of the subject sees itself as self-sufficient through the state (as had his privileged predecessors in the Roman *polis,*), in Christian medieval thought, the Christian is, in Dumont's terms, "an individual-in-relation-to-God." This means, then, that on the one hand man is essentially an outwardly individual. On the worldly level, however, man is not individuated, but a member of the commonwealth, a part of the social body. *Lebenswelt,* in other words, belongs to the Church.

The difficulty for Joan, as I have argued recently, is that she blurs the distinction between "Caesar" and God. That is, she sees Charles VII as king by divine right and understands this as an extension of her God's hierarchy. In contrast, she recognizes no role for herself in the commonwealth or social body, in the sense that she imagines herself to have only the fulfillment of her divine mission as her purpose (at least, in that portion of her life that we know). The power of the Church, or the Church Militant, is not a presence in the hegemony she recognizes. Fighting for Caesar through God, she refuses to adhere to the Church's demands because she sees them as countermanding her mission. In answering only to God, she is in the eyes of the Church refusing the Church Militant and recognizing only the Church Triumphant. Indeed, this was to be one of the final twelve charges leveled against her. For the Church probed Joan's thoughts again and again, to establish their "purity," just as surely as the midwives probed her many times to establish her virginity. Speculum into the *occulta,* the Church is unsuccessful in its violation and abandons its efforts with a blanket condemnation, motivated by the charge of disobedience.

It should not be forgotten that Joan's campaign had the effect of strengthening the monarchy at the expense of feudal lords, thus paving the way for the modern state. Her private relation to God, which she insists she has the right to keep so, is equally anachronistic: it is as if left over from an earlier Christianity, before the Church's seizure of *Lebenswelt.* This the Church sees clearly and makes brutally clear in the last article of Joan's condemnation. She is declared schismatic, "badly responding to the truth and authority of the Church." At one point, however, she tersely declares that she does not accept their judgment. To Cauchon she angrily says, "You say that you are my judge.

I do not know if you are. But be careful not to judge badly. And I am warn-ing you so that, if Our Lord punishes you for it, I will have done my duty in warning you."[16]

The clash of power registers could not be more overt. We are confronted here with two different notions of knowledge, two different hegemonies, two different understandings of the individual, two different concepts of the private. Her voices tell her to take everything in stride, not to avoid martyr-dom. "You will finally come to the kingdom of Paradise," they reassure her. She acknowledges, then, two kingdoms, the first existing by virtue of the sec-ond. that of her king and that of heaven. The Church is completely absent from this schema. and this absence becomes the Church's increasing obses-sion in the trial—more, finally, than the fact that Joan is a political danger. She remains stolid in refusing to bow to the Church's power, even at the expense of her life. It is not just that she does not want to; she actually does not un-derstand that power. When Cauchon asks her if her voices come from God, Joan's priorities are clear: "And I think that I am not telling you fully what I know; and I am more afraid of saying something which will displease them [the voices] than I am afraid of answering you."[17] Her secret then, that which is to remain *occultus,* is in her experience of a relation between her and God. "You say that if the Church wanted you to do the opposite of the command-ment you say from God," reads the last article of condemnation,

> that you would obey it for nothing in the world. . . . Given all things said on this, you do not want to submit to the judgement of the Church which is on earth, nor to any living man, but to God alone. And you say that you do not give these an-swers from your mind [*ex capite tuo*], but by God's commandment, even though the article of faith is that each person must believe in the Catholic Church, as has been often declared to you, and that every good Christian Catholic must submit all acts to the Church, especially with regard to revelations and such things.[18]

The clash of registers, then, arises around the question of who has the right to perform the hermeneutics of revelation. What I would add to this clash, however, which is more to the point for the purposes of the present vol-ume, is that by keeping such an experience of divine revelation private, and in refusing to bow to Church demands, and finally in enacting her divine orders in the political/social realm, Joan takes *Lebenswelt* back from the Church's purview. She does this, however, neither through the production of a mysti-cal text nor through speech, what Certeau calls a *modus loquendi.* Rather, Joan's mystical experience is one that wants to stay secret ("And I think that I am not telling you fully what I know") and resists all attempts to bring it into the light. Without text because she is illiterate and without speech because she is ventriloquized (the voices speak to her, in other words, such that her desire is always mediated by the voices' demands), Joan of Arc's form of the mystical can only be called apophatic. Thus:

1. Whereas the possessed woman says, "Something is speaking in me," Joan asserts that something is speaking *to* her. She cannot be placed in the economy of the possessed.

2. Visions, voices, and other manifestations of the divine are understood, in the Western Christian (in this case, specifically Catholic) tradition, as having to do with aspects of the faith. But Joan's experience of divine intervention is specifically political in its intent and pits Catholic (the French) against Catholic (Burgundians and the English). Thus the mission of Joan destabilizes the place of otherness. Moreover, on Joan's account, God seems forcefully to be taking the side of the French, which puts the English-dominated theologians from the University of Paris (Joan's judges) in a less than objective mode with respect to Joan's testimony.

3. Joan neither understands nor accepts the distinction between the Church Militant and the Church Triumphant. She is therefore openly more afraid of disobeying her voices than she is of disobeying the Church. When the chief magistrate, Cauchon, questions her about her voices, she is explicit: "And I am more afraid of saying something which will displease them [the voices], than I am of answering you."[19]

4. One might say that Joan wants experience to be the source of her relation to the divine. The Inquisition, however, accepts only the older notion of the mystical as a secret necessarily connected to exegetical concepts—the use over which they understand themselves as having complete monopoly. Thus, two hundred years earlier, Joan ushers in what Certeau sees as "new" to mysticism in the seventeenth century: experience as over text as the source of theologizing.

5. Such an insistence on experience as self-evident, or as evidence, on Joan's part, does not submit a *modus loquendi* to the court but, rather, a mode of being. The privacy of her relation to God, coupled with its projection onto *Lebenswelt*, is precisely what makes Joan an early modern. Her notion of subjectivity is not limited to her relation to God, nor is that subjectivity annulled in the social realm by the collectivity. The figure of Joan shifts the ontology of the subject in a manner prefiguring modernity.

6. The corollary of such a shift is the move from *occultus* as a secret to be glossed by the court to *occultus* as a mysticism to be guarded by the subject. Thus the apophatic language of Joan's pronouncements: Joan uses her voice to explain why she cannot speak. "I do not have permission to

tell you that," she repeats again and again to the court's interrogation. As with the possessed woman, in Certeau's words, Joan speaks "about a so-called ineffable experience which therefore *cannot be spoken about*."[20] But unlike those possessed women, Joan's voices do not speak in the indecipherable "flutterings" of proper names that the Church's discourse of demonology will decode but in French, as she attests, and with a perfectly lucid message. This apophasis has several facets in Joan's speech.

The court of the Inquisition insists on giving Joan's voices body and identity, and Joan acquiesces to this demand as if translating her experience into something the court will accept. Early in the trial, Joan refers to only one voice. But on 27 February and thereafter, having been endlessly pressed by the inquisitors as to the nature of that voice, she makes it plural and recognizable (into the virgin Saints Catherine and Margaret and the archangel Michael). It is as if by multiplying the voice and giving the ensuing figures specific traits—embodying them—she were giving the court a register it would acknowledge. Such a "translation" is yet another aspect of her apophatic experience, since by virtue of clarifying her visions, Joan ends up multiplying and blurring them. She always answers with a riddle. The court wants to know: Are the voices saints or angels? How does she recognize them? How are they clothed? Are they of the same age? Do they speak together or one at a time? Do they have sight? Do they have eyes? "You don't have that yet" [*Vous ne l'avez pas encore*], she says in response to the last of these questions. "I will not tell you any more about it now," she often replies, or (as we have seen), "Ask me on Saturday, then I will perhaps have something for you." All of these responses are ones of deferral ("not yet," "now," "then," "Saturday,") with the promise of a possible unlocking of the secret. Deferral becomes Joan's attempt to placate the court, since her experience does not suffice as evidence. Thus rather than an apophasis as denial, we rather have apophasis through deferral. Since the court insists that the ineffable, by definition that which cannot be spoken, be spoken, Joan responds with delaying tactics.

Or she hedges. The court, which will increasingly ask for a yes or no answer, at one point demands to know if Joan thinks she is in a state of grace. The question is a very dangerous one; both "yes" and "no" can be read as heretical. She famously answers, "If I am not, may God grant that I be so; and if I am, may He keep me there" [*Si je n'y suis, Dieu m'y veuille mettre, et si j'y suis, Dieu m'y veuille tenir*]. This is another tactic of apophasis: to respond by not responding.

Or she says she is not permitted by the voices to tell. "I do not have permission to tell you that, and I am more afraid of them than of you." Or that she is overwhelmed: "You burden me too much" [*Vous me chargez trop*], she says in the midst of yet another lengthy interrogation. In all of these cases the apophatic poses as *recusatio,* but the difference is crucial. *Recusatio* is a rhetorical strategy that denies even as it performs what is apparently rejected ("I come to bury Caesar, not to praise him" is the usual example). Joan's tactic of apophatic pronouncements, in contrast, pretends it can represent the ineffable even as she sidesteps responding directly ("Ask me Saturday"). Because private experience, if kept private, is not legitimized by the court as a possible source of mysticism, Joan has no choice but to use the language of the court (text, exegesis, hermeneutics, interpretation) as a means of denying its use in her case. But she also denies the Church its interpretative prerogative. Thus she will be cut from the Christian community: "like a rotten limb, we have rejected you and expelled you from the unity of the Church and have named you to the secular justice."[21] This cliché of heresy trials, however, and the execution of the defendant that follows, cannot excise the radical shift in mysticism that Joan's own voice performs. Part of the shift lies precisely in the fact that Joan refused to tell the Church her secret, and this the Church forgave finally far less than her actions on the battlefield.

Notes

1. Michel de Certeau, *The Mystic Fable: The Sixteenth and Seventeenth Centuries* (Chicago: University of Chicago Press, 1986), 1:114. The material covered here comes from my *For Fear of the Fire: Joan of Arc and the Limits of Subjectivity* (Chicago: University of Chicago Press, 2001). The present essay puts a different stress on the same material.

2. For a history of the notion of "mysticism" and of the word itself, see Louis Bouyer, "Mysticism: An Essay on the History of the Word," in *Understanding Mysticism,* ed. Richard Wood, O.P. (New York: Doubleday, 1980), 42–55. Bouyer points out that in Hellenistic religions, the secret that is truly mystical is not of knowledge but of rituals. The real heritage of Christian mysticism, Bouyer argues, is not pagan but rather "from the Bible and from the liturgy, particularly from the eucharistic liturgy" (45).

3. Amy Hollywood, *The Soul as Virgin Wife: Mechthild of Magdeburg, Marguerite Porete, and Meister Eckhart* (Notre Dame, Ind.: Notre Dame University Press, 1995), 21.

4. Certeau, *The Mystic Fable,* 96.

5. As will be clear, I do not mean apophatic in the usual sense: Joan's visions can be called cataphatic, for example. And yet the visions were first and primarily voices, so that in a sense Joan's experience of the divine can be understood as apophatic in the traditional sense as well.

6. Michel Foucault, *The Archeology of Knowledge and the Discourse of Language,* trans. A. M. Sheridan Smith (New York: Harper & Row, 1972), 6–7.

7. Georges Bataille, *The Trial of Gilles de Rais,* trans. Richard Robinson (Los Angeles: Amok, 1991), 19.

8. The full Latin text of both the trial of condemnation and of rehabilitation (twenty-five years later) with commentary is in Jules Quicherat, *Procès de condamnation et de réhabilitation de Jeanne d'Arc, dite la Pucelle* (Paris: J. Renouard & Cie, 1841–49). This is the standard edition. Quicherat's introduction to his edition, *Aperçus nouveaux sur Jeanne d'Arc,* was consid-

ered to be so important that it was published as a separate volume (Paris: J. Renouard & Cie, 1850). For a discussion of the manuscripts and translations, see Régine Pernoud, *Joan of Arc by Herself and by Her Witnesses* (New York and London: Scarborough House, 1994), 224–27 ff. See also my *For Fear of the Fire*, 119–21.

9. Sigmund Freud, "Psychoanalysis and the Establishment of the Facts in Legal Proceedings," in *The Standard Edition of the Complete Psychological Works of Sigmund Freud*, trans. and ed. James Strachey (London: Hogarth Press and the Institute of Psycho-analysis, 1953–54), 11:108.

10. Marcel Proust, *Swann's Way and within a Budding Grove*, trans. C. K. Moncrieff and Terence Kilmartin (New York: 1981), 1:49.

11. Georges Duby and Andrée Duby, *Le procès de Jeanne d'Arc* (Paris: Gallimard, 1995), 155. All translations are mine.

12. For this and other legal, technical aspects of the trial, see H. Ansgar Kelly, "The Right to Remain Silent: Before and after Joan of Arc," *Speculum* 68, no.4 (October 1993): 992–1026.

13. Duby and Duby, *Le procès de Jeanne d'Arc*, 29.

14. Kelly, "The Right to Remain Silent," 1022.

15. See Louis Dupré, *Passage to Modernity: An Essay in the Hermeneutics of Nature and Culture* (New Haven, Conn., and London: Yale University Press, 1993), 95. See also Louis Dumont, "A Modified View of Our Origins: The Christian Beginnings of Modern Individualism," in *The Category of the Person: Anthropology, Philosophy, History* (Cambridge: Cambridge University Press, 1985), 98.

16. Duby and Duby, *Le procès de Jeanne d'Arc*, 103.

17. Ibid., 46–47.

18. Ibid., 160.

19. Ibid., 103.

20. Michel de Certeau, *The Writing of History* (New York: Columbia University Press, 1988), 257.

21. Duby and Duby, *Le procès de Jeanne d'Arc*, 177.

Unitrinum Seu Triunum:
Nicholas of Cusa's Trinitarian Mysticism

BERNARD McGINN

In 1443 Johannes Wenck, professor of theology at Heidelberg, issued a sharp attack on Nicholas of Cusa's 1441 treatise *De docta ignorantia*. In his treatise, titled *De ignota litteratura,* the outraged professor, a firm adherent of Aristotelian reason, summarized his objections to the future cardinal with the accusation: "I don't know if in my lifetime I've ever seen a writer as destructive as this fellow on the issue of the divinity and the Trinity of Persons, that of the universe, that of Christ's Incarnation, that of the theological virtues, and that of the church."[1] Cusa's *Apologia doctae ignorantiae,* written six years later, countered Wenck by arguing that reason, though valid in its own realm, cannot attain the higher truths, such as those concerning the Trinity, that *docta ignorantia* reveals to the intellect. According to Cusa, the intellect that reaches learned ignorance will recognize that "the coincidence of supreme simplicity and indivisibility and of unity and Trinity" means that "when the Father is said to be a Person, the Son another Person, and the Holy Spirit a third Person, otherness cannot maintain its usual meaning, as when the word is used for otherness as divided and distinct from oneness."[2] In God there is no number and therefore he enjoys a mode of being that is beyond all modes as "indistinctly distinct" [*discretum indiscrete*].[3] Hence, as Cusa had put it earlier in the *De docta ignorantia*, "Join together what seems to be opposite . . . and you will not have one *and* three or the reverse, but "one-in-three" or a "three-in-one" [*unitrinum seu triunum*]: this is the Absolute Truth."[4]

Discussion of the Trinity is pervasive in Nicholas of Cusa's works, but the topic has attracted less attention than it deserves.[5] Rudolph Haubst's monograph of 1952 concentrated on the way in which the image of God as *uni-*

trinum seu triunum is manifested in the world.[6] Since then, other Cusa scholars have touched on aspects of his doctrine of the Trinity but usually in passing.[7] In a brief essay it will not be possible to do justice to such a major theme of the cardinal's thought. My intention is more limited in that I will focus on how Cusa understands the role of the Trinity in the process of mystical transformation.

Christian theology has always been essentially trinitarian. Confession that the one God is a Trinity of Father, Son, and Holy Spirit (however expressed and understood) has been central to Christian belief, worship, and practice from the start. If we take mysticism as that element within the Christian religion that concerns the preparation for, the attainment of, and the effects of what is described as an immediately conscious presence of God (often a presence realized in absence), then all Christian mysticism, like all classic Christian theology, is trinitarian, at least in the sense that the God sought and attained by the mystic is the God who is intended in the trinitarian formulas of belief.[8] But just as in dogmatic theology there are considerable differences between the theologians who remain content with passing on what the tradition has said and those who attempt to clarify and explore the dogmatic basis, so too in the history of the mystical element within Christianity some mystics have given the Trinity a more central role in their writings than others. Merely labeling a mystic "trinitarian" tells us little. It is more useful, if more difficult, to try to understand the role that the Trinity is given in the process by which the mystic comes to consciousness of the present/absent God.

Some Background to Cusa's Mathematics of the Trinity

Nicholas of Cusa's understanding of the trinitarian aspect of mystical transformation (as will be detailed below) is rooted in his teaching concerning the attributes of the three divine Persons as *unitas* (proper to the Father), *aequalitas* (proper to the Son), and *concordia* (proper to the Holy Spirit). Although this triad of attributes, especially when understood as terms distinctive of the Persons and not as terms common to the divine nature, was unusual, it had an ancient pedigree.[9] It is first found in an early work of Augustine of Hippo, book 1 of the *De doctrina christiana* written about 396. Here, in a discussion of the Trinity as the one *res* that can be truly loved and enjoyed for its own sake, the bishop provides a brief reflection on the common and proper divine attributes. He says: "The same eternity, immutability, majesty, and power are common to the three. In the Father there is unity, in the Son equality, in the Holy Spirit the agreement of unity and equality. And all three are one because of the Father, equal because of the Son, and connected because of the Holy Spirit."[10] In the following lines Augustine pauses to reflect on the nature of all speech about God, emphasizing the essential paradox involved in every term we apply to the divine realm. Even a negative term like *ineffabilis* is found wanting. He puts it this way: "God should not be said to be ineffable, because when this is said a statement is made. There results a form of verbal strife in that if the ineffable is what cannot be said, then what is called ineffable cannot be ineffable. This verbal strife is to be avoided by silence rather than resolved by speech."[11]

Augustine later abandoned the triad of *unitas-aequalitas-conexio* as a way of understanding the proper attributes of the three Persons of the Trinity (i.e., those that point to the Persons as such). It does not occur, for example, in his magisterial *De trinitate* (ca. 401–21), the source for so much subsequent trinitarian teaching and mysticism. However, anything that Augustine wrote usually had a history, and so it is not surprising that this form of transcendental trinitarian mathematics was to have an influence in later Latin theology.[12]

Fascination with numbers as a key to understanding the universe had deep roots in the societies of the ancient world, but it was brought to a special pitch in Greek philosophy, especially by the Pythagoreans and by Plato.[13] Unity, or "the One," as the source of all numbers, was the focus of this intellectual concern. In the *Republic* (7.525a) Plato had proclaimed that the "study of unity" [*to hen*] was one of the disciplines that helps convert the soul to the contemplation of true being. The *Parmenides,* the great philosopher's abstruse exploration of dialectics of the idea of the One [*to hen*], at least as interpreted by the Neoplatonists, became the foundation of what Etienne Gilson called the "metaphysics of the One"—a central chapter in the history of Christian metaphysical speculation.[14] So, when Augustine spoke of *unitas* as the proper denomination of the Father, he lent the weight of his authority to forms of metaphysical speculation different from his usual tack, which emphasized God as true being.[15] In the history of Western theology this text from the *De doctrina* facilitated readings of the bishop of Hippo that brought him close to thinkers who were more deeply involved with Neoplatonic "henology," such as Macrobius, Boethius, and Pseudo-Dionysius.

In the twelfth century, the Augustinian triad of *unitas-aequalitas-conexio/concordia* took its place in the trinitarian theology so intensely pursued in the nascent schools of northern Europe. The crucial figure in this regard was Thierry of Chartres, a famous master who taught at Paris and Chartres circa 1130s–1150s.[16] In his interpretation of the Hexaemeron entitled *De sex dierum operibus* (probably late 1130s), as well as in his commentaries on Boethius's *De trinitate* (late 1140s–1150), Thierry retrieved the Augustinian triad as a form of mathematical "proof" [*ratio necessaria*] of the Trinity, an analogue to the logical proof for God's existence advanced by Anselm in his *Proslogion*.[17] Thierry's attempt to show the inner agreement of the sciences of physics, mathematics, and theology—a unified field theory, as we might term it today—was the basis for his insistence that "there are four forms of demonstrations that lead humans to the knowledge of the Creator: arithmetical proofs, musical, geometrical, and astronomical."[18] The only one of these quadrivial proofs that is extant today is that from arithmetic. What is most striking about this demonstration (often advanced in Thierry's writings) is that it is not just an argument that God is the creator of the universe and that God is one, but it is meant to demonstrate that the "natural" mathematics of the created universe demands a transcendental mathematics of the Trinity. Investigation of the universe proves that the creator God must be three Persons understood as *unitas-aequalitas-conexio*. As Thierry put it in his *Lectiones in Boethii librum De trinitate:* "We speak of the Trinity in three ways—theologically, mathematically, and ethically. Mathematically speaking, Augustine says that unity is in the Father, equality in the Son, and the connection of unity and equality in the Holy Spirit."[19]

Nicholas of Cusa was directly inspired by Thierry's trinitarian mathematics. He read at least one of Thierry's Boethian commentaries and praised the (for him) anonymous author as "a man easily the foremost in genius of those I've read."[20] Cusa was especially drawn to Thierry because the Chartrian master had developed the Augustinian formula within the context of a negative theology based on Pseudo-Dionysius, as well as an understanding of the God-world relation in terms of the model of *complicatio-explicatio,* that is, a dialectic of the enfolding and unfolding of all things in and from God. According to Thierry, God is the Unity enfolding [*complicans*] in himself the universe in total simplicity, while at the same time unfolding [*explicans*] all things in their created particularity. Like Meister Eckhart and Cusa, Thierry also used the Neoplatonic dialectic of enfolding and unfolding to understanding how the human soul, as the microcosm, enfolds and unfolds all things knowable in and from itself. "The soul," he said, "is made according to the nature of the universe. Now she unfolds herself, as it were, and now she gathers herself into a certain simplicity, as when she is intelligibility. When she comes down from intelligibility, she enlarges herself, unfolding what she enfolded."[21] On the basis of texts like this we can understand why the Renaissance cardinal found inspiration for his thought in the writings of the twelfth-century schoolman.

Despite these affinities between Thierry of Chartres and Nicholas of Cusa, there is at least one major difference—Thierry did not draw out the mystical implications of the Augustinian formula. It remained on the level of doctrinal speculation for him and for most others who considered God as *unitas-aequalitas-concordia* in the twelfth and thirteenth centuries. Furthermore, Thierry understood the formula as an expression of the proper attributes of the three Persons, but most theologians (beginning with such authorities as Richard of St. Victor and Peter Lombard) understood the triad as an expression of what were called "appropriations," that is, attributes that were really common to all three Persons because they were identical with divinity, but that tradition had licensed to be applied in a metaphorical way to the individual Persons.

This appropriation model was the usual treatment found in the scholastics of the thirteenth century whom Cusa knew well. Thomas Aquinas, for instance, in his consideration of the appropriated trinitarian names in the first part of the *Summa theologiae* (Ia,39,8), gives a long explanation of why Augustine was justified in ascribing *unitas-aequalitas-concordia/connexio* to the Persons of the Trinity, without thereby locking these concepts into the truly "personal" attributes, such as *imago,* which for Aquinas is proper to the Second Person (Ia,35,1–2). The one High Scholastic theologian who made use of Thierry's formula in a way that suggests the triad is a form of proper attribution, and who also began to draw out the mystical implications of this transcendental mathematics, was a thinker well known to Cusa, Meister Eckhart.

Cusa's admiration for Eckhart is evident—in one of his marginal comments to *Codex Cusanus* 21 he says, "This Master is remarkable [*singularis*] in all his writings."[22] Eckhart's influence on many areas of Cusa's thought has been studied by a number of scholars.[23] In the case of trinitarian theology, unlike Thierry and Cusa, Eckhart did not develop full-scale quadrivial arguments for the Trinity based on Augustine's *unitas-aequalitas-concordia* formula. Nevertheless, he did know and employ the text in his own way—and within the context of a trinitarian mysticism. Eckhart's mystical appropriation of the transcendental mathematics of the Trinity forms an important link between Thierry and Nicholas of Cusa.

Eckhart's mysticism is fundamentally trinitarian in the sense that his preaching and writing were meant to encourage breakthrough [*durchbrechen*] to a life lived out of the realization that "God's ground and the soul's ground is one ground"—the ground that is dialectically both the Trinity of Persons and the "God beyond God" of the silent desert into which distinction never gazed.[24] In a number of passages in his Latin works Eckhart discusses the processions in the Trinity, emphasizing how the Father, to whom he ascribes the term *unitas* or "the One" [*unum*], gives rise to the other Persons. "Thus he who proceeds by a real procession [i.e., the Son] is the very essence of him who brings forth within the One, into the One, and the One himself [i.e., the Father]. He proceeds from him who brings forth insofar as the One who brings forth is one. This is why the saints very aptly attribute unity to the Father in the deity."[25] Here Eckhart is obviously echoing Augustine's *De doctrina christiana* text cited above.

In most of his treatments Eckhart attributes *unum* to the Father, *verum* to the Son, and *bonum* to the Holy Spirit, rather than using Augustine's formula itself.[26] But that the Son can be spoken of as the *aequalitas* of the Father, and the Holy Spirit the *concordia, conexio,* or *nexus* of the two, is evident in a key passage from the *Expositio in Evangelium secundum Iohannem* where Eckhart is analyzing the relation of the just person to Justice. He puts it as follows: "We often say, 'The just person insofar as he is just is Justice itself, and does the works of Justice.' The term 'insofar as' [*in quantum*] is a reduplication. Reduplication, as the word testifies, speaks of the bond [*nexus*] or ordering of two things. Reduplication expresses the folding together of two things, a fold or bond of two. Thus the Spirit, the third Person in the Trinity, is the bond of the two, the Father and the Son."[27] We might paraphrase this passage in the following way to bring out its inner affinity with Thierry's understanding of the Augustinian triad—"Unity-Justice insofar as it is the Equality of Unity-Justice is so by the Absolute Nexus or Connection of Unity-Justice."[28]

Mystical awareness of the paradox that "God is one without Unity, and three without Trinity," as Eckhart once put it, was the goal of his preaching.[29] The endlessly inventive verbal strategies of the Dominican preacher were meant to convey the realization that it is only by the exercise of subverting the claims of all language to adequacy through the dialectical fusion of opposites that we can come to the *docta ignorantia* that puts us in contact with God. As he says in one of his vernacular sermons: "Once I preached in Latin on Trinity Sunday and said: Distinction comes from Absolute Unity, that is, the distinction in the Trinity. Absolute Unity is the distinction and the distinction is the unity. The greater the distinction, the greater the unity, for it is the distinction without distinction. . . . The soul has a intelligible noetic being; therefore, where God is, the soul is, and where the soul is, God is."[30] The same concern for fusing unity [*unum*] and distinction [*trinum*] into one transformative and transcendental insight—the *unitrinum/triunum*—is evident in Cusa.

Nicholas of Cusa's Trinitarian Mysticism

The transcendental mathematics of the Trinity, originally explored by Thierry of Chartres and "complicated" if not fully "explicated" in Eckhart's mystical teaching, found its fullest expression in Cusa's writings. R. W. Southern once wrote that "Nicholas of Cusa, searching for jewels in the decaying body of scholasticism, ill-advisedly revived [the mathematical explanation of the Trinity] in the fifteenth century."[31] This judgment by a distinguished medievalist is unfortunately not based on any real evaluation either of the intention or the theological adequacy of the transcendental mathematics of the Trinity found in Cusa, Thierry, and Eckhart. Such peremptory dismissal of Cusa's trinitarianism is neither historically nor theologically justified.

In order to evaluate how Nicholas of Cusa's form of a transcendental mathematics of the Trinity was central to his understanding of mystical transformation we can begin with a brief overview of the cardinal's explicit treatments of the mystery of the triune God. A survey of more than fifty passages throughout his treatises where Cusa discourses on the Trinity reveals a rich variety of triadic formulas—triads that often do not make a clear distinction between appropriated and proper terms.[32] A full survey of all these formulas cannot be presented here, but it will come as no surprise to those who have read much of Cusa that the largest number (twenty of fifty-two in my tally) explicitly invoke the *unitas-aequalitas-conexio* theme.[33] Many others are reducible to it in obvious ways. One could even make the argument that all of the cardinal's expositions of the doctrine of the three Persons contain implicit variations on this fundamental insight into the Triunity.

How does Cusa understand *unitas-aequalitas-conexio?* We can begin from a consideration of the treatment in the *De docta ignorantia,* not because the exposition here is necessarily the most extensive or even the most subtle, but because it is representative of what was to follow and it is probably better known to the general reader.[34] Of the five passages on the Trinity found in *De docta ignorantia,* the most important comes early in the first book after his presentation of why "learned ignorance," based on the impossibility of any proportion between the infinite and the finite,[35] has no choice but to enter the realm of *coincidentia oppositorum* where the Minimum coincides with the Maximum beyond all affirmation and negation (*De docta ignorantia* I.4.11–12).[36] The Maximum, Cusa argues, is identical with the Absolute Oneness [*unitas absoluta*] that is beyond all number as its beginning and end (I.5.14). Exploring the implications of Absolute Oneness leads to the affirmation that it is absolutely necessary and also necessarily eternal (I.6.15–17). The discussion of eternity in chapter 7 is where Cusa begins to investigate the mystery of why the Eternal Unity must also be trinal [*trina*] in nature. The structure of the argument is a form of transcendental reduction. If otherness, inequality, and division are characteristic of everything we experience and know, and if otherness, inequality, and division demand a ground in what is not-other, not-unequal, not-divided, such a ground must be (*a*) eternal (because otherness, inequality, and division are temporal and finite); and (*b*) an Eternity that is both one and three.[37] Cusa concludes: "But because unity is eternal, equality is eternal, so too is connection; hence unity, equality and connection are one. This is that trinal unity which Pythagoras, the first of all philosophers and the glory of Italy and Greece, taught was to be adored."[38]

In the following three chapters, Cusa explores the relationship between "triunal Eternity" and Christian doctrine of the Trinity. The treatment of the eternal generation of *aequalitas unitatis* as *entitas,* or being, and the "form of being" (chap. 8), is close to several passages in Thierry of Chartres.[39] In discussing the eternal procession of *conexio* in chapter 9 Cusa makes it clear why this procession must be from both: "For Connection is not of one thing alone, but it proceeds from Unity into the Equality of Unity and from the Equality of Unity into Unity."[40] He notes that "our holiest doctors" (obviously including Augustine) have called *unitas* the Father, *aequalitas* the Son, and *conexio* the Holy Spirit, though these terms are only a "very distant likeness" [*distantissima similitudo*] taken from creatures (I.9.26). Finally, in chapter 10, Cusa reflects on how *intelligentia,* the knowing power superior to reason, attains to the realm of the coincidence of opposites where it can affirm that "Maximal Unity will never be correctly understood unless it is understood as trinal."[41]

Two important developments in chapter 10 demonstrate why this early treatment of the Trinity provides a good springboard into Cusa's later discussions. The first is his insistence that *docta ignorantia* brings one to understand three fundamental points about the maximal coincidence of all things in the One: "And then it understands that when anything whatsoever is in the One [1] it is one, and [2] the One itself is all things, and hence [3] whatever is in It is all things."[42] As Meister Eckhart once put in a lapidary formulation that Cusa copied out in a marginal reduplication: "In divinis quodlibet est in quolibet et maximum in minimo"; that is, "In God everything is in everything and the Maximum is in the Minimum."[43] The second issue that points to Cusa's later treatments is his suggestion that language about the Trinity as *unitas-aequalitas-conexio* can be illustrated by a number of "fitting examples" [*exemplis convenientibus*]. The first of these is the trinal nature of knowing analyzed as consisting in the knower [*intelligens*], what is known [*intelligibile*], and the act of knowing [*intelligere*]. These three are distinguishable in our realm of knowing. Raised to the level of the kind of knowing found in the Maximum, they form a "trinity of unity" (I.10.28).[44] This appeal to the act of understanding as a way of "seeing" the meaning of the Trinity provides a key for important aspects of Cusa's later thought on how the Christian appropriates the Trinity to attain eventually to face-to-face vision of God [*visio facialis*].

Several points are worth observing about Cusa's form of the argument for the necessity that the First Principle must be *unitrinum seu triunum*. Although both Thierry of Chartres and the *De septem septennis* (a twelfth-century Hermetic work) had ascribed eternity to triunal Absolute Necessity, they had not developed the argument specifically from the perspective of *eternitas* in the way in which Cusa did.[45] Also, at this stage Cusa asserted that philosophers like Pythagoras had grasped the trinitarian nature of the First Principle. Later in his career he revised this view, arguing in the *De beryllo* (1458), for example, that pagan thinkers had never attained to the knowledge of the supreme *conexio* that is the Holy Spirit.[46] Finally, despite three other discussions of the Trinity in itself found in the *De docta ignorantia*, there is no real consideration at this stage of mystical dimensions of speculation about the Trinity.[47]

Nicholas of Cusa, like Meister Eckhart and unlike Augustine, found a real, not a vestigial, presence of the Trinity in creation. To be sure, the Trinity is not present in the world as it is in the realm that lies on the other side of "the wall of the coincidence of opposites," as his evocative metaphor from the *De visione dei* puts it. Rather, the Trinity is the inner reality of all things in a contracted mode, as the treatment of the "Trinity of the Universe" in book 2 of *De docta ignorantia* demonstrates. In a discussion once again dependent on Thierry of Chartres, Nicholas argues in this book that "the unity of the universe is trinal, because it is from possibility, from the necessity of connection, and from the bond: what we can call potency, act, and bond."[48] Cusa's trinitarianism, like Eckhart's, is doubly dialectical, insisting not only that the Absolute One must be trinal but also that the immanence or indistinction of the *unitrinum* in all things is nothing other than the form its transcendence or distinction takes when it unfolds itself into what it creates.

The personal and transformative implications of this teaching become clear in the discussions of the Trinity in the *De coniecturis*, the early epistemological treatise (ca. 1441–43) in which Cusa explored the relation between how the divine mind creates all things and the human mind constructs the conceptual universe of its conjectures.[49] Cusa's analysis of knowing is not meant to be a purely abstract enterprise, any more than Augustine's *De trinitate* was just a dogmatic and speculative study of the Trinity. As he says, "The more we plumb the depths of our mind, whose single living center is the Divine Mind, the more closely we are being raised to become like it."[50] At the beginning of the work, Cusa announces that understanding the mind as "the principle of conjectures" reveals it as "a unitrinal principle," whose "*unity* enfolds in itself all multitude, and whose *equality* enfolds all magnitude, and whose *connection* enfolds all composition."[51] Two subsequent discussions expand on this trinitarian image in the soul, and the theme reaches a conclusion in the lengthy personal address Cusa makes to his patron, Cardinal Giulio Cesarini.[52]

Taking self-knowledge [*cognitio sui*] as the goal of his project, Cusa invites his supporter to grasp how "the humanity that is individually contracted in otherness is the otherness of a more Absolute Unity."[53] By means of the conjectural example of light, Cusa shows Cardinal Giulio how his own unity as knowing subject participates in the light of divinity in which unity, equality, and connection are all one and that it does so in an appropriate manner on each of the three levels of his apprehension—intellect, reason, and sense (II.17.172–76). This participation is actualized not only in grasping how the self participates in a contracted fashion in unitrinal light but also in how to understand the drive to create the speculative sciences, as well as the ratiocinative and sensible arts—that is, in every form of human knowing (II.17.177–78). The aim, however, is not just knowing more things but knowing the meaning of knowing, that is, apprehending how knowing makes one the "likeness of God," a unitrinal contraction of Absolute Unity, Equality, and Connection. This is nothing more or less than learning how to truly love God and to live the equality of his justice (II.17.179–84). As Cusa puts it:

> From yourself you can behold the godlike elections. For you see that God, who is the Infinite Connection, is not to be loved as some kind of contracted lovable thing, but as the most Absolute Infinite Love. In that love in which God is loved the Most Simple Unity and the Infinite Justice must also exist. It is also necessary that every love by which God is loved is less than that with which he can be loved. You also know that to love God is to be loved by God, for he is charity. The more that anyone loves God, the more he participates in divinity.[54]

This text, with its Eckhartian overtones, especially the stress given to the role of *iustitia* and the function of the Holy Spirit as the Person in whom the Father and Son love each other and in whom we too must love, is a good summary of the core of Cusa's trinitarian mysticism.[55]

The treatments of the Trinity found in Cusa's later writings (more than forty passages) display many variations, and in several cases deeper explorations, of the teaching found in these two early works. Nevertheless, these subsequent considerations do not, I believe, alter the foundations of Cusa's mystical trinitarianism. It is not possible to look at them all here, but a brief analysis of three key texts can serve to indicate aspects of the richness of the cardinal's later attempts to explore the role of the Trinity in mystical consciousness. The passages are drawn from the *De visione dei* (1453), the *De aequalitate* (1459), and the *De possest* (1460).

The *De visione dei,* Cusa's premier mystical text, focuses on the fascination with seeing God that percolates through the many treatises the cardinal composed in the final decade of his life.[56] The importance of the treatise for understanding Cusa's mysticism, as well as its role in late medieval debates about the nature of mysticism, has been much studied in recent years.[57] Here there is room to consider only the brief, but pregnant, section in which Cusa reflects on how the Trinity can be said to be in some way visible (chaps. 17 and 18).

The *De visione* does not employ the Augustinian triad of *unitas-aequalitas-conexio,* though Cusa uses an equivalent formulation in speaking of the Father, Son, and Holy Spirit as *unitas uniens-unitas unibilis-utriusque unio.* Rather, his argument in chapters 17 and 18 is based on an alternative form of the dialectical view of the Trinity, which picks up on the emphasis on love seen at the end of the *De coniecturis,* and discusses the Trinity as *amor amans-amor amabilis-utriusque nexus.*[58] In contrast to his earlier treatments, here Cusa's exposition of how we come to see God in experiencing and seeing love is framed within the discourse of prayer, in a manner close to Augustine's *Confessions.* "Seeing" means "seeing that" something is the case, not understanding it or being able to explain it in a conceptual way.[59] In his discussion, Cusa moves back and forth between (1) intellectual vision of the dialectical necessity that the three forms of love are one without number in the God who is *unitrinus et triunus* (17.77–78), and (2) exploration of how contracted human love, both self-love and love of others, reveals that all love participates in, but can never fully attain, the infinite divine mystery that resides in the paradise that lies on the other side of "the wall of coincidence" (17.78–79).[60]

What is especially significant about the *De visione* text is the way in which it connects this dialectical understanding of trinitarian love (the logic of which is not really different from the standard pattern of *unitas-aequalitas-conexio*) with some of the major themes of medieval mysticism that had not hitherto appeared in Cusa's writings—for example, the role of the spiritual senses, the nature of rapture, and the mode of union with God that is possible in this life.[61] In the case of rapture, Cusa surprises us by adding to the traditional appeal to Paul a rare description of personal mystical consciousness: "Trusting in your infinite goodness, I made an effort to be subject to a rapture so that I might see you who are invisible and who are the unrevealable revealed vision. You know how far I got; I do not. Your grace is sufficient for me. By it you assure me that you are incomprehensible, and that you raise me up into the firm hope that with you leading the way I will eventually come to enjoy you."[62] A more extensive treatment of the *De visione* would be needed to show how these traditional themes receive new meaning by being incorporated in Cusa's understanding of the dialectical mutuality of self-knowledge (which is also "self-seeing" and "self-presence") and knowledge of God: "Indeed, how will you give yourself to me, if you do not also give me to myself? And while I rest in this way in the silence of contemplation, you, O Lord, answer within the depths of my heart and say: 'Be your own and I will be yours.'"[63]

The *De aequalitate*, a Cusan meditation on John's Gospel, has been less studied than many of his other late treatises, but it is a subtle and powerful work, and one that features rich developments of his trinitarian thought.[64] The three discussions of the Trinity found in the work all contain unusual features.[65] The last and longest is especially noteworthy for its rethinking of the Augustinian trinitarian analogies from the last books of the *De trinitate*. Cusa begins by citing Augustine's triad of *memoria-intelligentia-voluntas*, identifying memory with the *principium*.[66] But he really wants to emphasize the absolute identity of the three, rather than their distinction, so he argues that *memoria* signifies at one and the same time the "intellectual and retentive memory," that is, the hidden a priori ground of all knowing, as well as the intelligence, or "intellect of memory" [*memoriae intellectus*], the power that reveals the hidden memory by its conversion to the intelligible species found therein. The will, then, is necessarily the will of both forms of memory simultaneously. Cusa also claims that the term *intellectus*, like memory, can be used of both Father and Son, as when the Intellect, as Father, is said to generate the Intellective Word. What this all comes down to is that *memoria* and *intellectus* are really equivalent to the perfect identity of *unitas* and *aequalitis* in the standard Augustinian mathematical formulas.[67]

In this treatise Cusa also goes deeper in his exploration of the mutuality of the divine knowing of Father and Son, as suggested in the gospel text, "No one knows the Son save the Father, nor does anyone know the Father save the Son" (Matt. 11:27). Because the Son "enfolds everything in himself," the Father knows himself and all other things in the act of generating the Son, while in the act of being generated the Son "knows all things in himself because he is the Word of the Father in whom the Father knows both himself and all things."[68] The interchangeability of *memoria* and *intellectus*, and the identity in distinction of the mutual knowledge of Father and Son lead the cardinal to a yet deeper meditation on his standard trinitarian presentation.

In the *De trinitate* Augustine had distinguished between the *verbum interius* and the *verbum exterius* in pursuing the analogy of the generation of the intellective word from *memoria*.[69] Cusa now reformulates this distinction, using *aequalitas* rather than *unitas* as the root term. A speaker, he tells us, understands an expressed word on the basis of the internal word generated from the intelligence that knows both itself and its external speech. If this intelligence is identified with "Absolute Equality," that is, the inalterability that precedes all change in being or becoming, then the internal word will be the *verbum aequalitatis*, that is, the expression in which Equality "intuits" its own *quidditas* and therefore that of all other things.[70] If Absolute Equality can be ascribed to the Father, and Equality of Equality to the Son, we can speak of the Holy Spirit as the Equality that is the Bond or Love of both.[71] Cusa goes on to show how this new terminology (i.e., *absoluta aequalitas-aequalitas aequalitatis-conexio*) both brings out the inner truth of traditional trinitarian language and also helps us to grasp the trinitarian structure of the whole "unfolded" universe in which contracted forms of *aequalitas* are found in all realities and in every discipline of thought.[72] He concludes by stressing the superiority of this argument to his earlier formulations, claiming that, "although Unity may seem to be the father of Equality, since Equality is unity multiplied by itself, as said in other places, nevertheless Absolute Equality enfolds Unity, for what is equal exists in one mode only."[73] More daringly, he even says that this new form of language about the Trinity is "much more precise" than that found in the Bible and the Fathers.[74]

The final text to be considered comes from one of Cusa's better-known late works, the *De possest*. This extensive treatment introduces several new formulations of the insights that had been developing in his thought for more than two decades. Nevertheless, there is really nothing substantially new in this discussion of the aging cardinal's efforts to discover the "most precise" name for *unitrinum-triunum*, especially in relation to the texts from the *De visione Dei* and the *De aequalitate*. As he grew older, the dialectical expression of Cusa's thought often seems to have become leaner and his formulations of insurpassibility of the wall of contradictions more extreme. The *De possest* offers an example of this tendency, along with the most detailed survey of the Trinity in the last works.[75]

In response to his interlocutor's request for a treatment of the Trinity, Nicholas confesses that his many "profound meditations" on the subject have only made it all the more clear to him that God escapes every concept. Still, after a typical geometrical illustration, Nicholas lays out a series of triadic arguments that start from the *principium mathematicae*, which is both one and three.[76] The succeeding discussion represents what we may call the Boethian dimension of this form of trinitarian thought, that is, the insistence on conceiving of the *unitrina deitas* as beyond numeration in the sense of being the *principium* of all numbers.[77] The major triad advanced by Cusa here (*potentia-actus–utriusque nexus*) is nothing more than the *unitas-aequalitas-conexio* demonstration in another mode. Lest we forget, though, Cusa underlines the fact that these mathematical formulations are far from precise: "The unity which is ascribed to God is not mathematical, but it is true and living, enfolding all things."[78] The final variations on the usual triads with which the cardinal concludes his treatment in this treatise are not mathematical, however, but are speculations about the trinitarian meaning of letters that could almost be taken for an early form of Christian Kabbala had they been produced a generation or two later.[79] Ingenious as these are, from the perspective of the major thrust of Cusa's distinctive trinitarian mysticism, they do not add much to what had already been expounded in the *De docta ignorantia* concerning the role of the Trinity as *unitas-aequalitias-conexio*.

In conclusion, we may ask what the significance of the trinitarian dimension of Cusa's mysticism really is. Viewing the mystical element as not more (but not less) than one dimension within a total religious belief system, and also conceiving of the trinitarian component as a necessary ground of Christian mysticism, allows us a perspective for assessing what the Trinity meant for Cardinal Nicholas. The sheer proliferation of his discussions of the Trinity, mostly centered on the mathematical "conjecture" of the *unitrinum/ triunum* God expressed as *unitas-aequalitas-conexio,* suggests that Cusa's mysticism was deeply trinitarian throughout his career. This is not to deny the traditional emphasis on the cardinal's christological approach to the *facialis visio* toward which believers advance during this life. But almost all of the great Christian mystical teachers have been both christological and trinitarian, though differing considerably in how they relate these two foundations of their faith.

We may ask, Is God really a "Trinity" for Cusa? Of course not in the deepest sense, because Trinity and Unity, and all human expressions, are no more than conjectures based on the inescapable task of the human intellect to continue to explore how its knowing necessarily conceives of itself and all reality as *unitrinum seu trinunum* and in that exploration to discover the only access that we have toward the divine mystery. Because God unfolds himself as Trinity and all knowing is grounded in this contracted Trinity, some knowledge of the *theos unitrinus* is found in every form of philosophy and religion.[80] But in his later years the cardinal was increasingly negative about the extent of knowledge of the Trinity found in the ancient philosophers. He insisted that although the Trinity can be naturally known, it is faith alone as revealed in Jesus Christ that allows confession of the Trinity to become the transformative act that leads on to vision.[81]

Cusa's trinitarian mysticism has both analogies to and significant differences from those who influenced him, especially Meister Eckhart. A full exploration is impossible here, but some tentative comments about his relation to his Dominican predecessor may serve to highlight one important conclusion regarding the cardinal's contribution to mysticism. Although Eckhart's view of the trinitarian ground of all reality was an important factor in Cusa's thought, anyone who has read these two thinkers carefully will admit that however much they shared a comparable metaphysical program (what Gilson called "the metaphysics of the One"), they differed in significant ways. Both thinkers insisted on the absolute unknowability of God, but they placed the mystery in different locations and expressed it through different linguistic strategies. Cusa, for example, did not explore the tension between the knowing and unknowing of God through the language of the hidden divine ground or desert beyond the three Persons of the Trinity—the "God beyond God"—as the German Dominican did.[82] Although he was interested in the divine Sonship we share in the Second Person of the Trinity, as the *De filiatione Dei* shows, Cusa did not explore in detail the birth of the Word in the soul, the dominant theme of Eckhart's vernacular preaching. This is not to say that there are not analogies to these themes in Cusa; the point is that the dialectical approach to trinitarian mysticism that Eckhart and Cusa used cannot, by definition, be uniform. How one presents in human speech the God who surpasses all speech and knowing can never be reduced to a single formula or a specific doctrinal statement. The genius of the *unitas-aequalitas-conexio* triad introduced by Augustine was that it suggested a form of speculative mathematics that defied the ordinary conventions of numeration and thus provided an entry into forms of thinking that led to the *docta ignorantia* in which deeper consciousness of God becomes possible.

Part of what makes Cusa such a stimulating exponent of this form of mysticism is his ability to both encourage and at the same time undercut the ways we speak about God. Across so many varied discussions, his energy never flagged in pursuit of the most incisive formulations for inducing the leap beyond the *murus coincidentiae* that represents the boundary of all that we can know and imagine in this life. As treatises like the *Idiota de mente et sapientia* demonstrate, Cusa, like Eckhart and other late medieval mystics, was convinced that this search was not just for the religious and learned elite but for all believers. The unlearned craftsman [*idiota*] could serve as the philosopher's instructor in the hunt for true wisdom.

The wisdom of the *idiota* needed both humility and courage. Cusa insists that when we speak of the Trinity, we must always be aware that the revealed language of *pater-filius–spiritus sanctus,* as well as the more theoretically precise language of *unitas-aequalitas-conexio* and its equivalents, is never more than a divine condescension—what contracted intellect allows us to say of the mystery beyond all comprehension. Here we return full circle to Augustine's reflections on ineffability from the beginning of the *De doctrina christiana.* It is hard to think that Cusa did not have this passage in mind when he wrote in the *De filiatione Dei:* "Whatever can be uttered does not express the ineffable; nevertheless, every expression tries to speak of [*fatur*] the ineffable."[83] Augustine the rhetorician did not explore this pregnant observation further but, rather, proceeded to create a theology whose linguistic exuberance, like that of Bernard of Clairvaux, conceals God at the same time that it attempts to make him present in excessive speech. Nicholas of Cusa, in contrast, deeply schooled in the traditions of negative theology found in Dionysius, Thierry, and Meister Eckhart, reveled in the paradoxes of speculative negation of negation. For those who still find the exigencies of apophaticism central to the mystical pursuit of God, Nicholas continues to present both an example and an inspiration.

Appendix: Trinitarian Discussions in Cusa's Treatises

The passages are listed chronologically. The various triads used are included. Abbreviations used are as follows: *u-a-c* = *unitas-aequalitas-conexio; p-f-ss* = *pater-filius–spiritus sanctus*).

I. *De docta ignorantia* (1440)
    A. 1.7–10
        1. *u-a-c* (1.7.18–9.26)
        2. *hoc-id-idem* (1.9.25)
        3. *unitas-iditas-identitas* (1.9.25)
        4. *p-f-ss* (1.9.26)
        5. *intelligens-intelligibile-intelligere* (1.10.28)
        6. *indivisio-discretio-conexio* (1.10.28)
        7. *principium sine principio–principium a principio–processio ab utroque* (1.10.28)
        8. *minimum-maximum-conexio* (1.10.28)
    B. 1.19–20
        1. *p-f-ss* (1.20.59)
    C. 1.24
        1. *u-a-c* (*amor*) (1.24.80)
        2. p-f-ss (1.24.80)
    D. 1.26
        1. *generans-genita-procedens* (1.26.87)
        2. *infinitas-species-usus* (1.26.87)

           3. *prin. sine principio–prin. a principio–processio ab utroque* (1.26.87)

           4. *u-a-c* (1.26.88)

           5. *p-f–ss* (1.26.88)

     E. 2.7

           1. *p-f–ss* (2.7.128)

           2. *u-a-c* (2.7.128–129)

II. *De coniecturis* (1441–43)

     A. 1.1.6: *u-a-c*

     B. 1.2.9: *u-a-c*

     C. 2.14.145: *u-a-c*

     D. 2.17.174–184

           1. *u-a-c* (2.17.174–81)

           2. *intellectus-intelligere–utriusque amor* (2.17.176)

III. *De filiatione dei* (1445)

     A. 3.69: *intellectus-intelligibile-intelligere*

     B. 4.76–77

           1. *p-f–ss*

           2. *principium-medium-finis*

IV. *De dato patris luminum* (1446)

     A. 4.108–5.122

           1. *virtus–verbum veritatis–perfectio* (4.109–5.112)

           2. *essentia-possibilitas-operatio* (5.112–13)

           3. *p-f–ss* (passim)

V. *Dialogus de genesi* (1447)

     A. 5.176–77: *pater-verbum-spiritus*

VI. *Apologiae doctae ignorantiae* (1449)

     A. 23–24: *p-f-ss*

VII. *Idiota de sapientia* (1450)

     A. 1.22: *u-a-c*

     B. 3.6.93–96: *u-a-c*

     C. 3.11.129–39

           1. *u-a-c* (129, 132, 139)

           2. *posse fieri–posse facere–utriusque nexus* (131)

VIII. *De visione dei* (1453)

     A. 17.75–18.83

           1. *amor amans–amor amabilis–utriusque nexus* (17.75–79, 18.81)

           2. *unitas uniens–unitas unibilis–utriusque unio* (17.76)

           3. *intellectus intelligens–intellectus intelligibilis–utriusque nexus* (18.82)

           4. *p-f–ss* (18.82)

     B. 19.85: *amor amans–amor amabilis–nexus*

     C. 20.88: *p-f–ss*

IX. *De pace fidei* (1453)

     A. 7–11

           1. *u-a-c* (7–8)

           2. *amans-amabile-amare* (8)

           3. *unitas-iditas-identitas* (8)

           4. *mens-sapientia–amor/voluntas* (8)

      5. *aeternitas ingenita–aeternitas genita–aeternitas neque ingenita neque genita* (10)

      6. *mens–verbum* (*sapientia*)*–spiritus* (*anima*) (8–10)

      7. *p-f-ss* (8, 10–11)

X. *Complementum theologicum* (1453)

    A. 3

      1. *inscriptus-scriptus–circumscriptus* (*circulus unitrinus infinitus*)

    B. 6

      1. *centrum-linea-circumferentia*

      2. *p-f-ss*

      3. *generans-genita-explicans*

      4. *principium sine principio–principium a principio–nexus*

      5. *u* (*entitas*)*-a-c*

XI. *De Beryllo* (1458)

    A. 33–42

      1. *u-a-c* (*nexus*) (33)

      2. *deus–conditor intellectus–anima mundi* (35, 37)

      3. *intellectus-verbum-delectatio* (39)

      4 *quo est–quid est–nexus* (39)

    B. 60: *maximus triangulus*

XII. *De aequalitate* (1459)

    A. ed. Gabriel, 366–68

      1. *syllogismus* in bArbArA

      2. *p-f-ss*

      3. *memoria-intellectus-voluntas*

    B. ed. Gabriel, 372–78

      1. *tempus intemporale in mente,* that is, *praeteritum-praesens-futurum*

      2. *memoria-intellectus-voluntas*

      3. *quia est–quid est–intentio finis*

    C. ed. Gabriel, 386–408

      1. *memoria-intelligentia-voluntas* (386)

      2. *quia est–quid est–intentio* (388–90)

      3. *intellectualis memoria–verbum–spiritus sanctus* (390–92)

      4. *p-f-ss* (390–92, 404)

      5. *absoluta aequalitas–aequalitas aequalitatis–nexus* (392–96)

      6. *aequalitas generans–aequalitas genita–aequalitas procedens* (396)

      7. *caritas intellectualis–caritas caritatis–caritas utriusque nexus* (396)

      8. *u-a-c* (402)

XIII. *De principio* (1459)

    A. 9–11

      1. *principium–principium principiatum–principiatum utriusque*

      2. *paternitas-filiatio–nexus amoris procedens*

    B. 14–15

      1. *causa tricausalis*

      2. *unum-intellectus–spiritus* (*anima*)

XIV. *De possest* (1460)

    A. 6–8

   G. 39.115–117: *posse facere–posse fieri–posse factum*
XIX. *Compendium theologiae* (1464)
   A. 10.29–31: *posse-aequalitas–unio potentissima*
   B. Epil. 45–46: *posse (unitas)–aequalitas-unio*
XX. *De apice theoriae* (1464)
   A. Epil. 25–28
      1. *mens memorans–mens intelligens–mens volens*
      2. *posse facere–posse fieri–posse conexionis*

Notes

1. *Le "De Ignota Litteratura" de Jean Wenck de Herrenberg contra Nicolas de Cuse*, ed. Edmond Vansteenberghe (Münster: Aschendorff, 1910), 41: "Nescio an diebus meis unicum scribam sicut hunc unquam viderim tam perniciosum, in materia divinitatis et trinitatis Personarum, in materia universitatis rerum, in materia Incarnacionis Christi, in materia virtutum theologicalium, in materia Ecclesie." For the further details of Wenck's attack on Cusa's teaching on the Trinity, see Vansteenberghe, ed., 25 and 34–35.

2. *Nicolai de Cusa Apologia Doctae Ignorantiae*, ed. Raymundus Klibansky (Leipzig: Meiner, 1932), 23.25–24.4: "Scilicet in coincidentia summae simplicitatis et indivisibilitatis atque unitatis et trinitatis. . . . Cum enim dicitur Patrem esse personam et Filium alteram et Spiritum sanctam tertiam, non potest alteritas significatum suum tenere, cum sit haec dictio imposita, ut significet alteritatem ab unitate divisam et distinctam."

3. *Apologia* 24.17: "Quis enim modum concipere possit discretum indiscrete." Cusa also uses the equivalent terms *distinctum-indistinctum,* as in *Apologia* 10.1–3: "Est singularitas singularitatum, et sic Deus dicitur singularis insingulariter sicut finis infinitus et interminus terminus et indistincta distinctio." See also *Nicolai de Cusa De docta ignorantia*, ed. Paulus Wilpert (Hamburg: Meiner, 1964), 76, I.19.57: "Nam ubi distinctio est indistinctio, trinitas est unitas. Et e converso, ubi indistinctio est distinctio, unitas est trinitas." Cusa here shows the influence of Meister Eckhart, especially the Dominican's Latin Sermo IV. Eckhart will be cited according to the critical edition, *Meister Eckhart: Die deutschen und lateinischen Werke* (Stuttgart: Kohlhammer, Deutsche Forschungsgemeinschaft, 1934–), using the abbreviations DW for the German works and LW for the Latin works, and citing volume and page. Sermo IV can be found in LW 4:22–32.

4. *De docta ignorantia* I.19.58 (ed. Wilpert, 78): "Coniunge igitur ista, quae videntur opposita, antecedenter, ut praedixi, et non habebis unum et tria vel e converso, sed unitrinum seu triunum. Et ista est veritas absoluta." The major discussions of the Trinity in *De docta ignorantia* are found in I.7.18–10.29, I.19.55–20.62, I.24.80–81, I.26.87–88. On the relation of the Trinity to the created universe, see II.7.127–31 and II.10.155.

5. This essay will restrict itself to Cusa's treatises, though the Trinity often appears in his sermons as well (see, e.g., Sermo XXII, "Dies sanctificatus," in *Nicolai de Cusa Opera omnia,* ed. Martin Bodewig [Hamburg: Meiner, 1984], 16 333–57). Nevertheless, a consideration of the sermons would go beyond what can be attempted in a short essay. Of Cusa's many theological tracts, only the brief *De quaerendo Deo* and the *De Deo abscondito,* as well as the *Coniectura de ultimis diebus,* contain no explicit mention of the Trinity.

6. Rudolf Haubst, *Das Bild des Einen und Dreienen Gottes in der Welt nach Nikolaus von Kues* (Trier: Paulinus, 1952). Haubst gives full attention both to the treatises and the sermons.

7. The recent treatment of Cusa's doctrine of the Trinity in Alexandre Ganoczy, *Der drei-*

einige Schöpfer: Trinitätstheologie und Synergie (Darmstadt: Wissenschaftliche Buchgesellschaft, 2001), chap. 5, also largely concerns how the Trinity is revealed in creation.

8. For this view of mysticism, see Bernard McGinn, *The Foundations of Mysticism: Origins through the Fifth Century* (New York: Crossroad, 1991), xiii–xx.

9. For the early development of this formula, see Bernard McGinn, "Does the Trinity Add Up? Transcendental Mathematics and Trinitarian Speculation," in *Praise No Less Than Charity: Studies in Honor of M. Chrysogonus Waddell, Monk of Gethsemani Abbey* ed. E. Rozanne Elder (Kalamazoo, Mich.: Cistercian Publications, 2002), 235–64.

10. Augustine, *De doctrina christiana,* ed. G. M. Green, Corpus Scriptorum Ecclesiasticorum Latinorum 80, sec. 6, pt. 6 (Vienna: Holder-Picheler-Tempsky, 1963), 10–11, I.5.12: "Eadem est tribus aeternitas, eadem incommutabilitas, eadem maiestas, eadem potestas. In patre unitas, in filio aequalitas, in spiritu sancto unitatis aequalitatisque concordia. Et tria haec unum omnia propter patrem, aequalia omnia propter filium, conexa omnia propter spiritum sanctum."

11. Ibid., I.6.13 (ed. Green, 10–11): "Ac per hoc ne ineffabilis quidem dicendus est deus, quia et hoc cum dicitur, aliquid dicitur. Et fit nescio qua pugna verborum, quoniam si illud est ineffabile quod dici non potest, non est ineffabile quod vel ineffabile dici potest. Quae pugna verborum silentio cavenda potius quam voce pacanda est."

12. The term "transcendental mathematics," employed here to describe the logic of Augustine's text, follows this form: the Absolute Oneness that is the Father (1) is the origin of the complete Equality of Oneness that is the Son (1 = 1), while the coequal Bond, Agreement, or Connection of the two, namely, the Holy Spirit (X), completes the perfection of the trinitarian mystery and is expressed in the formula 1 X 1.

13. Much has been written on the symbolism of numbers. For a cross-cultural introduction, see Annemarie Schimmel, *The Mystery of Numbers* (New York and Oxford: Oxford University Press, 1993).

14. Despite his opposition to the metaphysics of unity, E. Gilson's chapter "On Being and the One," in *Being and Some Philosophers* (Toronto: Pontifical Institute of Medieval Studies, 1949), remains one of the best surveys of this important tradition in Christian thought.

15. See, e.g., Emilie Zum Bruun, *St. Augustine: Being and Nothingness* (New York: Paragon House, 1988).

16. For an introduction to Thierry, see Peter Dronke, "Thierry of Chartres," in *A History of Twelfth-Century Western Philosophy,* ed. Peter Dronke (Cambridge: Cambridge University Press, 1988), 358–85.

17. Thierry's works have been edited by Nikolaus M. Häring, *Commentaries on Boethius by Thierry of Chartres and His School* (Toronto: Pontifical Institute of Medieval Studies, 1971). Thierry's teaching on the Trinity was first studied by M.-D. Chenu, "Une définition pythagoricienne de la verité au moyen âge," *Archives d'histoire doctrinale et littéraire du moyen âge* 28 (1961): 7–13; and Édouard Jeauneau, "Mathematiques et Trinité chez Thierry de Chartres," in *Die Metaphysik im Mittelalter: Ihr Ursprung und ihre Bedeutung,* Miscellanea Mediaevalia 2 (Berlin: De Gruyter, 1963), 289–95.

18. Thierry, *Tractatus de sex dierum operibus* in *Commentaries on Boethius,* ed. Häring, 568: Adsint igitur quatuor genera rationum que ducunt hominem ad cognitionem creatoris: scilicet arithmetice probationes et musicae et geometrice et astronomice.

19. Thierry, *Lectiones* VII.5, in *Commentaries on Boethius,* ed. Häring, 224: "Tribus enim modis de Trinitate loquimur: theologice scilicet mathematice et ethice. Et Augustinus quidem

mathematice dicit quod in Patre est unitas in Filio equalitas in Spiritu sancto unitatis equalitatisque conexio."

20. *Nicolai de Cusa Apologiae Doctae Ignorantiae,* ed. Klibansky, 24: "Vir facile omnium, quos legerim, ingenio clarissimus." Cusa certainly was familiar with Thierry's *Lectiones in Boethii Librum de Trinitate;* he may have known some of the other treatises as well.

21. This text comes from the *Glosa super Boethii Librum De Trinitate* II.12, in *Commentaries on Boethius,* ed. Häring, 271: "Ipsa facta est ad naturam rei uniuerse. Modo enim est quasi se explicat, modo in quandam se colligit simplicitatem: ut cum intelligibilitas est, a qua cum demittitur se ampliat euoluens quod implicuerat."

22. Donald F. Duclow, "Nicholas of Cusa in the Margins of Meister Eckhart: Codex Cusanus 21," in *Nicholas of Cusa in Search of God and Wisdom,* ed. Gerald Christianson and Thomas M. Izbicki (Leiden: Brill, 1991), 61.

23. For Eckhart's influence on Cusa, see Herbert Wackerzapp, *Der Einfluss Meister Eckharts auf die ersten philosophischen Schriften des Nikolaus von Kues (1440–1450),* ed. Josef Koch (Münster: Aschendorff, 1962); Josef Koch, "Nikolaus von Kues und Meister Eckhart: Randbemerkungen zu zwei in der Schrift *De coniecturis* gegebenen Problemen," *Das Cusanus-Jubiläum 1964,* ed. Rudolf Haubst (Mainz: Matthias-Grünewald-Verlag, 1964), 164–73; Rudolf Haubst, "Nikolaus von Kues als Interpret und Verteidiger Meister Eckharts," in *Freiheit und Gelassenheit: Meister Eckhart heute,* ed. Udo Kern (Munich: Beck, 1980), 75–96; Donald F. Duclow, "Nicholas of Cusa in the Margins of Meister Eckhart," 57–69; and Burkhard Mojsisch, "*Nichts* und *Negation:* Meister Eckhart und Nikolaus von Kues," in *Historia philosophiae medii aevi: Studien zur Geschichte der Philosophie des Mittelalters,* ed. Burkhard Mojsisch, 2 vols. (Amsterdam: G. R. Grüner, 1991), 1:675–93.

24. For more on the trinitarian character of Eckhart's mysticism, see Bernard McGinn, "A Prolegomenon to the Role of the Trinity in Meister Eckhart's Mysticism," *Eckhart Review* 6 (Spring 1997): 51–61, and *The Mystical Thought of Meister Eckhart: The Man from Whom God Hid Nothing* (New York: Crossroad, 2001), 75–100.

25. This text is from the *Liber parabolorum Geneseos,* n. 215 (LW 1:691): "Sed sic procedens reali processione est ipsa essentia producentis intra unum, in uno, et ipsum unum; procedit enim a producente in quantum producens unum est. Propter quod sancti optime patri in divinis attribuunt unitatem."

26. According to this pattern of *unum*-Father, *verum*-Son, and *bonum*-Holy Spirit, *esse* is ascribed to the divine essence or ground and *unum-verum-bonum* to the Persons. See, e.g., *Liber parabolorum Geneseos,* n. 12 (LW 1:483); and the *Expositio in Evangelium secundum Iohannem,* pars. 511–12, 516–18, 562 (LW 3:442–45, 446–48, 489–90). In at least one place, however, *unum* is ascribed to the essence and *ens-verum-bonum* is used of the three Persons (*Expositio in Evangelium secundum Iohannem,* pars. 359–60 [LW 3:304–6]).

27. *Expositio in Evangelium secundum Iohannem,* par. 438 (LW 3:376): "Dicimus et solemus dicere: iustus, in quantum iustus, est ipsa iustitia, facit opera iustitiae et similia. Li in quantum autem reduplicatio est; reduplicatio vero, sicut ipsum vocabulum testatur, dicit nexum et ordinem duorum; dicitur enim reduplicatio duorum replicatio, plica et nexus duorum. Sic spiritus, tertia in trinitate persona, nexus est duorum, patris et filii."

28. The reduplicating formula is found in both Eckhart and Cusa. In Cusa, e.g., see *De li non aliud* 5.18, which puts it this way: "Non aliud est non aliud quam non aliud" (see Jasper Hopkins, ed., *Nicholas of Cusa on God as Not-Other* [Minneapolis: University of Minnesota Press, 1979], 46). In Eckhart the *in quantum* principle is summarized thus in the Cologne

Defense: "Li 'in quantum,' reduplicatio scilicet, excludit omne aliud, omne alienum, etiam secundum rationem, a termino" (*Processus Coloniensis* I, n. 81 [LW 5:277]).

29. Sermo XI.2, n. 118 (LW 4:112): "Est enim unus sine trinitate, trinus sine unitate, sicut bonus sine qualitate," etc.

30. German sermon (Predigt) 10 (DW 1:173.1–12): "Ich predigete einest in latîne, und daz was an dem tage der drîvalticheit, dô sprach ich: der underscheit kumet von der einicheit, der underscheit in der drîvalticheit. Diu einicheit ist der underscheit, und der underscheit ist diu einicheit. Ie der underscheit mêr ist, ie diu einicheit mêr ist, wan daz ist underscheit âne underscheit. . . . Diu sêle hât ein vernünftic bekennelich wesen; dâ von, swâ got ist, dâ ist diu sêle, und swâ diu sêle ist, dâ ist got." The reference is not an exact fit with any particular passage in the surviving Latin Sermons for Trinity Sunday (II–IV), but the teaching is found in such passages as Sermo II, n. 14, and Sermo IV.1, n. 24 (LW 4:14 and 25). Similar passages can also found in Cusa, e.g., *De li non aliud* 5.18 (in *Nicholas of Cusa on God as Not-Other*, ed. Hopkins, 46): "Haec trinitas non sit aliud quam unitas, et unitas non sit aliud quam trinitas, quia tam trinitas quam unitas non sunt aliud quam simplex principium per 'non aliud' significatum."

31. R. W. Southern, *Platonism, Scholastic Method, and the School of Chartres*, Stenton Lecture for 1978 (Reading: University of Reading, 1979), 39.

32. A clear distinction between proper and appropriated trinitarian names is found in theologians like Thomas Aquinas, who adhered to a stricter demarcation between philosophy and theology, as well as a less absolute negative theology, than did Eckhart or Cusa. In thinkers like Eckhart and Cusa, however, apophatic exigence tends to fuse appropriation and property into the category of the useful metaphor. For insightful remarks on the theological location of Cusa's trinitarianism, see Haubst, *Das Bild*, 160.

33. It is interesting to note that in a late passage in the *De venatione sapientiae* 21.63 Cusa ascribes the triad to Augustine's *De trinitate* rather than to the *De doctrina christiana*.

For a list of Cusa's triadic formulas, see the appendix. There is also a listing in Eduard Zeller, *Cusanus-Konkordanz* (Munich: Hueber, 1960), 100–103, though my compilation expands on his.

34. The *De docta ignorantia*, written in 1439–40, does not mark the beginning of Cusa's knowledge of the triad *unitas-aequalitas–concordia/conexio*. For earlier uses, especially in the sermons, see Haubst, *Das Bild*, 42–49.

35. *De docta ignorantia* I.3.9 (ed. Wilpert, 12): "Quoniam ex se manifestum est infiniti ad finitum proportionem non esse, est et ex hoc clarissimum quod, ubi est reperire excedens et excessum, non deveniri ad maximum simpliciter, cum excedentia ex excessa finita sint." The conclusion of this argument was a position Cusa never backed away from: "Non potest igitur finitus intellectus rerum veritatem per similitudinem precise attingere" (ed. Wilpert, 13).

36. In his early works Cusa seems to say that the coincidence of opposites is where God is encountered, whereas in the later works the *coincidentia oppositorum* is better seen as the "limit situation" that allows *ratio* to transcend itself into the *intellectus*, which can attain the *visio Dei* that lies beyond the coincidence. See Werner Beierwaltes, "Deus Oppositio Oppositorum," *Salzburger Jahrbuch für Philosophie* 8 (1964): 175–85; and Donald F. Duclow, "Mystical Theology and Intellect in Nicholas of Cusa," *American Catholic Philosophical Quarterly* 64 (1990): 111–29. For a general account of the *coincidentia oppositorum* in Cusa, see Kurt Flasch, *Die Metaphysik des Einen bei Nikolaus von Kues* (Leiden: Brill, 1973), pt. 2.

37. The contrast among these three pairs of opposites—*unitas–alteritas/mutabilitas*,

equalitas-inequalitas and *conexio-divisio*—can also be found in Thierry of Chartres, e.g., *Commentum* 2.36–39, in *Commentaries on Boethius,* ed. Häring, 79–81.

38. *De docta ignorantia* I.7.21 (ed. Wilpert, 30): "Sed quia unitas aeterna est, aequalitas aeterna est, similiter et conexio, hinc unitas, aequalitas et conexio sunt unum. Et haec est illa trina unitas, quam Pythagoras, omnium philosophorum primus, Italiae et Graeciae decus, docuit adorandum." The reference to Pythagoras may come from the twelfth-century treatise known as the *De septem septennis* (PL 199:961C), which uses the Augustinian *unitas-aequalitas-conexio* in the context of a discussion of Pythagoras.

39. For example, Thierry, *Lectiones* 2.48 and 7.5–6, in *Commentaries on Boethius,* ed. Häring, 170, 224–25.

40. *De docta ignorantia* I.9.24 (ed. Wilpert, 32): "Neque enim conexio unius tantum est, sed ab unitate in aequalitatem unitatis [not *unitas* as in the text] procedit et ab unitatis aequalitate in unitatem."

41. Ibid., I.10.27 (ed. Wilpert, 36): "Maxima enim nequaquam recte intelligi poterit, si non intelligatur trina."

42. Ibid.: "Et tunc intelligitur, quando quodlibet in ipso uno intelligitur unum et ipsum unum omnia et per consequens quodlibet in ipso omnia."

43. Eckhart, *Lectiones et Sermones super Ecclesiastici,* n. 20 (LW 2:248). The axiom of *quodlibet esse in quolibet* was ascribed to Anaxagoras by Aristotle (*Physics* 1.4 [187b1]) and was often cited by Eckhart to indicate not mere physical interpenetration, as originally intended, but the dialectical coinherence of all things in God; see *Expositio in librum Exodi,* n. 16 (LW 2:22); *Expositio in librum Sapientiae,* n. 271 (LW 2:601); *Expositio in Evangelium secundum Iohannem,* n. 320 (LW 3:269); Sermo XXVII.2, n. 277, and XXX.1, n. 312 (LW 4:251 and 275).

44. Several other exempla are used: (1) *indivisio-discretio-conexio;* (2) *principium sine principio–principium a principio–processio ab utroque;* (3) *minimum-maximum-conexio* (1.10.28–29). In addition, *De docta ignorantia* 1.9.25 reformulates the basic triad in two related forms as: (4) *hoc-id-idem;* and (5) *unitas-iditas-identitas.* All of these formulations, with the exception of 1 and 3, have echoes in later discussions. See the appendix.

45. See *De septem septennis* (PL 199:961CD). *Eternitas* figures to some degree in the argument found in Thierry's *De sex dierum operibus* 30–47, in *Commentaries on Boethius,* ed. Häring 568.92–93, 570.42, 572.88–89 and 95, 574.57, 575.74. Since this text also names *alteritas-mutabilitas, inequalitas,* and *divisio* as the characteristics of created reality (see 568.86–88, 570.32, and 571.74), it may have been the ultimate source for Cusa's redeployment. See also *Commentum* 2.34, *Lectiones* 2.14, and *Glosa* 5.19–20, all , in *Commentaries on Boethius* (79, 159, and 297, respectively).

46. *Nicolai de Cusa De beryllo,* ed. J. G. Senger and C. Bormann, Nicolai de Cusa Opera omnia 11.1 (Hamburg: Meiner, 1988), no. 42 (48–49). On this shift in Cusa's thought, see F. Edward Cranz, "The Late Works of Nicholas of Cusa," *Nicholas of Cusa in Search of God and Wisdom,* ed. Christianson and Izbicki, 144–47.

47. These discussions include another major treatment: *De docta ignorantia* I.19.55–20.62 (ed. Wilpert, 72–82), considering the *aenigma* of the infinite triangle, which shows evidence of the use of Eckhart's Sermo IV on the Trinity in its employment of the dialectical language of indistinction and distinction. There are also two shorter considerations: (1) *De docta ignorantia* I.24.80–81 (ed. Wilpert, 102), treating *pater-filius–spiritus sanctus* under the category of affirmative theology; and (2) I.26.87–88 (ed. Wilpert, 110–11), which denies that any triad really belongs to God from the perspective of negative theology.

48. Ibid., II.7.130 (ed. Wilpert, 52): "Est igitur unitas universi trina, quoniam ex possi-

bilitate, necessitate complexionis et nexu, quae potentia, actus et nexus dici possunt." For these three terms, as well as the *quattuor modos universales essendi* that they imply, see Thierry of Chartres, *Lectiones* 2.9–14 in *Commentaries on Boethius,* ed. Häring, 157–59. For an extended treatment of this formula, see Haubst, *Das Bild,* 129–44.

49. For the definition of *coniectura* as *positiva assertio, in alteritate veritatis, uti est, participans,* see *Nicolai de Cusa De coniecturis,* ed. Josef Koch and Winfried Happ (Hamburg: Meiner, 1971), I.11.57 (66). For recent discussions of this work, see Clyde Lee Miller, "Nicholas of Cusa's *On Conjectures (De Coniecturis),*" in *Nicholas of Cusa in Search of God and Wisdom,* ed. Christianson and Izbicki, 119–40; and Wilhelm Dupré, "Absolute Truth and Conjectural Insight," in *Nicholas of Cusa on Christ and the Church: Essays in Memory of Chandler McCuskey Brooks for the American Cusanus Society,* ed. Gerald Christianson and Thomas M. Izbicki (Leiden: Brill, 1996), 323–38.

50. *De coniecturis* I.1.5 (ed. Koch and Happ, 8): "Ad cuius assimilationem tanto propinquius erigimur, quanto magis mentem nostram profundaverimus, cuius ipsa unicum vitale centrum exsistit." In one of his sermons, Cusa had cited a pseudo-Bernardine text to this effect: "Quantum in mei cognitione plus proficio, tantum in Deum proprius accedo" (cf. *Meditationes* 1 [PL 184:485]). See the discussion in Haubst, *Das Bild,* 34.

51. *De coniecturis* I.1.6 (ed. Koch and Happ, 8): "Quapropter unitas mentis in se omnem complicat multitudinem eiusque aequalitas omnem magnitudinem, sicut et conexio compositionem. Mens igitur unitrinum principium."

52. For the two expanded discussions on the trinitarian image in the soul, see ibid., I.2.9, and II.14.145 (ed. Koch and Happ, 12, 170–72).

53. Ibid., II.17.171 (ed. Koch and Happ, 202): "Humanitatem vero individualiter in alteritate contrahibilem alteritatem absolutioris esse unitatis."

54. Ibid., II.17.182 (ed. Koch and Happ, 214): "Ex te ipso igitur electiones deiformes intueri valebis. Nam conspicis deum, qui est infinita conexio, non ut contractum amabile aliquod diligendum, sed ut absolutissimum infinitum amorem. In eo igitur amore, quo deus diligitur, esse debet simplicissima unitas infinitaque iustitia. Necesse est igitur omnem amorem, quo deus amatur, minorem esse eo, quo amari potest. Cognoscis etiam hoc esse deum amare quod est amari a deo, cum deus sit caritas. Quanto igitur quis deum plus amaverit, tanto plus divinitatem participat."

55. See, esp., Eckhart, Sermo IV.1, n. 23–26 (LW 4:24–26).

56. Much has been written about this topic. See, e.g., the papers collected in *Das Sehen Gottes nach Nikolaus von Kues,* ed. Rudolf Haubst, Mitteilungen und Forschungsbeiträge der Cusanus-Gesellschaft 18 (Trier: Paulinus Verlag, 1989); and Alois M. Haas, *Deum mistice videre . . . in caligine coincidencie: Zum Verhältnis Nikolaus von Kues zur Mystik* (Basel-Frankfurt: Helbling, 1989). For more on my own view, see my "Seeing and Not-Seeing: Cusa's Place in the Western Mystical Tradition" (University of Chicago, Divinity School, 2003, typescript; forthcoming in a Cusa conference collection from Catholic University of America Press).

57. On the *De visione Dei,* see Jasper Hopkins, *Nicholas of Cusa's Dialectical Mysticism: Text, Translation, and Interpretive Study of De Visione Dei* (Minneapolis: Arthur Banning, 1985), as well as Clyde Lee Miller, "Nicholas of Cusa's *The Vision of God,*" in *An Introduction to the Medieval Mystics of Europe,* ed. Paul Szarmach (Albany: State University of New York Press, 1984), 293–312. See also Louis Dupré, "The Mystical Theology of Nicholas of Cusa's *De visione Dei,*" and Clyde Lee Miller, "God's Presence: Some Cusan Proposals"—both in *Nicholas of Cusa on Christ and the Church,* ed. Christianson and Izbicki, 205–20, 241–49, re-

spectively; and, esp., Michel de Certeau, "The Gaze of Nicholas of Cusa," *Diacritics: A Review of Contemporary Criticism* 3 (1987): 2–38.

58. *De visione* 17.75 (Hopkins, *Cusa's Dialectical Mysticism,* 204). This formulation certainly owes something to Augustine's exploration of the role of *amor* as a trinitarian analogy in *De trinitate* 8.5.14, and 9.1.2, but the stress on *non est autem infinitum multiplicabile* in line 10 suggests that Cusa must also have known Richard of St. Victor's discussion in his *De trinitate* 3.12–15. Another triad is briefly introduced in 18.82 (Hopkins, 216), one that goes back to the suggestion made in *De docta ignorantia* 1.10.28, the triad of God as *intellectus intelligens–intellectus intelligibilis–utriusque nexus.* There is a discussion of chap. 17 in Haubst, *Das Bild,* 79–81.

59. *Videre* and its forms appear thirty times in chap. 17 but only five times in chap. 18. *Videre* is used both in relation to seeing the trinal love that is God and seeing, or observing, our contracted form of this love. *Experior* and its equivalents (used three times) is only employed in relation to contracted love. Cusa contrasts *videre* with *concipere* in 17.76 and 78 (ed. Hopkins, 206.7–10, 208.5–6).

60. Regarding contracted human love, Cusa grants superiority to the self-love where we experience all three aspects—"Ego sum amans; ego sum amabilis; ego sum nexus" (17.79; ed. Hopkins, 210.1–15)—although not in an absolute manner. The love that goes forth to something outside, because it does not *necessarily* imply a response, is further from the *essentia amoris* (17.79; ed. Hopkins, 210.15–212.29).

On infinite divine mystery of paradise, see *De visione* 9.39 (ed. Hopkins, 160.7–11): "Et repperi locum, in quo revelate reperieris, cinctum contradictoriorum coincidentia. Et iste est murus paradisi in quo habitas, cuius portam custodit spiritus altissimus rationis, qui nisi vincatur, non patebit ingressus. Ultra igitur coincidentiam contradictoriorum videri poteris et nequaquam citra." On the *murus coincidentiae,* or *murus paradisi* image, see, among many studies, Rudolf Haubst, "Die erkenntnistheoretische und mystische Bedeutung der 'Mauer der Koinzidenz,'" *Mitteilungen und Forschungsbeiträge der Cusanus-Gesellschaft* 18 (1989): 167–95.

61. Union is the basic theme of chap. 20 where the language switches from the emphasis on seeing to that of *unio/uniri* (appearing thirteen times), which is seen as equivalent with *filiatio* (used six times). Here Cusa adopts the language of the soul as *sponsa,* also rare in his writings.

On the role of the spiritual senses, see *De visione* 17.80 (ed. Hopkins, 212.1–214.15).

62. Ibid., 17.80 (ed. Hopkins, 214.17–22): "Conatus sum me subicere raptui, confisus de infinita bonitate tua, ut viderem te invisibilem et visionem revelatam irrevelabilem. Quo autem perveni tu scis; ego autem nescio. Et sufficit mihi gratia tua, qua me certum reddis te incomprehensibilem esse, et erigis in spem firmam, quod ad fruitionem tui te duce perveniam." The passage is filled with verbal reminiscences of 2 Cor. 12:1–12, as well as Augustine's *Confessiones* 9.10. The passage, to be sure, is put in the mouth of the monk who is considering the implications of the omnivoyent, or all-seeing, icon, but some reference to Cusa himself cannot be totally excluded. For other mentions of *raptus,* see 16.74, 19.87 and 25.113 (ed. Hopkins, 202, 222, 266).

63. *De visione* 7.26 (ed. Hopkins, 144.13–146.16): "Immo quomodo dabis tu te mihi, si etiam me ipsum non dederis mihi? Et cum sic in silentio contemplationis quiesco, tu, domine, intra praecordia mea respondes dicens: 'Sis tu tuus et ego ero tuus.'" For insightful reflections on this theme, see Miller, "God's Presence: Some Cusan Proposals," 247–49.

64. There are brief comments in Haubst, *Das Bild*, 180–82 and 230–31. See also F. Edward Cranz, "The *De aequalitate* and the *De principio* of Nicholas of Cusa," in *Nicholas of Cusa on Christ and the Church*, ed. Christianson and Izbicki, 271–80.

65. For the *De aequalitate*, see the edition of Leo Gabriel in *Nikolaus von Kues: Philosophisch-Theologische Schriften* (Vienna: Herder, 1964), 3:358–416, citing by pages. The first discussion (366–68) uses the three equal *propositiones* of a syllogism in BARBARA as an analogy, while the second discussion (372–78) has a complex analysis of the three identical moments of *intemporale tempus in mente* developed out of Augustine's analysis of time in *Confessiones* 11. The third discussion is found at 386–408. At the end of this treatment, Cusa notes that all three are applications of *aequalitas* to the Trinity: "Et iuvo conceptum ex aequalitate, quam in tempore et anima et syllogismo praemisi."

66. See Augustine, *De trinitate* 9.3.3. For a treatment of this formula in Cusa's writings, esp. the sermons, see Haubst, *Das Bild*, 172–84.

67. *De aequalitate*, ed. Gabriel, 388–92.

68. Ibid., 392: "Cognoscit igitur verbum in se omnia, quia verbum patris, in quo pater et sese et omnia cognoscit."

69. For example, Augustine, *De trinitate* 15.12.22. For the role of the Augustinian *verbum interius* in the development of the trinitarian theology of Thomas Aquinas, see Bernard Lonergan, *Verbum: Word and Idea in Aquinas* (Notre Dame: University of Notre Dame, 1967), esp. the introduction (vii–xv).

70. *De aequalitate*, ed. Gabriel, 392–94: "Puta esto, quod intellectus loquentis sit absoluta aequalitas, verbum aequalitatis rationale, in quo se concipit, est conceptus simplex scilicet inalterabilis. . . . In eo conceptu seu verbo suam quidditatem intuetur aequalitas. . . . Tamen si aequalitas capitur pro absoluto inalterabili, omnem alteritatem praecedente in esse et posse, . . . tunc est aequalitas nomen primi aeterni principii."

71. Ibid., 396. Cusa at this point provides a brief description using *caritas* as the base term: "Ac si diceretur absoluta aequalitas est caritas. Est igitur caritas intellectualis de se generans conceptum essentiae suae, qui non potest esse nisi caritas caritatis, a quibus utique non potest nisi caritas, quae est utriusque nexus, procedere."

72. Ibid., 396–402.

73. Ibid., 402: "Et quamvis unitas videatur pater aequalitatis, quoniam aequalitas est semel sumpta unitas ut alibi habes, tamen aequalitas absoluta complicat unitatem. Id enim, quod est aequale, uno modo se habet."

74. Ibid., 404: "Si tuum in his exercitaveris intellectum et non ad vocabula, . . . multa praecisius semper prius tibi abscondita penetrabis. Nam id, quod de trinitate in sanctis scripturis et doctoribus ipsis [not *ipsas* as in the Gabriel edition] explanantibus legis, . . . utique dum ad dicta de aequalitate respicis melius et firmius fide capies."

75. The *De venatione sapientiae* contains a larger number of mentions of the Trinity, but the *De possest* text is the longest concerted investigation. For a discussion of the Trinity in the *De possest*, see Haubst, *Das Bild*, 250–54. For the *De possest*, I will use the edition of Jasper Hopkins as found in *A Concise Introduction to the Philosophy of Nicholas of Cusa* (Minneapolis: University of Minnesota Press, 1978), cited by section.

76. *De possest*, sec. 44 (Hopkins, *Philosophy of Nicholas of Cusa*, 112–14).

77. *De possest*, secs. 45–46 (Hopkins, *Philosophy of Nicholas of Cusa*, 114–16). Haubst, *Das Bild*, 252–54, uses this discussion to deny that Cusa has a conception of transcendental numbers like that found in Thomas Aquinas (e.g., *Summa theologiae* Ia,30,3). It seems to me that

Cusa does, indeed, have a role for transcendent numeration, but for him it expresses the *coincidentia oppositorum* and not the God who lies beyond the wall of coincidence.

78. *De possest,* sec. 50 (Hopkins, *Philosophy of Nicholas of Cusa,* 120): "Non enim unitas quae de deo dicitur est mathematica, sed est vera et viva omnia complicans."

79. These two illustrations (*aenigmata*) are as follows: (1) the *verbum abbreviatum,* i.e., three "minims" written as IN, where the *I* represents the *principium omnium,* while the *N* is the double, or equivalent *I,* and the juncture of the three in written form illustrates the *conexio* (*De possest,* secs. 54–56 [Hopkins, *Philosophy of Nicholas of Cusa,* 126–30]); and (2) the letter *E* considered as the *simplex vocalis unitrinus* when appearing in the formula *possE-Esse-nExus* (sec. 57, ed., 130–32). There is a brief discussion of these in Haubst, *Das Bild,* 302–4.

80. The formula *theos unitrinus* is found in another late treatise, the *De li non aliud* 23.105 (*Nicholas of Cusa on God as Not-Other,* ed. Hopkins, 132).

81. On the knowledge of the Trinity among the pagans and the role of faith, see Haubst, *Das Bild,* 304–12, and 327–31.

82. On the divine desert motif, see Bernard McGinn, "Ocean and Desert as Symbols of Mystical Absorption in the Christian Tradition," *Journal of Religion* 74 (1994): 155–81.

83. *De filiatione Dei* 4.73 (in *Nicolai de Cusa Opuscula,* vol. 1, ed. Paul Wilpert [Hamburg: Meiner, 1959], 54): "Omnia igitur quae effari possunt ineffabile non exprimunt, sed omnis elocutio ineffabile fatur."

Unmasking the Angel of Light: The Problem of Deception in Martin Luther and Teresa of Avila

SUSAN SCHREINER

In Reformation studies, interest in mysticism has been limited primarily to the study of the Radicals or to such topics as the influence of mysticism on Luther. However, an examination of central themes in sixteenth-century mysticism is crucial to understanding the age as a whole. This is because six-teenth-century mystical writings reflect those concerns so troubling to, and characteristic of, the entire Reformation era. Issues such as the drive toward the immediacy of experience, the concern with visions, the claim to the holy Spirit, and the desire for inner spiritual renewal are all mirrored among six-teenth-century mystics. But the mystical texts of this period also reveal a darker and more troubling side of sixteenth-century religion and attempts at reform. To date we have not paid sufficient attention to the ways in which mysticism also reflects such problematic issues as the adjudicating of experi-ential claims, detecting the role of the demonic, and that craving for certainty that haunted every aspect of early modern thought.

This essay explores the way in which the writings of people as diverse as Martin Luther and Saint Teresa of Avila reveal this overarching concern with certitude amid the demonic. But first some background is in order. To state the case much too broadly and briefly, the sixteenth-century Protestant and Catholic thinkers offered different forms of certainty. The mainline Protes-tant reformers expounded a doctrine of justification that promised the sub-jective or experiential certitude of salvation. Catholic opponents countered with a certainty based on visible authority; that is, the authority of the known, hierarchical, and centuries-old church. This church allowed the believer to know where the certainty of truth could be found. Most important, both sides claimed the Holy Spirit as the agent of certainty. Protestants described the Spirit as illuminating the heart and mind, thereby granting the certainty of salvation. The emergence of religious radicalism and the ongoing sacramental debates made this appeal to the Spirit very problematic. In response to this opposition, Protestants claimed the Spirit to authorize their biblical interpretation and thereby possess the certitude of authority. Catholics argued that unless one can know with certitude where the Spirit is, no one can claim any knowledge of truth. According to the Catholic argument, the Spirit is inseparable from the hierarchical church, a church that the Spirit has guided providentially for centuries. For Catholics, then, the questions of authority and ecclesiology (which were primarily questions of certitude) had to be answered before one could define doctrines of justification or of the sacraments. In addition to these debates, the collapse of traditional boundaries heightened the sixteenth-century concern with certainty. The interest in infinity from Cusa to Bruno, the impact of the Copernican hypothesis, and the colonialization of "New Spain" all raised the question of the certainty of human knowledge. Furthermore, the impact of historical thinking on the rise of skepticism intensified the struggle for certitude in the late sixteenth century.[1] We find in texts ranging from Luther through Shakespeare to Cervantes an apprehension about the difference between appearance, reality, and illusion. It is no wonder that many experienced this age as unsettling and disorienting. Stephen Greenblatt describes this feeling of disorientation as a feeling of "great unmooring," the sense that "fixed positions had become unstuck," and as an anxious awareness that the moral landscape was shifting. According to Greenblatt, religious polemicists demonstrated how "each other's religion—the very anchor of reality for millions of souls—was a cunning theatrical illusion, a demonic fantasy, a piece of poetry."[2] He concludes his analysis of Shakespeare's *Othello* by saying that this was a time when "truth itself is radically unstable."[3] The search for certainty was the natural reaction.

The underside of certainty, however, was the fear of deception, especially the horror of being deceived in matters concerning ultimate truth and salvation. Any number of figures could illustrate this issue but I have chosen only two very different thinkers: Martin Luther and Teresa of Avila. I have focused on these two thinkers because they stand as two very distant representatives of their age. One dates from the early sixteenth century and the other from late in that century. One was Protestant and the other was Catholic. Luther was learned in the theological tradition of the church. Teresa was not unlearned but knew no Latin. Both were reformers and both had to grapple with an era of division and turmoil. In their thought, we can detect a current that acts as an undertow to claims about certitude. Both thinkers betray an anxiety about the apparent "instability of truth," the feeling of "unmooring," and the ever-present fear of deception. Moreover, in these writers we see the certainty of truth authorized by the increasingly problematic appeal to experience. By juxtaposing these figures, who surprisingly share such common concerns, we are able to glimpse the pervasive presence of the sixteenth-century concern with certainty and deception.

Luther's thought is a classic example of how strident claims to certainty were fraught with a thoroughgoing concern with deception. From the outset, Luther's reform was challenged by various groups. Catholic opposition, the emergence of the religious radicalism, and the sacramental debates forced the question of deception to the forefront. In one form or another, all of his opponents asked the pointed question: "Are you alone wise?" As Eck wrote, "If the whole Scripture is so completely open, it is a wonder that the Holy Fathers who read it so frequently did not understand it for 1200 years, that if it was obscure to Augustine, Jerome, Bernard and Thomas, how will it be clear to Lutheran laymen?"[4]

In these questions, the issue of certainty and authority are clearly linked. To defend his own teaching, Luther had to account for the errors or deception of his opponents. An increasingly important explanation was that his enemies were diabolically inspired. Heiko A. Oberman and Mark U. Edwards have proven the centrality of demonology in Luther's theology and polemics.[5] His demonology also reveals the heart of his concern with deception. Moreover, Luther's demonology exactly paralleled his pneumatology. Just as the Holy Spirit was the agent of certitude, Satan was the agent of deception. The intensity of his preoccupation with the battle between certainty and deception is seen in his ardent fascination with the way in which Satan operated as the "father of lies."

To explain the method of Satan's deception, Luther tapped into a centuries-long teaching on the nature of evil. He explored the ancient insight that evil comes disguised as the good. The noble, sincere, religious, and pious appearance of evil gives the devil his seductive power to deceive. The literature of the desert fathers describes how the devil appeared to the saints as Christ.[6] So, too, Gerson began his 1401 treatise on discerning the spirits with the warning that Satan comes transformed as an angel of light. In so doing he was harkening back to book 12 of Augustine's *Literal Commentary on Genesis*. Repeatedly, Gerson tried to give criteria for distinguishing true from false visions so that one would not be deceived by the angelic-looking devil. As McGinn has shown, Satan's impersonation of Christ dominated the depictions of the Antichrist.[7] The biblical inspiration for the latter was 2 Thess. 9–12: "The coming of the lawless one by the activity of Satan will be with all power and with pretended signs and wonders, all wicked deception for those about to perish . . . God sends upon them a strong delusion to make them believe what is false" (RSV).

Luther was deeply affected by this biblical belief that God sends delusions by making evil mimic the good. He culled a series of verses to elaborate on this theme, including 2 Cor. 4:4: "The god of this world has blinded the minds of the unbelievers to keep them from seeing the light of the glory of Christ," and Gal. 3:1: "Who has bewitched you so that you do not obey the truth?" (Luther's translation). But no verse captivated Luther more than 2 Cor.11: 14: "For even Satan disguises himself as an angel of light." In this latter verse Luther found the perfect explanation for the effectiveness of Satan. According to Luther, Satan "puts on a most beautiful appearance," when he "captivates," "bewitches," "blinds," and "beguiles" the mind. Satan "dazzles" through "lovely thoughts and words" and gives the convincing appearance of wisdom and goodness. The devil is the "master of dissimulation, disguise, and pretense."[8]

Luther exploited this insight by arguing that Satan's effectiveness revolved around hiddenness. Scholars have long recognized the centrality of divine hiddenness in Luther's thought. But for Luther, an equally important counterpart to the hiddenness of God was the hiddenness of Satan. By transforming himself into an angel of light, the devil, like God, hides under a contrary; namely, by hiding under the appearance of holiness, truth, zeal, and faith. Satan can even appear as Christ himself. "The devil," Luther said, "so clothes and adorns himself with Christ's name and works and can pose and act in such a way that one could swear a thousand oaths that it is truly Christ himself, although in reality it is the Archenemy and the true Archantichrist." This Archenemy quoted Scripture, "under the guise and the name of Christ."[9] The devil "taught God, Christ, the Holy Spirit and Christendom."[10] Satan instructed about the sacraments and could inspire a life of good works. This "white devil" counseled people to trust the church of the apostles and the holy Fathers.[11] Luther insisted "the devil always adorns himself with such an angelic, yes such a divine form and appearance." The devil always "appears in the disguise of an angel of light and adorns his murdering with the beautiful trappings that are called piety and the worship of God."[12] The devil, Luther concluded, "insinuates himself into our hearts, not as one who is evil and false but as one who is good and the best, as an angel of light."[13]

Luther was keenly aware that the sin in deception was not primarily an act of will but, rather, was a noetic failure. He argued that although his opponents honestly believed they were inspired by the Spirit, they were, in reality, inspired by the devil. The Catholics and the "false brethren" did not simply refuse to understand; they were unable to understand. The Gospel of John explained why the whole world was wrong and he, Luther, alone seemed to be wise. Christ had foretold that the world "cannot understand" because it does not have the "Spirit of Truth." The "multitude" was incapable of recognizing the truth because, Luther said, they were under a "spell" in a "satanic illusion," in a "dream," under a "bewitchment of the spirit," and suffering from "spiritual blindness or madness."[14] Luther believed that humanity was locked into a world of satanic deception that seemed all too real. The "bewitchment of the spirit" even extended to a real but delusional certitude: "Nowadays [the ancient serpent] is showing his ability to do this in the fanatics, the Anabaptists and the Sacramentarians. With his tricks, he has so bewitched their minds that they are embracing lies, errors and horrible darkness as the most certain truth and the clearest light. . . . [The devil] works internally with plausible opinions and ideas about doctrine, by which, as I have said, he so dements the hearts of men that they would swear that their most vain and wicked dreams are the most certain truth.[15]" In Luther's view, the devil creates a world that is the mirror image of the truth. The hiddenness of God and the hiddenness of Satan are locked into a deadly contest between the real and the counterfeit. The individual is immersed in an illusion that seems more real than the truth. In Luther's frequent use of 2 Cor. 11:14 ("for even Satan disguises himself as an angel of light"), the world becomes a nightmare of mimicry, illusions, and deceptions that skillfully masquerade as reality. Evil parodies the good so authentically that all claims to certitude fall into a demonic perceptual chaos. To make matters worse, Luther depicts the paradoxical nature of God and Satan as they appear under the hiddenness of their contraries. Both God and Satan wear masks. The following passage illustrates dramatically that when the hiddenness of God confronts the hiddenness of Satan, the world becomes a tragic shadow play where the line between deception and reality, bewitchment and sight, truth and lies, threatens to disappear:

> God's faithfulness and truth always must first become a great lie before it becomes truth. The world calls this truth heresy. And we, too, are constantly tempted to believe that God would abandon us and not keep His Word; and in our hearts He begins to become a liar. In short, God cannot be God unless He first becomes a devil. . . . We cannot become God's children until we first become children of the devil. All that God speaks and does, the devil has to speak and do first. . . . Therefore it is actually the Spirit who enlightens and teaches us in the Word to believe differently. By the same token the lies of this world cannot become lies without first having become truth. . . . To summarize, the devil does not become and is not a

devil without having first been God. He does not become an angel of darkness un-less he has first been angel of light (2Cor. 11:14). For what the devil speaks and does must first have been said and done by God. . . . .I also know the devil's word must first become the delicate truth of God before it can become a lie. I must grant the devil his hour of godliness and ascribe the Satanic to our God.[16]

Luther delighted in this paradoxical description of reality. As a result he had to lay great stress on the "testing of the spirits." Luther's teaching of justifi-cation by faith did succeed in taking the burden of salvation off the back of the Christian. However, because of the subsequent crisis of authority, Luther left the believer with the heavy responsibility of discerning truth from false-hood and God from the demonic angel of light. This burden laid heavily on one surrounded by competing and conflicting claims to the illumination of the Spirit. Not surprisingly, 1 John 4:1 ("Beloved, do not believe every spirit, but test the spirits to see whether they are of God") took on an urgency in Luther's thought that reveals the crises of authority and certainty of his time. He continually warned his readers "we must be on our guard against the devil who can pose and masquerade in the form and name of Christ." The faithful had to unmask Satan of his angelic garb and reveal him as the devil.[17] To "test the spirits," was to plunge the believer into the battlefield between the Spirit of Truth and the Father of Lies. This testing required a depth of spiritual ex-perience and perception that could safely distinguish between these two op-ponents and thereby could choose salvation over damnation.

The necessity of detecting the demonic or testing the spirits became only more urgent in the course of the sixteenth century. The importance of dis-cerning between the spirits brings us also to the core of Teresa of Avila's writ-ings. But first, as Rowan Williams has shown, Teresa's theology cannot be un-derstood unless we see her as a "displaced person." As a woman, as a person of Jewish descent, as one who claimed ecstatic experiences and the authority to instruct, Teresa stood well outside the traditional hierarchical circles of le-gitimacy in the Spain of her day.[18] Teresa had to seek authority for her spiri-tual teachings in ways similar to the excommunicated Luther.

Teresa lived at a time when the fear of novelty, mysticism, and spiritualism had permeated Spanish society. She inherited the growing suspicion of the church and the Inquisition toward holy women, teaching in the vernacular, lay spirituality, and visionary experiences.[19] In particular, Teresa was vulnera-ble to the charge of *alumbradismo*. Although it is still problematic to speak of a unified doctrine of the *alumbrados,* certain teachings were identified with this group. These ideas included the technique of recollection (*recogimiento,* initiated by the Franciscans), the passive abandonment (*dejamiento*) of one's will to God, the despising of vocal prayer and an emphasis on only mental prayer, the state of quiet (*quietud*) or stillness of the soul, the private reading and teaching of Scripture, the inability to err, sinlessness and antinomianism, the stress on the love of God, and, for some, a desire for ecstatic experiences.

The investigation and trials of the *alumbrados* exemplified the larger concern of the Inquisition; namely, concerns about the flourishing of lay spirituality, claims to personal revelations, criticisms of the church, and the emphasis on individual unmediated access to God in prayer. These claims necessitated ecclesiastical control over ideas and experiences. Spirituality had to be reigned in and supervised. The 1559 Valdez Index prohibited almost all books on prayer and vernacular spiritual treatises.

The overarching problem was the preoccupation with experience, principally the authority being vested in personal or individual experience. The *alumbrados* were a part of that larger atmosphere shared by spiritualism, Italian evangelism, and radicalism that stressed the authority of the Spirit as experienced by the individual soul. As Alcaraz stated, "A saint says he whose knowledge is infused speaks as a man of experience, like one who has tasted honey and says it is sweet. He who has not tasted of it says it is sweet but he only has tasted it through knowledge. This is the difference between men."[20] Just as Luther was vulnerable to the charge of thinking he alone was wise, Teresa was vulnerable to the charge of *alumbradismo*. She claimed intimacy and union with God. She wrote of the presence of Christ in the interior depth of the soul. She spoke about passive contemplation (although, unlike Francisco de Osuna she denied that recollection and emptying could be achieved by human effort). She prized mental prayer and tried to demystify it by teaching that it was available to everyone. She also described her visions, raptures, locutions, and even levitations. Above all else, Teresa authorized her teaching declaring that "I can speak of what I have experience [*experiencia*] of."[21] Although she insisted on learned confessors, she continually struggled with those who feared or misjudged spiritual experiences: "And so many are wrong, as I said, in wanting to discern the spirits without having experience. I don't say that anyone who has not had spiritual experiences, provided he is a learned man, should not guide someone who has [had such experiences]. . . . He shouldn't kill himself or think that he understands what he doesn't, or suppress the spirit, for now in respect to the spirit, another greater Lord governs them; they are not without a Superior."[22] Like Luther, therefore, Teresa had to defend her authority. She was determined to distance herself from the *alumbrados*. Her quest for authority went beyond the issue of her gender. *The Book of Her Life* was composed with the apologetic purpose of showing that she could not be an *alumbrada* enthusiast as well as of ending any suspicions that her source of inspiration might be demonic. Nonetheless, Teresa's claim of legitimate authority and orthodoxy never blinded her to the ever present and real danger of deception. She knew that deception was a spiritual reality that one must always guard against. She never asserted the inability to err; on the contrary, she vividly recalled her own deceptions and walked warily lest she be deceived again. Teresa's main concern was to analyze the different stages of prayer, but in doing so she was equally anxious to warn about the deceptions that endangered the soul at every level. In her explanation of the Lord's prayer, Teresa interpreted the phrase "lead us not into temptation but deliver us from evil" to mean that one is praying to be delivered from deception.[23] Teresa's most commonly repeated prayer was that God protect against delusions. "Oh my Lord!" she prayed, "In your mercy do not consent to allow this soul to suffer deception. . . . Send light from the heavens, my Lord, that I might be able to enlighten these your servants . . . so that they might not be deceived by the devil transforming himself into an angel of light."[24]

Teresa knew that the most dangerous deceptions were caused by the devil. As did Luther, Teresa saw the devil's power in his ability to disguise himself; 2 Cor. 11:14 was once again the verse most commonly cited to explain the seductive power of Satan: "Believe, sisters, that the soldiers of Christ, those who experience contemplation and engage in prayer are eager to fight. . . . Those whom they fear . . . are the traitorous enemies, the devils who transfigure themselves into angels of light, who come disguised. Not until they have done much harm to the soul do they allow themselves to be recognized."[25] In *The Book of Her Life,* Teresa explained the deceptions that occur as one begins to receive supernatural gifts by saying: "It is always good that we walk with fear and caution. For, although the work may be from God, the devil at times can transform himself into an angel of light; and if the soul has not a great deal of experience, it will not discern the devil's work—and in fact, it must have so much experience that it needs to come close to the very summit of prayer to have such discernment."[26] Repeatedly, Teresa warned her readers not to let down their guard. As she said, "There are no enclosures so fenced in that the devil cannot enter." Teresa counseled always to "walk in fear" and "mark danger everywhere."[27] She cautioned that "we not grow careless in recognizing the wiles of the devil, and that we not be deceived by his changing himself into an angel of light. . . . He enters little by little, and until he has done the harm, we don't recognize him."[28]

Teresa's main anxiety was this inability to recognize the devil. Like Luther, Teresa also explained the diabolical transformation that took place when Satan "counterfeits [*contrahacer*] the spirit of light," "comes under the color of good," and feigns the gifts of God.[29] The devil can simulate almost all divine gifts. Hearing voices is dangerous and should always be validated by a confessor because of the devil's ability to mimic God's words. Satan meddles more in imaginative than in intellectual visions. The devil can create false peace, consolations, tears, visions, and locutions. The devil can even intrude on authentic spiritual gifts. He once made Teresa believe that a true vision of Christ was really diabolical in origin.[30]

Convinced that fallen humanity was the constant prey of demonic deceptions, both Teresa and Luther were then compelled to explain how one was to discern or to test the spirits. In so doing, they stood in a long line of thinkers who formulated criteria for the deception of false spirits and visions. To warn about the devil was not sufficient; the believer had to have signs to avoid Satan at every turn. Both Luther and Teresa tried to formulate objective and external standards by which they protected their teaching. However, in the end both relied primarily on the experience of certainty.

Against what he perceived to be an unconstrained spiritualism, Luther articulated certain supposedly objective standards: his theology of Word and Spirit, the necessity for a proper call, and his role as a Doctor of Holy Scripture.[31] The most familiar objective standard was, of course, conformity to the Word. Recognizing that everyone was claiming the Spirit, Luther argued that a doctrine must be tested: "If I see that it agrees with the words of Christ, I consider it true and good. But if it deviates . . . I declare, 'You are not the Holy Spirit; you are the devil.'"[32] But Luther knew it really was not that easy. His opponents not only claimed the Spirit, but they, too, argued on the basis of Scripture. The ancient insight was true: heretics and Satan always quote Scripture. The devil, Luther said, "tries to conjure up his phantoms. . . . First he employs all his craft and cunning to beguile the people. This he does with the very words of Holy Writ and under the guise of the name of Christ. Thus, all the schismatic spirits and heretics come clad in sheep's clothing; they use the same word, manner and mien, as though they were the true teachers of this way. They exalt nothing but Christ's honor and faith in Christ."[33]

Luther, of course, endlessly repeated his principle that all doctrine must be measured according to Scripture. Nevertheless, opposition on all fronts forced him to turn elsewhere to find a sure means for discerning deception. By following him, we arrive at the deeper core of Luther's struggle to test the spirits. Here we find recourse to a more subjective and clearly experiential language. The Spirit, Luther explained, effects a change within the believer, primarily a change in perception. The heart and the mind are renewed so that the believer possesses "spiritual insight." The so-called vision of the Spirit can undo the "spiritual witchcraft" of the devil. This spiritual renewal creates "the spiritual man who judges all things," described in 1 Cor. 2:15.[34] Moreover, this new spiritual insight grants subjective certainty in both the certitude of salvation and the certitude of authority. At this point, the affective language used to describe the subjective certitude of salvation is now applied by Luther to the certitude of authority:

> Through the spoken Word we receive fire and light, by which we are made new and different, and by which a new judgment, new sensations, and new drives arise in us. This change and new judgment are not the work of human reason or power; they are the gift and accomplishment of the Holy Spirit. . . . Therefore there is the greatest possible difference between us and the enemies and perverters of the Word: We, by the grace of God, are able to declare and judge with certainty, on the basis of the Word, about the will of God toward us, about all laws and doctrines, about our own lives and those of others . . . the papists and the fanatical spirits are unable to judge with certainty about anything. . . . In opposition to this perverse judgment of the world [which says that we are possessed by the devil] let us be satisfied with the testimony of our conscience, by which we know with certainty that it is a divine gift when we not only believe in Jesus Christ but proclaim and confess Him.[35]

Relying on John 16:13, Luther reiterates that the Holy Spirit is the "Spirit of Truth." In Luther's thought the Spirit is, above all else, "reliable." For Luther this meant that when one receives the true Spirit, he is given both the truth and the experiential certainty of that truth. Therefore, Luther explained, the Spirit makes the individual "certain and convinced of the truth."[36] The Spirit, Luther promised, "will confer the doctorate on you and call you doctors and masters who can determine with certainty what is a true and false doctrine in Christendom. . . . [The Spirit] will also make our faith certain, remove all doubt and enable us to judge all other spirits."[37]

The true Spirit is also the "Comforter" depicted in John 16:7. At this juncture Luther leads his reader directly to the examination of different spiritual experiences in order to "test the spirits." If the spirit is satanic, there is no comfort and the individual feels inward terror and sadness. The devil inwardly harasses and disquiets the soul, kills troubled consciences, and brings despair. The "experienced person," however, can recognize the devil by these feelings and thereby say: "'This is not my Lord, Christ; it is His enemy, the devil.' He indeed deceives pious hearts by disguising himself as, an angel of light (2 Cor. 11:14) . . . and pretends to be, Christ Himself. But this is the label which identifies him: he invariably leaves his stench behind him, that is, a faint, fearful, and disquieted conscience. . . . He delights in making hearts afraid, cowardly, and dejected."[38] Most important, the demonic spirit threatens damnation. Like Teresa, Luther interpreted the phrase "lead us not into temptation" as meaning a prayer not to be led into the deception of Satan.[39] For Luther, the ultimate deception was not a false vision or voice but doubt about one's salvation. Using the law and reminding the conscience of sin, the devil tempts and "bewitches" the believer with thoughts of God's continuing wrath, accusation, damnation.[40] There was no room in Luther's theology for the "pious doubt" of Catholicism. Rather, Luther tested the spirits by demonizing doubt; fear about salvation was now a satanic temptation.[41]

As the comforter, the Spirit erases doubt and leaves the inward feelings of "peace," "security," "courage," and "joy." But lest we believe that this feeling of peace and consolation is an irrefutable test of the spirits, Luther's attack on the antinomians warns against seeing Christ as one who consoles the conscience. Once again, the search for certitude is confounded by the ambivalent nature of experience. Nonetheless, Luther repeatedly insisted that the Son of man entered the world "to destroy doubt" about one's salvation.[42] To test the spirits, therefore, was to engage in the experiential battle between doubt and certainty.[43] For Luther, several verses described the victory of experiential certitude. John 14:20 ("In that day you will know that I am in My Father, and you are in Me and I in you") describes a union or merger between the believer and Christ that creates inner experiential certitude. Hence Luther wrote, "You will learn through the Holy Spirit and through your own experience that I am in the Father, that you are in Me and I in you and that we will always be closely united." Even more crucial was Gal. 4:6 ("And because you are sons, God has sent the Spirit of His Son into your hearts, crying 'Abba Father!'"). The term "Father" became a critical perceptual and polemical term for Luther; to see God as a Father (i.e., merciful) could not be the work of natural reason. Only faith creates this perception and is, therefore, evidence of the Spirit. Moreover, the ability to cry "Abba Father!" is testimony to an inner certainty that belongs only to the saved. The following passage is worth quoting in full because it demonstrates the centrality of certainty in Luther's thought:

> Therefore we should strive daily to move more and more from uncertainty to certainty; and we should make an effort to wipe out completely that wicked idea which has consumed the entire world, namely, that a man does not know whether he is in a state of grace. For if we are in doubt about our being in a state of grace and about our being pleasing to God for the sake of Christ, we are denying that Christ has redeemed us. . . .

Let us thank God, therefore, that we have been delivered from this monster of uncertainty and that now we can believe with certainty that the Holy Spirit is crying and issuing that sigh too deep for words in our hearts. . . .

Now that the plague of uncertainty, with which the entire church of the pope is infected, is driven away, let us believe with certainty that God is favorably disposed toward us, that we are pleasing to Him and of concern to Him on account of Christ . . . and that we have the Holy Spirit, who intercedes for us with a crying and a sighing too deep for words."[44]

Luther was irresistibly drawn to the experiential, affective language of interiority and immediacy in order to describe the certitude of the Spirit. Hence he spoke of a "feeling," "tasting," "sweetening," and "experiencing" in the heart of the believer. That which defeats doubt and instills assurance is an inner "feeling" or "experience" inspired by the Spirit. Luther continually spoke of the "experienced Christian" and of a faith that had to "make progress in experience."[45] This progress is precisely the growing experience of certitude. As stated above, "Therefore we should strive daily to move more and more from uncertainty to certainty."[46] Frequently, Luther depicted this progress in terms of a spiritual battle of conflicted experiences within the soul. The believer "feels" the temptations of the devil as well as the comfort of Christ. In fact, Luther said, "It is indeed a real Christian art to distinguish in the heat of battle between the suggestions of Christ and those of the devil. Only one who is experienced will realize the difficulty."[47] In the midst of this conflict the Christian must not judge according to his "own feelings" of sin but cling to the growing experience of certainty:

But the devil . . . assails and hinders us on all sides, in an attempt to check and obstruct the Word. At this point experience must enter in and enable a Christian to say: "To this point I have heard that Christ is my Savior, who conquered sin and death; and I believed this. Now my experience bears this out. . . . Now I see and know that He loves me. . . . Such experience makes a genuine and perfect man. . . . They [believers] thus experience that they are genuine Christians. Such experience engenders a sure hope which does not doubt that they are God's children and belong to Him."[48]

According to Luther, the person "trained by experience" emerges from the battle between the spirits with that internal certainty that only the true Spirit can give. To explain what the Christian must do in these periods of temptation, Luther marshaled all the language of experience and interiority at his disposal. The believer must "creep" to Christ in order to be completely "merged into [Christ]" and thereby "feel this comforting confidence and assurance." The believer must "lay hold" and "cling" to Christ and "experience" the Spirit of certitude "within the soul." Those who endure such trials finally "feel and experience peace." The Holy Spirit grants the experience that "sin, death and the devil" have been defeated.[49] Only these inner experiences and feelings of trial and combat cause the individual to experience inwardly "that he is a true and genuine Christian." Because one is "within Christ" and Christ is "within the heart," the justified person feels the certainty of being in a state of grace and can fight off the inner feelings of doubt and despair caused by Satan. The Spirit, then, inspires feelings of security, fearlessness, comfort, confidence, assurance, and, of course, certainty. In the end, therefore, Luther's ultimate criterion for 'testing the spirits" became the experience of certitude itself.

Teresa also searched for ways to distinguish the divine from the demonic. She, too, sought external standards. Conforming to the Church and to Scripture keeps the soul safe. And regardless of how problematic the concept of obedience is for Teresa, she nevertheless insists that conformity to the Church keeps one safe. Obeying the Lord is "the complete remedy against deception."[50] But like Luther, Teresa soon moved to experiential criteria. She flirted with the idea of the certainty of salvation but never adopted it. She continually emphasized the protection provided by humility.[51] The humble are much less likely to be deceived by the grandiose spiritual fabrications of the devil. However, Teresa also admitted that Satan could create a false humility in the soul.[52] Finally Teresa took the same step as Luther by arguing the spirits could be discerned by their experiential effects. In fact, Teresa cannot praise experience enough. She explained that only the person who had "long experience" could recognize the marks of satanic illusions.[53] The devil leaves the soul in spiritual dryness, disquiet, agitation, affliction, turbulence, and restlessness. The content of the delusion was not really the decisive issue because the devil could appear as an angel of light. The disturbing effects left in the soul, however, betray the demonic origin of the experience.[54]

A true spiritual experience can be judged as genuine by feelings within the soul that the devil cannot counterfeit. The divine spirit produces quiet, consolation, calm, clarity, assurance, virtue, and security.[55] Nonetheless, complicating the issue, Teresa also admitted that just as the devil can produce false humility, he could also create a false quiet, consolation, and vision.[56] And so Teresa continually struggled to find the definitive test of the spirits.[57] The most commonly cited proof for the authenticity of spiritual experience was, once again, the experience of certainty. As did Luther, Teresa specified certainty itself as the ultimate test. She explained repeatedly that after a true vision or locution she could "in no way doubt" that it was from God.[58] Teresa seems to argue that the soul should try to doubt the experience, try to convince itself that the experience is a deception. If that doubt cannot be sustained, then the experience is divine, "because of a certitude remaining in the soul that only God can put there." True spiritual experiences leave "a certitude so strong that an assurance is left that cannot be overcome."[59] In these experiences certainty literally triumphs over doubt.

The closer one travels to the sixth and seventh dwellings, the center of the soul or Interior Castle where Christ lives, the more certainty one feels. This part of the spiritual journey is definitely a journey toward an always-increasing certainty. Speaking of the prayer of union, Teresa said, "whoever does not receive this certitude does not experience union of the whole soul with God."[60] In the sixth dwelling, God bestows the intellectual vision that is "so certain and leaves us so much certitude . . . because in visions that come through the senses one can be deceived but not in the intellectual [vision]." With the intellectual vision, there "remains such great certitude that doubt has no force." In this intellectual vision, Teresa said, "True Wisdom has taken away the mind's dullness and leaves a certitude which lasts for some time, a certitude that this favor *is* from God."[61] Nevertheless, Teresa admitted, the spiritual battle between certainty and doubt can follow an intellectual vision. The devil can later "stir up doubts" that can shake the certitude of the soul. Still, Teresa insisted that "the more the devil fights against that certitude, the more certain the soul is that the devil could not have left it with so many blessings . . . for he cannot do so much in the interior of the soul."[62]

As one proceeds deeper into the soul's center, the closer one gets to the unassailable clarity and certainty of truth. In the final seventh dwelling of the Interior Castle, the Lord appears, the soul is made one with God, and the spiritual marriage takes place. The soul finally understands the deepest mysteries "in God himself." At this point the soul encounters Truth itself. "This truth," Teresa wrote, "which I say was given to my understanding, is in itself truth and it is without beginning or end; all other truths depend upon this truth."[63] The prayer "lead us not into temptation" is finally answered because the soul is delivered from deception. At this level the soul does not need to fear deception precisely because the devil cannot work here. "His majesty," Teresa explained, "communicates Himself in other ways that are more sublime and less dangerous because the devil, I believe, will be unable to counterfeit them."[64] She continued by saying that "the devil, in my opinion, and even one's own imagination, have little capacity at this level, and so the soul is left with profound satisfaction."[65] Finally, she concluded, "the soul is almost always in quiet. There is no fear that this sublime favor can be counterfeited by the devil but the soul is completely certain that the favor comes from God. His majesty reveals Himself to the soul and brings it to Himself in that place where, in my opinion, the devil will not dare enter, nor will the Lord allow him to enter."[66]

If these arguments about certainty seem circular, it might be reassuring to know that Inquisitors and polemicists such as Thomas More thought so too. The reliance on spiritual effects hardly seems helpful since the devil also can create quiet, consolations, visions, and even certitude itself. The fact that the devil always comes as "an angel of light" makes both the content and the spiritual experience itself a less than a reliable criterion. Most troubling, of course, is that in the end certainty guaranteed certainty. In his *Response to Luther,* Thomas More caricatured Luther's claim to certainty in a way that could apply to many sixteenth-century thinkers, including Teresa:

> By what reason, father, do you prove that you alone must be believed?
> Because I am certain, he says, that I have my teachings from heaven.
> By what means are you certain that you have your teachings from heaven?
> Because God has seized me unawares, he said, and carried me into the midst
>   of these turmoils?
> How do you know that God has seized you?
> Because I am certain, he says, that my teaching is from God.
> How do you know that?
> Because God has seized me.
> How do you know this?
> Because I am certain.
> How are you certain?
> Because I know.
> But how do you know?
> Because I am certain.[67]

The reader cannot help feeling sympathy with More's frustration. But the very circular, dizzying, and sometimes contradictory nature of the arguments only demonstrate the intensity of the problem. Both Luther and Teresa stand as symbols from the beginning and the end of this turbulent century. As symbols they represent and illuminate the sixteenth-century search for competing certainties: the certainty of salvation, the certainty of the Spirit, the certainty of the true church, the certainty of authority, the certainty of scriptural interpretation and doctrine, the certainty of the Spirit, and the certainty of mystical experience. In the midst of these many claims for certitude, both

Luther and Teresa were forced to confront the underside of the craving for certainty, namely, the threat of deception, particularly demonic delusion. The fact that both figures interpreted the prayer "lead us not into temptation" to mean "lead us not into deception" proves the centrality of this problem. In trying to extricate themselves from Satan's grasp, they tried to unmask the angel of light and thereby free themselves from the ever-present danger of deception. It was a problem they shared with their time. They grappled with the dilemma whose shadow even haunted Hamlet about the Ghost: "The spirit that I have seen may be the devil; and the devil hath power to assume a pleasing shape." Nonetheless, the certainty Luther and Teresa sought, and so insistently proclaimed, continued to be an uneasy and elusive certitude that never fully defeated the fear of deception and doubt, a fear that only continued to haunt subsequent generations.

Notes

1. Zachary Schiffman, *The Threshold of Modernity* (Baltimore: John Hopkins University Press, 1991).

2. Stephen Greenblatt, *Renaissance Self-Fashioning from More to Shakespeare* (Chicago: University of Chicago Press, 1980), 88, 113, 219.

3. Ibid., 254.

4. Johannes Eck, *Enchiridion locorum communium,* ed. P. Fraenkel, Corpus Catholicorum, vol. 34 (Münster: Aschendorff, 1979), IV.2. This question haunted Luther his entire life as is clear from his self-identification with Noah in his 1535 commentary on Genesis. Just as he, Luther, was assailed by the question, "Do you think that all the fathers were in error?" so, too, Noah was attacked by his generation. Noah also faced the question, "Is it you alone who is wise. . . Are all the rest of us in error. . . . Is it you alone who is not in error? Is it you alone who will not be condemned?"

5. Heiko A. Oberman, *Luther: Man between God and the Devil* (New Haven, Conn.: Yale University Press, 1992); Mark U. Edwards, *Luther and the False Brethren* (Stanford, Calif.: Stanford University Press, 1975), and *Luther's Last Battles* (Ithaca, N.Y.: Cornell University Press, 1983), 97–142.

6. Paschal Boland, O.S.B., S.T.L., *The Concept of Discretio spirituum in Jean Gerson's "De probatione spirituum" and "De distinctione verarum visionum a falsis,"* Catholic University of America Studies in Sacred Theology, 2d ser.; no. 112 (Washington D.C.: Catholic University of America Press, 1959), 117–18. For Gerson's works on this topic, see: Jean Gerson, *Oeuvres completes de Jean Gerson,* ed. Palémon Glorieux (Paris: Desclée, 1960). The treatise *De distinctione verarum visionum a falsis* is found in vol. 3. The treatise *De probatione spirituum* is found in vol. 9. For a thorough treatment of Gerson and other late-medieval thinkers on the discretion of the spirits, see Wendy Love Anderson, "Free Spirits, Presumptuous Women, and False Prophets: The Discernment of the Spirits in the Late Middle Ages" (Ph.D. diss., University of Chicago, 2002). See also Bernard McGinn, "Visions and Critiques of Visions in Thirteenth-Century Mysticism," in *Rending the Veil: Concealment and Secrecy in the History of Religions,* ed. Elliot Wolfson (New York: Seven Bridges Press, 1998).

7. Bernard McGinn, *AntiChrist: Two Thousand Years of the Human Fascination with Evil* (New York: HarperCollins, 1994).

8. *D. Martin Luthers Werke: Kritische Gesamtausgabe (Weimarer Ausgabe)*, ed. J. C. F. Knaake et al. (Weimar: H. Böhlaus Nachfolger, 1883–), 19.599.4–14, hereafter *WA; Luther's Works*, ed. Jaroslav Pelikan and Helmut T. Lehmann, 55 vols. (St. Louis: Concordia Publishing House; Philadelphia: Fortress Press, 1955–), 14:261, hereafter *LW*, and *On the Councils and the Church*, *LW* 41:85; *WA* 19.599.10–15.

9. *WA* 45.503.5–8; *LW* 24:46.

10. *WA* 45.503.2–11; *WA* 45.577.8–9; *LW* 24:46, 127

11. *WA* 40/1. 96.131, 130.32–131.20; *LW* 26:41, 65.

12. *WA* 46.14.9–10; *LW* 24:313.

13. *WA* 20.649.25–27.

14. *WA* 40/1.316.21–317.2; 319.19–320.24; 321.17–322.21; *WA* 45.716.9–15; *LW* 26:192, 194, 197–98; *LW* 24:280.

15. *WA* 40.316.26–29, 317.1–20; *LW* 26:192.

16. *WA* 31. 249.25–250.10; *LW* 14:31–32.

17. *WA* 46.13.17–18; *LW* 24:312. In the same passage Luther wrote, "Therefore we must pull off their masks and point out the true nature of the Gospel, Baptism and the ministry. The devil always adorns himself with such an angelic, yes, such a divine form and appearance, just as he makes a god of Himself when he speaks to Christ in Matt. 4. Here Christ himself must contend, not against man but against a god—not against the true God but against the devil, who uses God's name and adorns himself with divinity." Luther is employing a traditional theme but with his own originality. For a discussion of the illusions of the demonic, see Stuart Clark, *Thinking with Demons: The Idea of Witchcraft in Early Modern Europe* (Oxford: Oxford University Press, 1997), 80–93. Clark speaks of a "demonic inversion" that inverted values and turned particular things "upside down." Luther, in contrast, speaks more often, however, of an exact imitation. See also the 1583 version of Johann Weyer in *Witches, Devils, and Doctors in the Renaissance: Johann Weyer, "De praestigiis daemonum,"* trans. John Shea, Medieval and Renaissance Texts and Studies, vol. 73 (Binghamton, N.Y.: Medieval and Renaissance Texts and Studies, 1998).

18. Rowan Williams, *Teresa of Avila* (Harrisburg, Pa.: Morehouse Publishing, 1991), 37–38.

19. Gillian T. W. Ahlgren *Teresa of Avila and the Politics of Sanctity* (Ithaca, N.Y.: Cornell University Press, 1996). On the *alumbrados*, see Alastair Hamilton, *Heresy and Mysticism in Sixteenth-Century Spain: The Alumbrados* (Toronto: University of Toronto Press, 1992).

20. *Proceso de Alcarez*, fol. 224, cited by Hamilton, *Heresy and Mysticism in Sixteenth-Century Spain*, 38.

21. *The Book of Her Life* 8.5: "De lo que yo tengo experiencia puedo decir."

22. Ibid., 34.11.

23. *The Way of Perfection* 38.2.

24. *The Interior Castle* II.1.6; V.1.1.

25. *The Way of Perfection* 38.2.

26. *The Book Of Her Life* 14.8.

27. *The Interior Castle* VI.6.6, VI.6.8, V.4.10. English translations are from *The Collected Works of St. Teresa of Avila*, trans. Kieran Kavanaugh, O.C.D., and Otilio Rodriguez, O.C.D., 3 vols. (Washington, D.C.: ICS Publications, 1975–85).

28. *The Interior Castle* I.2.15.

29. *The Interior Castle* VI.3.16. See also *The Interior Castle* V.4.8: "I say that if this soul was always attached to God's will it is clear that it would not go astray. But the devil comes along with some skillful deception and under the color of good and confuses it with regard to little things and induces it to get taken up with some of them that he makes it think are good. Then little by little he darkens the intellect. . . . Until in one way or another he withdraws the soul from the will of God and brings it to his own." See also *The Interior Castle* VI.3.16.

30. *The Book of Her Life* 7.7.

31. Because of his explicit rejection of spiritualism and his appeal to the objective authority of Scripture, some Luther scholars have concluded that Luther was in no way a subjectivist. Michael Baylor has argued that, at the Diet of Worms, Luther appealed to reason and Scripture as "two objective and legitimate authorities." Hence he "was not a subjectivist in religion. The subjective sense of certainty with which he held his theological convictions did not function either formally or materially as a criterion for the truth of these convictions" (*Action and Person* [Leiden: E .J Brill, 1977], 267). Regin Prenter has argued that, because he insisted on the priority of the external sign, Luther's doctrine of Word and Spirit decisively separated him from the "enthusiasts" (*Spiritus Creator,* trans. John M. Jensen [Philadelphia: Muhlenberg Press, 1953], 205–53). B.A. Gerrish has pointed to Luther's "doctor consciousness," to his submission to the authority of Scripture, and to his belief in the duty of scholars to understand the Bible in accordance with the best biblical scholarship in order to argue that Luther was not appealing to a subjective conviction: "It is in fact, an appeal to objective standards" (*Continuing the Reformation* [Chicago: University of Chicago Press, 1993], 38–56).

However, the fact remains that when confronted by Catholics and the Radicals, Luther repeatedly insisted on his own inner experience of certainty, a certainty inspired by the Spirit and in conformity with the Word. Luther would have agreed with the judgments cited above but he was also sensitive to the fact that he often sounded uncomfortably close to his Radical opponents. Consequently he tried to distance himself as far as possible by defining his own objective criteria. But as George H. Williams astutely noted, "The vagaries [about the relationship of Word and Spirit] should not obscure from view the fact that a large element in the spiritualism of the Radical Reformation goes back to Luther himself and to a lesser extent, Zwingli" (*The Radical Reformation,* 3d ed., Sixteenth-Century Essays and Studies, vol. 15 [Kirksville, Mo.: Sixteenth Century Journal Publishers, 1992], 109–37, 1241–55.).

For more on this debate see Hermann Steinlein, "Luthers Doktorat: Zum 400 jahrigen Jubilaum desselben," *Neue kirchliche Zeitschrift* 23 (1912): 757–843. On this question, see also Bernhard Lohse, "Die Bleibende Bedeutung von Joseph Lortz 'Darstellung' Die Reformation in Deutschland" in *Zum Gedenken an Joseph Lortz (1887–1975),* ed. Rolf Decot and Rainer Vinke (Stuttgart: Franz Steiner, 1989), 337–51.

32. *WA* 45.622.30–31; *LW* 24:177.

33. *WA* 45.503.5–8; *LW* 24:46.

34. For citations and a discussion of this verse in the reformers, see Susan E. Schreiner, "'The Spiritual Man Judges All Things': Calvin and Exegetical Debates about Certainty in the Reformation," in *Biblical Interpretation in the Era of the Reformation,* ed. Richard A. Muller and John L. Thompson (Grand Rapids, Mich.: Wm. B. Eerdmans Publishing, 1996), 189–215.

35. *WA* 40.572.16–29; *LW* 26:375.

36. *WA* 45.727.33–728.1–4; *LW* 24: 293.

37. *WA* 45. 728.5–10; *LW* 24:293–94.

38. *WA* 45. 472.23–29; *LW* 24:13.

39. *WA* 40/1.321.17–20; *LW* 26:196.

40. *WA* 40.25.24–35; *WA* 40/1.319.25–321.12; *LW* 26:193–96.

41. *WA* 33.112.28–35, 563.21–565.26; *WA* 40.205.22–28, 299.3–5, 320.16–24; *WA* 40/2.42.33–35, 43.18–25; *WA* 43.459–462; *WA* 45.565.14–21; *LW* 33:75, 349–51; *LW* 26:114, 178, 195, 196; *LW* 27:33–34; *LW* 5:43; *LW* 24:114.

42. *WA* 43:462.1–5: "Therefore you must repel Satan from you with as few words as possible and say 'Get away from me Satan (Matt. 4:10). Do not instill doubt in me. The Son of god came into the world to destroy your work (1 John 3:8) and to destroy doubt'" (*LW* 5:49).

43. This is a frequently recurring theme in Luther's writings but the best passage is the commentary on Gal. 4:6: *WA* 40.577.20–579. See also *WA* 45.515–17, 597; *LW* 26:378–80. See also *WA* 45.515–17.597; *LW* 24:60–62.On Luther's view of the relationship between faith and experience, see Walther von Loewenich, *Luther's Theology of the Cross,* trans. Herbert J. A. Bouman (Minneapolis: Augsburg Publishing House, 1976), 77–88.

44. *WA* 40/1.579.17–24; *WA* 45.507.34; *LW* 26:380, 387, 388–89; *LW* 24:16, 51.

45. *WA* 45.507.34; *WA* 40.594.12: "Ista sine experientia non intelliguntur." *LW* 24:51; *LW* 26:390.

46. *WA* 40.579.17–24; *LW* 26:380.

47. *WA* 45.475.4–10; cf. *WA* 45.598.28–29, 599.10–16; *LW* 24:16, 150–52.

48. *WA* 45.599.23–24; *LW* 24:151.

49. *WA* 45.590.22–28, 591.29–36; *LW* 24:142–43.

50. *The Interior Castle* IV.3.2; *The Book of Her Life* 25.12–13.

51. *The Book of Her Life* 12.4, 7; 19.14.

52. *The Book of Her Life* 7.7; 30.9.

53. *The Interior Castle* VI.6.6.

54. *The Book of Her Life* 25.10–11, 30.9.

55. *The Interior Castle* VI.3.7–12, 17; VI.10.1.

56. *The Book of her Life* 7.1; 15.10; 19.2.

57. The most famous depiction of the authenticity of a spiritual gift is the "wound of love" by Bernini's sculpture. Only God can produce this "pain that was so great that it made me moan, and the sweetness of this greatest pain caused me was so superabundant that there is no desire capable of taking it away" (*The Book of Her Life* 29.13). Reflecting later on this experience, Teresa was assured to great certitude because "the devil never gives delightful pain like this" (*The Interior Castle* VI.2.6). In short, the paradoxical nature of the experience proved its divine origin; the devil can give delight but cannot join pain and delight together.

58. *The Interior Castle* V.1.8–10:

> For during the time of this union, it neither sees, nor hears, nor understands, because the union is always short. . . . God so places Himself in the interior of that soul that when it returns to itself it can in no way doubt that it was in God and God was in it. This truth remains with it so firmly that even though years go by without God granting that favor again. The soul can neither doubt nor forget that it was in God and God was in it. . . . Afterward it sees the truth clearly, not because of a vision but because of a certitude remaining in the soul that only God can put there.

See also *The Interior Castle* VI.2.1, 3, 6.; *The Book of Her Life* 18.14; 24.5; 27.2: "In the case of this [intellectual] vision . . . without being seen it is impressed with such clear knowledge that I don't think it can be doubted. The Lord desires to be so engraved upon the intellect that this vision can no more be doubted than what can be seen. . . . There remains such great certitude that the doubt has no force."

59. *The Interior Castle* VI.3.7; *The Book of Her Life* 18.14; *The Interior Castle* V.1.9.

60. *The Interior Castle* V.1.10.

61. *The Interior Castle* VI.9.10; see also *The Interior Castle* VI.8.3; *The Book of Her Life* 27.2–7.

62. *The Interior Castle* VI.9.10.

63. *The Book of Her Life* 40.4.

64. *The Interior Castle* VI.10.1.

65. Ibid., VI. 10. 8.

66. Ibid., VII.3.10.

67. Thomas More, *Response to Luther,* ed. John Headley, trans. Sister Scholastica Mandeville, vol. 5 of *The Complete Works of St. Thomas More,* 15 vols. (New Haven, Conn.: Yale University Press), 1307

From Ritual to Poetry: Herbert's Mystical Eucharist

REGINA M. SCHWARTZ

All things long for it. The intelligent long for it by way of knowledge, the lower strata by way of perception, the remainder by way of the stirrings of being alive—and it is praised by every name.

—Pseudo-Dionysius

In *The Disenchantment of the World,* Marcel Gauchet distinguishes two ways that meaning can be established: through the figure of the Other or the figure of the Self. In the premodern world, the believer himself does not actively establish meaning for all that is; it is given to him. What is given is understandings of aspects of his world including, among others, community, authority, materiality, justice, loss, and love. When we do not receive meaning from the Other—whether the premodern prior or the postmodern beyond—we tend to devise meaning actively; this is what Gauchet calls the figure of the Self. In the modern world, the figure of the Other is gradually replaced by the figure of the Self who defines, controls, possesses, and masters—that is, the modern subject. What had once been Other and inaccessible, unable to be grasped, is now comprehended, grasped, possessed, adored. This is the condition of idolatry, and in the early modern period many Reformers rejected transubstantiation and images claiming that they had become not mysteries, but idols, and they sought to restore the invisible God.

But if Gauchet and others are right about Protestantism ushering in secularization—"Christianity proves to have been *a religion for departing from religion*"—then the Reformation's efforts to destroy idols only produced new ones, the idols of metaphysics.[1] Here, the threat of idolatry is not from the visible God but from the thinkable Other, the concept. According to Jean-Luc Marion, metaphysics has subjected "the unconditional to the pre-conditions and limits of human thought and language. . . . In showing too much, in their pretension to equivalence with God himself, the necessarily limited concepts produced by metaphysics would in fact show too little, for God by definition would exceed every concept or definition."[2] For it is the "withdrawal of the divine [which] would perhaps constitute its ultimate form of revelation."[3] With Levinas and other postmodern thinkers, Marion is symptomatic of a new shift in emphasis, away from the figure of the Self toward the figure of the Other, or the Beyond. It has been inflected both philosophically and theologically, and in Levinas with his debt to Talmudic Judaism and Marion with his debt to Catholicism, phenomenological given-ness coalesces with the theological gifts of creation and redemption. Thus theologically inflected, the phenomenological *gegebenheit* receives a new reading in an ethical register. Here, it becomes not a question of perceiving or apperceiving a phenomenon through a reduction but of understanding all phenomena as well as one's own subjectivity as given. This gift is prior to our activity, our comprehension, and not available to our mastery. It evokes not manipulation but wonder, and more, responsibility. Before the "object" as understood by modernism, we feel compelled to analyze, comprehend, and use. Before the "gift" or, better, the "call" of postmodernism we feel com-pelled to receive with gratitude and respond with wonder. While elsewhere, I joined the widespread contemporary critique of religious idolatry in my critique of possession, here I want to elaborate a different religious legacy: not the legacy of possession but of dispossession, not of religious idolatry but of mystery.[4]

What the early modern poets were in touch with, because they could so keenly feel the loss of the sacramental, was the aching emptiness of a world without that divine meaning-filling. Abandoning the idol, they set to work to restore the "icon"—not the icon of eastern orthodoxy, not the visible icons of religion, but cultural icons that could point beyond themselves to the un-seeable. They asked how to think otherness without naming, comprehend-ing, controlling, institutionalizing; how to discover god, express wonder, in a work of human creativity. Even for Reformed poets who doctrinally rejected it, the mystery of transubstantiation did not disappear; the mystery became the province of poetry, as cultural critics from Matthew Arnold through George Steiner have so well understood. If the Reformation inaugurated the beginning of modernism and with it the loss of the Other, the death of God, and the birth of the modern Self, it also gave us ways of transfiguring into other cultural forms those values that—in another regime and in another register—religious ritual conveyed as God-given: meaning, love, charity, community, justice, a living universe, and mystery.

Mystical Poetry and Theology

The liturgy of the Eucharist is insistent in its emphasis on gratitude. The Greek e*ucharistia* is generally translated as "thanksgiving," but in contemporary parlance, thanksgiving has largely come to signify gratitude for a favor, for some *thing* received, while *eucharistia* suggests thanks giving, or praise, without reference to an object. In fact, the biblical psalms of thanksgiving have been distinguished, in just this way, from the hymns of praise; thanks for a particular favor or gift is contrasted to the generalized celebration of the psalms of praise.[5] Some have claimed that the earliest sense of *eucharistia* was, like the Hebraic *berakah,* a proclamation, a celebration of the *mirabilia Dei,* an expression of wonder. Such praise is not caught up in an economy of exchange, then, of thanks in return for a specific gift; nonetheless, it is a response—a response to revelation. As Hans Urs von Balthassar describes, "For God's revelation is not an object to be looked at: it is his action in and upon the world, and the world can only respond, and hence 'understand,' through action on its part."[6] That is, responses to revelation are in kind: when the focus of the revelation is the passion, the response is the Eucharist—God gives his body so that it may be given; when it is the Word, the response is the word: God gives the Scripture so that it may be given—we send up his psalms of praise. In this way, our most precious gift, praise, is indeed not ours. It is God's gift, as Marion has forcefully reminded us.[7]

While these modes of praise—Word and sacrament, Scripture and Eucharist—were always joined anyway, completely imprecated in one another, the Reformers stressed their connection polemically, with both Luther and Calvin describing the sacraments as the seal of the Word. With the Reformation's focus on Scripture reading, its Scripture translations, and (in England), its proliferation of translations of the psalms in particular (with Sir Philip Sidney and John Milton making their own contributions to that enterprise), with elaborate church choirs and organs replaced by psalm singing, a biblical liturgy was a key part of the cultural context that forged the period's devotional verse, a poetry constituted by hymns of praise that are deeply indebted to the Bible in vocabulary and form. George Herbert grew up in a household that, according to John Donne's account, sang psalms every Sunday evening, and he repeated that practice as a pastor at a rural village in Bemerton. While his contribution to English verse is already acknowledged to be biblical, I want to add that his understanding of language is, ironically in an age when the sacraments were under fire and undergoing rapid revision, sacramental. I will add that this was not felt as a contradiction, for it was the mystery of the sacrament more than its materiality that was so attractive to Reformation poets, and in all the doctrinal crossfire over the sacrament, its mystery was never in doubt.

The Eucharist was the very heart of mystery: here, the signifier and signified were identical, the subject knew no separation from the object of worship, the material and spiritual came together, transcendence was manifest in immanence, the past and present were united, remembering and reenacting knew no difference, the individual was joined to the community. Chrysostom spoke of the Eucharist as a mystery, Eusebius described the Eucharist as a "mystical liturgy," Gregory of Nyssa called it a "mystical action" and Gregory of Nazianzus called the altar a "mystical table." In the Apostolic Constitutions, the Eucharist is described as the "mystical sacrifice of the body and blood of Christ." The term was also used to describe the "discovery by faith of the mystery of Christ as the key to the scriptures." Gregory of Nazianzus writes, "I must be buried with Christ, rise again with him and inherit heaven with him, become God's son, become God! . . . That is for us the great mystery. That is what it means to us that God became incarnate, a poor man, for us. He came to raise up the flesh, to save his own image, to put men together again. He came to make us perfectly one in Christ who came to be perfectly one of us, to bestow on us all that he is."[8] He not only alludes to mystery; he evokes it: Christ came to bestow, not all that he *has,* but all that he *is* on man.

If poetry can embody this mystery, it is surely achieved in George Herbert's magnificent anthology of lyrics, *The Temple.*[9] A seventeenth-century Anglican pastor, Herbert has enjoyed widespread appreciation: he was called the "blessed Herbert" by a midcentury Puritan, the "divine" Herbert by a late-century Presbyterian, and during the Restoration, a Cambridge divine even wanted to canonize him. While *The Temple* is regarded by both early modern and postmodern readers as a triumph of literary imagination, in its own time it was also perceived as a source of religious inspiration and even as a model for practical devotion. In his *Poetry of Meditation,* Louis Martz said that it is "hardly too much" to call its main section, *The Church,* "a book of seventeenth-century psalmody."[10] Barbara Lewalski wrote that "Herbert seems to have conceived his book of lyrics as a book of Christian psalms, and his speaker as a new David, a Christian Psalmist."[11] Several have noted that among Herbert's precedents, it is Sir Philip Sidney *Psalms* (1–43) that are indeed the closest approximation in poetry to Herbert's *The Temple.*[12] Sidney's translations—which moved John Donne to write a poem in praise of them— were based on the Coverdale and Geneva Bibles and are marked by such simplicity of phrasing, and metrical variety (especially different stanza forms) that one critic was prompted to describe them as beginning a new school of English versification. In short, Herbert's *The Temple* was then and is now widely regarded as the greatest compendium of religious lyrics written in England's great age of religious poetry.

Along with other lyrics penned by other seventeenth-century poets, *The Temple* figures prominently in my argument that while the Reformation has been characterized as ushering in so many of the familiar features of modernism—a rising middle class, capitalism, nationalism, restructuring of the family, revisions of hierarchical authority, preoccupations with subjectivity, the advent of scientific empiricism—something else took place: the mystery that had been the province of religious ritual came to be vested in other cultural forms. One important site of this change was seventeenth-century verse: for all their doctrinal and stylistic differences, Milton, Donne, Herrick, Crashaw, Vaughan, and Herbert make similar claims for their verse. A new understanding of language emerges from these poets (one that I will ultimately show is, after all, not so new)—a language theory that is virtually "sacramental."[13]

While the famous debates by the magisterial Reformers over the sacraments were already a century old in seventeenth-century England, a series of bitter, divisive, doctrinal and liturgical battles continued to be waged. Most notable was the battle between those who, like Archbishop Laud, advocated the return to the "beauty of holiness," ceremonialism, sacramentalism, and those with more iconoclastic intentions who were offended by such so-called popish practices. The temptation to search the devotional verse of the period to ascertain the correct doctrinal label for each poet has not been resisted by critics; in fact, the old battles over liturgy and doctrine continue in twentieth-century literary studies, where the discussion has been dominated by the question of whether these poems are the products of a "Protestant poetics" or betray a doctrinal and even ceremonial debt to the Roman church. A session at the Modern Language Association convention in 1986 called "George Herbert's Theology: Nearer Geneva or Rome?" where critics squared off is symptomatic. But rather than worry more over labeling these poets—they are, after all, writing poetry and not systematic theologies—I have been focusing on their use of language and discovered that they were doing something startling: now that their theology insisted that the sacrifice be remembered, rather than reenacted in the communion, they are asking that their *poetry* carry the mystical force of the Sacrament.[14] Poetry is called upon to carry the performative power of liturgy. Ironically, of all places, Reformation poetry becomes the new cite of transubstantiation of the Word.

While theologians argued about the status of signs in the Eucharist—for Luther, Christ was in, with, and under the elements, for Calvin there was a "distinction without division" between Christ and the elements, and for Zwingli, the elements were metaphors only—the mysteries of the Eucharist gave Reformation poets little difficulty. Rejecting the ontological questions—how the accidents could stay the same and the substance change—they asked instead how the signifier, their word, which is the Word of God, could point to the mystery of man joining God, the mystery, that is, of the Eucharist. They asked, not, *what* does this word stand for, but *how* does this verse perform. If we were to follow their lead and move beyond metaphysical preoccupations, beyond onto-theology, we could learn much from their understanding of language as sacramental.

To trace the theological roots of their sign theory, however, we have to take a detour through Calvin's understanding of signs, for to the extent that anything about religious thought and practice in seventeenth-century England can be generalized, the understanding of signs informing the English church was, generally speaking, indebted to him. For Calvin, signs do not contain God but do lift you up to God; they are the very vehicle by which man is lifted up to participate in Christ. Alluding to Augustine, he wants to steer between two dangers, as he perceives them: one, that signs would be empty (the Zwinglian way, which harbors the threat of nihilism for Calvin, just as today postmodern sign theory does for some), the other, that they would be too full (that signs contain the thing itself; the Roman way, as he saw it). Toward the first, the empty sign, we would be wrong to think that signs are given in vain, to disparage or diminish their secret signification, excluding ourselves from the advantage that we ought to derive from them. In the other danger, they become idols by which we mistake the sign for the gift of the Spirit. Signs are effective because they are the gift by the Spirit, given to signal the gift of the Spirit. Book 4 of the *Institutes:* "If we do not elevate our minds beyond the visible sign, we transfer to the sacraments the praise of those benefits which are only conferred upon us by Christ alone, and that by the agency of the Holy Spirit, who makes us partakers of Christ himself—this is done by the instrumentality of the external signs which invite us to Christ."[15] Calvin is careful to stress the mystery of this process, the mystery of communion; speaking of "communion with Christ" in a letter to Peter Martyr (8 August 1555), he writes, "We become truly members of his body, and life flows into us from his as from the head. For in no other way does he reconcile us to God by the sacrifice of his death than because he is ours and we are one with him. . . . How this happens, I confess is something far above the measure of my intelligence. Hence I adore this mystery rather than labor to understand it."[16] Calvin's etymology for sacrament takes him immediately to mystery: "For whenever the author of . . . the New Testament wanted to render the Greek word, mystery [*musterion*], into Latin, especially where it related to Divine things, he used the word *sacramentum*." Examples follow of Calvin quoting the use of *musterion* in the epistle to the Ephesians (1:9, 3:3), the epistle to the Colossians (1:26, 27), and Timothy (3:16). "In all of these places," he continues, "where the word *musterion* is used, the author of that version has rendered it sacrament. He would not say *arcanum*, or secret, lest he should appear to degrade the majesty of the subject. Therefore he used the word sacrament for a sacred or Divine secret. . . . And it is well known, that baptism and the Lord's Supper, which the Latins denominate Sacraments, are called mysteries by the Greeks" (Inst. 14:2). When he stresses the mystery of the Eucharist, he is also stressing the mystery of signification, of sacramental signification, for what enables the sacramental union of *signum* and *res* is the mystery of Christ's gift, the mystery of faith conferred by the Spirit through the Gospel, a mystery grounded in the Word. Without that mystery, the sign is not effective, it is empty, a "vain and useless figure" in Augustine's phrase. If God

> had impressed memorials . . . on the sun, the stars, the earth, and stones they would all have been to us as sacraments. For why is the shapeless and the coined silver not of the same value seeing they are the same metal? Just because the former has nothing but its own nature, whereas the latter impressed with the public stamp, becomes money and receives a new value. And shall not the Lord be able to stamp His creatures with His word; that things which were formerly bare elements may become sacraments?
>
> (Inst. 4:14:18)

For Calvin, a sacrament is an act of God that "makes . . . divine mysteries lurk under things that are in themselves quite abject" (Inst. 4:19:2). What would make poetry sacramental, according to this logic, would be a mystery no less than the active agency of the Spirit.

The poets invoke just such agency, inviting the Spirit to turn their otherwise "shapeless" words into coined or valued ones. When George Herbert opens *The Temple* with an invocation of the mystery of the sacrifice, he thereby frames the ensuing poems as the offering he makes, an offering of praise, "singing the Name" as he says, apophatically, a gift he can give only because it was given to him.

> Lord, my first fruits present themselves to thee:
> Yet not mine neither, for from thee they came,

And must return. Accept of them, and mee.

And make us strive, who shall sing best they Name.

He is echoing the biblical liturgy for the offering of the first fruits of the harvest (Deut. 26:1–10), which concludes with, "And now behold, I have brought the first fruits of the land, which thou, O Lord, hast given me." Elsewhere, the fruits of the land become the "fruit of our lippes, giving thankes to his Name" (Heb. 13:15), and Paul even refers to Christ as the "first fruits": "Christ has been raised from the dead, the first fruits of those who have fallen asleep. . . . For as in Adam all die, so also in Christ shall all be made alive. But each in his own order: Christ the first fruits, then at his coming those who belong to Christ" (1 Cor. 15:20).

Here, the first fruits are Herbert's hymns of praise. Before we even enter *The Temple,* his entire collection of poems is framed thereby as an offering. When we do, he takes us through the church porch, where precepts are offered in verse: "A verse may find him, who a sermon flies/And turn delight into a sacrifice." And then to the heading before entering the church proper: "Thou, whom the former precepts have/Sprinkled and taught, how to behave/thy self in church; approach, and taste/The churches *mysticall* repast" (emphasis mine). And then, with the first poem of the section "The Church" proper as "The Altar," it is no wonder that the Eucharist has been called the very "marrow of Herbert's sensibility." In "The Altar," he repeats that he is offering his praise, his language itself, as a sacrifice, and he makes the explicit request that his verse be sanctified.

> A broken Altar, Lord, thy servant reares,
> Made of a heart, and cemented with teares:
> Whose parts are as thy hand did frame;
> No workmans tool hath touch'd the same.
> A heart alone
> Is such a stone
> As nothing but
> Thy power doth cut.
> Wherefore each part
> Of my hard heart
> Meets in this frame
> To praise thy Name
> That, if I chance to hold my peace,
> These stones to praise thee may not cease.
> O let thy blessed SACRIFICE be mine,
> And sanctify this ALTAR to be thine.

While the stones of the altar are the speaker's words, his praise, his tears, his heart, Herbert arranges them in the shape of an altar (the sacrament includes both the Word and the visible word, in Augustine's language), and the offering signals both divine grace and human gratitude. This insistent allusion to sacrifice—so explicitly deleted from the Anglican Eucharist—is no anomaly in Herbert's *Temple;* rather, the explicit offering of sacrifice is echoed in another verse, "Providence," in which Man "the world's high priest" presents "the sacrifice for all"—a sacrifice of praise. But what does it mean to write sacramental verse, to speak of *praise* as the sacrifice at the altar? Why does Herbert frame *The Temple* with the mystical repast? In the Eucharist, the sign points beyond itself by an agency beyond itself. This process informs the mystery of how language means, how language cannot contain what it points to, which is beyond itself.

In *A True Hymn* Herbert addresses just this problem. What would constitute a genuine offering of praise, a "true hymn"? "The fineness which a hymn or psalm affords/Is, when the soul unto the lines accords." Some congruence between the soul and the verse, but how is this possible? In the third stanza, the speaker says that when a poet wants "all mind, soul, strength and time" to be offered in a poem, he is justifiably disappointed if all he produces is a rhyme; and he offers just such a stanza—second rate verse that rhymes.

> He who craves all the minde,
> And all the soul, and strength, and time,
> If the words only ryme,
> Justly complains, that somewhat is behinde
> To make his verse, or write a hymne in kinde.

But this is not only banal rhyming verse, for the poet also offers another possibility, negatively. What he cannot say points to what he would say. The speaker repeats "somewhat"—"somewhat it fain would say," "somewhat is behind," "somewhat scant"—as if words are failing him, and "somewhat" is not even "some thing"; no category of being suffices as he gropes to describe the true hymn, and that hymn is not contained in this verse. This "somewhat" echoes Pseudo-Dionysius on the impossibility of naming the Divine for it is beyond all names. As it says in *The Divine Names,* "The sacred writers lift up a hymn of praise to this Good. They call it beautiful, beauty, love, and beloved. They give it the names which would convey that it is the source of loveliness and the flowering of grace."[17] But it is called beauty not because it *possesses* beauty—but because it *bestows* it, confers it. Similarly, the verse does not contain or possess praise, it confers it: simply put, it praises what it cannot even name.

The biblical texts this lyric echoes are Deut 6:5, "Thou shalt love the Lord thy God, with all thy heart, with all thy soul and with all thy might," and Luke 10:27, which changes it to "all thy heart, soul, strength, and mind." Herbert's poem speaks of minde, soul, strength and *time,* substituting poetic meter for heart. No wonder the poet is dissatisfied; meter and rhyme are no substitute for the heart. But if the heart is missing in this stanza, it appears twice in the final one:

> Whereas if th' heart be moved,
> Although the verse be somewhat scant,
> God doth supply the want.
> As when th' heart says (sighing to be approved)
> *O, could I love!* And stops: God writeth *Loved.*

If the verse is lacking, God supplies the want. What the poet cannot say is said by an Other. If the meter does not scan, God will complete it. And the verse demonstrates this in the last couplet, which does not scan without the addition of "Loved." The lyric is coauthored, by a human and a divine writer, and in this way becomes a "true hymn," giving what is already given. One obvious logical answer to the cry, "O could I Love" would be "you *can* love," but the request is granted in a different way: "you *are* loved." This is not only God's word in the lyric but also the divine logic explained in Scripture: "We love him because he first loved us" (1 John 4:19). The human effort is partial, unfinished, pointing to the need for intervention from Outside. If only he acknowledges that need with yearning for more, if the heart calls, "O could I love," it is answered, "Loved." Just as the mystery of divine love not only informs sacramental agency, it also makes a hymn "true" and a verse (do its) work. Pseudo-Dionysius writes of the Unnameable with all Names: "They especially call it *loving* toward humanity, because in one of its persons it accepted a true share of what it is we are, and thereby issued a call to man's lowly state to rise up to it."[18]

Herbert makes the connection between verse and apophatic theology explicit in *The Quidditee.* In scholastic philosophy, the quiddity was the nature or essence of a thing. Rather than describing that essence, grasping it, here his speaker can only describe the essence of verse through negations.

> My God, a verse is not a crown
> No point of honour, or gay suit,

> No hawk, or banquet, or renown,
> Nor a good sword, nor yet a lute.
>
> It cannot vault, or dance or play,
> It never was in France or Spain

Then, after all these negations that include courtly love poetry, heroic verse, Homeric epic, and Virgilian pastoral, he offers his affirmation of what verse is. Significantly, it has no predicate:

> But it is that which while I use
> I am with thee

"That which while I use": verse is not nameable as a thing; rather, it is a vehicle that takes him beyond, to God. The final lines echo Anselm's famous apophatic definition of God: "that which nothing greater can be thought," so if a "quiddity" is reached here in the defining process, it is a negative one.[19]

Mystical Theology and Poetry

It is no accident, I would argue, that Pseudo-Dionysius's *Mystical Theology* begins with a poem. That poem depicts an alternative revelation to the one at Sinai—not thunder and lightening but silence and darkness, not words graven on stone tablets soon dashed to pieces but a mystic Scripture whose words need not be cut or broken for they "lie simple," absolute and unchangeable, in the brilliant darkness of a hidden silence. To approach them, we too must be silent and blind: revelation only occurs when our senses and our understanding are left behind so that our sightless minds can be filled with treasures beyond—beyond being, divinity, goodness, and all beauty. This poem or hymn of praise constitutes a supplication and a celebration; the supplication—"lead us up beyond unknowing and light to the farthest peak"—indicates we are not yet there. Everything in the poem points beyond itself—from the invocation of the first line, "Somewhat Higher than any being," to the revelation conferred in the last, "treasures beyond all beauty." In no case does the verse contain what it points to. And this resistance to containing, this pointing beyond, this grasping and yearning and desiring more—more than the language can say, more than the hymn can express—is as much a part of sacramental signification as longing is part of praise. Herbert makes this function clear in *Providence,* where a sign cannot only point to one thing but more, and that excess is impelled by desire to praise; and in the providential scheme all things are impelled to praise.

> Each thing that is, although in use and name
> It go for one, hath many wayes in store
> To honour thee; and so each hymne thy fame
> Extolleth many ways, yet this one more.

Like God in Pseudo-Dionysius, verse has all names and no name.

Not only did Pseudo-Dionysius enjoy a resurgence of interest in seventeenth-century England, England had its own mystical tradition, including the *Cloud of Unknowing*, and this, combined with the influence of Calvin's Augustinian sign theory, his understanding of the mystery of the sacrament as an act of God "which makes divine mysteries lurk under things that are in themselves quite abject" (Inst. 4:19:2), could inform a mystical sacramental poetics. And so it is worth looking again, this time synoptically, at Pseudo-Dionysius's poem in *Mystical Theology:* "Trinity! Higher than any being, any divinity, any goodness! Lead us up!" says the prayer/poem, simultaneously praising and desiring. How can gratitude be expressed when the request is not yet granted? Lead us up, says Pseudo-Dionysius—amid his praise, but we are not yet led up, so why be grateful? Grateful for what? For desire, for what is given is this desire; hence, to feel desire is to be grateful, and when we express gratitude, we also express desire: this is the heart of a paradox that governs liturgical language.

"God is not governed by our desire," writes Henri de Lubac, "the relation is precisely the other way around—it is the giver who awakens desire . . . it remains true that once such a desire exists in the creature it becomes the sign, not merely of a possible gift from God, but of a certain gift. It is the evidence of a promise, inscribed and recognized in the being's very self."[20] This desiring subject, whose very heart is inscribed with want, is evidence of the promised gift; her desire and her praise become her offering. De Lubac writes that the longing for the beyond, the desire for God, that informs mystical theology is a symptom that humanity is called. It is the human response to the call. This is precisely the logic of Herbert's *The Altar,* where each part of the poet's heart, cut by God, desires only to praise, and so the poem is visibly shaped, not only like an altar but also to form the shape of the pronoun "I." In the end, the subject is the offering made at the altar. To live is to praise—it is the very purpose of life; the ancient Israelites understood death as the state when we can no longer praise. "For Sheol does not sing thy praise, Death does not celebrate thee" (Isaiah 38). "The dead, they do not praise Yahweh, nor any who sink to the silent land. But we, we will bless Yahweh from this time forth and for evermore" (Ps. 115:17).

If mystical theology invites us to think of praise as a gift that has been made to us, as an offering we return, as a ceaseless activity without a determinate subject or predicate, and as a pure expression of desire, praise is also, in a seeming paradox, a lament. For in the very act of lamenting, one already celebrates what she has: gratitude that there is a listener, someone to hear. This means that long before a request is honored, there is a prior response to it: the presupposition of responsiveness.[21] This prior return, as it were, is demonstrated in the biblical psalms. While Sigmund Mowinckel has separated psalms of lamentation from psalms of praise as heuristic structures, he acknowledges that the distinction does not hold liturgically. Even as the biblical speaker laments, he demonstrates his confidence that God will not fail him. And conversely, in the very act of celebrating God, the speaker expresses his longing for him. Furthermore, Mowinckel discerns that the vow contained in the psalms of lamentation indicates that they were offered in a cultic setting when some distress had been overcome, as a song of thanksgiving.[22] The *todha,* or thanksgiving psalm, had two functions: to offer testimony to the saving work of God and to thank God for that salvation. They begin with praise—"I will extol thee, Yahweh, for thou hast lifted me up" (Psalm 30)—and proceed to an account of affliction and an account of salvation: "On the very day I cried unto thee Thou answeredst me at once" (Psalm 138). The verb *hvdh,* generally translated as "to praise," properly means "to confess" or "to accept" so that praising includes a confession of unworthiness and acceptance of the judgment for that unworthiness. Gerhard von Rad points to the "avowal" component of praise: "In accepting a justly imposed judgment, the man confesses his transgression, and he clothes what he says in the mantle of an avowal, giving God the glory."[23] This is praise from the depths, like the praise of Jonah from the belly of the whale or the praise of the afflicted Job. Of such praise, the Bible says hauntingly, "God gives these songs in the night" (Job 35:10). It is the praise of Christ from the cross: "My God my God, why have you forsaken me?" he says, quoting Psalm 22, a psalm not only of lament but also of praise:

Why art thou so far from helping me,
from the words of my groaning?
my God, I cry by day, but thou dost not answer;
and by night, but find no rest.
enthroned on the praises of Israel.
In thee our fathers trusted;

they trusted, and thou didst
deliver them.
To thee they cried, and were saved;
in thee they trusted, and were not disappointed.

And then, toward its close: "I will tell of thy name to my brethren; in the midst of the congregation I will praise thee: You who fear the Lord, praise him! . . . For he has not despised or abhorred the affliction of the afflicted; and he has not hid his face from him, but has heard, when he cried to him."

Herbert's brief lyric "Bitter-sweet" compresses both understandings of praise that we find in the psalms, as lament and gratitude, lack and fullness, desire and love. That compression begins with the hyphenated title, one word that combines the bitterness of affliction and sweetness of praise:

Bitter-sweet
Ah my deare angrie Lord
Since thou dost love, yet strike:
Cast down, yet help afford;
Sure I will do the like.
I will complain, yet praise;
I will bewail, approve;
And all my sour-sweet days
I will lament, and love.

Psalm 126:6 is more succinct: "They that sow in tears shall reap in joy."

The "true hymn," for Herbert, is a call and an answer: "O could I love"; God writeth, "Loved." It is not an unheard lament, but a conversation, even if short and very much to the point. We see this call and response expressed dramatically in "The Collar," whose title puns on choler as anger, collar as a yoke, and finally, the caller, the One who calls. Initially, the speaker is frustrated, angry, unable to find fulfillment, lamenting about his constraints, when suddenly a voice breaks in:

But as I rav'd and grew more fierce and wilde
At every word
Me thoughts I heard one calling, Child!
And I reply'd, My Lord.

The conversation or dialogue has deep theological roots. The incarnation itself is described as part of a dialogue, a call to man that is framed so that man can respond. "Since the unknowing of what is beyond being is something above and beyond speech, mind, or being itself, one should ascribe to it an understanding beyond being. . . . In our reverent awe, let us be drawn together toward the divine splendor. For . . . the things of God are revealed to each mind in proportion to its capacities; and the divine goodness is such that, out of concern for our salvation, it deals out the immeasurable and infinite in limited measures."[24] We could understand these "limited measures" in two ways: the immeasurable is made proportionate to man in the incarnation, but the immeasurable is also given "limited measure" in the measures of poetry, another kind of incarnation: the Word made words. Hence, what follows in *Mystical Theology* could be an apt description of the metaphors in Herbert's poetry: "The Transcendent [comes to us] clothed in the terms of being, with shape and form on things which have neither, and numerous symbols are employed to convey the varied attributes of what is an imageless and supranatural simplicity. . . . We now grasp these things in the best way we can, and as they come to us, wrapped in the sacred veils of that love toward humanity with which scripture and traditions cover the truths of the mind with things derived from the realm of the senses." But if God offers a revelation proportionate to man's capacities, how could man respond? What could be our answer? The Eucharist, thanksgiving, the hymn of praise awakened by the desire that invites us beyond ourselves.

Again, the character of this interchange is a conversation—not a thunderous clap from the beyond that flattens the listener into shock; a conversation—not a devastation—not the kind of overwhelming ravishing that crushes, like Donne depicts in "Batter My Heart," where the speaker says to God, "nor ever chaste unless you ravish me"; a conversation—not a human call that echoes in a cavern, nor a lonely call that is unanswered, only deferred endlessly until it fades away. The mystery of this conversation "according to our proportion" is the mystery of the Eucharist, a mystery called "love" by both Pseudo-Dionysius and by George Herbert. Pseudo-Dionysius: "The sacred writers lift up a hymn of praise to this Good. They call it beautiful, beauty, love, and beloved. They give it the names which would convey that it is the source of loveliness and the flowering of grace." It is called beauty, he goes on to say, not because it possesses beauty but because it bestows it, confers love. . . . And there it is ahead of us as Goal, as the Beloved.[25]

"Love III"

Herbert's final poem in *The Temple*—the collection that begins with *The Altar* written by his heart, an altar that he asks to be sanctified so that he may receive the sacrifice that he subsequently offers—concludes by understanding that sacrifice as conversation. To be more precise, it is a conversation that is framed as an invitation to dinner. While the guest feels unworthy of the host, in the course of the conversation, the host lifts the guest up to her level, qualifying the guest to dine. Like all of Herbert's poetry, "Love III" is dense with biblical allusion. As he explains in his poem on the Scriptures, Holy Scriptures II, one allusion points to the next in an intertextuality that forms a virtual constellation of "stars," or biblical passages.

> Oh that I knew how all thy lights combine,
> And the configurations of their glorie!
> Seeing not only how each verse doth shine,
> But all the constellations of the storie.
> This verse marks that, and both do make a motion
> Unto a third, that ten leave off doth lie. . .

Herbert speaks Scripture in his poetry, but he does so in his own voice. It is as if, like Ezekiel, he had eaten the Scripture, made it a part of him, and it tasted like honey. That is precisely the image he invokes to open his other poem on the Bible, "Holy Scriptures I": "Oh Book! Infinite Sweetness! Let my heart Suck ev'ry letter."

Marked by an ease, a deceptive simplicity, even grace at presenting a deep theological and emotional drama, "Love" is often thought of as Herbert's quintessential poem: it derives some of its rich texture from the echo of many biblical passages describing God inviting man to a feast, including Sg. 2:4, "he brought me to the banqueting house, and his banner over me was love"; Twenty-third Psalm, where God is a gracious Host; Matt. 26:29, "I tell you I shall not drink again of this fruit of the vine until that day when I drink it new with you in my Father's kingdom"; Luke 12:37, where the master comes and serves his servants; Rev. 3:20, the promised messianic banquet, "Behold I stand at the door and knock; if any one hears my voice and opens the door, I will come in to him and eat with him, and he with me"; Matt. 22:1–10 and Luke 14:7–24, the parables of the great supper. Luke 14:7 is especially apt:

> Now he told a parable to those who were invited, when he marked how they chose the places of honor, saying to them, "When you are invited by any one to a marriage feast, do not sit down in a place of honor, lest a more eminent man than you be invited by him; and he who invited you both will come and say to you, 'Give place to this man' and then you will begin with shame to take the lowest place. [The setting of Herbert's poem follows.] But when you are invited, go and sit in

the lowest place, so that when your host comes, he may say to you, 'Friend, go up higher' then you will be honored in the presence of all who sit at table with you. For every one who exalts himself will be humbled and he who humbles himself will be exalted."

Herbert's unworthy guest alludes directly to Matthew's version of the parable, "the king said to his servants, The wedding is ready, but those invited were not worthy" (Matt. 22:8). But Herbert has changed the plot. The version in Luke 14:16 reads,

> A man once gave a great banquet, and invited many; and at the time for the banquet he sent his servant to say to those who had been invited, "Come; for all is now ready." But they all alike began to make excuses. The first said to him, "I have bought a field, and I must go out and see it; I pray you, have me excused." And another said, "I have bought five yoke of oxen, and I go to examine them; I pray you, have me excused." And another said, "I have married a wife, and therefore I cannot come." So the servant came and reported this to his master. Then the householder in anger said to his servant, "Go out quickly to the streets and lanes of the city, and bring in the poor and maimed and blind and lame." And the servant said, "Sir, what you commanded has been done, and still there is room." And the master said to the servant, "Go out to the highways and hedges, and compel people to come in, that my house may be filled. For I tell you, none of those men who were invited shall taste of my banquet."

Herbert clearly changes the plot.

In Herbert's version, Love does not simply invite a guest who, making excuses, refuses, is pronounced unworthy, and is then replaced by someone else because the host gives up on him. *Love will not be refused*. Like the lover in the Song of Songs, Love is not angered by rejection: "I opened to my beloved, but my beloved had withdrawn himself, and was gone." Instead, the lover is determined to win him back. Significantly, in Herbert, she invites him not only to her meal but into a conversation:

Love (III)
Love bade me welcome. Yet my soul drew back
　　　　Guilty of dust and sin.
Bur quick-eyed Love, observing me grow slack
　　　　From my first entrance in,
　　Drew nearer to me, sweetly questioning,
　　　　　If I lacked any thing.

A guest, I answered, worthy to be here:
        Love said, You shall be he.
I the unkind, ungrateful? Ah my dear,
        I cannot look on thee.
Love took my hand, and smiling did reply,
        Who made the eyes but I?

Truth Lord, but I have marred them: let my shame
        Go where it does deserve.
And know you not, says Love, who bore the Blame?
        My dear, then I will serve.
You must sit down, says Love, and taste my meat:
        So I did sit and eat.

Love asks, maternally, do you lack anything? In the course of this conversation, the guest disclaims that he is a worthy guest—he lacks "a guest worthy to be here." But Love designates that he is precisely that guest: "You shall be he." The guest responds by demurring, no, not me, I am not worthy to look on you, echoing the biblical injunction, "no one can look on the face of God and live." And then Love takes the guest by the hand and smiles, replying, "who made the eyes but I?" The guest is trying to back away and Love is holding on to him, continuing to engage him in conversation. The guest agrees that Love created him but insists that he has marred that created image. Alluding to the original sin, he wants to leave in shame; he feels he deserves exile, death, outer darkness. Love does not disagree: the image of God *has* been marred, shame *has* ensued, but Love reminds him that she has borne the blame and has thereby imputed worthiness to him. But this is not only a discussion about worthiness; rather, in the course of the conversation, the guest *becomes* worthy—worthy, first by acknowledging his lack of worth; worthy, then, by listening when he is told that his unworthiness has been accounted for; and worthy because he then understands that he belongs at the meal and wants to serve there. All of these change him—begin to qualify him—for the communion. The conversation becomes a conversion. Subjectivity is constituted in dialogue, in conversation. We cannot ask who is speaking and who is spoken to as though they are prior and independent of the conversation, for the addresser and addressee, host and guest, are only constituted as such in conversation. That is, the subjectivity of the guest is not reified before the conversation—as one who is unworthy—or after the conversation as one who is worthy; rather, it is forged actively in the very process of conversing. The speaker is "someone who receives an invitation." And who offers this invitation? Who is the host? God? Christ? Love? But what is Love? That which is welcoming, observing, questioning, taking a hand, smiling, insisting, and loving.

The feast of love to which God has invited man alludes to both the earthly communion with the implied pun on "host" and the heavenly marriage banquet it anticipates.[26] *The Book of Common Prayer* makes that very association, invoking the parables of the marriage feast and the wedding garment in the communion service. The prayer book exhorts those who are "negligent to come to the holy Communion," using the parable of the great supper:

> Ye know how grievous and unkind a thing it is, when a man hath prepared a rich feast, decked his table with all kind of provision, so that there lacketh nothing but the guests to sit downe, and yet they which be called (without any cause) most unthankfuly refuse to come. . . . If any man say, I am a grievous sinner, and therefore am afraide to come: wherefore then doe you not repent and amend? When God calleth you, be you not ashamed to say "yee will not come'"?[27]

In Herbert's version, the protestations of unworthiness are not dismissed, but they are not punished either. They are heard and answered in this conversation.

Another biblical allusion informs the final line of the poem. In Exodus, there is an alternative scene to the covenant given as tablets at Sinai: the ceremonial meal that the elders have at the top of the mountain. In contrast to the overwhelming theophany, the *mysterium tremendum* issuing in "I cannot look on thee" (Exod. 33:20), this scene describes the elders looking on God, sitting, and eating, with three spare verbs: "They looked on God, they sat and they ate." Unlike the violence of those who break the covenant even as it is given to them, these elders have been raised up to this peaceful communion.

Herbert understands love/communion as an invitation that is accepted, with the drama of the poem focusing with exquisite intensity on the invitation and the question of its acceptance—not on the menu. An invitation accepted, a call heard, a remark answered: none of these suggests the content of the conversation. Unlike so many theologians, Herbert shows no interest in defining the meal served—in addressing the issue of the Eucharistic elements—instead, he attends to the process of conversation itself, the calling and answering. What is at the heart of Herbert's mystery of the Eucharist is that an utterance could ever be heard, that a call could ever be answered, an offer ever received, an invitation ever be accepted, a conversation ever take place. For Herbert, then, an important aspect of this sacramental mystery is the mystery of language.

I am arguing that the way the English Reformed poets inaugurated modernity was not by turning away from the medieval mystery but by making language its chief vehicle in the transformation into other cultural forms. In their understanding of language, what is said and its relation to the referent—the sign to the signified—is less important than the activity of saying, than the conversation itself. In this model, language is not understood as the servant of ontology, of "standing for a thing"; in the language of conversation, some thing is not passed from one to another; rather some one hears when we call. What is heard is left indeterminate, but whatever it is, it is the only utterance we make while we live: praise expressed as the mysterious hypostasis of joy and pain. This becomes sacramental signification.

Much of the current discussion of sacrifice has turned to the question of the gift. We are told that the gift must be given with no expectation of return; for it to be a gift, that it must not be reciprocal. To give with an expectation of return is not to give a gift but to enter into a kind of contract or economic exchange.[28] I am joining those who caution against framing the discourse of the gift by economy. And I would add that we have much to gain by framing the question as Herbert did: not economically but linguistically, in the context of conversation. For when we shift the trope from gift to conversation, we no longer imagine an exchange of goods; instead, we think of a response that evokes a further response. There is a world of difference. According to Herbert, if we are unable to be heard, we are unable to speak.

> When my devotions could not pierce
> Thy silent ears;
> Then was my heart broken, as was my verse:
> My breast was full of fears
> And disorder
> . . . .
> And when we are heard, our petition is granted by that very hearing, and we
>   can once again voice our praise.
> Cheer and tune my heartless breast,
> Defer no time;
> That so thy favours granting my request,
> They and my mind may chime,
> And mend my rime.

With its understanding of signification as praise, mystical theology offered Herbert a language for gratitude that precedes and presupposes what we may really grateful for: speaking and being heard.

Like Herbert, postmodern thinkers are returning again to mysticism, to negative theology, and to its prime source, Pseudo-Dionysius, for these harbor solutions more radical than even the Reformation: the destruction of all idolatry, that is, all human efforts to comprehend, harness, and possess the domain of mystery. While their purpose is radical, their method is not. For their solution lies not in smashing or uprooting traditions. It is more modest: only to restore to the idols of our incessant use some of their mystery, that is, some of their rightful otherness. The restoration of invisibility to what had been imagined as transparent to understanding and to use, is necessary for an ethical response to the other. It is hoped that, after the "death of God," the death of the author, the end of metaphysics, the end of the subject, we will still have conversation—not between beings, but conversation as such, and that conversation will constitute us as calling and responding, as praising and hearing, and, finally, as loving.

Notes

I want to thank Chris Rebacz, Susan Schriener, David Tracy, and especially Jean-Luc Marion for their inspiration and support, as well as the volume editors, Michael Kessler and Chris Sheppard. This essay is part of a larger project on the translation of early modern sacramentalism into secular culture.

1. Marcel Gauchet, *The Disenchantment of the World: A Political History of Religion,* trans. Oscar Burge (Princeton, N.J.: Princeton University Press, 1997), 4; originally published as *Le désenchantement du monde* (Paris: Editions Gallimared, 1985).

2. Thomas Carlson's introduction to Jean-Luc Marion, *The Idol and Distance,* trans. Thomas Carlson (New York: Fordham University Press, 2001), xvi, xvii. See also Thomas Carlson, *Indiscretion: Finitude and the Naming of God* (Chicago: University of Chicago Press, 1999), 197–203.

3. Marion, *Idol and Distance,* 80.

4. My *The Curse of Cain: The Violent Legacy of Monotheism* (Chicago: University of Chicago Press, 1997) has sometimes been naively misread as an attack on religion rather than on idolatry and possession.

5. My debt is to the biblical understanding of praise as celebration, praise that is not part of an economic exchange or engages in the determinations that mark such exchanges. Here, I depart from Jacques Derrida's distinction between "praise" and "prayer" in which he assigns this noninstrumental role to prayer, and not to praise, in "Comment ne pas parler: Denegations," in *Psyche: Inventions de l'autre* (Paris: Galilee, 1987), 535–95, published in English as "How to Avoid Speaking: Denials," trans. Ken Frieden in *Languages of the Unsayable: The Play of Negativity in Literature and Literary Theory,* ed. Sanford Budick and Wolfgang Iser (New York: Columbia University Press, 1989). For Derrida, "The encomium qualifies God and *determines* prayer, determines the other, Him to whom it addresses itself, refer" 42. Derrida understands prayer as to, and praise as of, whereas in the Bible, praise is offered to without a request and prayer is a supplication for some thing. The exchange with Derrida ("On For-

giveness : A Roundtable Discussion with Jacques Derrida") on this issue can be found in *Questioning God*, ed. John Caputo, Mark Dooley, and Michael J Scanlon (Bloomington: Indiana University Press, 2001), 230–34.

6. Hans Urs von Balthassar, *Theo-drama: Theological Dramatic Theory* (San Francisco: Ignatius Press, 1988), 1:15.

7. Jean-Juc Marion, *God without Being,* trans. Thomas Carlson (Chicago: University of Chicago Press, 1991), published originally as *Dieu sans l'etre: Hors-texte* (Paris: Librairie Arthème Fayard, 1982).

8. Gregory of Nazianzus, *Laudem caesarii,* quoted in Louis Bouyer, *The Christian Mystery* (Edinburgh: T. & T. Clark, 1990), 168.

9. As the third poem on "love" in *The Temple,* it is often designated as "Love III." In reading "Love III" as a poem about the Eucharist, I am in line with the consensus among Herbert critics. Heather A. R. Asals, *Equivical Predication: George Herbert's Way to God* (Toronto: University of Toronto Press, 1981); Joseph Summers, *George Herbert* (London: Chatto & Windus, 1954), 88–89; Chana Bloch, *Spelling the Word* (Berkeley: University of California Press, 1985), 156–57; and Barbara Kiefer Lewalski, *Protestant Poetics and the Seventeenth-Century Religious Lyric* (Princeton, N.J.: Princeton University Press, 1979), 288. Richard Strier maintains that it is not about the Eucharist on the grounds that the poem speaks of sitting rather than kneeling to accept the meal ("Debating 'Love III'" panel at the Modern Language Association meeting, 1997), but that argument contradicted his otherwise consonant reading of Herbert in *Love Known: Theology and Experience in George Herbert's Poetry* (Chicago: University of Chicago Press, 1983), which stresses Herbert's theological debt to the Lutheran justification by faith.

10. Louis Martz, *The Poetry of Meditation,* rev. ed. (New Haven, Conn.: Yale University Press), 280. Chana Bloch and Heather Asals have also written of Herbert's poetry as psalmody, demonstrating the analogies between his verse and the biblical psalms.

11. Lewalski, *Protestant Poetics,* 300.

12. Sidney translated the first forty-three and his sister, the Countess of Pembroke, the rest, and they were printed in 1823; nonetheless, they were widely circulated in manuscript in Herbert's time.

13. This is further elaborated in my forthcoming book on sacramental poetry in early modern English.

14. Eleanor McNees anticipates this argument in her *Eucharistic Poetry* (Lewishburg, Pa.: Bucknell University Press, 1992).

15. Jean Calvin, *Institutes of the Christian Religion,* ed. J. T. McNeill, trans. Ford Lewis Battles, Library of Christian Classics, vol. 20(Philadelphia: Westminster Press, 1960); hereafter cited in text as Inst.

16. Calvin, Letter to Peter Martyr, (8 August 1555), cited in Ronald S. Wallace, *Calvin's Doctrine of the Word and Sacrament* (Edinburgh: Oliver & Boyd, 1953), 166.

17. Pseudo-Dionysius, *The Divine Names,* in *The Complete Works,* trans. Colm Luibheid (New York: Paulist Press, 1987), 701C.

18. Ibid., *The Divine Names,* chap. 1, 592A, 52.

19. Anselm, *Proslogion,* chap. 15, in *Monologion and Proslogion,* trans. Thomas Williams (Indianpolis: Hackett Publishing, 1995), 109.

20. Henri de Lubac, *The Mystery of the Supernatural,* trans. Rosemary Sheed (New York: Crossroad Herder, 1998), 207, originally published as *Mystère du surnatural* (Paris, 1967).

21. See Jean-Luc Marion, *Étant donné* (Paris: Presses Universitaires de France, 2000).

22. Sigmund Mowinckel, *The Psalms in Israel's Worship,* trans. D. R. Ap-Thomas, 2 vols. (Nashville: Abingdon Press, 1962), 2:30–43.

23. Gerhard von Rad, *Old Testament Theology* (New York: Harper & Row, 1962), vol. 1, originally published as *Theologie des Alten Testaments* (Munich: Kaiser Verlag, 1957).

24. Pseudo-Dionysius, *The Divine Names,* chap. 1, 588B, 49.

25. Ibid., 701C–704A.

26. Bloch, *Spelling the Word,* 100.

27. Church of England, *The Booke of Common Prayer* (London: Robert Barker, 1604).

28. Jacques Derrida, *The Gift of Death,* trans. David Wills (Chicago: University of Chicago Press, 1995), originally published as *Donner la mort* (Paris: Transition, 1999).

Mysticism and Catastrophe in Georges Bataille's *Atheological Summa*

AMY HOLLYWOOD

The opening lines of *Guilty,* the second volume of Georges Bataille's three-part *Atheological Summa,* mark the crucial, if often oblique, conjunction of historical events and mysticism in his wartime writings. (The textual history is complex, but these are the first lines to be written explicitly for this project.)

> The date on which I am beginning to write (September 5, 1939) is not a coincidence. I am beginning because of these events, but not in order to talk about them. I write these notes incapable of anything else. From now on it's necessary for me to let myself go to the movements of liberty, of caprice. Suddenly, the moment has come for me to speak without circumlocution.
>
> It is impossible for me to read—at least most books. I don't have the desire. Too much work tires me. My nerves are shattered. I get drunk a lot. I feel faithful to life if I eat and drink what I want. Life is an enchantment, a feast, a festival: an oppressing, unintelligible dream, adorned nevertheless with a charm that I enjoy. The sentiment of chance demands that I look a difficult fate in the face. It would not be about chance if there were not an incontestable madness.
>
> I began to read, standing on a crowded train, Angela of Foligno's *Book of Visions.*
>
> I'm copying it out, not knowing how to say how fiercely I burn—the veil is torn in two, I emerge from the fog in which my impotence flails.[1]

Bataille begins his exploration of ecstatic anguish at the moment when World War II begins and claims that the war itself necessitates his text. Despite "living like a pig in the eyes of Christians," moreover, Bataille finds his own tormented desire—the very anguish that compels him to write—reflected in Angela's pages. Angela, for Bataille the most important of the Christian mystics, surpasses him in the pursuit of abjection and ecstasy. He wants to be like her in her desire for and proximity to death: "I suffer from not myself burning to the point of coming close to death, so close that I inhale it like the breath of a loved being."[2]

War and mysticism, then, converge in Bataille's texts. Yet as these lines suggest, Bataille refers only elliptically to the war in *Inner Experience* and *Guilty*. He had, in fact, little direct experience of armed conflict. From 1939 to 1943, Bataille lived in relative isolation; increasingly ill, he moved between Paris and the French countryside.[3] The *Atheological Summa* itself suggests that only with the movement of Allied troops into France in 1944 did Bataille have any experience of war's violence and its effects on civilian bystanders.[4] *On Nietzsche,* the third volume of the *Atheological Summa,* contains journal entries that deal directly and at length with the effects of the war. Despite the relative paucity of direct reference to World War II, however, one must take seriously Bataille's claim that historical events precipitate his writing; moreover, one can see these catastrophes repeatedly emerging in the interstices of his texts.

What I hope to show here is that during a historical moment in which concrete political action seemed hopeless and the threat of death pervasive, Bataille turned to mysticism as an alternative form of community building. His inability to participate in the movements of history generates guilt at his own chance survival as well as his inaction.[5] In response, Bataille re-creates a mystical path of contemplation made up of "*compassion,* pain, and ecstasy."[6] Rather than marking a willed rejection of history, Bataille suggests that mysticism offers a form of community and action in the face of chance events that lie outside the control of individual subjects. (The introduction to *Guilty* points to Bataille's feeling of political impotence: "To ask oneself before another: how does he appease in himself the desire to be everything [*tout*]? . . . No longer to desire to be everything [*tout*] is to put everything [*tout*] into question.")[7]

Yet many of Bataille's contemporaries read his turn to mysticism as a form of intellectual and spiritual solipsism, a rejection of history, action, and politics for which they castigate him. Roger Caillois, with whom Bataille founded the prewar College of Sociology, is the first to claim that, in embracing mysticism, Bataille abandons politics and history. The charge is repeated by Jean-Paul Sartre in his 1943 review of *Inner Experience* (to which Bataille replies in an appendix to *On Nietzsche*). Rejecting Bataille's claim that nothingness and the unknowable radically destabilize the theological and soteriological assertions of traditional Christian mysticism, Sartre argues that Bataille reifies nothingness and makes it God. This nihilism, according to Sartre, is the result of Bataille's attempt to escape temporality, historicity, and responsibility through inner experience.

Caillois and Sartre set the tone for later commentators, who continually repeat this opposition between mysticism and politics. Francis Marmande, for example, argues in his fine study, *Georges Bataille politique,* that Bataille's multiple and fragmented body of writing can be tied together by its political aims. Marmande remains uneasy, however, with the *Atheological Summa.* On the one hand, Marmande writes, the turn to mysticism clearly marks a break with the flurry of prewar political activities in which Bataille engaged during the 1930s (participation in Boris Souvarine's Trotskyite Democratic Communist circle and its journal, *La Critique sociale;* the shorted-lived rapprochement with André Breton and the surrealists in *Contre Attaque;* the secret society *Acéphale* and the College of Sociology, both founded by Bataille in order to pursue the study of the sacred and its revitalization in the modern world, specifically as a response to fascism). Marmande doesn't limit politics, however, to such overt political activity—he insists that the resistance of Bataille's writing, his focus on the use of words rather than simply their meaning, is itself a form of antiauthoritarian and contestatory political engagement. (This will seem an attenuated understanding of politics to many.) *Inner Experience* maintains the refractory power of Bataille's writing, yet does so, Marmande argues, in response to "personal dramas and illness."[8] Marmande crucially ignores the centrality of historical events to Bataille's mystical "turn."

There is one dissenting voice in all of this—although he names neither Bataille nor, at least not explicitly, the particular historical moment in which Bataille's texts were produced.[9] In his 1972–73 seminar, *Encore,* Jacques Lacan (in)famously turns to the questions of love, "woman," history, and mysticism. Before associating his own work with mystical texts, he wants to make clear that mysticism is not to be associated with the early twentieth-century French religious and political right.[10] Nor does he associate mysticism with obscurantism and antinomianism as do many throughout the early twentieth century (including, at times, Bataille).

Me, I don't use the word mystic as Péguy used it. Mysticism is not all [*pas tout*] that which is not politics. It is something serious, about which certain people teach us, and most often women, or gifted people like saint John of the Cross—because one is not forced when one is male, to place oneself on the side of the [phallic function]. One can also place oneself on the side of the not all [*pas tout*]. There are men who are as good as women. It happens. And who at the same time feel good about it. Despite, I don't say their phallus, despite that which encumbers them under that title, they catch a glimpse, they sense the idea that there must be a jouissance that goes beyond. That's who one calls "mystics."[11]

Like those men who take the side of the "not all/whole"—who reject their place in a symbolic (cultural, political, and social realm) governed by the phallus (and hence, symbolically and literally, by men)—mysticism is itself "not all/whole". Rather than marking a nostalgia for lost plenitude and wholeness (supported by the conflation of imaginary and symbolic realms), mysticism (like psychoanalysis, according to Lacan) is the site in which such desires are renounced.[12] As such, it is not that which is not political but arguably the place where ethics (and a particular sort of politics?) receives its most stringent expression.

Lacan doesn't mention Georges Bataille in Seminar 20; yet I suspect that in naming those "men who are as good as women" in their renunciation of plenitude and wholeness, Lacan alludes to his longtime friend (who died in 1962). Even without such an explicit association, however, I think that Bataille's wartime writings can be usefully read in light of Lacan's understanding of mysticism as the "not all/whole", as a rejection of fantasies of wholeness and plenitude through which what Lacan calls "the real" is apprehended.[13] As Lacan shows in *Encore,* male subjectivity is supported in its illusory wholeness by the primacy of the phallus as signifier of mastery, meaning, and power; the gap between the penis and the phallus is real, and yet—as we all know—they look an awful lot alike. This resemblance gives greater verisimilitude to men's claims to overcome the gap in being that is intrinsic, Lacan argues, to every speaking subject. Only through a rejection of this fantasmatic association, however, can "the real"—what I will, following Lacan, associate with that in history unassimilable to its meaning-giving and salvific narratives—be apprehended.

Georges Bataille's *Inner Experience* and *Guilty* are markedly indebted to the mystical text most important to him, the *Book* of the thirteenth-century Umbrian Franciscan tertiary, Angela of Foligno.[14] Following Angela, Bataille offers an account of the modes of contemplation that lead to ecstasy. Bataille's texts can be read as his attempt to repeat Angela's experience, to bring himself "close to death."[15] Bataille writes for those who would themselves repeat Angela's excesses in the twentieth century, those who will create a new sacred community through embracing the not all and contemplating the real. In reading and rewriting (repeating) Angela's texts, moreover, Bataille creates a community with her in which the reader might also come to share. He argues that through contemplation, the laceration of subjectivity required by communication occurs. This communication grounds new communities, the work or action of Bataille's texts. So for Bataille, as for central portions of the medieval mystical tradition, contemplation is itself a form of action, one that generates a community brought together, paradoxically, through their shared contemplation of the real (what Bataille in *Guilty* refers to as the catastrophe, and which can be, as I will show, linked to contemporary discussions of trauma). Uncovering the relationship among *Inner Experience, Guilty,* and Angela's *Book* and through Angela's *Book* with broader Christian practices of meditation, then, offers important insight into the political, ethical, and religious import of Bataille's "project that is not a project" and will raise a new set of questions about the viability of these political, ethical, and religious claims.

Bataille begins his new mystical theology with a reminder to the reader of its divergences from the old. He writes that, like Maurice Blanchot's *Thomas the Obscure,* he seeks a new theology "which has only the unknown for its object."[16] Such a theology must

- have its principles and its end in the absence of salvation, in the renunciation of all hope,
- affirm of inner experience that it is authority (but all authority expiates itself),
- be contestation of itself and nonknowledge.[17]

Bataille wants to develop a mystical theology without God, an atheology in which God (as this concept is understood, according to Bataille, within the modern Christian West) is subverted through a radical experience of the limit and the unknowable, what, in *Guilty,* Bataille will call the catastrophe. He follows this call for a new mystical theology, then, with a series of chapters on God and the philosophical conceptions of God, knowledge, and totality found in Descartes and Hegel. I analyze in more detail elsewhere how the chapter entitled "God," which begins and ends with appeals to the mystics, effectively subverts traditional understandings of the divine object (as the source of plenitude and wholeness in which self-presence and meaning are guaranteed). Bataille uses the mystics' emphasis on desire and its unlimitability to this end.[18]

Bataille then introduces two digressions that are particularly indebted to Angela's *Book*—"First Digression on Ecstasy before an Object: The Point" and "Second Digression on Ecstasy in the Void." In characteristic fashion, these "digressions" are the heart of Bataille's book. Without here naming Angela, Bataille relies on a distinction central to her account of the twenty-sixth transformation of the soul. After having emphasized the role of suffering in her experience and its relationship to the sufferings of Christ in life and on the cross, Angela describes the relationship between that object-centered and desirous loving relationship and the encounter with darkness in which she is made into nonlove and lies in the abyss.

> When I am in that darkness I do not remember anything about anything human, or the God-man, or anything which has a form. Nevertheless, I see all and I see nothing. As what I have spoken of withdraws and stays with me, I see the God-man. He draws my soul with great gentleness and he sometimes says to me; "You are I and I am you." I see, then, those eyes and that face so gracious and attractive as he leans to embrace me. In short, what proceeds from those eyes and that face is what I said that I saw in that previous darkness which comes from within, and which delights me so that I can say nothing of it. When I am in the God-man my soul is alive. And I am in the God-man much more than in the other vision of seeing God with darkness. The soul is alive in that vision concerning the God-man. The vision with darkness, however, draws me so much more that there is no comparison.[19]

Angela here articulates the relationship between her experience of unity with Christ in his suffering and that with the divine abyss of darkness, nothingness, and unknowing. She asserts a relationship between these two forms of experience but doesn't completely elucidate the nature of the link between them.[20] She explains, however, that she sees the darkness in the eyes and face of Christ, suggesting a causal connection between her meditation and identification with the passion of Christ and her experience of the dissolution of self and other into ecstatic darkness.[21] Similarly, Bataille seeks to articulate the relationship between an ecstasy generated before an object and out of love for an other and that experienced in the void.

Bataille's conception of the self-subverting nature of the divine suggests that there will be no place for a positive object of meditation in his practice. But instead of rejecting such an object, Bataille reinterprets it, arguing that the object contemplated by the mystic is not a divine object of emulation but a projection of the self, a dramatization of the self's dissolution.[22] In making this claim, Bataille also draws out explicitly the relationship between ecstasy before an object and that before the void or darkness adumbrated by Angela.

> I will say this, although it is obscure: the object in the experience is first the projection of a dramatic loss of self. It is the image of the subject. The subject attempts

at first to go to one like itself. But having entered into inner experience, the subject is in quest of an object like itself, reduced to its interiority. In addition, the subject whose experience is in itself and from the beginning dramatic (it is loss of self)
needs to objectify this dramatic character. . . .

But it is only a question there of a fellow human being. The point, before me,
reduced to the most paltry simplicity, is a person. At each instant of experience, this
point can radiate arms, cry out, set itself ablaze.[23]

The extremity of the other's suffering leads not only to his or her own dissolution but also to that of the contemplator or viewer. It is through this laceration and loss of self that communication between the self and the other occurs. The practice of dramatization or meditation is a necessary (although not
sufficient) condition if one is to stand out of the self and open oneself to the
other—in other words, to attain ecstasy and communication.

Bataille explicitly ties ecstasy before the object to the practice of meditation described by Ignatius of Loyola and other Christian mystics. For Bataille,
the object of meditation is most often, as we will see, a series of photographs
of a Chinese torture victim. Bataille's allusions to Christian meditative practice, particularly the forms of meditative practice central to Angela, offer a key
to understanding his seemingly bizarre—and to many repulsive—practice of
meditating on these horrific images.

In a study of late medieval meditational practices and their relationship
to visionary literature, Denise Despres shows that Franciscan devotional
literature advocates a form of sensible meditational practice designed to be
penitential and participatory. Responding to the vexed question of the relationship between the active and contemplative lives, Franciscan authors emphasize that contemplation is itself a form of action and that living in accordance with the life of Christ itself a form of contemplation.[24] Rather than
standing in tension, meditation on the life of Christ brings about sensible
identification with Christ's suffering and hence true contrition (the emotional component) and the moral actions required by it. Meditation, then, as
Mary Carruthers brilliantly shows with regard to the early medieval monastic
culture out of which Franciscan practice emerges, is an art of memory and
memorialization. Memory is the key to both contemplative and active lives,
for both moral and religious dispositions are dependent on a well-stocked
and -ordered memory. Meditational practice, according to Carruthers, is a
type of memory work that generates emotion, which in turn facilitates the act
of memorialization. The beginning of the meditational life, for monastics,
Franciscans, and the lay audiences for whom Franciscans often wrote (among

them Angela of Foligno) lies in the inculcation of guilt (and with it contrition), which lead to further acts of meditation (including, for the Franciscans, actions imitative of Christ) through which that guilt is expiated.

This form of memory work and exegetical meditational practice is crucial to understanding the work of Angela of Foligno. Comparing Angela's *Book* to the late-thirteenth-century meditational primer *Meditations on the Life of Christ*, Robyn O'Sullivan demonstrates both Angela's debt to the Franciscan tradition and her divergences from it. For while thirteenth-century Franciscan authors typically call for the believer to identify with various witnesses of the events of Christ's life through the imaginative recreation of key moments in the Gospel narrative (perhaps reflecting a shift from monastic practice to texts designed for the laity), Angela moves from identification with Saint John and Mary, the mother of God, to identification with Christ himself. Like the thirteenth-century beguine mystics of northern Europe, Hadewijch and Mechthild of Magdeburg, Angela desires a relationship without mediation between herself and Christ. Angela's desire for mystical union with Christ and the Godhead is reflected in her meditational practice, which gradually elides the gap between onlooker and object.[25]

Angela's accounts of Christ's suffering, like those of many others in the later Middle Ages, attempt to explore fully the details of Christ's torture in order to make his suffering come alive for herself and for the reader. Meditation on the details of Christ's abjection is essential to the mystic's and the reader's identification with him.

> Once when I was meditating on the great suffering which Christ endured on the cross, I was considering the nails, which, I had heard it said, had driven a little bit of the flesh of his hands and feet into the wood. And I desired to see at least that small amount of Christ's flesh which the nails had driven into the wood. And then such was my sorrow over the pain that Christ had endured that I could no longer stand on my feet. I bent over and sat down; I stretched out my arms on the ground and inclined my head on them. Then Christ showed me his throat and arms.[26]

Angela does not just meditate on the figure of a crucified Christ but on the bits and pieces of his lacerated body. Moreover, the gap between herself as onlooker and the object of her contemplation is dissipated in the fragmentation of Christ's body. Attention to these fragments renders her body into the very cruciform pattern of Christ's torment, suggesting her complete identification with his suffering. Her suffering at the sight of the cross is immediate and inescapable (she tells us early in her book that she screams and cries out whenever she sees the cross) and ultimately the cross itself is permanently inscribed in her heart. Through the imaginative recreation of Christ's passion, Angela moves from sensible identification with his suffering body to its incorporation.[27] This fragmentation, incorporation, and repetition of Christ's suffering, moreover, leads to her joyful ecstasy.

Whereas Angela's *Book* suggests that she renders herself Christ-like through her identificatory meditations on Christ's suffering flesh, and hence potentially shares his redemptive activity, taking on a salvific role for herself and others (this is much more explicit in Hadewijch and Mechthild of Magdeburg), Bataille argues that the other is a projection of the self. Angela's desire to dissolve the self, to approach death, and open herself to the lacerating wounds required for communication are projected onto another, in this case, Christ. Bataille has recourse to other images: "In any case, we can only project the object-point by drama. I had recourse to upsetting images. In particular, I would gaze at the photographic image—or sometimes the memory I have of it—of a Chinese man who must have been tortured in my lifetime. Of this torture, I had had in the past a series of successive representations. In the end, the patient writhed, his chest flayed, arms and legs cut off at the elbows and at the knees. His hair standing on end, hideous, haggard, striped with blood, beautiful as a wasp."[28] Some of the most shocking aspects of Bataille's text repeat in the modern world (or as Bataille no doubt would put it, after the death of God) the Christian mystic's contemplation of Christ's suffering. The image of Christ on the cross is analogous to the photos of the cut-apart body of a torture victim (the contemporary figure of ignominy and abjection so central to *Inner Experience* and *Guilty*) on which Bataille meditates.

The move away from Christ occurs for a number of reasons. In order to reenact the meditative and writing practices of medieval mysticism, Bataille must defamiliarize the bodily torture of the crucifixion. More important, if the theocentrism and Christocentrism of Angela's experience is to be decentered, other images of woundedness and laceration must take the place of the Christ figure. The "object point," as Bataille tells us, is simply a "person," "a fellow human being": "The young and seductive Chinese man of whom I have spoken, left to the work of the executioner—I loved him with a love in which the sadistic instinct played no part: he communicated his pain to me or perhaps the excessive nature of his pain, and it was precisely that which I was seeking, not so as to take pleasure in it, but in order to ruin in me that which is opposed to ruin."[29] What is central about the cross, Bataille suggests, is not who is on it or the salvific nature of his suffering, but the suffering itself, which serves as the projected image through which the subject experiences his or her own dissolution. What we cannot ruin directly in ourselves, Bataille argues, we can (must?) ruin through identification with the other's bodily laceration.

The explosion of the other's body serves as a dramatization, leading to greater ecstasy in the void.[30] Here we see the move from ecstasy before the object, parallel to Angela's meditations on the figure of Christ, to ecstasy before the void, which is analogous to Angela's account of the darkness of the divine.

> The movement prior to the ecstasy of non-knowledge is the ecstasy before an object (whether the latter be the pure point—as the renouncing of dogmatic beliefs would have it—or some upsetting image). If this ecstasy before the object is at first given (as a "possible") and if I suppress afterwards the object—as "contestation" inevitably does—if for this reason I enter into anguish—into horror, into the night of non-knowledge—ecstasy is near and, when it sets in, sends me further into ruin than anything imaginable. If I had not known of the ecstasy before the object, I would not have reached ecstasy in night. But *initiated* as I was in the object—and my initiation had represented the furthest penetration of what is possible—I could, in night, only find a deeper ecstasy. From that moment night, non-knowledge, will each time be the path of ecstasy into which I will lose myself.[31]

Bataille's text itself attempts, like Angela's, to engender in writing and in the reader the dissolution of subject and object that is inner experience. Through this, communication occurs and a new community emerges—between Angela and Bataille, and between Bataille and his projected readers (and, more problematically, between the torture victim and Bataille). Moreover, Angela and her book become objects on to which Bataille can project his own dissolution, leading to the greater dissolution of self before the void. Arguably, Bataille in turn becomes such a figure for readers of his text.

These meditational practices—both those found in medieval texts such as the *Meditations on the Life of Christ* and Angela of Foligno's *Book* and Bataille's twentieth-century revisionings—bear a curious similarity to contemporary discussions of memory and traumatic suffering. Angela and Bataille both use meditational techniques to reenact and to experience sensibly, emotionally, and viscerally the extraordinary physical suffering of another; meditation on the fragmented body of torture victims gives rise to the dissolution of the subject and his or her lacerating openness to the other.

Whereas in the twentieth century, the literature on extraordinary suffering and its aftereffects primarily focuses on the victims of trauma and means of alleviating the hyperarousal, constriction of world, and intrusive memories that result from overwhelming events (and to ask why certain experiences give rise to such symptoms while other, seemingly similar experiences, do not), at least some meditational practices work to *generate* bodily memories in those not themselves immediately affected by the physical suffering memorialized (so perhaps it is better to speak of meditationally induced analogs of bodily memories).

This gives rise to a question not unlike that with which Sigmund Freud approached the compulsion to repeat traumatic memories among shell-shock victims. For Freud, who understood dreams and compulsions in terms of the desire for pleasure and its repression, compulsively repeated memories and dreams about physical horrors and the threat of death were inexplicable. This leads to his suggestion that there is a death drive in addition to and beyond the pleasure principle. Tied to his late theory of primary masochism, Freud suggests that there is a drive to escape subjectivity or to shatter the self that stands in tension with the pleasure principle (although arguably pleasure, untouched by the reality principle, itself dissolves subjectivity). For many contemporary theorists, the danger of Freud's view is that it ignores or covers over the harsh realities of victimization; if we read self-dissolution as desired, we are in danger of replacing trauma as inescapable suffering inflicted *on* human beings with masochism as the embrace of shattering affliction.[32] A similar dilemma, as I will show, haunts any reading of Angela's and Bataille's texts.

To get at the issues involved here, however, we first need to clarify the relationship between medieval and modern meditational practices and contemporary theories of bodily or traumatic memories. Pierre Janet introduced the distinction between narrative and traumatic memory as a way to highlight the abnormality of vivid, intrusive memories, laden with sensory and iconic motifs, common to survivors of traumatic events.

> [Normal memory] like all psychological phenomena, is an action; essentially it is the action of telling a story. . . . A situation has not been satisfactorily liquidated . . . until we have achieved, not merely an outward reaction through our movements, but also an inward reaction through the words we address to ourselves, through the organization of the recital of the event to others and to ourselves, and through the putting of this recital in its place as one of the chapters in our personal history. . . . Strictly speaking, then, one who retains a fixed idea of a happening

cannot be said to have a "memory". . . . it is only for convenience that we speak of it as a "traumatic memory."[33]

The highly sensory nature of these memories and absence of verbal narrative make them very similar to the memories of young children.[34] Yet unlike normal memories from early childhood, traumatic memories (and the associated phenomenon of traumatic dreams) are experienced as involuntary, having a "driven, tenacious quality," and repetitive dimension.[35] Current research suggests that in situations of hyperarousal, particularly those for which the subject is unable to prepare him- or herself, memory is encoded in a different, more viscerally experiential manner than normally. These bodily memories, then, are not assimilated to consciousness and thus impinge on it in uncontrollable and intrusive ways. The best available treatment for such memories seems to be narrativization, through which bodily memories are relived and reordered in meaningful narrative forms.[36]

Thus researchers, psychiatrists, and psychotherapists working with trauma survivors have developed complex therapies of reenactment and narrativization in which subjects remember in controlled environments, enabling them to order and make sense out of their experience: "Out of the fragmented components of frozen imagery and sensation, patient and therapist slowly reassemble an organized, detailed, verbal account, oriented in time and historical context. The narrative includes not only the event itself but also the survivor's response to it and the responses of important people in her life. . . . The completed narrative must include a full and vivid description of the traumatic imagery. . . . The ultimate goal, however, is to put the story, including its imagery, into words." Psychiatrist and psychotherapist Judith Herman, who offers this account of the therapeutic process involved in recovery from post-traumatic stress disorder (PTSD), also insists that the (re)creation of a narrative of the traumatic event "includes a systematic review of the meaning of the event." The survivor must "reconstruct a system of belief that makes sense of her undeserved suffering"; such a system of belief, to be effective, must also result in action, often involving social activism against suffering and injustice.[37]

Medieval meditational practices reverse this pattern, moving through narrative memory in order, through imaginative re-creation, to induce sensory and emotive suffering and horror in the face of catastrophic loss—in this case the death of the God-man on the cross. Medieval memory work involves making one's own this historically distant yet cosmologically and soteriologically central event, inducing something like traumatic memories of events that have not occurred to the subject but to Christ. We see this, for example, in Angela's focus on the gruesome details of Christ's crucifixion, through which she makes present, emotionally and sensorily vibrant, the experience of Christ's suffering. Moreover, Angela stresses the extent to which these emotive and visceral responses become involuntary and inescapable. This sensory and emotionally laden contemplation generates the guilt of survival and with it contrition and the penitential acts that will—in theory—allay that guilt. Angela thus moves from intense sorrow at Christ's suffering to the desire not simply to witness but also to share in the suffering, even to intensify it: "Then I would beg him to grant me this grace, namely, that since Christ had been crucified on the wood of the cross, that I be crucified in a gully, or in some very vile place, and by a very vile instrument. Moreover, since I did not desire to die as the saints had died, that he make me die a slower and even more vile death than theirs. I could not imagine a death vile enough to match my desire."[38] This desire is answered on the spiritual level, making Angela's suffering soul itself an object of contemplation for the reader: "Concerning the torments of the soul which demons inflicted upon her, she found herself incapable of finding any other comparison than that of a man hanged by the neck who, with his hands tied behind him and his eyes blindfolded, remains dangling on the gallows and yet lives, with no help, no support, no remedy, swinging in the empty air."[39] Angela's repeated accounts of her own abject suffering and her desire for suffering and death, moreover, suggest the viability of Bataille's claim that the image of the suffering Christ serves as a projection through which the subject comes to experience her own dissolution.[40] Angela seems less intent on the "recovery" made possible through narrativization (in this case the soteriological narrative of Christianity) than in a dissolution of self desired "beyond the pleasure principle," although arguably, the Christian narrative allows for both simultaneously, as Angela is lost in Christ and through sharing in his suffering keeps her own—and the world's—guilt.

So we see that a central feature of traumatic memory, its lack of a meaning-giving narrative framework, is generally absent from the work of medieval meditation, for in monastic meditative texts and in Franciscan meditational guides the narrative of salvation history is the constant backdrop against which Jesus' life and death is reenacted. In this context, the making visceral of Christ's suffering in the soul (and, at least occasionally, on the body with phenomenon like the stigmata) of the believer is a means of inducing emotion only in order to redeploy that suffering toward certain narrative and salvific ends. Medieval meditational techniques, in this reading, induce something like traumatic memory—or perhaps better, make visceral the catastrophe of God's death on the cross—only in order to relocate and redeploy that bodily response within the terms of salvation history. The central question raised by Angela's text is whether in her case the reenactment of the divine catastrophe of the cross doesn't overwhelm the redemptive framing story, bringing her closer, once again, to Bataille than her place within the Christian tradition might initially suggest.

Without denying the power and efficacy of narrativization, then, both Angela's and Bataille's texts raise the question of that which is left out of Herman's therapeutic account and my use of it to read medieval meditational practices—the refusal, on the part of many survivors of traumatic or catastrophic events, to accept any palliating or explanatory narrative for their suffering. Victims often express the fear that the imposition of salvific or other explanatory narratives onto their experience undercuts the onlooker's ability to understand and identify with the severity of their suffering.[41] In addition, a sense of obligation to cosufferers who have not survived sometimes gives rise to an explicitly *ethical* rejection of meaning-giving narratives.[42] Finally, the guilt often associated with survival can block healing, as it is understood by Herman and other psychotherapists. Bataille, with his rejection of salvific narratives and insistence on the dissolution of subjectivity in the face of bodily trauma, uses meditational practices of traumatic recreation not in order to inculcate and then allay guilt but, rather, to intensify and embrace anguish. Given his distance from the catastrophes of war and experiences of bodily torture like those on which he meditates, however, we must ask whether Bataille's pursuit of bodily memory and the concomitant dissolution of the subject marks, as Sartre and others suggest, mere self-indulgence and escapism from the demands of history.

Cathy Caruth argues that literary and philosophical accounts of trauma raise the question of whether trauma is an "encounter with death, or the ongoing experience of having survived it"[43] Caruth's account of trauma focuses on the onlooker, the one who encounters overwhelming events, unassimilable to consciousness, and hence always returned to in an attempt to make sense out of experience. In almost all of Caruth's examples, that onlooker remains physically untouched by the witnessed catastrophe. I think this understanding of trauma must be carefully differentiated from that central to contemporary clinical literature like Herman's, which focuses on those who have themselves *undergone* extraordinary physical suffering.[44] In addition, this distinction also suggests another, between the individual's encounter with violence and suffering and such events as experienced within larger social, political, and historical networks. To this end, I will differentiate between those who encounter catastrophe (borrowing a term crucial to Bataille) from the contemporary clinical use of the term trauma, which focuses on the individual and his or her responses to life-threatening acts of violence.

Following Lacan, Caruth argues that the onlooker's refusal to accept redemptive narratives marks the ethical nature of traumatic memory itself:

> The accidental in trauma is a revelation of a basic, ethical dilemma at the heart of consciousness itself insofar as it is essentially related to death, and particularly to the death of others. Ultimately, then, the story of father and child [in Freud's account of a father's dream after the death of his son] is, for Lacan, the story of an impossible responsibility of consciousness in its own originating relation to others, and specifically to the death of others. As an awakening, the ethical relation to the real is the revelation of this impossible demand at the heart of human consciousness.[45]

This is what Lacan refers to as the "ethical *relation* to the real," a mode of encounter that refuses salvific narratives insofar as they cover over the other's death and the accidental nature of one's own survival.[46] At the heart of the individual's experience of the other's death, then, lies an ethical intuition about the social nature of existence.

This helps elucidate Bataille's repetition, throughout the *Atheological Summa* and particularly in the aptly named *Guilty*, of the themes of chance and ecstasy. At one point in *Guilty* this takes the form of fascination with the sturdy hooks he sees placed half way up a roof. (These hooks are used to hold in place poles that keep snow from falling off the roof.)

> I saw big, solid hooks on a roof, placed half way up. Suppose a man falls from the roof, perhaps [*par chance*] he could grab hold of one of them with his arm or leg. Precipitated from the roof of a house, I would crash into the ground. But if a hook were there, I could stop myself on the way down!

> A bit later I might say to myself: "One day an architect planned that hook without which I would be dead. I ought to be dead: it isn't so at all, I am alive, someone put a hook there."
>
> My presence and my life would be ineluctable: but I don't know what of the impossible, of the inconceivable, would be its principle.
>
> I understand now, imagining to myself the momentum of the fall, that nothing exists in the world without meeting a hook.[47]

This hook comes to represent the contingency of Bataille's survival; neither the war nor his illness kill him (although these issues aren't raised explicitly by

Bataille). There's no reason for him to be alive, nor can he make his life meaningful—all he can do is witness to its contingency. And in embracing chance, he stands outside of himself in ecstasy: "THE OBJECT OF ECSTASY IS THE ABSENCE OF RESPONSE FROM OUTSIDE. THE INEXPLICABLE PRESENCE OF MAN IS THE RESPONSE THAT THE WILL GIVES ITSELF, SUSPENDED OVER THE VOID OF AN UNINTELLIGIBLE NIGHT; THAT NIGHT, FROM ONE END TO THE OTHER, HAS THE IMPUDENCE OF A HOOK."[48] Chance is the hook on which existence falls. It's without meaning and offers no answer to the question of human existence other than its own facticity. The abruptness of this facticity, the absence of response in the response, is ecstasy. Ecstasy is here engendered through meditation on the absence of response to the "why" of his own survival. Yet when the object of ecstasy is the other, we are brought back to our earlier question concerning Bataille's practice of meditating on photographs of a Chinese man, the victim of a horrifying torture, and the ethical challenge this practice offers the reader.

> I just looked at two photographs of torture. These images have become familiar to me; one of them, nevertheless, is so horrible that it makes my heart skip a beat.
>
> I must have had to stop writing. I was, as I often am, sitting before an open window; I had just sat down when I fell into a sort of ecstasy. This time, I no longer doubted, as I did painfully the previous night, that such a state was more intense than erotic pleasure. I see nothing: *that* is neither visible nor sensible. *That* makes me sad and heavy not to die. If I picture, in my anguish, all I have loved, I must imagine furtive realities to which my love attached itself like so many clouds behind which *what is there* hid itself. Ecstatic images betray. *What is there* comes entirely from fright. Fright makes it happen: a violent fracas is required for *it to be there*.[49]

This ecstatic standing outside of the self is experienced as laceration, agony, and anguish, a rendering of the self in the face of the real: "When an image of torture falls before my eyes, I can, in my fright, turn away. But I am, if I look at it, *outside of myself*. . . . The horrible sight of torture opens the sphere in which is enclosed (is delimited) my personal particularity, it opens it violently, it lacerates it."[50]

For Bataille, inner experience begins with dramatization and meditation on "images of explosion and of being lacerated—ripped to pieces."[51] Meditation on the wounded body of the other lacerates the onlooker's subjectivity; Bataille argues that woundedness and its recognition is necessary to opening one human being to the other. The greater this woundedness and laceration, the more the self is exploded and ripped apart, the fuller is the communication that occurs between the nonself and the now ruined other. The crucial question remains as to why openness to the other and communication are understood as woundedness.[52] But the ways in which Bataille discusses his meditational practices in *Guilty*, a more anguished and personal text than *Inner Experience*, suggests that the question might be posed in another way—perhaps Bataille is attempting to communicate a kind of experience unassimilable to traditional narrative forms and normal language use.[53] The distinction between narrative memory and catastrophic memory is useful here, for it helps us see that for Bataille the writings of the mystics (and of Nietzsche), like the photographs of the Chinese torture victim, communicate realities that stand outside of everyday experience or, at least, what we like to believe about everyday experience. For Bataille, these texts and images force the onlooker/reader to recognize the anguishing real hidden by everyday talk and the illusions of wholeness and unity on which it depends.[54] *Inner Experience, Guilty,* and *On Nietzsche*, written in the midst of the historical catastrophes confronting Bataille from 1939 to 1944, attempt to find a way to communicate catastrophic suffering without succumbing either to salvific and compensatory narratives or to dissolution, silence, and death.

One might argue, however, that it is wrong to read Bataille's compulsion in light of historical catastrophe, for his texts elide history in its specificity. The time, place, and context of the Chinese man's torture and execution is only briefly alluded to and plays no role in Bataille's meditative practice, and Bataille refuses to focus directly on contemporary European events.[55] Bataille then is able to move rapidly from the traumatic dismemberment of the torture victim to the chance nature of human existence, reading the tortured body as emblematic of the human condition (and this reflects the move, described in *Inner Experience*, from ecstasy before an object to that before the void). This ignores the stark *differences* between Bataille's bodily experience and that of the dismembered Chinese man and conflates, far too rapidly, contingency with violence and horror. Seen in another way, however, Bataille asks readers to look at this dismembered body, in all its unnamed specificity, and recognize that *only* chance keeps that body from being their own. From this perspective, Bataille's move becomes less ethically dubious. Yet I still hesitate over the "only," for while such horrors can befall any body, should we ignore the concrete ethical, political, and historical dimensions that engender many such events?

To uncover these dimensions, to ask how such events occur and how they can be stopped, is to provide a narrative and historical context for them, precisely the move Bataille eschews. Read in light of medieval meditational practices centered on the crucifixion, in which narrative memory plays a key role, Bataille's renunciation of such narratives becomes particularly stark. We can see what Bataille rejects in those practices and the ramifications of his denial. He offers guilt without redemption, anguish without salvation. Bataille implies that the specificity of the real (*this* body, in pieces) must take precedence over any narrative contextualization; to put this more strongly, Bataille suggests that narrative and historical contextualization is (necessarily? can be if it takes soteriological form?) a way of evading the real. This points to two ways of understanding history within Bataille's text: as those narratives that give meaning and direction to human action and that which remains unassimilable to such narratives.

In her discussion of contemporary academic attempts to speak for the other, the dead victims of catastrophic events, Patricia Yaeger cogently questions what is at stake for us in such ventriloquizing moves.[56] Despite her insistence that we maintain a nervous vigilance against accepting too readily our ability to speak for the other, she maintains this model of "speaking for." Bataille, on the contrary, never pretends to speak for the other; rather his texts demonstrate a compulsion to see the speechless body. Rather than providing the context in which demands for justice might be made, the sight of the speechless body rejects meaning and any historical or soteriological framework in which the fragmented body might be turned into or read as a sign. Bataille attempts to give an account of *communication* in and through the lacerating reality of the other's suffering that does not embrace any salvific narrative, that doesn't reduce the suffering other to his or her "use" value (as heroic emblem, call for political action, etc.). (Yet this body *communicates* only through the mediation of the photographer, raising crucial issues about agency, fictionality, and the real.) It's hard to see this as a *sufficient* form of action—and there is the real danger that with this rejection of soteriological narratives, historical and cultural memory will be annihilated—yet it may be a necessary contestation of more immediately "useful" political projects. Just as there are two conceptions of history standing alongside each other in Bataille's text, perhaps we should distinguish between two conceptions of action and two politics, one that would contest power and injustice through narrativization and the other that would contest those very narrativizations themselves in the name of that which is unassimilable to redemptive political projects—the bodies of those who can never again be made whole.[57]

Yet isn't Bataille using violent imagery toward contemplative ends and thereby appropriating others' real, bodily suffering for his own "ecstasy"?[58] The more closely we associate ecstasy with pleasure (the tendency of many critics), the more troubling this becomes.[59] In a line of interpretation that I have followed out elsewhere, Bataille's account of ecstasy can be understood in light of Lacan's theory of jouissance and its deployment by Jean Laplanche and Leo Bersani. One can thus read ecstasy in terms of Freud's late account of primary masochism, as a self-shattering that lies beyond the pleasure principle and yet is itself *desired*. In both the masochistic and the catastrophic line of interpretation, Bataille's "compulsion to repeat" the encounter with extraordinary physical suffering has nothing to do with the obvious pleasure of mastering seemingly unmasterable horrors. Whatever ecstasy is, it is not simply pleasure, and I take seriously Bataille's repeated claim that ecstasy is anguish (although an anguish accompanied by the joy of communication). This still leaves me with the question of masochistic desire and its relationship to the ethical compulsion to confront the real (with the ramifications that encounter carries for subjectivity). Here I've offered an account of Bataille's wartime writing as sparked by an imperative to witness to the other's physical dissolution and to accept the dissolution of the self—the anguished ecstatic standing outside of oneself—that this witnessing demands. There is another reading of this desire, however, as a desire to *escape* from the self that uses the other's physical suffering as a means to this ecstatic end.

War is a catastrophe to which Bataille, in oddly indirect fashion, bears witness (and the role of World War II in these texts needs further elaboration); yet in a troubling way, the constant threat of death, like the death of Christ on the cross for Angela, leads to ecstatic communication and community.

> Instead of avoiding laceration, I'll deepen it. The sight of torture/execution staggers me, but quickly enough I support it with indifference. Now I invoke innumerable tortures/executions of a multitude in agony. Finally (or maybe all at once) human immensity promises a horror without limit.
>
> Cruelly, I stretch out the laceration: at that moment, I attain the point of ecstasy.
>
> *Compassion*, suffering, and ecstasy mingle together [*se composent*].[60]

Bataille is compelled to face catastrophe in order to communicate it, yet only the meditative embrace, even intensification, of catastrophe *enables* communication.

Just this insistence, throughout the wartime writings, on the necessity of communication points to Bataille's demand that the self not be fully dissolved (and, I would argue, that new forms of memorialization be established).[61] Regardless of his critics' claims, Bataille does not desire death (either his own or that of the other). He recognizes that to speak of communication, one must have a self-lingering on the edges of dissolution, the explosion cannot be literal, and the catastrophe cannot be physically reenacted if it is to be communicated. The torture victim cannot himself speak and cannot write (although Bataille doesn't purport to speak for him so much as to bear, subjectively and in writing, the consequences of *witnessing* his suffering). Bataille desires to live within death's breath; he is compelled to witness (to) the other's physical dissolution, through which the chance nature of existence is made known; he provides a model of dissolving subjectivity for others, one that witnesses to the void without reenacting physical dissolution. Yet we must ask again whether he desires to witness *to* the other's suffering, or simply to *witness* it, as the spark for his own, less literal, dissolution. Bataille's texts here encapsulate the ambiguity of witnessing—What is the source of this desire? The ethical call of the other, whose suffering demands attention? Or the desire for self-shattering anguish and ecstasy? For some late medieval women, like Angela of Foligno, Hadewijch, and Mechthild of Magdeburg, the two come together in Christ. The soul shattered in contemplation of Christ's suffering body, attends, in and as Christ, to the suffering of others. Without that divine, salvific ground can we ever bring together love of the other and the desire for self-dissolution? Does communication itself provide the new ground for their convergence? And after Bataille, can we ever again, so easily, distinguish between the two?[62]

In his attempt to articulate that which cannot be assimilated into meaning-giving and salvific narratives, Bataille speaks from the side of the "not all/whole," what Lacan reads as femininity.[63] Bataille argues, moreover, that Angela of Foligno speaks from that place, despite the dogmatic utterances that pull her text toward the conflation of imaginary and symbolic governing any soteriological discourse. Lacan's critics claim that his account of femininity and masculinity as they occur within linguistic and cultural realms governed by the phallus reinscribes women's silence. Yet Lacan insists that women can, albeit with difficulty, speak from the side of the masculine; he also suggests, more important (perhaps here following Bataille), that there is another mode of communication that emerges from the side of the feminine. Lacan merely alludes to the writings of the thirteenth-century beguine Hadewijch and suggests that his own writings are of a similar sort. Attention to the operations and difficulties of Bataille's writing practice clarifies what is at stake in this attempt to speak from the side of the "not all/whole." Most crucially, from the standpoint of the masculine subject, the "not all/whole" is figured as death and silence. The question is how to speak from the side of the "not all/whole," how to maintain a voice that can be heard, to break the silence imposed on the feminine within a masculine economy.

Angela and Bataille communicate by dramatizing the dissolution of the "masculinized" subject through its encounter with the catastrophes of the real.[64] These catastrophic events, in turn, demand that the subject forfeit his or her illusory wholeness and plenitude. If we accept, provisionally, the terms of Lacan's analysis (as I have done in this essay), we still must ask to what extent this act of self-negation differs for men and women. To dramatize the dissolution of an illusorily whole subject requires that one have such a subjectivity to begin with. For Angela, this is only possible through her projection of self onto the God-man. The authority of her text, moreover, is dependent on this act of memorializing identification. Angela's projection onto the God-man serves the double function of authorization and dissolution. For Bataille, who as a white, educated, European male occupies the position of authorized speaking subject without challenge, the object point of meditation serves only as the image of dissolution. The fact that Bataille meditates on the image of a Chinese man, moreover, suggests an orientalizing gaze in which the other's body-in-pieces is inscribed as feminine. In other words, the gendered terms of the phallic economy are not challenged by Bataille's texts, despite his embrace of a feminized position. The history of Angela's *Book*— its mediation by male scribes and the subsequent doubts about Angela's voice and authority (to the point that one scholar now questions whether there was an Angela of Foligno)—suggests that without such a direct challenge to the phallic economy, women and other marginalized people speaking from the side of the "feminine" are easily rendered silent once again.[65]

Notes

1. Georges Bataille, *Oeuvres Complètes* (Paris: Gallimard, 1973), 5:245, and the translated version is *Guilty*, trans. Bruce Boone (San Francisco: Lapis Press, 1988), 11. Although I will give page numbers for both the French and the English, the translations are my own.

2. Bataille, *Oeuvres Complètes*, 5:246, *Guilty*, 12.

3. For Bataille's isolation, his movements from 1939 to 1942, and the diagnosis of tuberculosis, see Michel Surya, *Georges Bataille: La mort à l'oeuvre* (Paris: Gallimard, 1991), 363–65.

4. As Susan Suleiman points out, however, Bataille would have been aware of numerous acts of Nazi violence against the resistance and Jews, despite the fact he does not mention such events in the *Atheological Summa*. Susan Suleiman, "Bataille in the Streets: The Search for Virility in the 1930s," in *Bataille: Writing the Sacred*, ed. Carolyn Bailey Gill (New York: Routledge, 1995), 44, n. 23.

5. For recent debates about Bataille's political commitments before, during, and after the war, see Suleiman, "Bataille in the Streets"; Allan Stoekl, "Truman's Apotheosis: Bataille, 'Planisme,' and Headlessness," *Yale French Studies* 78 (1990): 181–205; Carolyn Dean, *The*

Self and Its Pleasures: Bataille, Lacan, and the History of the Decentered Subject (Ithaca, N.Y.: Cornell University Press, 1992), 222–31; and Denis Hollier, *Absent without Leave: French Literature and the Threat of War,* trans. Catherine Porter (Cambridge, Mass.: Harvard University Press, 1997), 76–93.

6. Bataille, *Oeuvres Complètes,* 5:273, *Guilty,* 36.

7. Bataille, *Oeuvres Complètes,* 5:10; *Guilty,* xxxii.

8. Francis Marmande, *Georges Bataille politique* (Lyon: Presses Universitaires de Lyon, 1985), 8.

9. Three other dissenting voices, who insist on historically contextualizing Bataille's work, have been influential on the reading I offer here. Suleiman, "Bataille in the Street"; Hollier, *Absent without Leave;* and Alexander Irwin, "Saints of the Impossible: Politics, Violence, and the Sacred in Georges Bataille and Simone Weil" (Ph.D. diss., Harvard University, 1997).

10. On the ambivalent legacy of Charles Péguy, "socialist, republican, Dreyfusard, severe critic of anti-Semitism, Catholic mystic" and yet, paradoxically, read as a forebear by French fascists before and during the Second World War, see David Carroll, *French Literary Fascism: Nationalism, Anti-Semitism, and the Ideology of Culture* (Princeton, N.J.: Princeton University Press, 1995), 42–70. For this characterization of Péguy, see 44. It is against this backdrop that I imagine Lacan cites Péguy.

11. Jacques Lacan, *Encore, 1972–1973,* Le Seminaire, vol. 20 (Paris: Seuil, 1975), 70.

12. Lacan argues in *Encore* that the work of analytic practice, insofar as it can be formulated, is to separate the imaginary and symbolic realms, the object *a* and the Other, so that the "real" can emerge. In this his writings are like those of the mystics.

13. The real is also tied to the symptom and hence to hysteria. From Charcot to Irigaray, hysteria and mysticism are linked by this convergence in the real.

14. Since this *Book* is so central to Bataille's wartime writing, it's worth briefly highlighting its tremendous complexity. Modern editors divide Angela's *Book* into two texts, the *Memorial,* which is a relatively coherent narrative of Angela's religious experience from the time of her conversion, organized into a series of steps or "transformations" of the soul, and the *Instructions,* a group of visions, letters, and hagiographical accounts emanating from Angela and her circle. Bataille focuses his attention on the *Memorial,* although he also discusses the *Instructions'* account of Angela's final words. The *Memorial* raises central textual and authorial problems, as well as problems of translation, for it is the work of a scribe, Brother A., who tells us that he took down Angela's Umbrian dialect, translating rapidly into Latin. When he reads portions of this text back to Angela, she invariably complains about its brevity, dryness, and lack of accuracy, at times claiming not to recognize her own words in his (and did he read to her in Latin or translate her words back into the original Umbrian dialect?). The importance of Brother A. to the production of the *Memorial* is still hotly contested, with some going so far as to argue that we cannot posit Angela's authorship and that the text is so mediated as to offer little concrete information about Angela herself. For Bataille, however, Angela was the author of her *Book,* and I will proceed with my discussion on Bataille's terms.

For the critical edition and a modern English translation, see Angela of Foligno, *Il Libro della Beata Angela da Foligno,* ed. Ludger Thier and Abele Calufetti (Grottaferrata: Collegii S. Bonaventurae ad Claras Aquas, 1985), and *Complete Works,* trans. Paul Lachance (Mahway, N.J.: Paulist Press, 1993). Bataille generally cites the *Book* through the 1927 edition and translation of M. J. Ferré, which gives the Latin text facing a French translation. In the portions cited by Bataille, this edition and translation do not substantively differ from the critical edition of Ludger Thier and Abele Calufetti on which Paul Lachance's recent English translation is based.

15. Bataille suggests in his preface to the book that readings of *Inner Experience* should focus on pt. 2, "The Torment/Torture," and the final brief section, which contains two poems ("Gloria in excelsis mihi" and "God"); only these were "written with necessity" rather than with "the laudable concern of creating a book" (*Oeuvres Complètes*, 5:9–10, and the translated version is *Inner Experience*, trans. Leslie Anne Boldt [Albany: State University of New York Press, 1988], xxxi). "The Torment/Torture" offers an account of inner experience and "Post-Scriptum to the Torment/Torture (or the New Mystical Theology)" describes the methods used to attain it (although Bataille insists that no method alone can promise inner experience). Given the more explicit debt to Angela in the latter, I will focus my attention on it here. I believe, however, that Angela is crucial to all of *Inner Experience* and *Guilty*.

16. Bataille, *Oeuvres Complètes*, 5:120; *Inner Experience*, 102.

17. Bataille, *Oeuvres Complètes*, 5:120; *Inner Experience*, 102.

18. See Amy Hollywood, "'Beautiful as a wasp': Angela of Foligno and Georges Bataille," *Harvard Theological Review* 92, no. 2 (1999): 225–27.

19. Angela of Foligno, *Il Libro*, 362, *Complete Works*, 205. I have used Lachance's translation.

20. For a theological elucidation of Angela's work, see Paul Lachance, *The Spiritual Journey of the Blessed Angela of Foligno according to the Memorial of Frater A.* (Rome: Pontificium Athenaeum Antonianum, 1984).

21. This would be similar to the relationship between suffering with Christ in his humanity and being divine with God articulated by the thirteenth-century beguine mystic, Hadewijch. See Hadewijch, *Complete Works*, trans. Mother Columba Hart (New York: Crossroads, 1980).

22. This suggests further the importance for Bataille of thinking about God as projection of human desire. The point is not that God is "merely" humanity but, rather, that this process of projection is necessary to attaining inner experience.

23. Bataille, *Oeuvres Complètes*, 5:137, *Inner Experience*, 118.

24. Denise Despres, *Ghostly Sights: Visual Meditation in Late Medieval Literature* (Norman, Okla.: Pilgrim Books, 1989), 9.

25. In the Middle Ages, visual images were routinely used for meditational purposes. What are the implications of the use of photography in this context? See Mary Carruthers, *The Craft of Thought: Meditation, Rhetoric, and the Making of Images, 400–1200* (Cambridge: Cambridge University Press, 1999); Jeffrey Hamburger, *The Rothschild Canticles: Art and Mysticism in Flanders and the Rhineland, circa 1300* (New Haven, Conn.: Yale University Press, 1990), *Nuns as Artists: The Visual Culture of a Medieval Convent* (Berkeley: University of California Press, 1997), and *The Visual and the Visionary* (New York: Zone Books, 1999).

26. Angela of Foligno, *Il Libro*, 192–94, *Complete Works*, 145–46.

27. Is this a melancholic incorporation? What relationship is there to embodied memory and the development of a *habitus*? Also see Cathy Caruth on the film *Hiroshima mon amour*: "Her refusal is thus carried out in the body's fragmentation, in the separation of her hands from the rest of her corporeal self and in the communication with her lover's death through the sucking of her own blood. It is thus utterly deprived of sight and understanding, and only as a fragment, that the body can become, for the woman, the faithful monument to a death" (*Unclaimed Experience: Narrative, Trauma, and History* [Baltimore: Johns Hopkins, 1996], 31).

28. Bataille, *Oeuvres Complètes*, 5:139, *Inner Experience*, 119. I think it is crucial that these are photographs, as I hope to discuss elsewhere.

29. Bataille, *Oeuvres Complètes*, 5:140, *Inner Experience*, 120. His identification is not with the sadistic torture (God, in earlier formulations?), but perhaps a masochistic identification with the tortured person (if we take the passage to be disavowing sadism alone, not every pleasure at all). This suggests that to disavow God is to disavow sadistic pleasure. Yet what is the masochist without the sadist? Merely a victim of chance? And later, Bataille will claim that there is a link between sadism and ecstasy. See Georges Bataille, *The Tears of Eros*, trans. Peter Connors (San Francisco: City Lights, 1988).

30. For suggestive comments about the distinction between dramatization and narrativization, see Mieke Bal's introduction to *Acts of Memory: Cultural Recall in the Present*, ed. Mieke Bal, Jonathan Crewe, and Leo Spitzer (Hanover, N.H.: University Press of New England, 1999).

31. Bataille, *Oeuvres Complètes*, 5:144; *Inner Experience*, 123–24.

32. This is related to the claim that Freud never adequately distinguishes between repression and dissociation. See Bessel A. Van Der Volk and Onno Van Der Hart, "The Intrusive Past: The Flexibility of Memory and the Engraving of Trauma," in *Trauma: Explorations in Memory*, ed. Cathy Caruth (Baltimore: Johns Hopkins, 1995), 168–69.

33. Pierre Janet, *Psychological Healing*, trans. E. Paul and C. Paul (New York: Macmillan, 1925), 1:661–63, as cited by Judith Herman, *Trauma and Recovery* (New York: Basic Books, 1992), 37.

34. As Herman reports, researchers suggest possible neurophysiological causes for such memories; further research would be needed to determine whether meditational practices might elicit a similar set of neurophsyiological responses. Yet the intrusive and repetitious nature of traumatic memory is precisely what is induced through meditational practices, suggesting that there may be no physical relationship between the phenomena.

35. Herman, *Trauma and Recovery*, 41.

36. Although there is some work now being done also with psychotropic drugs and other medications, they seem not to have the same clinical success. How successful is narrativization? What kind of clinical evidence exists? Putting in form palatable for whom? One sees many cases in which narratives themselves are obsessively repeated. Does this suggest that other emotional work is required? Or can't ever be completed? And to what extent does the reception of the narrative play a role in recovery?

37. Herman, *Trauma and Recovery*, 177, 178.

38. Angela of Foligno, *Il Libro*, 144, *Complete Works*, 128. See also *Il Libro*, 206–8; *Complete Works*, 150–51.

39. Angela of Foligno, *Il Libro*, 338, *Complete Works*, 197. This is just one of many similar images of abjection found throughout Angela's *Memorial*. See *Il Libro*, 144, 206–8, 242, 302–4, *Complete Works*, 128, 150–51, 162–63, 184–85.

40. We should not forget, however, that Angela's book was recorded by a scribe who translated her words into Latin. Similar translations by male scribes of women's texts suggest that this emphasis on the external suffering and asceticism of medieval women may be a hagiographical trope rather than an accurate reflection of mystical experience. In this reading, Angela's suffering body might be seen as an "object" on to which her readers can project themselves. See Amy Hollywood, "Inside Out: Beatrice of Nazareth and Her Hagiographers," in *Gendered Voices: Medieval Saints and Their Interpreters*, ed. Catherine Mooney (Philadelphia: University of Pennsylvania Press, 1999), 78–98.

41. On the dangers of overidentification and retraumatization, see Dominick LaCapra, *Representing the Holocaust: History, Theory, Trauma* (Ithaca, N.Y.: Cornell University Press, 1994), 198–200. These issues will have to be explored further.

42. For powerful examples among Holocaust survivors and an examination of the ethical ramifications of this refusal, see Lawrence Langer, *Holocaust Testimonies: The Ruins of Memory* (New Haven, Conn.: Yale University Press, 1991). The work of memorialization surrounding the Holocaust is specific to that event; yet a similar refusal to accept meaning-giving narratives can be found among victims of less historically overdetermined forms of trauma.

43. Caruth, *Unclaimed Experience,* 7.

44. This distinction cannot be made too sharply, however, as witnessing violent crimes often gives rise to PTSD, and the lines between psychological and physical violence can be difficult to determine.

45. Caruth, *Unclaimed Experience,* 104.

46. Lacan, *Encore,* 102.

47. Bataille, *Oeuvres Complètes,* 5:315, *Guilty,* 74.

48. Bataille, *Oeuvres Complètes,* 5:320, *Guilty,* 78.

49. Bataille, *Oeuvres Complètes,* 5:268–69, *Guilty,* 32.

50. Bataille, *Oeuvres Complètes,* 5:272, *Guilty,* 35.

51. Bataille, *Oeuvres Complètes,* 5, 269, *Guilty ,* 32. I have here used Boone's evocative translation. The slide between image and reality is, I think, intentional, as is that between physical and subjective dissolution. These moves point to crucial issues concerning fictionality and writing in Bataille's approach to catastrophe that I explore in my *Sensible Ecstasy: Mysticism, Sexual Difference, and the Demands of History* (Chicago: University of Chicago Press, 2002), 88–110.

52. Many would read this as a gendered conception of communication and the imaginary wholeness of the self, in which any openness is conceived as a wound. Irigaray compellingly makes this critique, although in relation to Lacan rather than Bataille. In response, she attempts to articulate a conception of fluid subjectivity that does not understand openness as a wound. See, e.g., Luce Irigaray, *Speculum of the Other Woman,* trans. Gillian C. Gill (Ithaca, N.Y.: Cornell University Press, 1985), and *Sexes and Genealogies,* trans. Gillian C. Gill (New York: Columbia University Press, 1993). Although I find much in this reading compelling, I wonder what we do with the emphasis on woundedness within medieval women mystics like Angela. Do we read this solely in terms of their complicity with a masculinist religion? Or are there other issues aside from sexual difference playing into this account of subjectivity? In the case of Bataille, as I'm arguing here, I think that there is a historically specific dimension to his emphasis on violence and laceration.

53. In the longer version of this chapter I analyze a number of Bataille's discussions of his meditational practices in *Guilty.* See Hollywood, *Sensible Ecstasy,* chap. 1.

54. The *Diagnostic and Statistical Manual of Mental Disorder* designates trauma as an event that is "outside the range of human experience," despite the fact that this is clearly not the case (American Psychiatric Association, *Diagnostic and Statistical Manual of Mental Disorder,* 3d ed., rev. [Washington, D.C.: American Psychiatric Association, 1987], 250). See also Laura S. Brown, "Not Outside the Range: One Feminist Perspective on Psychic Trauma," in *Trauma,* ed. Caruth, 100–112.

55. Much more must be said about this refusal, as well as about the way the events of World War II haunt Bataille's wartime writings, despite his assertion that he will not write directly of the war that sparks his texts.

56. Patricia Yaeger, "Consuming Trauma; Or, The Pleasures of Merely Circulating," *Journal x* 1 (1997): 225–51.

57. Bataille himself suggests such a reading in a postwar review of John Hershey's account of survivors' stories from Hiroshima.

> At this point the first aspect of an attitude stands out: the man of sovereign sensibility, looking misfortune in the face, no longer immediately says, "At all costs let us do away with it," but first, "Let us live it." Let us lift, in the instant, a form of life to the level of the worst.
>
> But no one, for all that, gives up doing away with what one can.

Georges Bataille, "Concerning the Accounts Given by the Residents of Hiroshima" in *Trauma,* ed. Caruth, 232, and *Oeuvres Complètes,* 11:185, translation modified. The focus on Hiroshima is worthy of note and needs further elaboration.

58. And yet, Bataille himself, despite his own objections, is engaged in a project (albeit a "project without project"). Has he avoided "using" the other's suffering toward that (non)end?

59. For recent examples of critics closely associating ecstasy with pleasure, see Jill Robbins, *Altered Reading: Levinas and Literature* (Chicago: University of Chicago Press, 1999), 97; and Edith Wyschogrod, *An Ethics of Remembrance: History, Heterology, and the Nameless Others* (Chicago: University of Chicago Press, 1998), 235, 247. To what extent is this critique grounded in questions first posed by Jean-Luc Nancy? See Jean-Luc Nancy, "The Unsacrificeable," *Yale French Studies* 79 (1991): 34–38, and *The Inoperative Community,* ed. Peter Connors (Minneapolis: University of Minnesota Press, 1991). To what extent do they focus on dangers of prewar writings on sacrifice in ways that ignore Bataille's own evolving attitudes? The relationship between Bataille's attitudes toward sacrifice before and after the war and that found in these wartime writings requires further exploration as do the links made after the war between eroticism and mysticism, particularly with regard to the writings of Sade. Is the ethical effaced in these texts? And/or reinscribed within them in even more problematic ways?

60. Bataille, *Oeuvres Complètes,* 5:273–74, *Guilty,* 36.

61. Much more is needed on what this new form of memorialization might look like, with Bataille's writing practice and its relationship to that which is memorialized serving as a guide. Just as there are two conceptions of history and politics that minimally need to operate together, so there are probably two conceptions of memory that can be extrapolated from Bataille's work. A reading of Georges Bataille, *On Nietzsche,* trans. Bruce Boone (New York: Paragon House, 1992) will help elaborate this point.

62. Wyschogrod argues that Bataille's ecstatic mysticism is unacceptable as a way to think exteriority because, in it, the pursuit of ecstasy is "unconstrained by the responsibility of one for the other." She suggests instead a language of "the cataclysm, a power that overpowers, constrained by language so as to resist mythologization as sheer will to power" (*An Ethics of Remembrance,* 247). Yet as I have argued, in Bataille catastrophe and ecstasy—at least for the onlooker—are inextricably mingled. We might hope for more restrained ways to meet the excesses of history—or ones less suspect of themselves inducing the excesses they encounter. Bataille casts doubt on the possibility of such a pure witness.

63. This move needs to be further contextualized in terms of Bataille's early emphasis on virility. Although Bataille's wartime writings, as Suleiman shows, at times question aspects of "femininity," I find this significantly less pervasive than in his work from the 1930s. At the same time, as I will argue, the subject's laceration seems dependent on its preexisting masculinity.

See Suleiman, "Bataille in the Street," esp. 40–43; and also, Carolyn Dean, *Self and Its Pleasures*, 242–45.

64. Through the separation of the object *a* and the Other, to use Lacan's terms?

65. For the complex textual history concerning Angela, see Catherine Mooney, "The Authorial Role of Brother A. in the Composition of Angela of Foligno's Revelations," in *Creative Women in Medieval and Early Modern Europe: A Religious and Artistic Renaissance,* ed. E. Ann Matter and John Coakley (Philadelphia: University of Pennsylvania Press, 1994), 34–63. For the question about Angela's existence, see Jacques Dalarun, "Angèle de Foligno a-t-elle existé?" in *"Alla Signorina": Mélanges offerts à Noëlle de La Blanchardière* (Rome: École française de Rome, 1995), 59–97.

"The Experience of Nonexperience"

KEVIN HART

1

When Maurice Blanchot went to Vézelay in the July of 1962 to attend the funeral of Georges Bataille, he took with him "a large wreath of flowers."[1] Any student of French literature who has visited this little cemetery knows that it is neither as full of blossoms nor as closely supervised as the public gardens of Tarbes; it bears no sign forbidding visitors to carry in flowers, as Jean Paulhan claimed to have seen at the Jardin Massey, and no notice restricting entry only to those with flowers, as he believed should be there. If Paulhan was also at the funeral, it is unlikely that Blanchot would have spoken with him at any length: the two had fallen out over the Algerian insurrection in May 1958.[2] Long before, though, just a year after he had met Bataille, Blanchot had been greatly excited by Paulhan's *Les Fleurs de Tarbes* (1941).[3] In his regular column for *Journal des débats* he hailed it as "one of the most important works of contemporary literary criticism" and presented a version of his long review as his first critical volume, *Comment la littérature est-elle possible?* (1942).[4]

From the Romantics to the surrealists, Paulhan argued, writers have prized originality, purity, or rupture as the enabling condition of literature, while downplaying language as an imperfect medium and a purveyor of cliché. But these "terrorists" are mistaken, he said, for one can never tell for sure whether an arresting line represents an original thought or is a function of an exotic trope. Our only hope of apprehending reality is by acknowledging the inevitability of rhetoric and agreeing to treat tropes as tropes. In his dashing debut as a critic, Blanchot reads *Les Fleurs de Tarbes* far beyond its apparent meaning, suggesting that Paulhan does far more than commend a purified rhetoric.[5] Rather, he reveals himself to be a revolutionary of a Copernican or Kantian kind in demonstrating, through a "secret book" contained between the lines of the one he had written, that consciousness forever turns around flowers. Authors are always terrorists, Blanchot insists, yet while they reject commonplaces and conventions—all the traditional "flowers of eloquence"—even the most violent of them nonetheless relies on these flowers and their deceitfulness. What seems to render literature impossible turns out to be its condition of possibility. Or, to avoid the implication that this transcendental condition forms a firm ground, we should say that literature is produced by contesting what enables it.

Commonplaces generate ambiguities, Paulhan argued in 1941, and Blanchot fully agreed with him. Yet by the time of "Littérature et le droit à la mort" (1947–48), Blanchot had come to think that literature's constitutive ambiguities have their ground and abyss in death.[6] An early remark by Hegel on the power of language provides him with a starting point: "Adam's first act, which made him master of the animals, was to give them names, that is, he annihilated them in their existence (as existing creatures)."[7] Language can destroy the singularity of any being—this tabby cat curled up beside my feet, for example—while preserving its being in general as an idea (the concept "cat"). A remarkable power of the negative is therefore revealed to be at work in language. In the terms that Hegel establishes in *The Phenomenology of Mind* (1807), nature is the self-alienation of the idea, the realm of finitude. Any linguistic representation of nature will negate whatever characterizes its finitude and thereby disclose the universal: a movement that, for Hegel, revealed "the divine nature" of language.[8] Like others of the day, Blanchot was influenced by the "French Hegel" of the late thirties and early forties, especially by Alexandre Kojève's anthropological reading of the archphilosopher.[9] Unlike others, though, Blanchot vigorously recast this reading at the level of the transcendental. Death is the enabling condition of being an animal, while consciousness of mortality is what distinguishes humans from animals. In other words: I am because I will die, and I am human because I know I will die. Our relation with death is not wholly taken up with the possibility of being human, however. Art reveals to us a realm in which nothing truly begins or ends: in Bernini's sculpture, Apollo will never grasp Daphne; in *The Prelude* the young Wordsworth will forever skate on a frozen lake and hear the melancholy echoes of his friends' cries. Art does not indicate a space of death, for there is no traction for the dialectic to gain a hold; nor is it a space of eternal life, for art is the realm of the imaginary where being is perpetuated as nothingness. Rather, it is a space of endless dying. That we have art tells us,

Blanchot thinks, that human beings are related to death not only as possibility but also as impossibility.

So, on the one hand, death is the force of determination: it generates meaning and comprehension, and Blanchot insists that without it life would be absurd.[10] On the other hand, it opens us to indetermination: we are exposed to meaninglessness and incompletion without end. As the hero of Blanchot's first novel, *Thomas l'obscur* (1941), discovers to his horror, "He was really dead and at the same time rejected from the reality of death."[11] Because death abides in language, and as Hegel saw, sustains "the life of mind," this fundamental ambiguity cannot be eliminated.[12] Before Heidegger ventured the thought that "language speaks," Blanchot had proposed that it is not only an author who speaks in a piece of writing but also death, and we can never be sure if it is affirming being or perpetrating the absence of being.[13] This is preeminently true in literature, Blanchot suggests, for literature is nothing other than language allowing ambiguity to flourish. In reading an ode by Hölderlin or a story by Kafka, one experiences a process of negativity, a work and a power, which yields meaning. Also, though, one must respond to an empty depth in the work where every possibility has been exhausted, where there is nothing to negate, and only pointless repetition occurs. Considered transcendentally, death is the source of ambiguity, and literature is its privileged way of unveiling and reveiling itself. Yet considered as a phenomenon, death is a quotidian event; it asks for conventional signs of mourning like carrying a wreath of flowers into a cemetery and, in a far more complex manner, of other flowers being brought back into the world of the living.

Bataille's death quickly called forth two remarkable pieces of eloquence from Blanchot. "L'Amitié," a moving tribute to his friendship with the dead man, appeared in the October number of *Les Lettres nouvelles,* and "L'Expérience-limite," an analysis of what he took to be his friend's animating theme, was published that same month in Paulhan's journal, *La Nouvelle revue française.*[14] Each text approaches the same concern: how to think an extreme alterity, the invisible and vertical movement of death that escapes all representation. In "L'Amitié" death is glossed in a manner familiar to readers of "Littérature et le droit à la mort" as the "unforeseeable that speaks when he speaks," and the main concern is raised as a question, "Who was the subject of this experience?"[15] In what had by then become a Heideggerian gesture, we are told that when heard properly the question answers itself. Language speaks: the subject is not an "I" but a "Who?"[16] Less lyrical in mood and mode, "L'Expérience-limite" does not rely on hearing either death or language speak. In an attempt to clarify Bataille's raptures, Blanchot sets a short remark that is as tantalizing as any lyrical utterance in a paragraph by itself: "The experience of nonexperience."[17]

I would like to organize a brief reading of Blanchot around this odd expression, "experience of nonexperience," partly because I suspect that it informs all his writing in one way or another and partly because it condenses a number of problems encountered in studies of mysticism. Despite what Jean-Paul Sartre says about *L'Expérience intérieure* (1943), Bataille is not a "new mystic," not even when we overhear him advising himself "to take a flower and look at it until harmony," then speaking of "a *vision,* an *interior vision* maintained by a necessity undergone in silence."[18] Nor is Blanchot a mystic, not even of an atheistic kind, despite the allure of "A Primal Scene?" For that tiny *récit* does not so much reveal an unknown god as the complete absence of any God or god.[19] And yet, as we shall see, Bataille was not entirely mistaken to identify a "new theology" in his friend's first novel.

2

In asking "How is literature possible?" Blanchot invites us to recall Kant's guiding question, "How is experience possible?" Kant showed that the categories of the understanding were the only means by which any consciousness could legitimately claim experience. And if we credit the references to Paulhan's Copernican or Kantian revolution, Blanchot is presumably suggesting that commonplaces and conventions are the only means by which any literature can be written.[20] The analogy between the two revolutions limps, however, for Blanchot does not adduce a firm ground on which we might build an epistemology of literature but instead shows that literature contests whatever enables it. When it comes to writing there will never be a clean division between theory and practice.[21] And it follows that, in Blanchot's recasting of Kant's question, "literature" does not simply replace "experience."

Terrorists pride themselves on the authenticity and vitality of their experiences, and deride conventions precisely because, as Blanchot puts it, these are nothing but "tired rules, these rules themselves, like any form, being the result of earlier experiences [*expériences*]."[22] Seen in this way, the writer's situation is a conflict between experience and nonexperience. Both Paulhan and Blanchot realize that the struggle is specular—for when properly understood rhetoric is nothing other than "perfected terror"—and beset with mutual infiltrations and internal strife. To read *Les Fleurs de Tarbes* well would be to learn that in literature experience is always and already a nonexperience. Authenticity, individuality, *Erlebnis:* all these are compromised by an author's inevitable negotiations with convention. At the same time, however, Blanchot allows the possibility that nonexperience is always and already an experience. Only in the act of writing does an author brush against a limit of existence, risk peril, and return to ordinary life changed, having undergone an unsettling passage that we call *Erfahrung* or experience.

I will return to this final point. Beforehand, I wish to explore another analogy between Kant's *Critiques* and Paulhan's "secret book." That Kant wrote the first *Critique* in order to protect faith from unwelcome incursions of reason is well known, and it is equally well known that beginning with *Dreams of a Spirit-Seer* (1766) he set himself fiercely against all mysticism. In the first *Critique* (1781), possible experience is secured by foreclosing on all immediate experience of the divinity. In the second *Critique* (1788), we are warned not to carry over intuitions from the sense world to the intelligible world lest we change what was intended merely as a symbol into a schema and consequently generate a "mysticism of practical reason."[23] And in *Religion within the Limits of Reason Alone* (1793), we are relentlessly shown how anything that smacks of the mystical must be relegated to the status of *parerga*, supplements to rational religion. There can be no doubt about it: the critical philosophy is resolutely directed against mysticism, as Kant understood it. Of course, whether he understood it correctly or even fully is another question.

When Blanchot reads Paulhan, he notes how the terrorist searches for an "inexpressible reality" with which he desires "virginal contact" or, by a "prodigious asceticism," tries "to be in direct contact with the secret world" or the "veiled world." Even the writer who agrees to use rhetoric's "renewed means" does so because it promises "contact with the virgin newness of things." If one knows Paulhan at all well, this language should not come as a surprise. Earlier he had suggested that "one must return to the mystics. Of all the philosophers, only they openly put their philosophy to the test and *realise* it."[24] And he had hinted of experiences or thoughts he had enjoyed or suffered, "which one achieves in a flash and which one cannot sustain, but from which, once they have appeared, infinitely unfold the apparent world with its brightness and darkness, its joys and filthinesses."[25] Nothing in *Les Fleurs de Tarbes* contradicts this kind of event. Indeed, Paulhan seems to have entertained the idea that his book gave some insight into the divine Word.[26] Could anything be further from the critical philosophy? Also unlike Kant, Paulhan does not establish limits for possible experience. His argument merely renders the recovery of any representation of such an experience suspect, for by his reasoning one could never tell whether the text reported an experience or flaunted a trope.

Blanchot knew nothing of Paulhan's experiences when he was writing *Comment la littérature est-elle possible?* although he would have been fascinated by them. In 1942, the year his first study of Paulhan appeared, he discussed Meister Eckhart in his column "Chronique de la vie intellectuelle," and the following year he contributed articles on Nicholas of Cusa and Angelus Silesius.[27] When we read that the cardinal never attains "inner experience" and that Eckhart gains a finer sense of "nonknowledge" than the author of *De docta ignorantia* (completed in 1440) we realize that both writers are being viewed from the perspective of Bataille. Indeed, Blanchot's review of *L'Expérience intérieure* marks the end of his initial interest in mysticism.[28] There we learn that although Bataille's ecstasies seem to be mystical they are nothing of the sort. They do not rely on "religious presuppositions," which "often change" the experience and "in giving it a meaning or a direction [*un sens*], determine it." Years later, when reflecting on Paulhan's life and death, Blanchot will similarly read his friend's raptures under the sign of inner experience rather than mysticism.[29] Yet in the early 1940s he is undecided whether to abandon or preserve the word "mystical." Discussing French religious verse, he tells us that the "true mystical poems of our language, those born of an inner discovery, of a ravishing, of a revelatory anxiety, have been construed outside the religious traditions."[30]

Blanchot does not specify exactly which "religious presuppositions" the mystics make. Yet they are negatively implied by his account of inner experience: mystical experience is a singular relation of the human being with God; the object of this encounter is transcendent; the experience consists of a fusion of subject and object; it occurs immediately and is to be reckoned a success because it yields meaning. Now it would be hard to read Origen, Meister Eckhart, the *Cloud* author, or Saint John of the Cross and still claim that Blanchot has isolated essential traits of mysticism. When Origen, for example, writes of "knowing God" he is thinking of *theopoiesis*, not making a cognitivist claim; and, although in this area one should walk in fear of generalizations, the mystics tend to figure knowledge of God by way of relation with him.[31] And if Origen is a reliable witness, this relationship is marked by the elusiveness and playfulness of God more than by comprehension of him.[32] However, anyone familiar with the critical philosophy would find it easy to recognize these traits as those that Kant associated with mysticism. Nowhere is this more evident than in Kant's and Blanchot's quiet insistence that mysticism presupposes a particular kind of experience, one that appears to be convertible to determinate knowledge. When we inquire what characterizes inner experience we learn that it is transgressive (rather than transcendent), a relation without relation (rather than an immediate fusion), and results in nonknowledge (rather than knowledge). That said, Blanchot does not simply mirror Kant's rejection of mysticism. For the German philosopher, no ineffable experience is legitimate for human beings by dint of the structure of our consciousness. Yet ineffability for Blanchot does not turn on immediacy and transcendence (as for Kant) or immediacy and singularity (as for Hegel) but around the limit that reveals itself when someone lives as the "last man," contesting every possibility, even one's death. One consequence of this understanding of things is that for Blanchot ineffable experience is both legitimate and partly legible in texts about it. Even religious experience is not rigorously excluded from this experience, for as we have seen he concedes that "religious presuppositions . . . *often* change [emphasis mine]" the experience of an agent and ascribe a value to it. It follows that some religious presuppositions do not shape the experience in advance, and Blanchot's admiring column on Meister Eckhart leads one to think of the *doctor ecstaticus* in precisely this way.

It is understandable, then, that toward the end of his reflections on *L'Expérience intérieure* we are told that "it is not forbidden to discourse to try to take responsibility for what escapes it." This translation from experience to text can never be satisfying. All the same, it is valuable because it "retains an essential part of authenticity to the extent that it imitates the movement of challenge which it borrows." Of course, the text is "an unfaithful depository" that must be denounced by what it translates; and so the text ends up doubling itself "with another that supports and effaces it through a kind of permanent demi-refutation."[33] As with Paulhan, Bataille has also written a "secret book" that countermines the public book we read and admire. The two critical strategies are not quite the same, however. When Blanchot discovers that Paulhan has written a phased counterpart to *Les Fleurs de Tarbes,* one that undoes terrorist claims to sheer presence by reference to the necessity of repeating empty forms, we have glimpsed an early instance of deconstruction. Yet when Blanchot reads Bataille he does not find a mode of nonexperience that hollows out experience and unsettles its claim to presence. Rather, he finds and prizes an experience that cannot be assimilated to the human subject. We might ponder whether this is a reading at odds with deconstruction or whether we glimpse a style of deconstruction that some of the mystics would recognize.

3

What does it mean to speak of experience of nonexperience? Three kinds of answer come to mind. The first is an evocation of a limit experience, which of course may or may not converge with the categories traditionally used when speaking of mysticism. At a fairly high level of abstraction, it is one thing to speak of experiencing God, as the mystics do, and another to speak with Karl

Jaspers of *Grenzsituationen* or with David Tracy of positive limit situations.[34] In practice it is not always easy to distinguish them, and to claim as a matter of principle that there is no chance of a thorough differentiation places one squarely in a far-flung camp of theological liberalism. A line can begin to be drawn, of course. For one can note that in the Western church mystical writings seldom use or mention the word "experience" before the twelfth century, and in any case the extraordinary events that we might now classify as experiences are scarcely valued by those who enjoy or suffer them.[35] Bataille, however, explicitly prizes the word "experience" and qualifies it by "inner" in a way that, at first blush, links him with an understanding of mysticism he inherited from nineteenth-century French spirituality. If a closer reading of Bataille makes us realize that he read quite deeply in the medieval mystics— Meister Eckhart and the Pseudo-Denys, Angela of Foligno and John of the Cross—it does not eliminate the nineteenth-century emphasis on experience with which he approached them.[36]

The matter becomes all the more complicated when one realizes that attempts to specify mystical or limit experiences could be reset to describe or prescribe normative behavior. Thus Saint Benedict's vision of the world contained within a single glance can be used to guide a phenomenological description of the liturgy. For Jean-Yves Lacoste, the ordinary Christian pilgrim can transgress the distinction between "earth" and "world" and can therefore occupy a nonplace that exceeds the totality of all places. Since earth and world form the a priori conditions of experience [*expérience*], liturgical experience involves nonexperience.[37] The "liturgical night" is a "liturgical *désoeuvrement*," Lacoste says in a manner reminiscent of Blanchot, although unlike Blanchot he stresses that experiential aridity in no way denies God's proximity to the one who prays.[38] To take a rather different example, Karl Rahner argues that what is immanent in God is also economic, revealed in the incarnation of Christ; and on this basis he elaborates a theology in which our experience of God occurs at the limit of ordinary human expressions of desolation and faith, hope and love. Our experience of God would involve nonexperience to the extent that it answers to the structures of the knowing subject but would be experience insofar as our movement toward the divine Mystery in faith, hope, and love is always an index of transcendence.[39] Similarly, while Bataille prizes rapturous communications with death, usually by way of alcohol or sex, Blanchot quietly reworks these discrete events so that they are part and parcel of daily life. On his account, the impossible does not haunt the extremes of life but shadows each and every event in life, "as though its other dimension."[40] If we cannot name this neutral outside, this specter of death as the impossibility of dying, at least we can respond to it; and this vigilant response is what Blanchot, in dialogue with Simone Weil, calls "attention."[41]

The second way of hearing experience of nonexperience is with the ear of faith. Indeed, it is not only Maurice Blanchot but also Hans Urs von Balthasar who uses this expression, and he does so while placing himself at a great distance from Karl Rahner's theology. Faith, here, is not to be approached by way of the heights and depths of our daily lives. Rather, it is "the surrender of one's own experience to the experience of Christ, and Christ's experience is one of kenotic humiliation and self-renunciation." Such is his understanding of how ordinary Christians are to live. It is in "mysticism," a word von Balthasar carefully wraps in quotation marks, that "every deeper experience [*Erfahrung*] of God will be a deeper entering into [*Einfahren*] the 'nonexperience' of faith, into the loving renunciation of experience." The allusion is to the "dark nights" of Saint John of the Cross that are, he says, "precisely an '*experience* of nonexperience,' or an experience of the negative, privative mode of experience, as a participation in the total archetypal experience of the Old and New Testaments."[42] Here mystical experience is regarded as extraordinary not because it falls under the rubric of a theological positivism, whose coordinates it largely ignores, but because it is Christian renunciation lived in a more rigorous and intense fashion than can be asked of the faithful. The ground of the *via negativa* is held to be biblical rather than personal.

Before going on, it is worth noting that renunciation of experience can readily be rethought as a movement away from mysticism. This is how Karl Barth, to whose theology von Balthasar was very close in some respects, understood things.[43] "In fact, our experience is that which we have not experienced," he observed in the second edition of his *Romans*.[44] Then, in the *Church Dogmatics*, the paradox is explained. Faith is granted by God "unveiling His veiling," and mysticism is characterized by the expectation that this process will continue. By contrast, faith is worked out in a radical reversal, an affirmation of the God "who is veiled in His veiling."[45] Unlike the mystic, the ordinary believer passes from God to the Word of God, and Barth tells us that "in faith men have real experience of the Word of God," not because there is a point of connection between them and revelation but because a capacity for faith is granted by God.[46] This encounter with the Word is dynamic: we are continually "in movement from the experience felt at one time, from the thought grasped at one time, to the opposite experience and thought, because hearing the Word of God always consists of a simultaneous hearing of the one in the other and the other in the one." There can be no end to this movement, and this open relation with the eschatological message of the gospel is precisely what Barth means by "Christian experience."[47] Although the believer does not experience God in the awakening of faith, as liberal Protestants from Schleiermacher to Harnack imagined, he or she is assured of an excessive experience of the Word of God.

The third way of inflecting experience of nonexperience is in terms of ethics. For Emmanuel Lévinas, language is not to be regarded as a correlation of thought and being but rather as a disruption of that correlation. Before anything else, language is a saying that testifies to the passing of the infinite through the other person; it is "a way of signifying before all experience."[48] In consequence, my relations with the other person will inevitably turn on an experience of nonexperience. Lévinas and Blanchot agree that this is in no way a mystical ecstasy, which they all too quickly construe as fusion, nor is it susceptible to dialectical sublation. In Hegel's terms, the experience of non-experience is quite simply not an experience at all.[49] Certainly it would not be a "lived event." Put positively, as Lévinas and Blanchot would wish, the ex-perience is of two parties brought into relationship without a unity being achieved. There could be no unity precisely because the relationship is, as Lévinas says, asymmetric or, as Blanchot prefers, doubly dissymmetric.[50] If the passing of God (Lévinas) or friendship (Blanchot) is not a lived event it is, as we learn in *L'Écriture du disastre* (1980), "already nonexperience." Yet Blanchot underlines that nonexperience, as understood here, contains the es-sential trait of experience. For "negation does not deprive it of the peril of what, already past, happens."[51]

4

When von Balthasar evokes the "*experience* of nonexperience" he does so in order to clarify the affectivity of "the dark night of the soul" as endured by Saint John of the Cross. When Blanchot uses the same expression, it is by way of evoking what he calls "the *other* night," that which reveals and veils itself when death is encountered as the impossibility of dying. Blanchot is highly circumspect when talking about Bataille's ecstasy, for "its decisive trait is that the one who experiences it [*l'éprouve*] is no longer there when he experiences it [*l'éprouve*], is therefore no longer there in order to experience it [*l'éprou-ver*]." This relation of experience and nonexperience is not a recent histori-cal problem, he admits, and he refers us to the mystics, all of whom, especially Saint John of the Cross, have known that "memory, considered as personal, could only be doubtful."[52] Sanjuanist mysticism is accordingly "foreign to all *Erlebnis*," and the possibility arises that inner and mystical experience are both instances of *Erfahrung*. By no means would this include all claims to mystical experience. Distinctions would need to be drawn in order to make decent sense of a work like the Pseudo-Macarian *Homilies,* on the one hand, and testimony like that of Mechthild of Magdeburg, on the other.[53] Yet the possibility of approaching inner and mystical experience by way of *Erfahrung* is intriguing for two reasons: first, because it allows an opportunity of speaking more precisely about a modern displacement of mystical theology, one associated with Bataille and Blanchot, and second, because it offers a way of responding to the claim, vigorously asserted by Denys Turner, that mysticism, rather than forming a body of positive or negative experiences, properly consists in the "deconstructions" of "experiences *of* the negative."[54] I shall consider each in turn.

In literature, for Blanchot, *Erlebnis* is proscribed by virtue of the author's inevitable relations with convention; and yet, as we have seen, there remains the possibility that nonexperience is always and already an experience in the sense of *Erfahrung.* If we read Blanchot to find out exactly what he means by "experience," we would first of all find him speaking of it in a dialectical fashion. Pondering Lautréamont, he tells us that "it has become familiar to us that the most self-conscious writer . . . institutes between his work and his lucidity a movement of composition and of reciprocal development . . . that we call *experience* [*expérience*] and at the end of which the work not only will have made use of the spirit but will have served it."[55] Here, in 1948, Blanchot is writing in a language redolent of Hegel in which there is only one kind of experience, that which passes from consciousness and returns to modify it. If we move forward just a few years, to 1955, we find Blanchot using "expérience" a little more warily. One trouble with this word, he admits, is that it "tends to make us think that literature is tied to a particular psychological phenomenon" and that it would have a "lived experience [*vécu*]" that would be the "essence of poetry." Yet there is a "literary experience [*expérience*]" that flies over experience and that experiences [*épreuve*] what cannot be experienced." As though literature had the power to bracket itself, it opens "another space" that is "above or below existence."[56]

Over the years Blanchot condenses these thoughts to the claim that a poem forms "the trace of what has not taken place."[57] At the very least it is a decisive rejection of the Romantic idea that a literary work represents an act of genius. Be that as it may, we can ask, If literary experience is not a translation of lived or imagined experience, what then is it? On Blanchot's analysis, in the act of composition, writers are fascinated by what precedes writing. It is reality we want, and when that is taken from us by writing (as Hegel saw), we become drawn to the silent origin of the work in hand that has been posited by the act of writing (as Hegel did not see). This origin marks a "dead time" that does not respect the flow of past, present, and future; and, like death, it torments us by withdrawing as we come closer to it. Blanchot regards this endless approach to what has never existed as a "radical reversal" of death: it is death as the impossibility of dying. He dubs it the "original experience," and we recognize it as an experience of nonexperience. To yield to the fascination of this approach would be to consign whatever is being written to pointless repetition: the origin must be forced into a beginning if a work is to be composed. And yet unless one experiences the dark gaze of the origin, no work will be produced, for literature is constituted by putting itself into question. It follows that literature—or, as he will come to say, writing—is always double, like Thomas, at once experience and nonexperience, death as possibility and as the impossibility of dying.

When reflecting on Bataille's ecstasies, Blanchot is quick to point out that no individual would be sufficient for an inner experience to occur. This experience *is* communication with others, not an affirmation of a particular content but an affirmation of affirmation. The individual's selfhood is fissured, and no fusion takes place.[58] Without breaking faith with Bataille's ecstasies, Blanchot rethinks them at the level of experience as such. Ecstasy is thereby reworked as "the *other* relation," which interrupts being and which characterizes friendship and writing. In *L'Expérience intérieure* itself, Bataille had spoken of *Thomas l'obscur* as the only other text "where the questions of the new theology (which has only the unknown as object) are pressing, although they remain hidden."[59] The "new theology" here is not a reflection on the absence of God but on the approach of the original experience. As we have seen, the experience of nonexperience is generated by the quest for what writing destroys. Rather than discover that pristine world, however, we find ourselves on a detour that exposes us to the neutral relation, which many years later he will characterize as the "eternal follower that precedes."[60] Since this is death as the impossibility of dying, we may say that the new theology is an eschatological irrealism. Far from answering to a transcendent deity, it broods on a quasi-transcendentality to which all writing exposes itself. What it shows, and what neither literary critics nor theologians have sufficiently realized, is that in terms of textual effects it little matters whether one is responding to the transcendent or the transcendental. Perhaps this begins to account for the uneasy pathos of the postmodern. Or, to turn the matter around, perhaps this is why so much theological writing on the mystics seems naive to literary critics. One other consequence that needs to be drawn is this: if Bataille casts himself as displaced mystic and Blanchot as theologian, Blanchot gradually responds by doubting that the distinction has any weight. Experiences interest him less and less, experience more and more.

5

In recent years the distinction between mysticism and mystical theology has been shown to be divided, equivocal, and at times frankly misleading.[61] From the fact that no mention is made of an author enjoying mystical experience it does not follow that no experience has been granted. It was never the intention of an Origen or a Pseudo-Dionysius to speak of particular experiences, although, to be sure, a careful reader can find testimony even in their writings. Of course, a knowledge of literary form makes any student of mystical writings extremely cautious of deducing a body of experience from a text, even when those texts speak openly of union. As soon as there is a negotiation with form, genre, and rhetoric, there is an experience of nonexperience, and no author can avoid entering into these negotiations. Especially when it comes to apophatic writings, one might well wonder whether mystics are the greatest of all rhetoricians or the most fiercesome of all terrorists. Or, on reflection, one might ponder whether they are concerned with experience at all.

In saying that I am of course alluding to Denys Turner's *The Darkness of God* (1995). As a whole, this study has the logical structure of a hasty induction, but balancing Turner's individual insights against the scope of his thesis is not my theme here. My interest is best indicated by Turner's claim that when evoking the dark nights Saint John of the Cross is not concerned with "that which cannot itself be experienced" but with its "'experiential feedback.'"[62] The dark nights are not metaphors of particular experiences but of "a dialectical *critique* of experientialist tendencies," and the claim is that the nights are not first-order descriptions but second-order reflections.[63] Contemporary reading of mystical writings is bedeviled, it seems, by confusing these first- and second-order levels. Before pondering any of the larger questions that Turner's study raises, one might well wonder how he can pass from regarding the second-order discourse as a "dialectical *critique*" to claiming it to consist of "deconstructions."[64] For deconstruction is neither dialectical nor a critique, and it tends to undo hard and fast distinctions such as that between first- and second-order discourses. Yet I do not think that Turner is merely flourishing a word he does not understand.

In a discussion of the Areopagite toward the start of his book, we are told that the cataphatic and the apophatic are "mutually cancelling forces" that "crack open the surface of language" and that "it is through the fissures in our discourse that the darkness of the apophatic is glimpsed."[65] Turner's prose style is usually very English indeed: at times one might be forgiven for thinking one is reading a G. E. Moore interested in mysticism. Yet here Turner's phrasing recalls *soixante-huit* French criticism, and his absorption with this style prevents him from giving as accurate an account of mystical language as one would like. For the cataphatic and apophatic do not cancel each other so much as engage one another. It is not the positive and the negative annihilating one another that makes mystical texts so intriguing, rather the patterns of textual disturbance that are set up by their engagements. That said, Turner shows that to read a mystical text adequately we must pass from the *liber experientiae*, so attractive to we moderns, to another book that exposes the negativity of experience. It is as though Turner were writing a study called *How Is Mystical Literature Possible?* and its import would be that it occurs by a process of self-contestation. Mystical literature would be written not by dint of experiences but by calling experiences into question, and the inevitable Copernican revolution would be that, in mysticism, experience turns around nonexperience. It would be, as he says, "feedback."

It is a pleasant thought, just close enough to reality to gesture toward some truths. For I suspect that Turner has written two books, one that launches a critique by way of first- and second-order distinctions and another that proposes a deconstruction. My sense as a reader of medieval mystical writings is that there are no firm first- and second-order levels of discourse and that the apophatic and cataphatic engage one another without ceasing.[66] And so it is the second book, one that seems to have defeated its author, that interests me the more. Were one to give Turner a hand and continue writing his second book, one would find that many mystics are indeed wary of *Erlebnis* though few would reject *Erfahrung*. Perhaps one would find that many of the mystics touch on an *Erfahrung* that keeps opening before them, exposing them to new heights and depths that cannot be translated into an *Erlebnis* and, perhaps, does not ever settle into a discrete experience. An experience of God is never altogether closed because even the slightest encounter with the divinity yields endless meditation and endless prompts to action in the world.

In saying this, I do not mean to say that "experience of God" isolates a particular kind of experience. All experience is constituted as an aporia in that it involves reference to a model and possible reference to that which is unforeseen. Experience of God differs from this general rubric only in that the possibility is realized and strengthened: divine action is not only unforeseen but also unforeseeable. Jacques Derrida tells us, rightly, that the aporia is a negative form: it upsets all positive programs and therefore offers no security of consolation or knowledge.[67] The sheer amount of testimony by mystics should suffice to indicate that they know they have encountered God, but of all people they know what they do not know. Their experience of God remains open to meditation, perhaps all the more so once they have written about it and experienced language. The rest of us do not know what we do not know, and as often as not we close our nonexperience of God as tightly as we can. I think Barth was aware of this when he spoke so eloquently of experiencing the Word of God. That is sufficiently disturbing, I think; and all the rest is not so much darkness as openness.

Notes

1. Christophe Bident, *Maurice Blanchot, Partenaire invisible: Essai biographique* (Seyssel: Champ Vallon, 1998), 409, n. 2.

2. According to Jean Piel, "Trois hommes, en tout, ont enterré Bataille: Blanchot, Leris et moi" ("*Critique,* l'histoire souterraine de l'intelligence contemporaine," *Libération* [13–14 December 1980], 21). Blanchot indicates that he and Paulhan had fallen out over the Algerian situation in "La facilité de mourir," in *L'Amitié* (Paris: Gallimard, 1971), 172.

3. Jean Paulhan, *Les Fleurs de Tarbes, ou la Terreur dans les lettres* (Paris: Gallimard, 1941).

4. Maurice Blanchot, "La Terreur dans les lettres," Chronique de la vie intellectuelle, *Journal des débats* (21 October 1941). Two further installments of this review appeared in the November and December of 1941 and formed the basis for *Comment la littérature est-elle possible?* which appeared with José Corti in 1942. A shorter version of the study appeared in *Faux pas* (Paris: Gallimard, 1943).

5. On 1 December 1941, Jean Paulhan wrote to Francis Ponge, "Mais vexé de n'avoir pas les 3 articles des *Débats* (!) sur les *Fleurs,* qu'on me dit bien meilleurs que les *Fleurs*" (Jean Paulhan and Francis Ponge, *Correspondance, 1923–1968,* ed. Claire Boaretto, vol. 1, *1923–1946* (Paris: Gallimard, 1986), 263. For Paulhan's private strictures on Blanchot's reading of *Les Fleurs de Tarbes,* see his letter to Julian Benda of April 1945, in *Choix de lettres,* ed. Dominique Aury et al. (Paris: Gallimard, 1992), 2:412.

6. See Blanchot, "La littérature et le droit à la mort," in *La Part du feu* (Paris: Gallimard, 1949), 330. The essay first appeared in *Critique* 18 (November 1947) and 20 (January 1948).

7. Blanchot, *La Part du feu,* 312. Blanchot quotes from G. W. F. Hegel, *System of Ethical Life and First Philosophy of Spirit,* ed. and trans. H. S. Harris and T. M. Knox (Albany: State University of New York Press, 1979), 221–22.

8. G. W. F. Hegel, *The Phenomenology of Mind,* trans. J. B. Baillie, introduction by George Lichtheim (New York: Harper & Row, 1967), 160.

9. We know that Blanchot was familiar with Jean Hyppolite's *Genèse et structure de la Phénoménologie de l'Esprit de Hegel* (Paris: Aubier, 1946); and Alexandre Kojève's *Introduction à la lecture de Hegel* (Paris: Gallimard, 1947). Which other commentaries, if any, on Hegel he had read is unknown. However, since there was a steady publication of articles and books about Hegel in France of the mid-1940s it is not unlikely that he was familiar with texts such as Maurice Merleau-Ponty's "Une conférence de J. Hyppolite: L'Existentialisme chez Hegel," *Les Temps Modernes,* vol. 1, no. 7 (1945); and Henri Niel, *De la médiation dans la philosophie de Hegel* (Paris: Aubier, 1945).

10. Blanchot, "La Littérature et le droit à la mort," 313.

11. Blanchot, *Thomas l'obscur* (Paris: Gallimard, 1941), 48. The same expression was kept when Blanchot recast the *roman* as a *récit* in 1950. The name Thomas means "twin" in Aramaic or Syriac, and here the Thomas who has died encounters his twin for whom death is the impossibility of dying.

12. Hegel, *The Phenomenology of Mind*, 93.

13. Heidegger proposed that "Language speaks" in "Die Sprache," which was first presented on 7 October 1950 and was published in *Unterwegs zur Sprache* (Pfullingen: Neske, 1959).

14. Blanchot, "Pour Georges Bataille: l'amitié," *Les Lettres Nouvelles* 29 (1962): 7–12, reprinted in *L'Amitié*, 326–30, and "L'Expérience-limite," *La Nouvelle revue française* 118 (1962): 577–92, reprinted in *L'Entretien infini* (Paris: Gallimard, 1969), 300–313.

15. Blanchot, *L'Amitié*, 328, 327.

16. Ibid., 328.

17. Blanchot, *L'Entretien infini*, 311.

18. See Jean-Paul Sartre's essay on *L'Expérience intérieure*, "Un nouveau mystique," in *Situations* (Paris: Gallimard, 1947), 1:143–88. Georges Bataille, "Le Coupable: Found Fragments on Laure" in Laure, in *The Collected Writings*, trans. Jeanine Herman (San Francisco: City Lights Books, 1995), 258. This passage would need to be read alongside Bataille's "Le langage des fleurs" in his *Oeuvres complètes*, 12 vols (Paris: Gallimard, 1970–88), 1:173–78.

19. Blanchot's *récit* may be found in *L'Écriture du désastre* (Paris: Gallimard, 1980), 117. Blanchot quietly alludes to Heidegger's reading of Hölderlin, "Poetically Man Dwells," which may be found in Heidegger's *Poetry, Language, Thought*, trans. Albert Hofstadter (New York: Harper & Row, 1975), 223. Also, see my "Blanchot's 'Primal Scene,'" chap. 2 of my *The Dark Gaze: Maurice Blanchot and the Sacred*, forthcoming.

20. See Blanchot, *Comment la littérature est-elle possible?* 23.

21. Consider Blanchot on criticism: "'Critique,' au sens où nous l'entendons, serait déjà plus proche (mains l'approximation reste trompeuse) du sens kantien: de même que la raison critique de Kant est l'interrogation des conditions de possibilité de l'expérience scientifique, de même la critique est liée à la recherche de la possibilité de l'expérience littéraire, mais cette recherche n'est pas une recherche seulement théorique, elle est le sens par lequel l'expérience littéraire se constitue, et se constitue en éprouvant, en contestant, par la création, sa possibilité" ("Qu'en est-il de la critique?" in *Lautréamont et Sade* [Paris: Les Éditions de Minuit, 1963], 13).

22. *Blanchot, Comment la littérature est-elle possible?* 20.

23. Immanuel Kant, *Critique of Practical Reason*, trans. Lewis White Beck (Indianapolis: Bobbs-Merrill, 1956), 73.

24. Jean Paulhan, *Le Clair et l'obscur*, preface by Philippe Jaccottet (Cognac: Le temps qu'il fait, 1983), 100. The essay first appeared in *La Nouvelle NRF,* nos. 64 and 66 (1958).

25. Pauhlan, *Le Clair et l'obscur,* 116. Also see Paulhan's "Lettres à Madame ***": "Voici, pour l'essential: c'est qu'il est parfaitement chimérique de chercher à connaître Dieu directement. Ce qui se passe, il me semble, c'est qu'il arrive dans la vie à chacun de nous, dans certains instants privilégiés, de nous trouver au contact de ce qui passe nos calculs, nos réflexions, notre raison, bref du Divin" (*Nouvelle revue français* 228 [1971]: 80).

26. In his inscription of Francis Ponge's copy of *Fleurs*, Paulhan quotes Augustine's remarks in *On the Trinity* to the effect that whoever grasps a word before it is spoken and allowed

to generate images begins to see the divine Word. See Paulhan and Ponge, *Correspondance,* 1:265. Paulhan asks Henri Pourrat in November 1941 if he knows the passage from Augustine. See *Choix de lettres,* ed. Aury et al., vol. 2.

27. Blanchot, "Maître Eckhart," *Journal des débats* (4 November 1942), "Nicolas De Cues," *Journal des débats* (6 January 1943), and "La mystique d'Angélus Silesius," *Journal des débats* (6 October 1943).

28. Blanchot, "L'expérience intérieure," *Journal des débats* (5 May 1943).

29. See Blanchot "La facilité de mourir," in *L'Amitié.* The essay first appeared in *Nouvelle revue française,* vol. 197 (May 1969). At the Colloque de Cerisy consecrated to Paulhan in 1973, the question of Paulhan's mysticism was raised by way of an appeal to Blanchot's authority. See "Paulhan mystique?" in *Jean Paulhan le souterrain* (Paris: Union Générale d'Éditions, 1976), 371–88.

30. Blanchot, "La poésie religieuse," *Journal des débats* (9 June 1943).

31. Andrew Louth makes the point about Origen very clearly in relation to the *Commentary on John.* See Louth, *The Origins of the Christian Mystical Tradition: From Plato to Denys* (Oxford: Clarendon Press, 1981), 73.

32. I have in mind the following well-known passage in Origen's first homily on the Song of Songs: "God is my witness that I have often perceived the Bridegroom drawing near me and being most intensely present with me; then suddenly He has withdrawn and I could not find Him, though I sought to do so. I long, therefore, for Him to come again, and sometimes He does so. Then, when He has appeared and I lay hold of Him, He slips away once more; and, when He has so slipped away, my search for Him begins anew" (*The Song of Songs: Commentary and Homilies,* trans. R. P. Lawson [London: Longmans, Green & Co., 1957], 280).

33. Blanchot, "L'Expérience intérieure, in *Faux pas* (Paris: Gallimard, 1943), 52.

34. See Karl Jaspers, *Philosophy,* 3 vols (Chicago: University of Chicago Press, 1970), vol. 2, pt. 3, chap. 7; and David Tracy, *Blessed Rage for Order: The New Pluralism in Theology,* new ed. (Chicago: University of Chicago Press, 1996), 105–9.

35. The point is well made by Bernard McGinn in his *The Presence of God: A History of Western Christian Mysticism,* vol. 2, *The Growth of Mysticism* (New York: Crossroad, 1994), 81. Of course, *peira* occurs in Eastern works before the twelfth century; it is used frequently in the Pseudo-Macarian *Homilies,* e.g.

36. For Bataille's interest in the mystics, see Pierre Prévost, *Rencontre Georges Bataille* (Paris: Jean-Michel Place, 1987), 100–101. Also see my "Art or Mysticism?" the first chapter of my forthcoming study, *The Dark Gaze.*

37. For the recasting of the vision of Saint Benedict, see Jean-Yves Lacoste, *Expérience et Absolu* (Paris: Presses Universitaires de France, 1994), secs. 9–15, entitled "Lieu et non-lieu." In the chapter that follows that one, Lacoste examines the theme of "non-expérience."

38. Ibid., 178. *Désoeuvrement* is one of Blanchot's signature words. See, for instance, his *récit, Celui qui ne m'accompagnait pas* (Paris: Gallimard, 1953), 70, or *L'Espace littéraire* (Paris: Gallimard, 1955), 16.

39. See Karl Rahner, *Foundations of Christian Faith: An Introduction to the Idea of Christianity,* trans. William V. Dych (New York: Seabury, 1978), 20–21.

40. Blanchot develops this thought in *L'Entretien infini,* 68–69. It appears to have first been raised in a letter to Bataille of 24 January[1962]. See Georges Bataille, *Choix de lettres, 1917–1962,* ed. Michel Surya (Paris: Gallimard, 1997), 596.

41. See Blanchot, "L'Affirmation (le désir, le malheur)," in *L'Entretien infini,* 153–79.

42. Hans Urs von Balthasar, *The Glory of the Lord: A Theological Aesthetics,* vol. 1, *Seeing*

the Form, ed. Joseph Fessio SJ and John Riches, trans. Erasmo Leiva-Merikakis (San Francisco: Ignatius Press, 1982), 412–13. Also see von Balthasar's essay "Experience God?" in his *New Elucidations,* trans. Sister Mary Theresilde Skerry (San Francisco: Ignatius Press, 1986).

43. See Hans Urs von Balthasar, *The Theology of Karl Barth,* trans. John Drury (New York: Holt, Rinehart & Winston, 1971).

44. Karl Barth, *Epistle to the Romans,* trans. Edwyn C. Hoskyns (Oxford: Oxford University Press, 1933), 110; cf. 299. Also see Barth's *The Göttingen Dogmatics: Instruction in the Christian Religion,* ed. Hannelotte Reiffen, trans. Geoffrey W. Bromiley (Grand Rapids, Mich.: William B. Eerdmans, 1991), 1:67. In his old age Barth observes: "A confession of faith, religious experience as such, is good. There is no faith without experience. But a candidate for the ministry speaks of *faith,* not of experience as such. He gives an answer to what he has heard of the Word of God" (*Karl Barth's Table Talk,* recorded and ed. John D. Godsey [Edinburgh: Oliver & Boyd, 1963], 38).

45. Karl Barth, *Church Dogmatics,* trans. G. T. Thomson (Edinburgh: T. & T. Clark, 1936), vol. 1, pt. 1:203. Barth later asserts that "mysticism is esoteric atheism" (*Church Dogmatics,* ed. G. W. Bromiley and T. F. Torrance, trans. G. T. Thomson and Harold Knight [Edinburgh: T. & T. Clark, 1956], vol. 1, pt. 2:322).

46. Ibid., vol. 1, pt. 1:272.

47. Ibid., 237.

48. Emmanuel Lévinas, "Dieu et la philosophie," in *De Dieu qui vient à l'idée,* 2d ed., rev. and enlarged (Paris: J. Vrin, 1986), 122.

49. Hegel defines "experience" [*Erfahrung*] as the "very process by which the element that is immediate, inexperienced, i.e. abstract—whether it be in the form of sense or of a bare thought—externalizes itself, and then comes back to itself from this state of estrangement, and by so doing is at length set forth in its concrete nature and real truth, and becomes too a possession of consciousness" (*Phenomenology of Mind,* 96).

50. For Blanchot's suggestion that Lévinas's word "asymmetry" be replaced by "double dissymmetry," see *L'Entretien infini,* 100.

51. Blanchot, *L'Écriture du désastre* (Paris: Gallimard, 1980), 85. On this topic, see the second chapter of my *The Dark Gaze.*

52. Blanchot, *La Communauté inavouable* (Paris: Les Éditions de Minuit, 1983), 37. Blanchot appears to be thinking of Saint John of the Cross's comments on memory and imagination in *The Living Flame of Love:* "Neither should there be any fear because the memory is void of forms and figures. Since God is formless and figureless, the memory walks safely when empty of form and figure, and it draws closer to God. The more it leans on the imagination, the farther away it moves from God" (in *The Collected Works of St. John of the Cross,* trans. Kieran Kavanaugh and Otilio Rodriguez [Washington, D.C.: Institute of Carmelite Studies Publications, 1979], 630).

53. Consider, e.g., the following from the Pseudo-Macarius's fourth homily: "Should anyone only strive to be pleasing to him and be acceptable, he certainly will see the heavenly good things in actual experience. He will have an experience of the unspeakable delights and truly immense riches of God which 'eye have not seen nor ear heard nor has it entered into the mind of man to conceive' (1 Cor 2: 9)" (*The Fifty Spiritual Homilies and the "Great Letter,"* trans. and ed. George A. Maloney, S.J., preface by Kallistos Ware, Classics of Western Spirituality (New York: Paulist Press, 1992), 55. Also consider Mechthild's testimony: "The more the Infinite God unlifts the unfirm soul, the more this wondrous experience makes her lose sight of the earthly kingdom, and she forgets that she was ever a part of it" (Mechthild

von Magdeburg, *Flowing Life of the Divinity,* ed. Susan Clark, trans. Christiane Mesch Galvani, Garland Library of Medieval Literature, vol. 72, ser. B (New York: Garland Publishing, 1991), 7.

54. Denys Turner, *The Darkness of God: Negativity in Christian Mysticism* (Cambridge: Cambridge University Press, 1995), 259.

55. Blanchot, *Lautréamont et Sade,* 90. "Lautréamont ou l'espérance d'une tête" first appeared in *Cahiers d'art* 1 (1948): 69–71.

56. Blanchot, "À toute extrémité," *La Nouvelle NRF* 26 (1955): 290. This essay was later cannibalized by Blanchot and recast in *Le Livre à venir* (Paris: Gallimard, 1959), 147–48, and *L'Espace littérature* (Paris: Gallimard, 1955), 105–9. In neither book, though, is Blanchot as clear about what he takes "expérience" to be as in the original version of "À toute extrémité."

57. Blanchot, *L'Écriture du désastre,* 205. Philippe Lacoue-Labarthe develops the thought in his *La Poésie comme l'expérience* (Paris: Christian Bourgois, 1986), 30–32.

58. See Blanchot, *La Communauté inavouable,* 35.

59. Bataille, *Oeuvres complètes,* 5:120.

60. Blanchot, *Le Pas au-delà* (Paris: Gallimard, 1973), 106.

61. See, e.g., Michel de Certeau, *The Mystic Fable,* vol. 1, *The Sixteenth and Seventeenth Centuries,* trans. Michael B. Smith (Chicago: University of Chicago Press, 1992); Bernard McGinn, *The Presence of God,* 1:xvii–xviii; and Mark A. McIntosh, *Mystical Theology* (Oxford: Basil Blackwell, 1998).

62. Turner, *The Darkness of God,* 250.

63. Ibid., 227.

64. Ibid., 227, 259.

65. Ibid., 33.

66. I am thankful to Bernard McGinn for drawing my attention, after I presented this paper at the University of Chicago, to his review of Denys Turner's book in *Journal of Religion* 77, no. 2 (April 1997): 309–11. Although they come from rather different directions, our approaches to Turner's book converge.

67. See Jacques Derrrida, *Apories* (Paris: Galilée, 1996), 42.

Locating the Mystical Subject

THOMAS A. CARLSON

In what follows, I want to locate the mystical subject in at least two senses. I want first to locate our fascination with the "mystical" as a subject of inquiry in relation to that modern world that can seem to be thoroughly "de-mystified," void of any mystical presence at all, thanks to the self-assertion of a purely human reason that, by comprehending itself and its world, aims to manipulate and master that world technologically—above all in the technologies of image that come so fully to frame our world today. I want then, in turn, to locate a mystical or "apophatic" subject within some of those classic traditions of Christian theology where the human creature is seen ultimately not as self-transparent master of its world but as incomprehensible image of an incomprehensible God, who himself becomes visible—as invisible—in and through a world that is thoroughly theophanic.

Can these two subjects and their worlds, the technological and the mystical, shed any light on one another? I want to suggest that they might—insofar as we can discern not only a shadow of the mystical subject in today's technological world but also a figure of the technological subject already in more traditional mystical cosmologies.

It is a commonplace of twentieth-century thought that we live in a world that is demystified by the force of technology and by the rationalized thinking that grounds such technology. Two classic examples come quickly to mind here. As Max Weber argues in his 1918 lecture "Science as a Vocation," modernity's rationalized approach to reality presupposes that "there are no mysterious or incalculable forces that come into play" in our dealings with the world and that, accordingly, "one can, in principle, master all things by calculation. This means that the world is disenchanted."[1] Walter Benjamin, in his well-known 1936 essay "The Work of Art in the Age of Mechanical Reproduction," argues, more specifically, that the technologies of image reproduction in the modern world alter the limits of time and space to such a degree that they erase the uniqueness and distance that alone might preserve the "aura" or sacrality of things.[2] From perspectives such as those of Weber and Benjamin, we see a model of the modern human subject as one who, through its rational and technological self-assertion, empties the world of mystical presence—precisely by taking over the very production or framing of that world, a production or framing that appears nowhere more powerfully than in those technologies of image that today not only mediate reality to us but indeed prove to be inseparable or even indistinguishable from reality itself.[3]

The subject who stands behind this scientific and technological construction of reality is analyzed with considerable force—and influence—by Martin Heidegger already in his 1938 lecture titled "Age of the World Picture" [*Die Zeit des Weltbildes*]. There, Heidegger asserts that "the fundamental event of the modern age is the conquest of the world as picture [*die Eroberung der Welt als Bild*]."[4] In speaking of this modern "conquest," Heidegger does not mean first to signal the technologies of image production that do in fact dominate our world today but rather the subject on whom those technologies would be founded—namely, the human subject who, by representing the world to itself, positions itself as the ground and measure of being. In the human subject's representing production [*vorstellende Herstellen*], "man contends for the position in which he can be that particular being who gives the measure and draws up the guidelines for everything that is."[5] The age of the world as picture is the age of the human as subject who relates to the world first and foremost as ob-ject, as that which the subject sets or places [*stellt*] before [*vor*] itself through the operation of representation [*Vorstellung*] in such a way that the world is thereby subjected to the subject's calculative project of manipulation and mastery.[6] When the human subject becomes the "relational center" [*Bezugsmitte*] of all that is, "man brings into play his unlimited power for calculating, planning, and molding all things."[7]

A decisive sign of this struggle to conquer the world as picture appears most notably in the science and technology that make possible a manipulation of space and time. Heidegger articulates this project of manipulation, which gives way to the unthinkably massive modern systems of calculation and planning, in terms of what he calls the "gigantic" or the "immense" [*das*

Riesige]—which emerges through the unlimited extension of technologies that master both the minute and the enormous:

> A sign of this event [of the conquest of the world as picture] is that everywhere and in the most varied forms and disguises the gigantic [*das Riesige*] is making its appearance. In so doing, it evidences itself simultaneously in the tendency toward the increasingly small. We have only to think of numbers in atomic physics. The gigantic presses forward in a form that actually makes it seem to disappear—in the annihilation of great distances by the airplane, in the setting before us of foreign and remote worlds in their everydayness, which is produced at random through radio by the flick of the hand [*Handgriff*].[8]

Arising at the technological intersection of the atomic and the cosmic, the "gigantic" or the "immense"—which Heidegger will later understand in terms of the "monstrous"—becomes most present in its disappearance, which "takes place" to the degree that distance is annihilated and the remote becomes the everyday—without our actually noticing.[9] This self-effacing presence of "the gigantic" is embodied for Heidegger in the global extension of technologies that are driven by "the planetary imperialism of technologically organized man," wherein a planetary reach emerges very literally at my fingertips: through a mere flick of the hand, its grasp extended immeasurably through the prostheses of electronic technology, spatial and temporal distance increasingly disappear.[10] It almost goes without saying that the hand that in Heidegger becomes an index for the entire modern system of technological prostheses is tied to the image today even more intimately than Heidegger could have imagined.[11]

Heidegger argues, then, and electronic culture today might seem to confirm, that the conquest of the world as picture occurs with the position of the human as subject; the immanence of that human subject and its rationality, in turn, would seem to imply the abandonment or negation of transcendence and its mystery—and, indeed, on Heidegger's view, the modern age conceives of truth no longer in terms of any revelation, Christian or otherwise, but in terms of the self-certainty of the representing subject.[12] Such a denial of revelation signals, more broadly, a "loss of the gods" that would recall Benjamin's decay of the aura or Weber's "disenchantment of the world"— or more deeply the death of God as it appears not only in Nietzsche but already in Hegel: along with the position of the human as representing subject, along with rational science and machine technology, the "loss of the gods" [*Entgötterung*] must be seen, Heidegger insists, as an essential phenomenon of the modern age.[13]

This "loss," however, constitutes a peculiar "phenomenon" insofar as it signals—much like "the gigantic" of which it is an essential dimension—the presence of an absence. In the culture of the modern subject who would master the world according to the logic of representation and through the technologies grounded in such a logic, which seem to overcome the limits of space and time, the mystery of transcendence can indeed seem to "appear" only through its sheer absence. Such a culture, then, would appear to be a culture of absolute immanence or even "total presence," a culture de-mystified by a subject who, most notably in the technologies of all-consuming light and image, seems to comprehend all.

As Don DeLillo's recent novel *Underworld* puts it, through the voice of an old-school nun who is at once repulsed and fascinated by the force of tele-visual technology, "you touch a button and all the things concealed from you for centuries come flying into the remotest room. It's an epidemic of seeing. No conceivable recess goes unscanned. In the uterus, under the ocean, to the lost halls of the human brain. And if you can see it, you can catch it."[14]

Because the culture consumed by such an epidemic is one in which all can in-deed seem to be made manifest—and thus available, calculable, and manip-ulable—it can seem to afford no recess of darkness or mystery, no distance or transcendence, and in this sense it could rightly be termed an "apocalyptic" culture of "total presence." One of the most forceful and sustained efforts to embrace such a culture theologically remains, of course, that of Thomas J. J. Altizer, who, within his deeply Hegelian reading of Nietzsche, welcomes the advent of an apocalyptic totality that is to be affirmed as "all in all."

As Altizer has insisted for thirty years now, such an apocalyptic totality would be defined by the deepest anonymity of God, which is itself answered by a new anonymity of the human. The human subject who was "the center of a uniquely Western self-consciousness," the subject who comes to birth (with Paul and Augustine) as a unique, interior "I" only in relation to the "pure otherness" of its God, has been "eroded under the impact of the mod-ern realization of the death of God. Thence it has disappeared in our late modern imaginative and conceptual enactments, and is now becoming truly invisible in a new mass consciousness and society."[15] In a culture that embod-ies the death of God, Altizer insists, anonymity befalls the human through a dissolution of the unique, interior subject, and such anonymity would come to expression in the new "universal humanity" of modern mass consciousness and society.

The import of such mass anonymity in Altizer recalls Heidegger's analyses of the "collective," which, with the "gigantic," comes into force through modern humanity's liberation from revelation: "Certainly the modern age has, as a consequence of the liberation of man, introduced subjectivism and individualism. But it remains just as certain that no age before this one has produced a comparable objectivism and that in no age before this has the non-individual, in the form of the collective, come to acceptance as valid."[16] The modern liberation of the human subject from any god or revelation—which occurs in and through the rise of distinctively modern, totalizing systems of calculation and planning—would be tied intimately to an objectivism and anonymity of the collective.[17] Such objectivism and anonymity, in turn, would go hand in hand with the technological imperialism for which "uniformity becomes the surest instrument of total, i.e., technological, rule over the earth. The modern freedom of subjectivity vanishes totally in the objectivity commensurate with it."[18] In Altizer, we find a theological response to just this situation: "If only in its totality, or its dawning totality," Altizer writes, "the very uniqueness of our world is inseparable from a dissolution or erasure of all interior consciousness. There is now far more objective knowledge and objective actuality than ever before, but a subjective interiority has never been so precarious, just as a genuinely human future has never been so totally in question."[19]

The totalizing force of the objectivism and collectivism that Heidegger notes in modernity's technological imperialism goes hand in hand, for Altizer, with the erasure of human interiority that itself corresponds to the death of God. What one could see as a kind of "negative" theology in Altizer is answered, then, by a kind of negative anthropology, for "just as a purely anonymous vision is impossible apart from the loss or dissolution of an interior and immanent center, so likewise is it impossible apart from the loss or reversal of a transcendent ground or center."[20]

For Altizer, the death of the transcendent God implies a death or dissolution of the interior self, and such a dissolution would be spoken most fully by the anonymity of modern mass culture—which comes to light most notably in the all-consuming culture of technological image, where distinctions between surface and depth, exteriority and interiority, immanence and transcendence are themselves unsettled. Such anonymity, then, would be the anonymity of an "electronic humanity," and it would be tied—this paradox is key—to an unrestrained polyonymy: "A new 'electronic' humanity is now manifest as postmodernity," Altizer writes, "a humanity whose depth is indistinguishable from its surface or mask, and this is an anonymous humanity if only because it is a nameless humanity. Its actual name is everyone and no one at once, an everyone who can only be no one."[21] "Everyone" and "no one," the endlessly named and finally unnamed, the all and the nothing, coincide here in the new universality of a mass society, a universality that collapses the distinction between transcendence and immanence and becomes actual through the light and power of electronic technologies.

As already in Heidegger, Benjamin, or Weber, these technologies are defined for Altizer by their apparent transcendence of space and time: Altizer's "total presence"—finding now its very body and life in the polyonymous anonymity of an electronic or virtual humanity—would involve a "simultaneity in which time itself is a wholly abstract or simulated time, and most abstract to the extent that it is simultaneous. So likewise are we being overwhelmed by a ubiquity of space, a space that is omnidirectional, without any actual direction or perspective. Thereby center as center has truly disappeared, just as circumference as circumference has disappeared."[22] Within the electronic simultaneity and ubiquity that Altizer signals here, both of which appear already in Heidegger, any discrete place or location (spatial or temporal) is finally dis-placed or dis-located, and in light of such spatiotemporal displacement, Altizer can glimpse a hint of the mystical God whose center is everywhere and circumference nowhere. At the same time, however, he will want clearly to distinguish this modern ubiquity and simultaneity, which arise only "with the modern realization of the death of God," from those of any "traditional" mystical God who might be identified as such.[23] I want here to resist this overly clear distinction by stepping back a moment toward some of the mystics themselves.

To make this step, I will address briefly the dialectic of immanence and transcendence in those traditions of speculative mysticism in the West that derive most notably from the sixth-century Eastern monk Pseudo-Dionysius (ca. 500) and that prove central to the aesthetics and metaphysics of light and image in medieval thinking and spirituality.[24] If we live today in a world consumed by technologies of image and light, might we gain any perspective on that world through a comparison of it with the cosmos of mystical light and image that emerges in the Dionysian traditions?

Much as in Altizer's dialectic of everyone and no one, of the endlessly named and the finally nameless, so can we find in the Dionysian traditions a dialectic of immanence and transcendence according to which God is both all in all and nothing in anything, named infinitely and infinitely nameless, everywhere and nowhere, illuminating all and beyond all in a brilliant darkness. As developed by thinkers from John Scotus Eriugena (ca. 810–877) through Meister Eckhart (ca. 1260–1327) to Nicholas of Cusa (1401–64), this dialectic seeks to indicate that God is distinct precisely by his indistinction, different thanks to his indifference, absent in his presence—in short, transcendent through his incomprehensible immanence.[25]

To elucidate this dialectic here, I will focus on Eriugena, who is decisive not only for having transmitted the Dionysian corpus and conceptuality into the Latin West, but also, in line with my more specific concerns, for developing more thoroughly and systematically than Dionysius himself does the interplay between an apophatic or mystical cosmology (which Dionysius's theology does elaborate) and a correspondingly apophatic or mystical anthropology (which Dionysius leaves more implicit).[26]

The core dialectic of Eriugena's masterwork *On the Division of Nature*, or the *Periphyseon*, stands in πρόοδος, ἐπιστροφή, μονή.[27] According to that dialectic, the superessential cause of all things moves through all things as immanent to them and stands beyond all things as transcendent of them. As cause, the divine is all in all—and so addressed, metaphorically, by affirmative theology; and as superessential the divine is nothing in anything—and so most properly addressed by negative theology.[28] In short, "He is all things as the Cause of all things, embracing and holding beforehand all beginnings, all endings, all existent things, and He is above all things as the Super-ὤν which is superessentially before all things."[29]

In his treatment of this dialectic, Eriugena argues not only that the divine cause manifests itself in all created things, but indeed that it creates itself in and through that which it creates:[30] "Whoever looks into the meaning of these words will find that they teach, indeed proclaim, nothing else but that God is the maker of all things and is made in all things."[31] For Eriugena, this self-creation of the divine—and it alone—gives the subsistence of creatures: "For when it is said that it creates itself, the true meaning is nothing else but that it is establishing the natures of things [*nisi naturas rerum condere*]. For the creation [*creatio*] of itself, that is, the manifestation [*manifestatio*] of itself in something, is surely that by which all things subsist [*omnium existentium profecto est substitutio*]."[32] Creation itself, then, the whole of the intelligible and sensible world, is for Eriugena the self-creation and the self-manifestation of the divine.

Such a self-manifesting self-creation occurs for Eriugena in a two-leveled descent of the divine—"from itself into itself, as though from nothing into something"—which structures the overall dialectic of procession, return, and remaining.[33] In a first moment, the superessential God descends into the intelligible causes of all things, which God generates within himself through his Word, which is the beginning of all essence, life, and intelligence, and in a second moment God descends into the effects created through those causes within the world that is both intelligible and sensible; because all things issue from the incomprehensible simplicity or Nothingness of the superessential God, all things actually remain in and return to that simplicity or Nothingness:

> Descending from the superessentiality of His Nature, in which He is said not to be, He is created by Himself in the primordial causes and becomes the beginning of all essence, of all life, of all intelligence, and of all things which the gnostic contemplation considers in the primordial causes; then, descending from the primordial causes which occupy a kind of intermediate position between God and the creature, that is, between the ineffable superessentiality which surpasses all understanding and the substantially manifest nature which is visible to pure minds, He is made in their effects and is openly revealed in His theophanies; then He proceeds through the manifold forms of the effects to the lowest order of the whole nature, in which bodies are contained; *and thus going forth into all things in order He makes all things and is made in all things, and returns into Himself, calling all things back into Himself, and while He is made in all things, He does not cease to be above all things and thus makes all things from nothing*, that is, He produces from His Superessentiality essences, from His Supervitality lives, from His Superintellectuality intellects, *from the negation of all things which are and are not the affirmations of all things which are and are not.*[34]

Thus, interpreting the cosmic dialectic of divine immanence and transcendence as divine *self*-creation, Eriugena, like Dionysius, can see all of the cosmos as an infinitely varied showing or appearance of God. Just as the Scripture in which God reveals himself opens the way to an endless variety of possible readings, where one meaning leads to the next within an endless exegetical *transitus* toward the absolutely simple and inaccessible source of all meaning, so the cosmos offers an endless multiplicity of theophanies that can be read to show the invisible God from as many different angles as there are holy souls to desire God's appearance.[35]

Within this theophanic play of the cosmos, where God's self-manifestation is actually self-creation, Eriugena emphasizes, further, the fundamentally cocreative interplay between Creator and creature: "We ought not to understand God and the creature as two things distinct from one another," Eriugena insists, "but as one and the same. For both the creature, by subsisting, is in God; and God, by manifesting Himself, in a marvelous and ineffable manner creates Himself in the creature."[36] Much like G. W. F. Hegel, though with an apophatic intention that is deeply absent in Hegel, Eriugena insists that God realizes himself in and through the creature, just as the creature finds its subsistence in God; God achieves self-consciousness in and through the creature's consciousness of God.[37] It is in these dynamic, cocreative terms that "the Creator of all things" is "created in all things"—which means that every creature is at bottom a paradoxical theophany, from the celestial essences down to the very last bodies of the visible world.[38] All of creation offers a field of luminous appearance that makes manifest the inaccessible darkness of the superessential.[39]

Operating according to the paradox of God's brilliant darkness, wherein the invisible becomes visible, the theophanic in Eriugena follows the Dionysian logic of "dissimilar similarity," and thus it proves equally theocryptic:

> For everything that is understood and sensed is nothing else but the apparition of what is not apparent, the manifestation of the hidden, the affirmation of the negated, the comprehension of the incomprehensible, the utterance of the unutterable, the access to the inaccessible, the understanding of the unintelligible, the body of the bodiless, the essence of the superessential, the form of the formless, the measure of the measureless, the number of the unnumbered, the weight of the weightless, the materialization of the spiritual, the visibility of the invisible, the place of that which is in no place, the time of the timeless, the definition of the infinite, the circumscription of the uncircumscribed.[40]

In sum, the theophanic self-creation of God constitutes a movement from the transcendence of superessential Nothingness, which is absolutely simple and incomprehensible, into the manifold immanence of all created things, which can be known; that immanence, however, is always an immanence *of* the transcendent, and it can therefore ultimately signal only the impossible appearance of the inapparent—the limited and knowable determinacy of God's absolutely unlimited and unknowable indeterminacy.[41]

Significantly, Eriugena seeks to elucidate the logic of theophanic self-creation, where the something of creation, which we can know, issues from the self-negation of the divine Nothingness, which we cannot know, through the "example" of our own human nature—and at this point, the indispensable and very powerful anthropological dimension of Eriugena's theological project becomes quite clear:

> For our own intellect [*intellectus*] too, although in itself it is invisible and incomprehensible [*invisibilis et incomprehensibilis*], yet becomes both manifest and comprehensible [*et manifestatur et comprehenditur*] by certain signs [*signis*] when it is materialized in sounds and letters and also indications as though in sorts of bodies; and while it becomes externally apparent in this way [*et dum sic extrinsecus*

apparet] it still remains internally invisible [*semper intrinsicus invisibilis permanet*], *and* while it breaks out into various figures comprehensible to the senses it never abandons the incomprehensible state of its nature; and before it becomes outwardly apparent it moves itself within itself; and thus it is both silent and cries out, and while it is silent it cries out and while it is crying out it is silent; and invisible it is seen and while it is being seen it is invisible; and uncircumscribed it is circumscribed, and while it is being circumscribed it continues to be uncircumscribed.[42]

The theophanic God, who through self-creation makes manifest his uncreated invisibility, is mirrored by the human intellect, which, in itself indefinite and invisible, defines and shows itself through its self-expression, all the while remaining indefinite and invisible. In both cases, I think, Eriugena is finally pointing to the incomprehensible ground of creativity itself, the mystery of creation ex nihilo.

Now, this human example is not really just an example, since it is based in Eriugena's core understanding of the human subject as incomprehensible image of the incomprehensible God. While every creature in Eriugena constitutes an appearance of God (or a theophany), the human creature alone constitutes an image (or *imago*) of God—and it constitutes an image of God not simply to the degree that the human intellect, like the divine, becomes self-conscious in and through its own self-expression but, even more, insofar as the human intellect, again like the divine, ultimately proves through that very self-consciousness—or in the deepest ground of that self-consciousness—to be incomprehensible to itself.[43] The human image of the divine is distinctive in that it is both self-conscious and incomprehensible to itself or, indeed, incomprehensible in its self-consciousness. Eriugena's apophatic anthropology, insisting as it does on the incomprehensible image of the divine in the human, here comes to play a decisive theological role, for in knowing the deepest incomprehensibility of the human, we come in fact to know the true incomprehensibility of God. In both cases, the divine and the human, such incomprehensibility is at the same time the ground of self-consciousness, for it is the incomprehensibility of a Nothingness which is the ground of that creation in and through which alone self-consciousness is realized.

Here, Eriugena's apophatic anthropology complements his apophatic theology: neither God nor the human subject created in His Image can comprehend what they themselves are—even as they achieve, through their own self-creative self-expression, a self-conscious awareness that they are:

For the human mind [*mens*] does know itself [*et seipsam novit*], and again does not know itself [*et seipsam non novit*]. For it knows that it is [*quia est*], but does not know what it is [*quid est*]. And, as we have taught in earlier books, it is this which reveals most clearly the Image of God to be in man [*maxime imago Dei esse in homine docetur*]. For just as God is comprehensible in the sense that it can be deduced from His creation that he is, and incomprehensible because it cannot be comprehended by any intellect whether human or angelic nor even by Himself [*nec a seipso*] what He is, seeing that He is not a what but superessential [*quia non est quid, quippe superessentialis*]: so to the human mind it is given to know only one thing, that it is—but as to what it is no sort of notion is permitted it.[44]

As becomes clear in this passage, Eriugena wants to insist not only that the human cannot comprehend God, nor even simply that the human created in the image of the incomprehensible God is itself incomprehensible—but also, in full consistency with these first two principles, that even God finally cannot comprehend himself.[45] In light of such thoroughgoing divine ignorance Eriugena can insist that "the human mind is more honored in its ignorance than in its knowledge," for in that ignorance above all the image of the divine in the human achieves its perfection. And so it is that "the ignorance in it of what it is is more praiseworthy than the knowledge that it is, just as the negation of God accords better with the praise of His nature than the affirmation."[46]

Eriugena's apophatic celebration of ignorance—both theological and anthropological—is intended here to mark the manner in which both the divine and human substance ultimately exceed or transcend all ten of the categories or "predicables" delimited by that "shrewdest of the Greeks," Aristotle.[47] One of those categories, however, assumes a particular importance: that of place, *locus,* or τόπος (and its twin, time). In seeking to articulate the excess of the divine and its image over the categories, Eriugena emphasizes above all the impossibility of locating either the divine or the human substance, and he does so because it is above all *locus* that marks the kind of limitation, circumscription, or definition that alone make knowledge (or discourse) possible: "The Divine Likeness in the human mind is most clearly discerned," Eriugena insists, when it is "not known what it is"—precisely because "if it were known to be something, then at once it would be limited by some definition, and thereby would cease to be a complete expression of the Image of its Creator, who is absolutely unlimited and contained within no definition [*qui omnino incircumscriptus est, et in nullo intelligitur*], because He is infinite, beyond all that may be said or comprehended, superessential [*quia infinitus est, super omne, quod dicitur et intelligitur, superessentialis*]."[48] The superessential God who remains beyond all that can be spoken or understood is a God beyond the definition or circumscription of any place (or time); indeed, he is for Eriugena the placeless place of all places, "present to all things by his immeasurable circumambience of them"—and thus in that very presence to all things beyond those things.[49] Since knowledge for Eriugena implies the definition or location of the object known, the unknowable God and its human image alike stand beyond all location.

At the same time, such definition or location is the condition of all creation. Thus, insofar as self-creation implies definition or location, even as it issues from—and returns to—a nothingness that cannot be defined or located, we can see in the movement of self-creation an intersection between self-awareness and ignorance of self.[50] That is, the creative intellect (human or divine) must define or locate that which it—only thereby—comes to know, and in that which it comes to know it achieves its own self-consciousness or self-awareness, its very subsistence; at the same time, however, the same creative intellect necessarily exceeds or stands beyond that which it creates, and to that degree it remains beyond all location and thus incomprehensible—even to itself. The ground of definition and knowledge here is itself indefinable and unknowable.

This interplay between the self-consciousness and self-ignorance of creative intellect, between knowable creation in all its multiplicity and the unknowable simplicity of creation's ground, comes to light most forcefully in Eriugena where the divine and the human are most essentially united—in the Word of God as Reason or Cause of the universe:

> The Word of God is the creative Reason and Cause of the established universe, simple and in itself infinitely multiple; simple, because the universe of all things is in Him an indivisible and inseparable One, or rather the indivisible and inseparable unity of all things is the Word of God since He is all things; and not unreasonably understood to be multiple because He is diffused through all things to infinity, and that diffusion is the subsistence of all things. For He spreads mightily from end to end and sweetly disposes all things. Also in the Psalm: "His speech runneth swiftly."
>
> By "speech" [*sermo*] the prophet meant the Word [*verbum*] of the Father which runs swiftly through all things in order that all things may be. For its multiple and infinite course through all things is the subsistence [*subsistentia*] of all things.[51]

As the self-expression of God, the Word creates all things and is created in all things; it is the creative Wisdom [*sapientia creatrix*] of the Father whose providence "proceeds into all things and comes into being in all things and contains all things, and yet because of its preeminent self-identity it is not anything in anything through anything, but transcends all things".[52] The core

Eriugenian dialectic of immanence and transcendence here comes to expression through the Word that is the center of God's self-expression: the God who as Word runs through all things and is their subsistence at the same time remains transcendently simple in Himself. As beginning, middle, and end of all things, the Word is both creative and salvific ground—and consistent with the twofold descent of God addressed above, the creative and salvific aspects of the Word are marked in God's double cry of it. As Don Duclow nicely summarizes: "The Father cries out through the Word, and this cry first establishes all created natures. . . . The Word's second cry occurs through the flesh and constitutes the Incarnation, which sets in motion the return of all things to God."[53]

Now, in this understanding of the Word as that which "runs" through all things so as to make them be and bring them back into God, Eriugena is alluding to one of two etymologies that he invokes elsewhere to articulate the meaning of the Greek name for God: if θεός derives from the verb θέω, or "I run," he reasons, then it articulates the sense in which God "runs *throughout all things* and . . . by His running fills out all things, as it is written: 'His Word runneth swiftly'" if θεός derives from the verb θεωρῶ, "I see," then it articulates the sense in which God "sees in Himself all things that are [while] He looks upon nothing that is outside Himself because outside Him there is nothing."[54] The God who runs through all things to make them be is also the God who creates and sustains all things by seeing all things in himself—and himself in all things. As maker and made, seer and seen, the God who expresses himself through his Word is at once most present and most hidden, all things in all and nothing in nothing.[55] The ineffable intellectual light present to all but contained by none, He is, in short, the placeless "place of all places" that can be defined neither by itself nor by any other intellect, the placeless place from which all things proceed and to which all things return.[56]

In this light we can situate the end of Eriugena's entire vision: the unification [*adunatio*] of the world with God in and through the human subject implies a deification (or theosis) achieved only insofar as the human creature, in perfect likeness with God, transcends all location through "the ascent beyond places and times," for those "*who participate* in the eternal and infinite beatitude will be encompassed neither by place nor by time."[57]

Now, I want to emphasize that the human subject who would be capable of such transcendence over place and time is not only the subject who proves incomprehensible to itself; it is also—to the very same degree—the subject who comprehends all of creation, which it can transcend thanks only to that comprehension. In this regard, a significant conjunction emerges in Eriugena's anthropology between the ultimately unknowing subject, on the one hand, and a certain all-knowing subject, on the other hand—the subject, precisely, made in the image of the incomprehensible God who himself sees and comprehends all by his presence. I want quickly to highlight this conjunction because I think it may eventually shed some interesting light on the technological subject of modern culture.

The fact that the human is created in God's image means for Eriugena not only that the human mind is ultimately incomprehensible to itself but also that the same human mind, like the divine, contains within itself all of creation. God "has created in man all creatures visible and invisible" [*omnem quidem creaturam visibilem et invisibilem in homine fecit*] in the sense that the "notion of nature, created in the human mind and possessed by it" is the "substance of the very things of which it is the notion, just as in the Divine Mind the notion of the whole created Universe is the incommunicable substance of the whole."[58] It is this comprehension of all creation that signals the distinctive transcendence of the human who is created in the image of God.

God wills to make every creature in man, Eriugena argues, "because He wished to make [man] in His image and likeness, so that, just as the primal Archetype transcends all by the excellence of His Essence, so His image should transcend all created things in dignity and grace."[59] The incomprehensible transcendence of the divine that contains all things within itself is imaged, then, in the transcendence of the human creature who comprehends all creation even as it remains incomprehensible to itself. This means, in short, that the apophatic or unknowing subject in Eriugena is also an all-comprehending subject.[60]

One should also note here that the apophatic subject who comprehends all creation is a subject who, by means of that comprehension, comes to dominate that which it comprehends. "For how," Eriugena asks, "could man be given dominion [over] the things of which he had not the concept? For his dominion over them would go astray if he did not know the things which he was to rule" [*Quomodo enim dominatus eorum homini daretur, quorum notionem non haberet? Siquidem dominatus illius erraret, si ea, quae regeret, nesciret*]." In a strange kind of resonance with the modern subject analyzed in Heidegger (or embodied in Hegel), man here rules creation through the knowledge that grasps or takes hold of it.

Even further, this domination is achieved through a knowledge that is understood above all in terms of sight—and in terms of the linguistic power that Eriugena can associate with sight. Notably in his exegesis of Gen. 2:19, where Adam sees and thereby names every beast, Eriugena emphasizes that scripture uses the verb "to see" [*videre*] because sight signals the power of understanding [*intelligere*] which alone gives rule or dominion [*dominatus*] over that which is understood, a rule or dominion itself enacted through the power of naming.[62] Just as God is θεός because he "sees" all things in himself and himself in all things, so the human subject sees all of creation in order to comprehend, name, and dominate it.

The emergent model here of an ultimately unknowing subject who at the same time comprehends and dominates all creation—through sight and language—is certainly not Eriugena's innovation, and we can find at least one significant precedent for this model in the theologian who perhaps most substantially informs Eriugena's apophatic anthropology: the fourth-century Cappadocian Gregory of Nyssa (ca. 335–ca. 394).

In his treatise from 379, "On the Creation of Man" (περι κατασκευής ἀνθρώπου/*De hominis opificio*), which Eriugena translated into Latin and refers to more simply as "The Image," Gregory presents the two aspects of the human subject that I have just marked out in Eriugena: the created subject who proves incomprehensible in the manner of its Creator is also a subject intended by that Creator to dominate the world through the comprehension of sight, the rational power of language—and finally, for Gregory, the technological self-assertion that proves both possible and necessary only for a subject of language who sees and comprehends all.

The anthropological insight of Gregory's treatise that is most significant for Eriugena's thinking appears in chap. 11, where Gregory argues that "since one of the properties of the divine essence is its incomprehensible character [το ἀκατάληπτον τῆς οὐσίας], in that also the image must resemble its model [ἀνάγκη πᾶσα καὶ ἐν τούτ την εἰκόνα προς το αρχέτυπον ἔχειν την μίμησιν]."[63] The God whose essence or οὐσία is incomprehensible (ἀκατάληπτον) is a God not to be grasped (or seized or conquered) by thought (and these are all possible meanings of ἀκατάληπτον —from the a-privative and καταλαμβάνω, to seize upon, lay hold of, take possession of; to hold in, keep down or under check; to catch, overtake, hence to discover, detect, find).[64] The human subject who understands its God as ultimately incomprehensible is itself the image of that God and so proves incomprehensible to itself (or indeed unconquerable, unable to seize or possess itself). To the degree that "we do not manage to know the nature of our own mind," we constitute the perfect image of our Creator.[65] At the same time, however, as in Eriugena, the subject who cannot know its own nature at the same time relates to creation through an all-inclusive vision of comprehension and dominion.

Indeed, in seeking to emphasize the full mimesis between Creator and creature, or between archetype and icon, Gregory notes that "the Divinity sees all, hears all, scrutinizes all. You also, through sight and hearing, possess a hold over things [ἔχεις καὶ συ την δι' ὄψεως καὶ ἀχοῆς τῶν ὄντων

ἀντίληψιν], and you possess a thinking [or intellect] that examines and scrutinizes the universe [καὶ τὴν ζητικήν τε και διερευνητικν τῶν ὄντων διά
νοιαν]."⁶⁶ The power of sight is tied here, as in Eriugena, to the intellectual
comprehension—indeed, possession—that gives a control or dominion.

Such comprehension and dominion are not unqualified, however. For
while Gregory argues that God made man "appear in this world" precisely "in
order to be both the contemplator [θεατην] and the master [κύριον] of the
marvels [θαυμάτων] of the universe," he also goes on to indicate that the
enjoyment of those marvels "should give to man the understanding [την
σύνεσιν] of the one who provides them, while the grandiose beauty of what
he sees places him on the tracks of the ineffable and inexpressible power of
the Creator [τήν ἄρρητον τε και ὑπερ λόγον τοῦ πεποιηκότος δύναμιν]."⁶⁷
Here we can note a very interesting conjunction, much like that we saw in
Eriugena, between an all-knowing, all-seeing subject and a subject for whom
the ground of knowing, or the God who gives that which is to be known, is
incomprehensible. The one who, as κύριος, masters or possesses the universe
in and through the contemplation of a spectator (θεατής) at the same time
finds, through that very contemplation, a trace of the incomprehensible and
ineffable (that which is ὑπερ λόγον and ἄρρητος). The mastery of sight here
comes up against the incomprehensible that literally cannot be mastered.

A certain mastery there is, however, and Gregory is clear on this: the
human creature appears in his treatise as master and possessor, lord and king
(κύριος, βασιλεύς)—and he does so in the very measure of his freedom, for
as autonomous and independent master of his own will, he is created in the
image of the God who, though incomprehensible, or as incomprehensible,
is nevertheless understood to rule all.⁶⁸ The human creature here is an image
of God not only insofar as the creature proves, like the Creator, incomprehensible to itself, but also, at the same time, insofar as the creature proves,
again like the Creator, to be the one who commands all creation through the
royal power of freedom: "Creation in the image [εἰκόνα] of the nature that
governs all [τῆς δυναστευούσης τῶν πάντων φύσεως] shows precisely that
it has from the start a royal nature [βασιλίδα . . . την φύσιν]. Thus, human nature [ἡ ἀνθρωπίνη φύσις], created to dominate the world [προς την ἀρχην
ἄλλων], because of its resemblance with the Universal King [δια τῆς προς
τον βασιλέα τοῦ παντος ὁμοιότητος], was made as a living image [εἰκων]
who participates in the archetype both in dignity and in name."⁶⁹ Incomprehensible icon of the incomprehensible archetype, the human creature
also mimics the king of all in its freedom and dominion. Indeed, as Jean
Daniélou emphasizes, freedom is the attribute par excellence of the human
who is created in the image of the divine—and that freedom is marked pri

marily by the interrelated traits of self-determination and domination over the universe.[70]

The freedom, then, that marks our resemblance with God implies a control or possession both of self and of world—and such freedom, I want to emphasize, exercises its rule over others in and through a technological capacity and a linguistic power enjoyed only by that creature who is capable, literally, of technological manipulation.

Having asserted that man is created for the very purpose of comprehending the universe both in sight and in thought, in order there also to find a trace of the incomprehensible, Gregory goes on to explain and celebrate humanity's technological ingenuity and the domination it ensures. The explanation begins by noting a physical poverty that forces rational innovation, for man "comes into the world stripped of any natural protections, without arms [ἄπλος—from τό ὅπλον, any tool or instrument, which in the plural refers especially to implements of war, arms] and in poverty [πένης], lacking everything needed to satisfy the needs of life."[71] Lacking most notably the natural arms or instruments of war (τα ὅπλα) that one can see in the animal's horn or hoof, claw or stinger, man is forced to innovate technologically in such a way that his power eventually exceeds—and controls—that of other creatures. "What appears to be a deficiency of our nature," Gregory can thus argue, "is in fact an encouragement to dominate [προς το κρατεῖν] that which is near us."[72]

Man therefore "works the iron that he uses for war [προς τον πόλεμον]," and through "the ingenuity of his *techné* [ἡ τέχνη δι᾽ ἐπινοίας ποιησαμένη] [he] gives wings to arrows and, by means of the bow, turns to our use the speed of the bird."[73] As these key passages attest, the purpose of man's mastery over creation is realized for Gregory through the ingenuity of a thinking that takes control of space and time by technological means, which, most interestingly, harness the speed of flight and thus allow man both to diminish distance and to realize action at a distance.[74] All of this becomes possible thanks to the physical poverty or deficiency that forces rational, technological innovation.

At the same time, while emphasizing that poverty, Gregory will note that the physical makeup of man includes also both the sign and the means of man's dominion—in that which most directly embodies man's rational capacity: the hands.[75] "Anyone who would see in the use of hands that which is proper to a rational [λογικῆς] nature would not be mistaken," Gregory reasons, not only because the hands make possible the rational self-expression or self-embodiment exemplified in writing but even more fundamentally because the hands alone free the mouth for language.[76]

The linguistic subject in Gregory is made possible only through the endowment of hands, and thus the linguistic subject is at the same time the subject who can manipulate and rule the world technologically. As much as technological manipulation, the hands signal for Gregory language or logic itself—λόγος]—and thus the dignity and power of the linguistic or rational subject who alone exercises a technological rule: "One can undoubtedly list by the thousands the needs of life for which the finesse of these instruments, which suffice for everything [προς πᾶσαν τέχνην και πᾶσαν ἐνέργειαν], has served man in peace as in war; however, it is above all else for language [τοῦ λόγου] that nature added the hands to our body."[77]

In sum, then, in this key source for Eriugena's apophatic anthropology, where we saw an intriguing intersection between all-encompassing vision and ultimate unknowing, we find again an all-encompassing vision of the cosmos in and through which the incomprehensible appears—but to a comprehending subject who, through the hand and through the rational, linguistic capacity signaled by the hand, masters that cosmos technologically.

If we can see here an all-knowing technological subject in unexpectedly close proximity to the apophatic or mystical subject of unknowing, might we also see, conversely, a hint of the mystical or unknowing subject in today's technological world?

Like the totality of the mystical cosmos in Eriugena, or already in Dionysius, a cosmos wherein created souls endlessly desire and seek out—but never fully or finally capture—the superessential "Cause" that reveals itself concealedly through that cosmos, so the technological world of all-consuming image today can seem to contain a subject unable to comprehend or to represent the ultimate causality of its world—a subject who seems, for that very reason, to be driven by ever renewed desire to generate and to consume (to posit and remove, to affirm and deny) ever new images in which desire never quite finds satiety. As in the mystical cosmos, where the desire for God passes through infinite layers of theophanic appearance without ever reaching an end, so in the world of technological image, the subject remains ever on the move, passing constantly from image to image, within an endless proliferation of connections, associations, and displacements.

Such an endless displacement of the desiring subject within today's world of endless technological image could be registered at several different levels, most all of which would concern some disjunction between the individual experience we can know and the incomprehensible totalities or systems— above all the technological—that we might imagine to determine the "place" of such experience. As Jacques Derrida has recently put it, evoking explicitly a "transcendence" in "tele-technology," "because one increasingly *uses* artifacts and prostheses of which one is totally ignorant, in a growing disproportion between knowledge and know-how, the space of such technical experience tends to become more animistic, magical, mystical."[78] Whereas in Gregory the ultimately unknowing subject is also the all-knowing subject of technological rule, here in Derrida, the seemingly all-knowing subject of technological rule proves to be more and more unknowing—operating in a quasi-mystical space opened by the disjunction or disproportion between practical know-how and scientific comprehension. The emergence of such a space, of course, was glimpsed already by our theorists of technology in the earlier half of the twentieth century: Weber already saw that, in a world disenchanted through modern rationalization, we come to rely ever more essentially on forms of knowledge we do not ourselves possess and on technological powers we do not in fact control; Benjamin likewise saw that the technologies of image reproduction become so fundamental to the framing of our reality that we can no longer even see or comprehend them in our experience of that reality, and finally, Heidegger, already in his 1938 essay, was able to see that "what is gigantic" in the modern system of the representing subject, "and what can seemingly always be calculated completely, becomes, precisely through this, incalculable [*zum Unberechenbaren*]."[79] He then goes on to indicate that "this becoming incalculable remains the invisible shadow that is cast around all things everywhere when man has been transformed into *subjectum* and the world into picture."[80] That is, the modern system of the calculating, technological subject opens a space that ultimately eludes the subject's planning and calculation because it eludes the subject's power of representation: "By means of this shadow [of the incalculable] the modern world extends itself out into a space withdrawn from representation" [*in einen der Vorstellung entzogenen Raum*].[81] As Samuel Weber helpfully glosses, this shadow of the gigantic "prevents [things] from ever being put fully into their proper places, that is, being fully depicted. This shadow is not simply external to the world as picture; it is an inseparable part of it. . . . ['Shadow' here] designates what escapes and eludes the calculating plans of total representation, of which it is at the same time the condition of possibility."[82] Much as in Eriugena or Gregory, where the incomprehensible substance or essence of the human intellect is the ground of possibility for the human comprehension of all that is, so here the space that cannot be contained by the totalizing representation of the technological subject becomes the groundless ground of such representation. Just as the all-knowing subject in Eriugena and Gregory turns out to dwell in unexpected proximity to the subject of unknowing who cannot be located, so the representing subject who grounds modern technology here dwells in unexpected proximity to a space that cannot be fixed, set, or placed through representation.[83]

In this light, the quasi-mystical space opened by today's "delocalizing tele-technoscience," or already the shadow that emerges with the gigantic in Heidegger, might evoke sufficiently the uncircumscribable place of all places or the brilliant darkness of Eriugena's cosmology to suggest that a strange shadow of the mystical subject and its God may somehow appear in the experience of today's technological subject.[84]

Where might we glimpse such an appearance? In what figures of incomprehensible totality might we seek such a shadow? The figures of global totality are, at present, inescapably technological figures, and among those I would highlight two. We might think, of course, almost automatically, of the World Wide Web or the Internet, figures of an electronic and telematic light system in which "iconic" interconnection approaches both infinite complexity and unthinkable unity—altering or even erasing the limits of time and place themselves. Or we might think—with growing urgency—of the thermonuclear bomb, the image of an unthinkable power or potential whose actualization would bind us universally and instantaneously in some unknowable fusion of invisible light and fire. These two figures of a purely rationalized human self-assertion, two figures, one might assume, of a total de-mystification of the world by a self-grounding and self-transparent modern subject, might signal also a displacement or dislocation of that subject—indeed, a dislocation in which that subject would confront some shadow of the mystical.

Such a shadow appears brilliantly, I think, in Don DeLillo's *Underworld*, a novel not only permeated by our modern obsessions with sight and comprehension and systematic manipulation but also haunted by aura and angels and the mystical body. In *Underworld*'s closing pages DeLillo imagines the intersection or fusion of both these totalizing technologies—the computer and the bomb—and he does so by narrating the experience of one old-school nun, Sister Alma Edgar, a bride of Christ either dying or already dead (and a twin of the all-seeing J. Edgar), who, entering the "miracle" of the Internet, "where everybody is everywhere at once," faces the kind of pure exposure, indeed the ubiquity and simultaneity, known in the total presence of Altizer's "electronic humanity": "She is not naked exactly but she is open—exposed to every connection you can make on the world wide web," and she discovers that "there is no space or time out here, or in here, or wherever she is. There are only connections. Everything is connected. All human knowledge gathered and linked, hyperlinked, this site leading to that, this fact referenced to that, a keystroke, a mouse-click, a password—world without end, amen."[85] Caught up in the totality of the web's endless interconnection, which gathers all human knowledge as if in some all-seeing vision and keeps it literally ready-to-hand, the bride of Christ encounters a ubiquity and simultaneity that seem to unsettle place and time. Like the endlessly multiple perspectives of Eriugena's theophanic cosmos, which both shows and hides all, so here the endlessly multiple images and connections of the net draw the bride of Christ onward, leading her, through an endless displacement, into a totality that approaches the mystical. And so she can wonder, as one might of the mystical God—or the mystical subject—in their relation to the mystical cosmos, "Is cyberspace a thing within the world or is it the other way around? Which contains the other, and how can you tell for sure?" [86] Are all things in God or is God in all things? Does the intellect contain all that it creates, or is the intellect contained by all that creates it? A believer, Sister Alma Edgar is, of course, convinced that "she is in cyberspace, not heaven"—but her conviction is uneasy, for "she feels the grip of systems. This is why she's so uneasy. There is a presence here, a thing implied, something vast and bright . . . it's a glow, a lustrous rushing force that seems to flow from a billion distant net nodes."[87]

Caught in this rushing force and glow, in this presence vast and bright, implied and thus elusive, running like Eriugena's God through all that might be seen, DeLillo's bride of Christ approaches, through this first technological figure of totality, a second: the thermonuclear bomb. "When you decide on a whim to visit the H-bomb page, she begins to understand. Everything in your computer, the plastic, silicon and mylar, every logical operation and processing function, the memory, the hardware, the software, the ones and zeroes, the triads inside the pixels that form the on-screen image—it all culminates here."[88] It "all" culminates "here," the narrator tells us—all knowledge and power merge here, the atomic and the cosmic intersect here, on the screen whose bottomless light gives endless image, a screen where technological totalization, the logical consequence of Heidegger's "planetary imperialism of technologically organized man," is given as a blinding vision:

First a dawnlight, a great aurora glory massing on the color monitor. Every thermonuclear bomb ever tested, all the data gathered from each shot, code name, yield, test site, Eniwetok, Lop Nor, Novaya Zemyla, the foreignness, the otherness of remote populations implied in the place names, Mururoa, Kazakhstan, Siberia, and the wreathwork of extraordinary detail, firing systems and delivery systems, equations and graphs and schematic cross sections, shot after shot, summoned at a click, a hit, Bravo, Romeo, Greenhouse Dog—and Sister is basically in it.

She sees the flash, the thermal pulse. . . . She stands in the flash and feels the power. She sees the spray plume. She sees the fireball climbing, the superheated sphere of burning gas that can blind a person with its beauty, its dripping christ-blood colors, solar golds and reds. She sees the shock wave and hears the high winds and feels the power of false faith, the faith of paranoia, then the mushroom cloud spreads around her, the pulverized mass of radioactive debris, eight miles high, ten miles, twenty, with skirted stem and platinum cap.

The jewels roll out of her eyes and she sees God.[89]

Here on the screen of light where all becomes connection and connection becomes all—where every image, hyperlinked, points beyond itself within some uncircumscribable totality, some incomprehensible unity, where inside is out and outside in, where the mere flick of a hand gives "shot after shot, bomb after bomb," where the bomb itself takes name after name and calls up place after place, signaling all the places of unthinkable displacement—here the figure of ultimate fusion, dripping in "christblood" colors, becomes an image of blinding beauty, like that of the divine radiance in Eriugena, before which angels are blown back and shield their faces, like that of the God who blinds with his holiness, the God whom no one can see without dying.[90]

"No, wait, sorry. It is a Soviet bomb she sees, the largest yield in history. . . preserved in the computer that helped build it."[91] The bride of Christ, the old-school believer, comes to her senses, of course, for she knows false faith and she sees that this blinding beauty dripping in christblood colors, this "end" in which "everything is connected," this technological erasure of place and time, is not God.[92] Of course: it is surely not likely that this nun would find on such a screen, in such an all-consuming vision of human reason and human self-assertion, any shadow of the mystical. Such a total light, after all, would leave no shadow.

And yet, like the God whose purest light is unimaginable darkness, whose immanence is transcendence, these images of technological totality can seem to signal that which would comprehend the human subject more than the subject would comprehend it. While born of human reason and human self-assertion, such technological totality can nevertheless seem to absorb and escape us—with nothing beyond.

If a strange shadow of the mystical God appears here, could that be because all creatures are indeed theophanies, or because the creative self-expression of God, which issues from and returns to Nothingness, is imaged perfectly in the creative self-expression of the human? If a shadow of the mystical subject appears here, could that be because the mystical subject who is ultimately unknowing is also a subject who comprehends all and masters all technologically? How far is the distance between the molded iron and flying arrow in Gregory and DeLillo's nuclear warhead? In face of Sister Alma Edgar's all-consuming vision, could we truly affirm with Eriugena that God is the all in all that returns to Nothing? If so, then we would have to read in a whole new light, and in at least two ways, Eriugena's assertion that "there is no other end of this world, but the ascent beyond places and times of all those who shall receive the glory of . . . deification."[93]

Notes

1. Max Weber, "Science as a Vocation," in *From Max Weber: Essays in Sociology*, ed. H. H. Gerth and C. Wright Mills (New York: Oxford University Press, 1946), 139.

2. Walter Benjamin, "The Work of Art in the Age of Mechanical Reproduction," in *Illuminations*, ed. Hannah Arendt (New York: Schocken Books, 1968). On the significant proximities between Benjamin and Heidegger, many of which resonate here in my own essay, see, esp., Samuel Weber, "Mass Mediauras; Or, Art, Aura, and Media in the Work of Walter Benjamin," in *Walter Benjamin: Theoretical Questions*, ed. David Ferris (Stanford, Calif.: Stanford University Press, 1996).

3. As would hold thinkers as diverse as Jean Baudrillard, Mark C. Taylor, and Jean-Luc Marion. See, e.g., Jean Baudrillard, *Simulacres et simulation* (Paris: Editions Galilée, 1981); Mark C. Taylor, *Hiding* (Chicago: University of Chicago Press, 1997); and Jean-Luc Marion, *La Croisée du visible* (Paris: Presses Universitaires de France, 1991).

4. Martin Heidegger, "The Age of the World Picture," in *The Question concerning Technology and Other Essays*, trans. William Lovitt (New York: Harper & Row, 1977), 134 published in German as "Die Zeit des Weltbildes," in *Holzwege*, vol. 5 of *Gesamtausgabe* (Frankfurt am Main: Vittorio Klostermann, 1977), 94.

5. Heidegger, "World Picture," 134, "Die Zeit des Weltbildes," 94.

6. The modern subject's attempt to construct or produce the world as "image" is central to that subject's struggle to master the world as ob-ject, and in this sense the becoming image of the world and the becoming subject of man are for Heidegger one and the same event ("World Picture," 132, "Die Zeit des Weltbildes," 92).

7. Heidegger, "World Picture," 135, "Die Zeit des Weltbildes," 94. On *Bezugsmitte*, see "World Picture 128, "Die Zeit des Weltbildes," 88.

8. Heidegger, "World Picture," 135, "Die Zeit des Weltbildes," 95.

9. In his 1953 essay "The Question concerning Technology," Heidegger signals the "monstrousness" that reigns when nature—above all in the form of energy—is ordered and approached in terms of the availability and manipulability of "standing reserve." See "The Question concerning Technology," in *Basic Writings*, ed. David F. Krell (New York: Harper & Row, 1977), esp. 297–303.

10. Consistent with the logic of this disappearing presence/present disappearance, the reverse is also the case: in the movement where the distant is made close, the close becomes distant—as Heidegger notes, e.g., in his 1955 "Memorial Address": "All that with which mod-

ern techniques of communication stimulate, assail, and drive man—all that is already much closer to man today than his fields around his farmstead, closer than the sky over the earth, closer than the change from night to day, closer than the conventions and customs of his village, than the traditions of his native world" (in *Discourse on Thinking,* trans. J. M. Anderson and E. Hans Freund (New York: Harper & Row, 1966), 48. The quote is from Heidegger, "World Picture," 152, "Die Zeit des Weltbildes," 111.

11. As Samuel Weber suggests, the picture today "gets" us more than we "get the picture": "But in a world on the verge, traversed and indeed constituted out of such circulating series of images, it is difficult to establish the kind of set and secure position that Benjamin initially associates with the aura and Heidegger with the world picture. These are pictures that you do *not* get—you are gotten by them" ("Mass Mediauras," 45).

12. For Heidegger, the distinctively modern claim of human subjectivity to found truth as (self-)certainty "originates in that emancipation of man in which he frees himself from obligation to Christian revelational truth [*Offenbarungswahrheit*] and Church doctrine to a legislating for himself that takes its stand upon itself [*zu der auf sich selbst stellenden Gesetzgebung für sich selbst*]" ("World Picture," 148, "Die Zeit des Weltbildes," 107).

13. Heidegger, "World Picture," 116, "Die Zeit des Weltbildes," 76.

14. Don DeLillo, *Underworld* (New York: Scribner, 1997), 812.

15. Thomas J. J. Altizer, *The Contemporary Jesus* (Albany: State University of New York Press, 1997), 187.

16. Heidegger, "World Picture," 128, "Die Zeit des Weltbildes," 88. In Heidegger, the anonymity of the collective goes back, of course, to the problem of inauthenticity and "the They" [*das Man*] in *Being and Time.* In relation to Heidegger's concern with the collective mass and technological society, Benjamin would also prove helpful, insofar as he links the "decay of the aura" to the logic of mass society and to the statistical thinking associated with that logic: "To pry an object from its shell, to destroy its aura, is the mark of a perception whose 'sense of the universal equality of things' has increased to such a degree that it extracts it even from a unique object by means of reproduction. Thus is manifested in the field of perception what in the theoretical sphere is noticeable in the increasing importance of statistics. The adjustment of reality to the masses and of the masses to reality is a process of unlimited scope, as much for thinking as for perception" (Benjamin, "The Work of Art in the Age of Mechanical Reproduction," 223). For a provocative reflection on statistical mass and numeric thinking, see Annie Dillard's essay "The Wreck of Time: Taking Our Century's Measure," *Harper's* (January 1998).

17. "'We get the picture' concerning something does not mean only that what is, is set before us, is represented to us, in general, but that what is stands before us—in all that belongs to it and all that stands together in it—as a system" (Heidegger, "World Picture," 129, "Die Zeit des Weltbildes," 89).

18. Heidegger, "World Picture," 152–53.

19. Altizer, *Contemporary Jesus,* 203–4.

20. Thomas J. J. Altizer, *Total Presence: The Language of Jesus and the Language of Today* (New York: Seabury Press, 1980), 35–36.

21. Altizer, *Contemporary Jesus,* 187.22. Ibid., 196.

23. Ibid. Both in the tie between polyonymous anonymity and spatiotemporal displacement and in the distinction between modern and traditional forms of ubiquity and simultaneity, Altizer stands in agreement with numerous thinkers of the various post-ages (above all, the post-Heideggerian and poststructuralist) for whom the presence of the God or gods

can be seen today only as an absence, their givenness given only as loss or abandon. In this direction, Jean-Luc Nancy would be exemplary when, in his work on the topic of "divine places," he evokes an immediate presence or excessive "denuding" that finally constitutes an absence or desertion (*Des Lieux divins* [Mauvezin: Editions Trans-Euro-Repress, 1987]). In a different sense, Jean-Luc Marion's treatment of givenness and abandon would also resonate significantly here (esp. as it appears in *Etant donné: Essai d'une phénoménologie de la donation* (Paris: Presses Universitaires de France, 1997). For further discussion of Nancy and Marion in relation to Altizer, see my "Unlikely Shadows: Transcendence in Image and Immanence" (in *Transcendence,* ed. Regina Schwartz [New York: Routledge, 2003], in press).

24. One can see the emergence of such an aesthetic in the abbey church at St. Denis, whose Abbot Suger took his inspiration for the church design directly and explicitly from Dionysian theology. On Dionysius, the church at St. Denis, and the emergence of the Gothic light aesthetic, see Otto von Simson, *The Gothic Cathedral* (Princeton, N.J.: Princeton University Press, 1988), esp. 21–141; and Georges Duby, *Medieval Art: Europe of the Cathedrals, 1140–1280* (Geneva: Editions d'Art Albert Skira S.A., 1995), esp. 7–55.

25. On this dialectic of transcendence and immanence in Eckhart, see, e.g., his treatment of it—in terms of dissimilarity and similarity—within his commentary on Exodus's prohibition against fashioning any likeness of God (Exod. 20:4): "You should know that nothing is as dissimilar as the Creator and any creature. In the second place, nothing is as similar as the Creator and any creature. And in the third place, nothing is as equally dissimilar and similar to anything else as God and the creature are dissimilar and similar in the same degree" (*Commentary on Exodus,* sec. 112); "What is as dissimilar and similar to something else as that whose 'dissimilitude' is its very 'similitude,' whose indistinction is its very distinction? . . . Therefore, because he is distinguished by indistinction, is assimilated by dissimilitude, the more dissimilar he is the more similar he becomes (*Commentary on Exodus,* sec. 117). Passages from Eckhart can be found in Bernard McGinn, ed., *Meister Eckhart: Teacher and Preacher* (New York: Paulist Press, 1986). In Cusa, see, e.g., *On Learned Ignorance,* which approaches the issue in terms of the coincidence of opposites—the maximum and minimum:

> Oppositions, therefore, apply only to those things that admit greater and a lesser, and they apply in different ways, but never to the absolutely maximum, for it is above all opposition. Therefore, because the absolutely maximum is absolutely and actually all that can be, and it is without opposition to such an extent that the minimum coincides with the maximum, it is above all affirmation and negation. It both is and is not all that is conceived to be, and it both is and is not all that is conceived not to be. But it is a 'this' in such a way that it is all things, and it is all things in such a way that it is none of them.
>
> (in Nicholas of Cusa: Selected Spiritual Writings, trans. H. Lawrence Bond [New York: Paulist Press, 1997], I.2.12)

26. Creatively appropriating the Dionysian cosmology, Eriugena ties that cosmic vision inextricably to a treatment of the human subject, so that one can see Eriugena's thought "from start to finish" as providing "an account of how the cosmos, through the mediation of the human subject, returns to its fullest possible unification (*adunatio*) with the hidden God" (Bernard McGinn, *The Growth of Mysticism,* vol. 2 of *The Presence of God* [New York: Crossroad, 1994], 81).

27. Johannes Scotus Eriugena, *Periphyseon = The Division of Nature,* trans. I. P. Sheldon Williams, rev. John J. O'Meara (Montreal: Editions Bellarmin, 1987). All citations will be given according to the Migne pagination, as follows: bk., p., col. Citations of the Latin original

are taken, for bks. 1 and 2, from I. P. Sheldon Williams, ed:, *Periphyseon (De Divisione Naturae)* (Dublin: Dublin Institute for Advanced Studies, 1968, 1972), and, for all other books, from J. P. Migne, ed., *Patrologiae Cursus Completus Series Latina,* vol. 122 (Paris: Migne, 1853).

28. Eriugena, *Periphyseon* I.458B, I.458A–B.

29. Ibid., III.682D.

30. Eriugena explicitly attributes the teaching that God both makes and is made in creation to Pseudo-Dionysius: "Therefore God *is* everything that truly is because He Himself makes all things and is made in all things, as St. Dionysius the Areopagite says" (*Periphyseon* III.633A).

31. Ibid., III.682D.

32. Ibid., I.455A–B.

33. Ibid., III.681C.

34. Ibid., III.683A–B; emphasis added. Eriugena will elaborate this scheme in both Christocentric terms (which I address below) and, correlatively, in trinitarian terms (which nevertheless insist on the utter incomprehensibility and mystery of divine Unity and Trinity): "Now, [the holy theologians] called the condition [i.e., the relation] of the Unbegotten Substance to the Begotten Substance Father, the condition of the Begotten to the Unbegotten Substance Son, and the condition of the Proceeding Substance to the Unbegotten and to the Begotten Substance Holy Spirit" (ibid., I.456B; see also II.570B). Signaling God in himself, in his causes, and in the effects of those causes, the three persons of the Trinity are answered in turn by three motions of the soul: the simplicity of mind "moves about the unknown God"; the movement of reason "'defines the unknown' God 'as Cause' of all"; and the movement of sense "comes into contact with that which is outside her as though by certain signs and reforms within herself the reasons of visible things" (ibid., II.572C–573B). The soul answers in this way to God precisely because it constitutes the image of that God—and as Eriugena will insist, there is no difference here between the image and its exemplar "except in respect of subject. For the most high Trinity subsists substantially through itself and is created out of no cause, while the trinity of our nature is made by it, Which through Itself is eternal, out of nothing, in Its image and likeness" (ibid., II.598B). As Eriugena will put it, the Exemplar is God by nature, while the image is God by grace, and the passage from image to exemplar involves the threefold movement of purification, illumination, and perfection (see, e.g., ibid., II.585C, II.598B–C).

35. As McGinn points out, "John stressed that creation and scripture were two parallel manifestations of the hidden God" (*Growth of Mysticism,* 93), and he "often used the term *transitus* ('dynamic passage from one state to another' would be a possible translation) to describe the process of how the exegete moves through the infinity of textual meanings to the hidden divine unitary source" (*Growth of Mysticism,* 94). For an extended discussion of spiritual exegesis in Eriugena, see McGinn, "The Originality of Eriugena's Spiritual Exegesis," in *Iohannes Scottus Eriugena: The Bible and Hermeneutics,* ed. Gerd Van Riel, Carlos Steel, and James McEvoy (Leuven: University Press, 1996). Werner Beierwaltes emphasizes that this movement of human *transitus,* wherein the believer passes through the infinity of God's scriptural and cosmic showings to return into God himself, answers to the divine *transitus* that is the very nature of both divine and created being: "Transition expresses an essential feature of divine being: the movement in which it develops itself and creates the world" ("Language and Its Object," in *Jean-Scot Ecrivain,* ed. G.-H. Allard [Montreal: Editions Bellarmin, 1986], 224).

Regarding the endless multiplicity of theophanies, see Eriugena, *Periphyseon* III.679A or I.448C–D: "For as great as is the number of the elect, so great will be the number of the mansions; as much as shall be the multiplication of holy souls, so much will be the possession of divine theophanies."

36. Eriugena, *Periphyseon* III.678C.

37. For a clear instance of this in Hegel, see, e.g., *Lectures on the Philosophy of Religion:* "Finite consciousness knows God only to the extent that God knows himself in it" (*Lectures on the Philosophy of Religion: One-Volume Edition—the Lectures of 1827*, ed. Peter Hodgson; trans. R. F. Brown, P. C. Hodgson, and J. M. Stewart [Berkeley: University of California Press, 1988], 392, n. 3). On the "apophatic erasure" that Hegel effects in his reading of the speculative mystics, see Cyril O'Regan's *The Heterodox Hegel* (Albany: State University of New York Press, 1994). On Eriugena and German idealism, see esp. the fine study by Dermot Moran, *The Philosophy of John Scotus Eriugena* (Cambridge: Cambridge University Press, 1989); and, for a brief treatment, Werner Beierwaltes, "The Revaluation of John Scottus Eriugena in German Idealism," in *The Mind of Eriugena*, ed. John J. O'Meara and Ludwig Bieler (Dublin: Irish University Press, 1973), 190–99.

38. Given that the creator of all things is created in all things, divine self-manifestation signals not simply the Incarnation but indeed more broadly "the ineffable descent of the Supreme Goodness, which is Unity and Trinity, into the things that are so as to make them be, indeed so as itself to be, in all things from the highest to the lowest, ever eternal, ever made, by itself in itself eternal, by itself in itself made" (Eriugena, *Periphyseon* III.678D).

For the paradoxical theophany of all creatures, see Eriugena, *Periphyseon* III.681A–B

39. Several commentators have made this point with some force. See, e.g., Don Duclow: "Conceived as theophany, the entire created order becomes a field of translucent symbols which yield knowledge of the divine nature, even thought this position knowledge [*sic*] remains metaphorical and partial throughout" ("Divine Nothingness and Self-Creation in John Scotus Eriugena," *Journal of Religion* 57, no. 2 [April 1977]: 118). On Eriugena's significance to medieval aesthetics and art, see Werner Beierwaltes, "Negati Affirmatio: Welt als Metapher/Zur Grundlegung einer mittelalterlichen Ästhetik durch Johannes Scotus Eriugena," in *Jean Scot Erigène et l'histoire de la philosophie*, ed. Centre national de la recherche scientifique (Paris: Editions du Centre National de la Recherche Scientifique, 1977); and Yves Christie, "Influences et Retentissement de l'Oeuvre de Jean Scot sur l'Art Médiéval: Bilan et Perspectives," in *Eriugena Redivivus*, ed. Werner Beierwaltes (Heidelberg: Carl Winter-Universitätsverlag, 1987).

On the field of luminous appearance, see , e.g., Eriugena, *Periphyseon* III.681B.

40. Eriugena, *Periphyseon* III.633A–B. See also III.678C:

> And God, by manifesting Himself, in a marvelous and ineffable manner creates Himself in the creature, the invisible making Himself visible and the incomprehensible comprehensible and the hidden revealed and the unknown known and being without form and species formed and specific and the superessential essential and the supernatural natural and the simple composite and the accident-free subject to accident [and accident] and the infinite finite, and the uncircumscribed circumscribed and the supratemporal temporal and the Creator of all things created in all things and the Maker of al things made in all things, and Eternal he begins to be, and immobile He moves into all things and becomes in all things all things.

41. As Don Duclow puts it, "the divine *nihil* constitutes the ground for theophanic self-

creation, which in turn cannot be thought apart from the transcendence which it manifests in the otherness of created essence and being" ("Divine Nothingness and Self-Creation," 119).

42. Eriugena, *Periphyseon* III.633B–C.

43. McGinn puts all of this quite well:

> If all things are God manifested, then humanity is God manifested in the most special way. It is the true and only *imago Dei*, because, like its divine source, it does not know *what* it is (it is not a *what* at all), but it does know *that* it is—namely, it possesses self-consciousness. Thus, the primacy of negative theology in Eriugena is complemented by his negative anthropology: Humanity does not know God, but God does not know God either (in the sense of knowing or defining a *what*); and humanity does not know itself, nor does God know humanity insofar as it is one with the divine mind that is the cause of itself. This brilliant anthropological turn, hinted at in Gregory's *The Image,* was brought to full and daring systematic expression in the Irishman's writings. It is the ground for a remarkable elevation of humanity (at least the idea of humanity) to a divine and co-creative status.
>
> Growth of Mysticism, 105

44. Eriugena, *Periphyseon* IV, 771B. To elucidate more fully this interplay between the human creature's self-consciousness and its ultimate incomprehensibility to itself, one would have to note that Eriugena distinguishes two aspects of the human substance: as created among the intelligible Causes in God, that substance is utterly simple and thus incomprehensible; as generated among the effects of those Causes, however, the human substance takes on the kind of determination that renders it comprehensible, as indicated by IV.771A: "No, I should not say that there are two substances, but one which may be conceived under two aspects. Under one aspect the human substance is perceived as created among the intelligible Causes, under the other as generated among their effects; under the former free from all mutability, under the latter subject to change; under the former simple, involved in no accidents, it eludes all reason and intelligence; under the latter it receives a kind of composition of quantities and qualities and whatever else can be understood in relation to it, whereby it becomes apprehensible to the mind." Having made this distinction, however, Eriugena finally insists, apophatically, on the ultimate incomprehensibility of the human substance—at the level both of generated effect and of created cause: "So it is that what is one and the same [substance] can be thought of as twofold because there are two ways of looking at it, yet everywhere it preserves its incomprehensibility [*ubique tamen suam incomprehensibilitem custodit*], in the effects as in the causes [*in causis dico et in effectibus*], and whether it is endowed with accidents or abides in its naked simplicity: under neither set of circumstances is it subject to created sense or intellect nor even the knowledge of itself as to what it is [*nec a seipsa intelligitur quid sit*]" (IV.771A).

45. For a concise and rigorous analysis of these three theses—with an insistence on their essential interconnection—see Bernard McGinn, "The Negative Element in the Anthropology of John the Scot," in *Jean Scot Erigène,* ed. Centre national de la recherche scientifique, 315–25.

46. Eriugena, *Periphyseon* IV.771C.

47. Ibid., I.463A.

48. Ibid., IV.771C–D.

49. Ibid., I.523B. On the placelessness of God's causal presence, see also, e.g., ibid., I.468D–469A: "For everything that is in the world must move in time and be defined in

place; even place itself is defined and time itself moves. But God neither moves nor is defined. For (He is) the Place of places by which all places are defined, and since He is not fixed in place but gives place to all things within Him, He is not place but More-than-place. For he is defined by nothing, but defines all things: therefore He is the Cause of all things." The inextricable tie between definition and location runs throughout Eriugena's thinking, for "place is definition and definition is place" (ibid., I.485B); place, indeed, "is simply the natural definition of each creature, within which it is wholly contained and beyond which it by no means extends: and from this it is given to understand that whether one call it place or limit or term or definition or circumscription, one and the same thing is denoted, namely the confine of a finite creature" (ibid., I.483C); and place is tied, again inextricably, to time, the two of which in tandem marking the conditions of existence and knowledge: "For it is impossible to conceive place if time *is withdrawn*, as it is impossible for time to be defined without *understanding it in connexion* with place. For these are included among the things which are always found inseparably together; and without these no essence which has received being through generation can by any means *exist or be known*. Therefore the essence of all existing things is local and temporal, and thus it can in no way be known except in place and time and under place and time" (ibid., I.481C).

50. As Marta Cristiani nicely puts it, one can see throughout Eriugena "the clearest affirmation that *place* is identified with the activity of the human, angelic or divine intellect that localizes and circumscribes beings, that knows reality thanks to that very act, thanks to that power of definition, which is considered at the same time as the power of *creation*," in *The Mind of Eriugena,* ed. O'Meara and Bieler, 47.

51. Eriugena, *Periphyseon* III.642C–D.

52. Ibid., III.646C, III.646A, III.644D.

53. Duclow, "Divine Nothingness and Self-Creation," 122. On this double cry, see also McGinn, *Growth of Mysticism,* 108.

54. Eriugena, *Periphyseon* I.452C.

55. Ibid., III.677C, 668C.

56. See especially those passages such as ibid., II.592C–D: "The Divine Nature is without any place, although it provides place within itself for all things which are from it, and for that reason is called the Place of all things; but it is unable to provide place for itself because it is infinite and uncircumscribed and does not allow itself to be located, that is, defined and circumscribed, by any intellect nor by itself. For from it, being infinite and more than infinite, all finites and infinites proceed, and to it, being infinite and more than infinite, they return"; or III.643C: "For who, taking thought for the truth, would believe or think that God had prepared for Himself places through which he might diffuse Himself, He who is contained in no place since He is the common place of all things and therefore, as Place of places, is held by no place?"

57. Ibid., I.482D.

58. Ibid., IV.763D, 769A. See also IV.764A: "No part of [the sensible world] is found, either corporal or incorporeal, which does not subsist created in man, which does not perceive through him, which does not live through him, which is not incorporated in him."

59. Ibid., IV.764A.

60. Indeed, the concept of man "stands above all definition" to the extent that "it has been given him to possess the concept of all things which were either created his equals or which he was instructed to govern" (ibid., IV.768 D), for man possesses the concept of all

things only insofar as he constitutes the perfect image of the incomprehensible God who knows all.

61. Ibid., IV.768D.

62. Eriguena's interpretation of Gen. 2:19 reads: "Therefore, having formed out of the earth every beast of the field and every bird of the heavens, the Lord brought them unto Adam to see what he would call them: and whatsoever Adam called every living soul that is its name" (ibid., IV.768D–769A).

He goes on to discuss the use of the verb *videre:* "It says 'to see,' that is, to understand what he would call them. For if he did not understand, how would he be able to call them rightly? [*si enim non intelligeret, quomodo recte vocare posset?*] But what he called anything that is its name, that is, it is the very notion of the living soul" (ibid., IV.769A). To call or to name here is to understand, and to understand is to see in such a way as to comprehend in a concept [*notio*]—and thereby secure dominion.

63. Gregory of Nyssa, *On the Creation of Man* will be cited here according to the pagination of J.-P. Migne, ed., *Patrologiae Cursus Completus Series Graeca,* vol. 44, 156B. In my translations I have relied on the original Greek and on the French translation, *La Création de l'homme,* trans. Jean Laplace, notes by Jean Daniélou (Paris: Editions du Cerf, 1944).

64. *Liddell and Scott's Greek-English Lexicon* (Oxford: Oxford University Press, 1987).

65. Gregory of Nyssa, *On the Creation of Man* 156B.

66. Ibid., 137C. The sense of possession is indicated twice here, in the verb ἔχεις and in the noun ἀντίληψις, which, though often rightly translated as "perception," can mean also a laying hold of something, a seizure, or an attack.

67. Ibid., 133A.

68. Ibid., 136C.

69. Ibid.

70. Daniélou, in his notes to Gregory of Nyssa's *La Création de l'homme* (43–44):

What, according to Gregory, are the characteristics of this state of freedom? We can bring them down to two: self-determination and domination over the universe. . . . We resemble God through our purity and virtue; but we can acquire that state only through the mediation of freedom. Without freedom, our perfection would be imposed on us and it would no longer be divine. For "to have the initiative in one's acts is to be equal with God" (*De mortuis,* P.G. 46, 524 a). Without this self-determination, man would be "stripped of the honor that makes him equal to God" (*ibid.*). Freedom is therefore inherent to our spiritual nature. Spirit means not only self-knowledge, but essentially self-possession. We will never be the images of God if we do not freely make our destiny.

This independence makes man "king of the universe." . . . This is why [the creature] is made to "know" all, to "scrutinize" all, to subject all to itself.

71. Gregory of Nyssa, *On the Creation of Man* 140D.

72. As Daniélou notes, "the same idea had already been developed by Origen: man was created in nudity and indigence ἐνδεής, as distinct from animals, because he is λογικός: he must conquer his food and the world thanks to his intelligence (*Contr. Cels.,* IV 76; P.G. XI, 1148 B). It is a sign of his greatness. This optimistic view, of Stoic origin, is opposed to the pessimism of the Epicureans" (in Gregory of Nyssa's *La Création de l'homme,* 103, n. 1). For the Stoic celebration of man's rational-technological capacities—and esp. the power of the hands that will prove key in Gregory—see Cicero (who relies on Posidonius), *De natura deorum,*

II.150–52, which is preceded by a celebration of reason and speech (II.147–49); see also Daniélou, 102, n. 1.

73. Gregory of Nyssa, *On the Creation of Man* 141D, 144A. Man also "bends to his use the wing of the birds, so that by his ingenuity he has at his disposal the speed of flight" (141D).

74. ἐπίνοια, the power of thought, inventiveness, design, is tied closely here to τέχνη.

75. A physical sign of man's dominion is seen also in the stature of a being who stands upright and looks to the heaven above—in an attitude that "renders [man] apt for rule and signifies his royal power" (Gregory of Nyssa, *On the Creation of Man* 144B).

76. Ibid., 144b–c.

77. Ibid., 148c–d.

78. Jacques Derrida, "Faith and Knowledge: The Two Sources of 'Religion' at the Limits of Reason Alone," in *Religion,* ed. Jacques Derrida and G. Vattimo (Stanford, Calif.: Stanford University Press, 1998), 2, 56.

79. For example, as Max Weber indicates, "unless he is a physicist, one who rides on the streetcar has no idea how the car happened to get into motion. And he does not need to know. He is satisfied that he may 'count' on the behavior of the streetcar, and he orients his conduct according to this expectation; but he knows nothing about what it takes to produce such a car so that it can move" (*op. cit.,* 139).

As Benjamin notes, in a discussion of film that could be extended today, "the equipment free aspect of reality here has become the height of artifice; the sight of immediate reality has become an orchid in the land of technology" ("The Work of Art," 233). Heidegger, "World Picture," 135, "Die Zeit des Weltbildes," 95.

80. Heidegger, "World Picture," 135, "Die Zeit des Weltbildes," 95.

81. Heidegger, "World Picture," 135, "Die Zeit des Weltbildes," 96.

82. Samuel Weber, "Mass Mediauras," 31.

83. In the space of just such a disproportion, where experience sees the reemergence of a certain mystery, image would proliferate without end—and it would do so according to the logic that Fredric Jameson has elucidated in his analyses of postmodern culture: the irreducible play of "figuration" in the deeply superficial world of late capitalism (or of the "tele-technology" related to it) signals "some sense that these new and enormous global realities are inaccessible to any individual subject or consciousness . . . which is to say that those fundamental realities are somehow ultimately unrepresentable or, to use the Althusserian phrase, are something like an absent cause, one that can never emerge into the presence of perception." The individual caught in the grip of today's incomprehensible technological (and economic) totalities consumes—and is consumed by—an endless stream of image that remains endless, precisely, because the causality of those totalities can never be brought fully to consciousness or representation. See Fredric Jameson, *Postmodernism; Or, The Cultural Logic of Late Capitalism* (Durham, N.C.: Duke University Press, 1991), 411.

84. "Delocalizing tele-technoscience" is from Derrida, "Faith and Knowledge," 56.

85. DeLillo, *Underworld,* 808, 824–25.

86. DeLillo, *Underworld,* 826. This would echo Taylor's assertion in *Hiding* that virtual reality is not so much "a specific technology" as it is "an effective figure of the postmodern condition" (301).

87. DeLillo, *Underworld,* 825.

88. Ibid.

89. Ibid.

90. Eriugena, *Periphyseon* III.668A–B.

91. DeLillo, *Underworld*, 826.

92. For reasons quite different from those of Sister Alma Edgar, but no less interesting in light of our concerns here with freedom and creativity, Martin Amis will also insist—in his essay titled "Thinkability"—on the final distinction between these two powers that can stand in such strange proximity:

> Meanwhile [nuclear weapons] squat on our spiritual lives. There may be a nuclear "priesthood," but we are the supplicants, and we have no faith. The warheads are our godheads. Nuclear weapons could bring about the Book of Revelation in a matter of hours; they could do it today. Of course, no dead will rise; nothing will be revealed (*nothing* meaning two things, the absence of everything and a thing called *nothing*). Events that we call "acts of God"—floods, earthquakes, eruptions—are flesh wounds compared to the human act of nuclear war: a million Hiroshimas. Like God, nuclear weapons are free creations of the human mind. Unlike God, nuclear weapons are real. And they are here.

(In *Einstein's Monsters* [New York: Vintage Books, 1987], 27) It bears noting here that the recent edition of Revelation published by Pocket Canons (which had once been planned to contain an introduction by Will Self) has for its cover image the photo of a mushroom cloud.

93. Eriugena, *Periphyseon* I.482C–D: "Nec alium hujus mundi finem fore, quam ut omnes, qui gloriam theoseos, id est, deificationis accepturi sunt, ultra loca et tempora ascendant."

Afterword:
A Reflection on *Mystics: Presence and Aporia*

DAVID TRACY

I begin these brief, indeed cryptic, reflections by recalling Bernard McGinn's survey of the many definitions of mysticism at the conclusion of his first volume on the history of Christian mysticism, *The Presence of God*. He concluded that survey with a definition of his own that Christian mysticism is the consciousness or awareness of the presence or absence of God. That definition, specifically the choice of "awareness" or "consciousness" rather than "experience" or "knowledge," seems to me both appropriate and very helpful. For McGinn understands "consciousness," as do I, in the terms of our common mentor, Bernard Lonergan. For Lonergan consciousness is awareness, not knowledge or experience. There are different modes and types of awareness: from the awareness when one is dreaming to that when one is awake. The latter "awake" awareness, moreover, structures itself as experience, understanding, and reflective consciousness issuing in critical judgment and decision. McGinn's innovation, by using Lonergan, clarifies what can and cannot count as mystical awareness and frees one from the enormous confusions occasioned by the choice of either "experience" or "knowledge" for describing mysticism in so much of the literature or mysticism.

I would like to employ this Lonerganian definition of awareness in some reflections on the foregoing chapters here in order to address two distinct forms of awareness of the presence or absence of God. Although I am discussing distinctly Christian mysticism, this distinction may be more widely applied to theistic mysticism, as studies of Jewish mysticism, for instance, have shown. However, first, recall how two forms of analogous secular awareness (sometimes of God, at other times of the Void or the Open) can be present in both philosophy and tragedy. Both these two kinds of secular awareness are also present in this collection. In the modern period, starting with Nietzsche's debate on the relationship of tragedy and philosophy, a principal question has been whether philosophy eliminated tragedy as the central mode of Western sensibility by what Nietzsche called philosophy's "optimism of reason." One might also say, with some of the new Nietzscheans, including Bataille and Blanchot (and those others discussed in this collection by Hart, Hollywood, Meltzer, and Schwartz) that one now finds less explicit reflection on tragedy itself than on those limit experiences or nonexperiences that tragedy discloses, especially dying and death or, most especially with Levinas, the innocent suffering of the other. This latter awareness also demands attention for understanding mysticism adequately.

To ask how philosophy relates to tragedy, as Nietzsche did, is to ask us to rethink our Greek origins, especially the reception of Plato by Neoplatonism and the nascent Neoplatonic aspects of Plato himself. I cannot defend my interpretation here, but I am persuaded contra Nietzsche that Plato is not, in fact, a rejecter of tragedy. At crucial moments one finds a tragic spirit in Plato, especially in one of the most influential of his texts, the *Timaeus*. The resonances of the *Timaeus* with Aeschylus's *Oresteia* are remarkable and in need of further critical reflection. Such reflection can challenge, philosophically, Nietzsche's *The Birth of Tragedy* and continue on with the new Nietzscheans' thoughts on death, dying, and innocent suffering. In Christian theology, the same kind of distinction between tragedy/philosophy holds in the classical distinction between the cosmic Christianity of Eastern Orthodoxy and the troubled anthropology of Western Augustinian Christianity. The latter, in turn, is linked to theological reflections on redemption in Western Catholicism and Protestantism. The first distinction between Eastern and Western Christianity in terms of awareness, therefore, can be reformulated as a principal awareness of creation (the East) and redemption (the West). Western Catholic thought, at its best, for example, can be interpreted as an attempted mediation between the presence/creation awareness tradition of Orthodoxy and the absence/redemption awareness of Reformed Christianity. Moreover, there is a further distinction within the West itself between the Catholic and Protestant emphasis: between a Catholic emphasis on nature/grace (recently rethought by such figures as De Lubac and Rahner) and Reformed emphasis on sin/grace (recently rethought by such theologians as Karl Barth and Paul Tillich). Both theological positions, Catholic nature/grace and Protestant sin/grace, are already present in the thought of the West's greatest thinker, Augustine.

And so both philosophical and theological debates on presence and absence, and their possible relationships in Western Christian mysticism, are among the most important concerns still facing Western Christian thought. For example, we need to reread and rethink Augustine both in his early, more Platonic Christian work (where nature/grace is emphasized in both logos and in terms of eros and agape) and in his later anti-Pelagian work (where Augustine shifts his emphasis to the relationship between sin and grace). The latter emphasis was famously taken up by the Reformers. One result of that shift is clear: Protestantism has mostly (with exceptions such as Schleiermacher and Tillich) related rather uneasily to the Christian mystical tradition. This rejection was first inspired by Luther's original embrace of Dionysius and his later violent break with him.

Moreover, there are different forms of negativity itself in the Western mystical tradition. There is not only the cognitively oriented apophatic negativity associated, for example, with Meister Eckhart's understanding of the primacy of detachment over love. There is also the distinct negativity of existential dereliction in Suso, John of the Cross, Teresa of Avila, and perhaps Luther himself (see Schreiner). This latter is a reflective awareness of suffering, especially innocent suffering, and allows for some Christian theological retrieval and transformation of the classic tragic vision. It is crucial, I believe, that the two forms of awareness represented in secular thought by philosophy and tragedy are also present in Western religious thought. On the one hand, one finds a meditative and contemplative awareness that, when intensified, is well described as mystical. Here we must recognize, of course, both the cataphatic, positive awareness of divine presence (as the Good) and the apophatic, negative awareness of divine absence (as Unknowable). On the other hand, one finds a prophetic awareness focused on evil injustice and suffering that, when intensified, becomes apocalyptic: when prophecy fails, apocalyptic takes over.

Both kinds of mystical awareness in their most intensified modes can be expressed today by languages of fragmentation. Thus when meditative and contemplative awareness becomes intense it fragments any totality into the paradoxical introduction of apophatic language. And when the prophetic becomes apocalyptic we find fragmented understandings of history: as in Luther's reading of history not as continuity but rather as a series of apocalyptically disruptive and interruptive moments. Even nature can be viewed not as a cosmic book of glory and beauty but, in Luther's experiences of thunderstorms and so on, a negative awareness of the Hidden God in nature that forces the Christian to flee to the cross. Similarly, the early modern Pascal experienced an awareness of terror at the silence of infinite space. But Pascal must here be compared and contrasted with the even earlier Nicholas of Cusa for whom an awareness of infinity opens the thinker up to positive possibilities of mystical awareness in the Dionysian tradition.

One question provoked by these essays, therefore, is whether one can justifiably link these two senses of awareness as other than a descriptive juxtaposition. Here postmodern thought on mysticism seems genuinely helpful. Postmodern thinkers, for example, often use the provocative category of the Impossible. Both prophetic and mystical awareness are thus viewed as disclosing kinds of Impossibility (i.e., impossible to the limits of modern rationality). The category The Impossible can relate mystical awareness to postmodern discussions of death and dying, innocent suffering, limit experiences, radical alterity, and, positively, the Good beyond Being. And the God beyond Being as analyzed by Jean-Luc Marion as well as his category of the saturated phenomenon have also proved fruitful to think though a mystical awareness related to the category of the Impossible. I have tried elsewhere (the forthcoming *This Side of God*) to develop a theory of the fragment in order to relate contemporary accounts of mystical awareness and prophetic awareness to postmodern secular thought partly under the sign of the Impossible.

Like Simone Weil, I prefer to begin thinking about our awareness of God with an account of human and historical awareness of innocent suffering. Weil first presents her account of this awareness in her brilliant reading of the nature of Greek tragedy as expressed in the *Iliad,* the central formative text of the West. By focusing one's awareness on (she would say focusing one's attention on) innocent suffering, one opens up the possibility of experiencing and reflecting on the overwhelming situation of massive global suffering. It is not only in the heroes of Sophocles or Aeschylus that one finds the possibility of becoming aware of such phenomena as the saturated, indeed excessive, phenomenon of tragedy. On further reflection, as in Weil, one may also find in classical tragedy a sense of justice as a kind of equilibrium and a profound sense of compassion. Thus one becomes aware in Homer of a beauty that abides in tragedy. Indeed, no sunset is more beautiful in Homer than that at the moment just before a hero dies and knows that he or she is going to die.

What Weil suggests—though she never says so explicitly—is that one can begin mysticism with a tragic sense of innocent suffering. For biblical peoples, that means starting in a way that Weil never understood, with the prophetic/ apocalyptic centers of the Jewish, Christian, and Islamic traditions. Then one can move well, very well indeed, to moments of compassion, love, and beauty, and even on to the great Platonic discussions in the *Republic* of the Good beyond Being, and in the *Symposium* of the Beautiful Itself, which happens "suddenly," just as Alexander Golitzin shows, mystical awareness also happens suddenly in Dionysian thought. If such a suggestion is plausible, then we need not juxtapose these two moments of awareness. Rather, we may be able to see how they intrinsically relate, for example, in the Gospels. The Christian Gospels are four, after all, not a homogenized one that many seem to think of as "the Gospel." The difference between a Mark and a John is as significant as the difference between a Sophocles and a Plato. It is this kind of relationship that we may now embrace as we rethink these two kinds of awareness in mystical texts as well.

The Mystical Theology and *The Divine Names* of Dionysius the Areopagite, for example, must now be read, as Dionysian scholars have shown, by seeing the positive cataphatic namings and the negative apophatic namings never on their own but as embedded in their liturgical and christological contexts: in textual forms, in relationship to *The Celestial* and the *Ecclesiastical Hierarchies*. For *The Mystical Theology* can no longer be interpreted solely on its own, unless through willful misprision. Why not now also read those Dionysian texts, as Maximus the Confessor implies, in relationship to the whole christological complex (incarnation, cross, Resurrection, second coming). Would that Martin Luther had seen the implication of "cross" in the Dionysian texts—it is there—Western mysticism might have had a significantly different journey.

Mystical awareness is, for many today, entered principally through the negative apophatic moments of suffering and cross and only then to the kind of "yes," which, as Karl Barth insisted in his deathbed letter to Emil Brunner, is the final word of a Christian to every great "no." If you prefer secular writers to Barth, there is perhaps the greatest "yes" in modern literature: the words James Joyce gives to Molly Bloom at the end of *Ulysses,* just before he would enter the nightworld of *Finnegan's Wake,* "Yes, she said yes I will, yes. . . ." No one—even the most cataphatic mystics—need fear the loss of that "yes" if they would begin their reflections where so much of the best contemporary thought now begins them: the innocent suffering of others. The focus is not on the self but on the other: for Christians, especially those oppressed and marginalized others disclosed in the Cross of Jesus Christ, disclosed for all in the relentless horror of the suffering of millions in our tortured and disruptive history. Otherwise a new forgetfulness will continue to affect too much Western thought and practice, even at times its greatest mystical thought. It need not be so if both moments of awareness are kept in mind. Otherwise even mystics—along with artists, our greatest hope as a culture—may be moved into another "reservation of the spirit." We must resist that move.

Contributors

THOMAS A. CARLSON is associate professor in the Department of Religious Studies at the University of California, Santa Barbara. He is the author of *Indiscretion: Finitude and the Naming of God* (1999) and translator of several works by Jean-Luc Marion, including *God without Being* (1991), *Reduction and Donation: Investigations of Husserl, Heidegger, and Phenomenology* (1998), and *The Idol and Distance* (2001).

ALEXANDER GOLITZIN, professor of theology at Marquette University, specializes in the origins of the Eastern Christian ascetical and mystical tradition, with particular emphasis on continuities with and parallels to, respectively, intertestamental and Rabbinic Judaism. His recent books are *New Light from the Holy Mountain* (1996), *Et introibo ad altare dei: The Mystagogy of Dionysius Areopagita* (1994), *St. Symeon the New Theologian on the Mystical Life: The Ethical Discourses,* in three volumes (1995–97), and, with Michael Prokurat and Michael Peterson, *Historical Dictionary of the Orthodox Church* (1996).

KEVIN HART is professor of English at the University of Notre Dame. He is the author of *The Trespass of the Sign* (1989), *A. D. Hope* (1992), and *Samuel Johnson and the Culture of Property* (1999) and the editor of *The Oxford Book of Australian Religious Verse* (1994). He is also the author of seven collections of poetry, most recently, *Flame Tree: Selected Poems* (2002).

AMY HOLLYWOOD, professor of the History of Christianity at the University of Chicago, is the author of *The Soul as Virgin Wife: Mechthild of Magdeburg, Marguerite*

Porete, and Meister Eckhart (1995) and *Sensible Ecstasy: Mysticism, Sexual Difference, and the Demands of History* (2001).

MICHAEL KESSLER, a graduate of the University of Chicago, has been visiting assistant professor of philosophy at Purdue University and an instructor at the University of Chicago.

JEAN-LUC MARION is professor of philosophy at the University of Paris IV—Sorbonne and John Nuveen Professor at the University of Chicago Divinity School, Department of Philosophy, and the Committee on Social Thought. He is the author of *Sur l'ontologie grise de Descartes* (1975), *Sur la théologie blanche de Descartes* (1981), *God without Being* (1991), *Reduction and Givenness* (1998), *Cartesian Question* (1999), *On Descartes' Metaphysical Prism* (1999), *The Idol and the Distance: Five Studies* (2001), *Being Given* (2002), and *Prolegomena to Charity* (2002).

BERNARD McGINN is the Naomi Shenstone Donnelley Professor in the Divinity School of the University of Chicago. He is currently at work on the fourth volume of his history of mysticism entitled *The Presence of God*.

FRANÇOISE MELTZER is professor in the departments of comparative literature, romance languages and literatures, the Divinity School, and the College at the University of Chicago. Her most recent book is *For Fear of the Fire: Joan of Arc and the Limits of Subjectivity* (2001), and she is coeditor of *Critical Inquiry*.

SUSAN SCHREINER is associate professor of the history of Christianity and of theology at the University of Chicago Divinity School. She is the author of *Where Shall Wisdom Be Found? Calvin's Exegesis of Job from Medieval and Modern Perspectives* (1994).

REGINA M. SCHWARTZ is professor of English, comparative literature, and religious studies at Northwestern University and director of the Institute of Religion and Global Violence. She is the author of *The Curse of Cain: The Violent Legacy of Monotheism* (1997) and of *Remembering and Repeating: On Milton's Theology and Poetics,* coeditor of *Desire in the Renaissance: Literature and Psychoanalysis* (1994) and of *The Postmodern Bible* (1995), and editor of *The Book and the Text: The Bible and Literary Theory* (1990). Her collection *Transcendence* is forthcoming from Routledge in 2003.

CHRISTIAN SHEPPARD is an instructor in the University of Chicago's Basic Program. His work has appeared in *Transcendence* and *Ronald Johnson: Life and Work*.

DAVID TRACY is the Andrew Thomas Greeley and Grace McNichols Greeley Distinguished Service Professor of Catholic Studies and professor of theology and of the philosophy of religion in the Divinity School and the Committee on Social Thought at the University of Chicago. His publications include *Blessed Rage for Order: The New Pluralism in Theology* (1975), *The Analogical Imagination: Christian Theology and the Culture of Pluralism* (1981), *Plurality and Ambiguity: Hermeneutics, Religions, and Hope* (1987), and *On Naming the Present: Reflections on God, Hermeneutics, and Church* (1994). His latest book, *This Side of God*, based on the 2000 Gifford lectures, is forthcoming.

Index